Lived Religion in America

Lived Religion in America

TOWARD A HISTORY OF PRACTICE

Edited by David D. Hall

PRINCETON UNIVERSITY PRESS

PRINCETON, NEW JERSEY

Library of Congress Cataloging-in-Publication Data

Lived religion in America : toward a history
of practice / edited by David D. Hall.
p.   cm.
Includes bibliographical references and index.
ISBN 0-691-01674-7 (alk. paper)
ISBN 0-691-01673-9 (pbk. : alk. paper)
1. United States—Religion.   I. Hall, David D.
BL2525.L58   1998
200′.973—DC21   97-9421   CIP

This book has been composed in Galliard

Chapter Eight in this volume has been previously published in R. Marie Griffith,
God's Daughters: Evangelical Women and the Power of Submission (Berkeley:
University yof California Press, 1997); copyright © 1997 The Regents of
the University of California. Used by permission.

Princeton University Press books are printed
on acid-free paper and meet the guidelines
for permanence and durability of the Committee
on Production Guidelines for Book Longevity
of the Council on Library Resources

http://pup.princeton.edu

Printed in the United States of America

1   3   5   7   9   10   8   6   4   2

1   3   5   7   9   10   8   6   4   2
(Pbk.)

CONTENTS

Introduction by David D. Hall   vii

CHAPTER ONE
Everyday Miracles: The Study of Lived Religion
  Robert Orsi   3

CHAPTER TWO
"What Scripture Tells Me": Spontaneity and Regulation within
the Catholic Charismatic Renewal
  Danièle Hervieu-Léger   22

CHAPTER THREE
Family Strategies and Religious Practice: Baptism and the Lord's
Supper in Early New England
  Anne S. Brown and David D. Hall   41

CHAPTER FOUR
Practices of Exchange: From Market Culture to Gift Economy
in the Interpretation of American Religion
  Leigh Eric Schmidt   69

CHAPTER FIVE
Lived Religion and the Dead: The Cremation Movement in
Gilded Age America
  Stephen Prothero   92

CHAPTER SIX
Coffee, Mrs. Cowman, and the Devotional Life of Women
Reading in the Desert
  Cheryl Forbes   116

CHAPTER SEVEN
The Uses of Ojibwa Hymn-Singing at White Earth: Toward a
History of Practice
  Michael McNally   133

CHAPTER EIGHT
Submissive Wives, Wounded Daughters, and Female Soldiers:
Prayer and Christian Womanhood in Women's Aglow Fellowship
  R. Marie Griffith   160

CHAPTER NINE
Golden Rule Christianity: Lived Religion in the American
Mainstream
Nancy T. Ammerman 196

CHAPTER TEN
Getting (Not Too) Close to Nature: Modern Homesteading
as Lived Religion in America
Rebecca Kneale Gould 217

Contributors 243

Index 245

INTRODUCTION

DAVID D. HALL

THE ESSAYS brought together in *Lived Religion in America* advance a way of doing American religious history. The name for this approach is "lived religion," a shorthand phrase that has long been current in the French tradition of the sociology of religion (*la religion veçue*) but is relatively novel in the American context. As we use it in this volume, the phrase is rooted less in sociology than in cultural and ethnographical approaches to the study of religion and American religious history that have come to the fore in recent years. Some of the case studies in *Lived Religion in America* are explicitly ethnographic. Others, however, approach their subjects through sociology, history, and the close reading of texts. In the two essays that open the book, the historian Robert Orsi and the sociologist Danièle Hervieu-Léger reflect on broader aspects of lived religion, Orsi in the course of responding to the case studies and Hervieu-Léger in reviewing how modes of inquiry have evolved within the French tradition since the Second World War. Her report, which concludes with a case study of the charismatic movement within French Catholicism, is in keeping with a central aim of this volume and the project out of which it grew: to expand our ways of thinking about American religious history by enlisting perspectives—in this instance, a tradition of inquiry largely unknown to historians of religion in America—from outside the field.

The project that lies behind *Lived Religion in America* has encompassed both an experimental course on lived religion and a conference at Harvard Divinity School in September 1994 at which these essays were initially presented. These activities were made possible by the generosity of the Religion Division of the Lilly Endowment, which in a "workplan" prepared a few years ago for Protestantism and American Culture affirmed that the Division intended to promote the study of "daily life," especially among Protestant laity. Although not explicitly articulated in the workplan, another goal was to encourage reflection on "practice" as the center or focus of the Christian life.

In their own way, historians of religion in America have begun to call for attention to the same matters, usually in the context of observing that, while we know a great deal about the history of theology and (say) church and state, we know next-to-nothing about religion as practiced and precious little about the everyday thinking and doing of lay men and women.

The purpose of the lived religion project was to gain some ground on both of these matters, though in the event our agenda began to evolve. Each of the case studies that follow is about the laity, some as members of churches or groups (like Hervieu-Léger's Catholic charismatics), with close ties to the institutional church, others in a space of their own devising, in two instances—the cremationists described by Stephen Prothero and the "back to nature" homesteaders Rebecca Gould has studied—deliberately turning away from orthodox and organized religion. Despite the importance of the laity in these essays, their creativity and participation are only a small part of the answer, and possibly a problematic one at that, to the question, what is lived religion—or better, what has been the history of lived religion in America? For these essays are really about a wider reorientation rooted in a rethinking of what constitutes religion.

This rethinking is due, in part, to the inquiries that lie behind the term "popular religion." Much in use among historians of the Reformation, the concept of popular religion emerged as these historians began to ask how the theology of the Protestant Reformers was translated into behavior in local parishes. How were Luther and Calvin understood, and how did the educational and disciplining dimensions of the Reformation fare in these settings? Though historians do not agree on the answers to these questions, most have realized that the Luther of everyday, popular religion was sometimes a strangely magical figure and that campaigns of social discipline were only intermittently effective. Popular religion has therefore come to signify the space that emerged between official or learned Christianity and profane (or "pagan") culture. In this space lay men and women enjoyed a certain measure of autonomy; here they became actors in their own right, fashioning (or refashioning) religious practices in accordance with local circumstances. Another aspect of this space is that religion encompassed a range of possibilities, some with the sanction of official religion and others not, or perhaps ambiguously so. The concept of popular religion has thus made it possible for historians to expand the scope of belief and practice beyond what was authorized by the institutional church. To say this differently, historians of the Reformation (and also of the Middle Ages) have underscored the politics of religious practice: on the one hand a politics of regulation from the center, often with some measure of success; on the other an extraordinary array of practices arising out of custom, improvisation, and resistance.

This way of doing religious history has entered into the concept of lived religion as we use it in the case studies that follow. To this older and still vital mode of inquiry we owe a questioning of boundaries, a sympathy for the extra-ecclesial, and a recognition of the laity as actors in their own right. So too, these case studies embody a kindred effort to reclaim and

establish the importance of texts and activities that all too readily are ignored or trivialized—for example, Mrs. Cowman's *Streams in the Desert*
and the healings undertaken by Women's Aglow.

Where lived religion goes its own way is in breaking with the distinction
between high and low that seems inevitably to recur in studies of popular
religion. That is, these case studies are not built around a structure of
opposition. Nor do they displace the institutional or normative perspectives on practice, as historians of popular religion so commonly do. The
essay on church membership in early New England that Anne S. Brown
and I have written comes close to having such a structure, for we acknowledge that the clergy were sometimes angered by the patterns of behavior
we describe. Yet our purpose is also to demonstrate that the clergy were
complicitous in the ways of thinking and doing that we map, complicitous
because they, too, were caught up in the same dilemmas and because they
realized that the looser meanings of baptism and saint that came to prevail
were advantageous in allowing their congregations to grow. Working in
the very different historiographical context of Native American religious
history—in his case study, Ojibwa who were converted to Christianity by
Protestant missionaries in the nineteenth century, and who have sustained
into our own times a tradition of hymn-singing—Michael McNally is concerned to avoid another characteristic set of oppositions, in this instance
the alternatives of missionary imperialism and a naturalized rendering of
"native" religion. The close analyses of "meaning" and the attention to
ambivalence and contradiction that recur in these essays also sidestep the
divisions of high and low, elite and popular.

Lived religion as we pursue it in these case studies builds on other lines
of inquiry. One of these is the sociological tradition of the community
study, which for Nancy T. Ammerman becomes the study of congregations.[1] Another is ritual studies, which casts a long, influential shadow
over several of the essays. A third is the cultural or symbolic anthropology
that in America we associate with Clifford Geertz. That in some of these
essays so much attention is paid to the play of meaning may seem to contradict the implications of *lived* religion, as though this term were confined to what people do. But in keeping with the trajectory of practical
and theoretical work in recent decades—here, Hervieu-Léger's review of
the French tradition is pertinent—the case studies that follow are prem-
ised on the assumption that behavior cannot be understood apart from
meaning, or what sometimes is loosely designated as "culture." In this
respect these case studies descend not only from Geertz but, more immediately, from the work of certain students of American religious history who, in the 1980s, were turning to the language and analytical framework of ritual theory (relying as much, perhaps, on Victor Turner as on

Geertz). The long, central chapter of Robert Orsi's *The Madonna of 115th Street* in which he elaborates on "The Meanings of the Devotion to the Madonna of 115th Street" remains perhaps the single most important example of this way of doing history—that is, of explicating the multiple, overlapping, even contradictory meanings embodied in a symbolic figure.

Several of our case studies employ a kindred mode of analysis. Leigh Eric Schmidt's essay on the gift in nineteenth-century Protestantism is about a complex of meanings that infused the burgeoning of gift-giving practices within everyday religious culture. Anne S. Brown and I reflect on ambiguities in the symbolism of "covenant," ambiguities that were played out in how people made decisions about participating in the sacraments of baptism and the Lord's Supper. In the course of describing hymn-singing and "back-to-nature" homesteading, McNally and Rebecca Kneale Gould unfold the extraordinary freight of meaning conveyed by each of these modes of practice. As described by Stephen Prothero, the details of the cremation carried out in Washington, Pennsylvania, reveal a sense of ritualization among those who planned the event, which they cloaked in a repertory of symbols conveying (as do some of the actions of Gould's homesteaders) expectations of immortality.

This attention to meaning and ritualization is complemented in two of the case studies by a focus on narrative. The close reading that Cheryl Forbes undertakes of Mrs. Cowman's *Streams in the Desert* reveals an unexpected story, a narrative pattern of difficulty and darkness never fully to be overcome in this world. In light of this narrative pattern, the devotional practice of daily reading takes on a new significance. The stories recounted in the meetings and publications of Women's Aglow are even more fully charged with the difficulties of what goes wrong in marriages and parenting. Here too, however, the narrative form subsumes these difficulties into a larger structure of healing.[2]

This quick sketch of the lines of thinking that converge in these essays should make it clear that the study of lived religion does not depend on any single method or discipline. As useful and rewarding as participant-observation is for Gould, Griffith, McNally, Hervieu-Léger, and (in a slightly different way) Ammerman, the rest of us have had to depend on recovering our evidence from the past. One imperative for any student of lived religion—an old-fashioned imperative, to be sure, but doubly pertinent in this context—is to acknowledge as fully as possible the play of meaning. It is tempting to abridge, even to censure, the messiness that leaks into everyday life—to insist that the Puritans cannot be authentically religious if they depart from one particular understanding of covenant, that Ammerman's liberals are not really Christians, or that the members of Women's Aglow are hopelessly regressive because they tolerate certain forms of patriarchy. No doubt the contributors to this collection have their own ways of being censorious, but I think it fair to say that each of us has struggled against this instinct in the course of representing our subjects as they live with and work through multiple realms of meaning.

Though it is surely the case that no single key unlocks the door to lived religion, one term—"practice"—does have particular importance. The complicated history of this term within Western philosophy and social theory is not resolved or for that matter explicitly addressed in the essays that follow. Where they may be said to enter this long conversation is at the point many others reached in the 1980s, an interest in "culture in action."[3] As most of us use the term, it encompasses the tensions, the ongoing struggle of definition, which are constituted within every religious tradition and that are always present in how people choose to act. Practice thus suggests that any synthesis is provisional. Moreover, practice always bears the marks of both regulation and what, for want of a better word, we may term resistance. It is not wholly one or the other.[4] It is in practice, so construed, that the Christian Ojibwa sustain their faith and a sense of being native; that the colonists in New England enact both the purity of the sacraments and a family strategy of inheritance and incorporation; and that participants in Women's Aglow transform, even while accepting, the obligations of sacrifice and submission.

Lived religion as an approach to the past and to the present opens up a rich array of possibilities for historians. For one, it brings into the foreground the age-old question of change. Speaking of the postwar generation of researchers in France, Hervieu-Léger remarks that they shared the "observation of the measurable collapse of the world of observances within which the lived religion of the French had organized itself for centuries." Other historical moments may not have this magnitude or be as readily apparent until we develop a more comprehensive map of practices. Among the steps in this direction is Leigh Eric Schmidt's narrative of the rise and fall of sacramental feasts in the Church of Scotland; he has also described the reshaping of the Protestant (or American) calendar that began to unfold in the middle of the nineteenth century.[5] It may also be that certain paradigms of change deserve to be rethought, as Anne S. Brown and I attempt with "declension" in early New England in light of the practices we describe. Not only is there much work to do on these times of transition; we also need to translate the great "isms" of church history into modalities of practice—say, the practices that distinguish or were central to Protestant liberalism as it arose in the late nineteenth century, as distinct from practices that were characteristic of other movements in that period. The time-bound shape of practice surely looks different if we view it from the standpoint of women's participation, as several of the essays that follow suggest. It may also look different if we inquire into regulation (to borrow a term from Hervieu-Léger) or take seriously the perspective of the theologian.

Let me close by returning to the Lilly workplan. It should be clear that lived religion as I have described it is an imperfect tool for getting at the "person in the pew," for the fullness of any person's religious practice cannot be summed up by what happens in a single location. Meredith McGuire's remark in *Ritual Healing in Suburban America* that, on any given day, a suburban housewife in the Northeast United States employs five different theologies of healing is an apt reminder of the compounding of possibilities in modern times.[6] Because lived religion is (as Hervieu-Léger suggests) "fluid, mobile, and incompletely structured," the essays in *Lived Religion in America* do more, or possibly less, than was entertained by the authors of the Lilly workplan. Nonetheless, these essays all acknowledge the imperative of charting the practices of the laity. As Orsi warns us, this imperative can evolve into an overemphasis on agency. Yet these essays surely reveal that regulation is ongoing within the most fluid of movements. To cite but one example, regulation inheres in the structure of certain master narratives, as happens among the women who gather to share stories of misfortune and healing and, we may also imagine, among the readers of Mrs. Cowman's *Streams in the Desert* and the participants in homesteading. Let me acknowledge, however, that it remains a challenging task to think historically about the normative and regulating dimensions of lived religion.

The lived religion project at Harvard Divinity School has depended not only on the Religious Division of the Lilly Endowment, for which support I thank especially Craig Dykstra and Dorothy Bass, but also on the community of doctoral students in various departments and programs at Harvard who are interested in American religious history. As officially constituted, the project in lived religion relied as well on the advice of scholars from other institutions. I want to thank those who participated in the first phase of these consultations: Nancy Ammerman, Yvonne Chireau, Sarah Coakley, Roland Delattre, Richard W. Fox, Charles Hambrick-Stowe, Robert Orsi, Leigh Eric Schmidt. The conference in September 1994 included a presentation by Lawrence Sullivan on space that is being published elsewhere. Sarah Coakley, Roland Delattre, Caroline Ford, Richard Fox, Marilyn Grunkemeyer, and Charles Hambrick-Stowe served as commentators at the conference. R. Marie Griffith helped plan the conference and the course that preceded it, and Christopher Coble also gave much practical assistance. I want to thank in particular the doctoral students and faculty who have given so much to the entire project: David Bains, Christopher Coble, Margaret Gillespie, Rebecca Kneale Gould, R. Marie Griffith, Stephen Holmes, John McGreevy, Michael McNally, John O'Keefe, Karen Marie Yust. Lauren Bryant expertly abetted the revision of the conference papers. The support and encouragement of the dean of the Divinity School, Ronald Thiemann, has been crucial.

Notes

1. A genre to which Ammerman has contributed an excellent case study, *Bible Believers: Fundamentalists in the Modern World* (New Brunswick, N.J.: Rutgers University Press, 1987). In the course that I taught at Harvard Divinity School on lived religion, we also came to appreciate an anthropologically oriented town study by Carol J. Greenhouse, *Praying for Justice: Faith, Order, and Community in an American Town* (Ithaca, N.Y.: Cornell University Press, 1986). Perhaps the most informative exercise in the course has been to analyze an entire year's worth of a parish weekly newsletter, in this instance the (UCC) Church of the Apostles, Lancaster, Pa.

2. Narrative is also at the center of James L. Peacock and Ruel W. Tyson Jr., *Pilgrims of Paradox: Calvinism and Experience among the Primitive Baptists of the Blue Ridge* (Washington, D.C.: Smithsonian Institution, 1989).

3. See Sherry B. Ortner, "Theory in Anthropology since the Sixties," *Comparative Studies in Society and History* 26 (1984): 126–66 (a reference I owe to Tim Morehouse); Alasdair MacIntyre, *After Virtue: A Study in Moral Theory* (Notre Dame, Ind.: University of Notre Dame Press, 1981).

4. I owe some of this language to John McGreevy.

5. Leigh Eric Schmidt, *Holy Fairs: Scottish Communions and American Revivals in the Early Modern Period* (Princeton, N.J.: Princeton University Press, 1989); idem, *Consumer Rites: The Buying and Selling of American Holidays* (Princeton, N.J.: Princeton University Press, 1995).

6. Meredith B. McGuire, *Ritual Healing in Suburban America* (New Brunswick, N.J.: Rutgers University Press, 1988).

Lived Religion in America

Chapter One

EVERYDAY MIRACLES: THE STUDY OF LIVED RELIGION

Robert Orsi

THE ROMAN CATHOLIC CHURCH of St. Lucy at the corner of Bronx-wood and Mace avenues in the North Bronx boasts a huge outdoor construction of rocks and plants that "replicates," according to a bro-chure available at the parish, the topography of the countryside in Lourdes, France, where in 1858 a woman in white appeared to a girl named Bernadette and announced herself to be the "Immaculate Concep-tion." St. Lucy's is famous throughout New York City for this reproduc-tion. The site, which is in a working-class Italian American neighborhood, is popularly known as the Bronx Lourdes. The grotto was built in 1939 at the peak of a vogue among American Catholics for copying European locations of Mary's appearances.[1] "It looked like someone's patio had exploded," a woman from the area recalled of the days of the grotto's construction. "People brought in stone and cement . . . everyone helped. Some of the women who knew handicrafts helped in decorating and painting the statues; the men did the heavy work."[2]

A stream of cold, clear New York water pours down the face of the grotto from a pipe hidden (but only just) in the rocks. Bernadette's woman in white had pointed to a spot on the dry ground and told the girl to dig there. Bernadette clawed the earth on her hands and knees until a spring of muddy water bubbled to the surface between her fingers. Pil-grims to Lourdes bathe in pools fed by Saint Bernadette's miraculous spring, hoping for relief from physical distress; small bottles of the pre-cious liquid—in the shape of the woman in white, capped with a little blue crown—are sent or taken away from Lourdes to heal and console distant sufferers.[3] Lourdes water is the most powerful of modern Catholic devo-tional media. The water in the Bronx is treated by those who come for it as Lourdes water, and it is also believed to be miraculously efficacious.

An endless procession of cars pulls up to the grotto on warm spring and summer afternoons (the water is shut off in cold weather). Migrants from Jamaica, Trinidad, the West Indies, the Dominican Republic, and Puerto Rico, along with African Americans from Manhattan and the South Bronx, have moved into the neighborhoods around St. Lucy's in the past thirty years, and the grotto has become a popular place for pilgrims from these communities, even those who are not Catholic, together with second-, third-, and now even fourth-generation European American Catholics from all over the Northeast. "There's no color barrier here," a young Trinidadian woman told me as we sat together in front of the statues of the Virgin and Bernadette two summers ago, watching people come and go at the grotto. Visitors were holding white plastic gallon jugs, paper cups, and glass tumblers beneath the stream flowing out from the rocks at the feet of the Immaculate Conception. They drank water there and took water home with them; they made the Sign of the Cross with dripping hands and ladled scoops of water onto their heads for a "blessing," a Puerto Rican woman explained to me. An older woman obviously in serious physical distress spent the afternoon sipping glass after glass of holy water, chatting in the meantime with her son, daughter-in-law, and grandchildren who were keeping her company. Bending under the open hoods of cars parked just outside the chain-link fence surrounding the grotto—which gives the site the look of a city playground—men in shorts and t-shirts filled their radiators with Bronx Lourdes water for protection on the road.

I was standing one afternoon at the foot of the rocks watching the family of a very old woman who could not walk lift her out of her wheelchair so she could hold a cup to the grotto water herself. A woman beside me noticed that I did not have anything with me to drink from and offered me her own pink plastic container. (To sip directly from the stream as it tumbles over the rocks means getting drenched. Many people do this, but I did not want to spend the afternoon wet.) The woman urged me to drink. "It's sweeter than regular water," she said, better than "water-fountain water." She watched me fill the cup and drink the water down and then she prodded me, "See what I mean?" The water was indeed refreshing on the hot, humid day.

"Where does the water come from?" I asked her.

At the time the grotto was constructed (and the water pipe fitted out in the rocks), a rumor went around among some local devout that builders had—miraculously—discovered a spring of fresh water under the Bronx pavement. This was clearly an effort to establish a literal parallel with Lourdes, but it was also a bid to raise the stakes of reproduction so high as to deny it: if there was indeed a miraculous spring here in the Bronx clay, then this was a holy site in its own right. I was wondering when I asked about the water's source if the woman I was talking with would mention this belief.

"What do you mean, where does the water come from?" She looked at me sharply, apprehensively, as if she were suddenly afraid that I was the sort of excessively, perhaps dangerously, pious man who believed in such crazy rumors and discussed them with women at shrines. "It's city water—it comes from the reservoir, I guess," wherever city water comes from, she added. But wasn't it the sweetest water I'd ever tasted? Later I was told by one of the caretakers at the grotto that no one really believed the story about the underground spring; everyone knows exactly where the water comes from and everyone maintains the water is holy and powerful.

Students in my class on U.S. urban religions are offended by the practices that take place at St. Lucy's. They are especially outraged that the people involved consider these practices "religious." The last time I introduced this material one student called what went on at St. Lucy's "a lot of crap," an unusual breach of classroom etiquette and uncharacteristic of the student but indicative of the anger provoked by the images I was showing. Another said that what people did at St. Lucy's was "abusive." Not all students were this vocal with their criticism, but not one student in all the years I have taught this course in the Midwest has ever been willing to say that the practices at St. Lucy's are of obvious importance to the people who do them and therefore worthy of our serious attention. The image of holy water being poured into car engines is especially disturbing to students, an instance of the general blurring of categories they want to keep distinct (sacred/profane; spirit/matter; transcendent/immanent; nature/machine) which occurs at St. Lucy's. What happens at the Bronx grotto is literally inadmissable, intolerable, in a religion classroom, because it is not "religion," but defilement—the *other* of the sacred and of religion. This is felt by students of all denominations, even by Catholics who might be expected to approach such idioms more sympathetically.

The peculiarly mixed consciousness of pilgrims to the Bronx Lourdes— evident in the woman's response to my query about the source of the holy water—represents the limit of the students' willingness to care about this other world. It is willfully perverse, they insist, to call holy what you know to be not, or pathetically self-delusional, or else an example of religious chicanery. It is ridiculous to pray at an imitation—and therefore, in their view, ersatz—sacred site. These reactions mark—and authorize—a commonly recognized border between what is and what is not "the religious" with great intensity and passion. St. Lucy's occasions a mandatory mapping of the cultural landscape.[4]

So if this is not religion, what is? I ask my students. Religion is concerned with the "sacred," not the profane, according to notes I have kept of how students answered this question in reaction against St. Lucy's. The sacred has "nothing to do with the quotidian," but rather "draws attention away from itself" toward something higher, greater. Religion is not "selfish" (this oft-repeated stricture indicates the moral ground of the re-

jection of St. Lucy's rituals), not preoccupied with "material things."
(Students are invariably upset, I have learned over the years, whenever
money makes an appearance in the space of the sacred.) Religious feelings—and no one doubts that there is a discrete category of feelings called
"religious"—represent a "higher state of consciousness," a "union of the
one with the one," that sends "shivers down the spine" of a sort different
from the shivering of wet grotto pilgrims.[5] What passes for religion at St.
Lucy's is too earthy and "quotidian," conceptually mixed, experientially
indeterminate. Students are so dismayed by St. Lucy's that they call it
"boring," which I read as the shutting down of their curiosity and engagement and as an expression of their conceptual frustration. The goings-on
at the Bronx Lourdes lack the romance of great religious faith. St. Lucy's
is too mired in matter. "Religion" necessarily and normatively exists in an
either/or relationship with everything else.

Challenged to examine the assumptions that lead them to feel the way
they do about St. Lucy's, my students come up with a fairly comprehensive account of what "religion" means in modern post-Reformation, post-
Enlightenment, capitalist, post-Conciliar (for contemporary Catholics),
Anglo-American Christian culture. This is what they have heard "religion" is since childhood from their pastors, their grade school and high
school teachers, and, a little later on, their therapists. "Religion" so defined is legally tolerable in the United States and socially acceptable.[6] Psy-
chologists call it "mature" (as opposed to infantile) faith and liberal clerics
of all faiths and denominations enshrine it as the highest attainment of
religious life. "Religion" is private and interior, not shamelessly public;
mystical, not ritualistic; intellectually consistent and reasonable, not ambivalent and contradictory. "Religion" is a matter of decision, choice, and
personal commitment, not of sipping water from a city aqueduct that is
somehow connected to the water an invisible being directed an ignorant
child toward a hundred years ago. "Religion" is ethical, not "selfish";
transcendent, not present in things. Religion is concerned, tautologically,
with religious matters, not with what Sartre has called the "equivocal giv-
ens of experience."[7] So pervasive is this account of religion in the United
States, and so normative, that there is no mention of Lourdes grottoes
nor of the other practices associated with the Virgin and saints in recent
histories of American Catholicism, just as there is no mention of the
everyday religious practices of American Protestants in most studies of
American religion either.

It is exactly with practices "in which faith and materiality . . . commin-
gle," as Leigh Eric Schmidt describes nineteenth-century American Protestant gift tokens, that the authors in this volume are concerned. They
insist that something called "religion" cannot be neatly separated from
the other practices of everyday life, from the ways that human beings work

on the landscape, for example, or dispose of corpses, or arrange for the security of their offspring. Nor can "religion" be separated from the material circumstances in which specific instances of religious imagination and behavior arise and to which they respond. "Lived religion" is an awkward neologism, but I like it because it recalls the phrase "lived experience" used by existentialists for men and women "everywhere *where [they are]*," as Sartre has written, "at . . . work, in [their] home[s], in the street."[8] Workplaces, homes, and streets—as well as churches, temples, shrines, class meetings, and other more immediately recognizable sites of religious activity—are the places where humans make something of the worlds they have found themselves thrown into, and, in turn, it is through these subtle, intimate, quotidian actions on the world that meanings are made, known, and verified. "Religion" is best approached, according to the scholars in this collection, by meeting men and women at this daily task, in all the spaces of their experience. The essays in this volume invite a redirection of religious scholarship away from traditions—the great hypostatized constructs of "Protestantism," "Catholicism," and so on—and likewise away from the denominational focus that has so preoccupied scholars of American religions, toward a study of how particular people, in particular places and times, live in, with, through, and against the religious idioms available to them in culture—*all* the idioms, including (often enough) those not explicitly their "own." The shared methodology of this collection is radically or phenomenologically empiricist, concerned with what people *do* with religious practice, what they make with it of themselves and their worlds. It is further assumed by the authors gathered here that religious practice is polysemous and that it is constituted—assembled—by cultural bricolage.

The essays propose, therefore, that to study lived religion entails a fundamental rethinking of what religion is and of what it means to be "religious." Religion is not only not sui generis, distinct from other dimensions of experience called "profane." Religion comes into being in an ongoing, dynamic relationship with the realities of everyday life. Four things are necessary to understand religious practice: (1) a sense of the range of idiomatic possibility and limitation in a culture—the limits of what can be desired, fantasized, imagined, and felt; (2) an understanding of the knowledges of the body in the culture, a clear sense of what has been embodied in the corporeality of the people who participate in religious practices, what their tongues, skin, ears, "know"; (3) an understanding of the structures of social experience—marriage and kinship patterns, moral and juridical responsibilities and expectations, the allocation of valued resources, and so on; and (4) a sense of what sorts of characteristic tensions erupt within these particular structures. The essays in this collection set religion precisely in this densely configured context. A

shorthand designation for the reorientation proposed in this volume
would be to call it a materialist phenomenology of religion. But this term
is not satisfactory because it preserves the dualism of matter and religion,
sacred and profane, whereas scholars of "lived religion" seek a more dynamic integration of religion and experience.

David D. Hall and Anne S. Brown make this approach to religion clear-
est in their study of infant baptisms in colonial New England. An earlier
generation of historians of American Puritanism saw "the world" as the
implacable other of Puritan spirituality. The facts of biology, for example,
or the changing material circumstances of the colonists were understood
as that against which Puritan theology had to contend and to which it had
to adapt. The story was usually told as one of declension and spiritual
betrayal. This is the influence of neo-orthodoxy on American religious
historiography: religion exists in contradiction or tension with the world,
in but not of it. But for Hall and Brown, "the social" is the necessary
dialectical partner of "the religious." Religious creativity is not intransi-
tive. It is action on the world, made necessary and possible by particular
circumstances in the world. "Religion" is not *in* or *of* the world, nor simply *against* but *through* the world. Theologically caught between "a covenant that blessed family preservation," on the one hand, and the covenant
of grace "that inserted the doctrine of a limited atonement into the relationship between parents and children," on the other, Puritans actively,
creatively—religiously—negotiated their way through the contradictions
between theology and experience, faith and the world, by means of infant
baptism, which was existentially necessary though ecclesiologically meaningless in Puritan terms.

Men and women do not merely inherit religious idioms, nor is religion
a fixed dimension of one's being, the permanent attainment of a stable
self. People appropriate religious idioms as they need them, in response
to particular circumstances. All religious ideas and impulses are of the
moment, invented, taken, borrowed, and improvised at the intersections
of life. Nancy T. Ammerman's comment that Golden Rule Christians
"draw from Scripture their own inspiration and motivation and guidance
for life in this world" can stand as a description of religious creativity generally. R. Marie Griffith talks about the "reworking" of the notion of
submission in practice and Schmidt points us toward the "complex motivations of religious actors as they meet, associate, sacrifice, struggle,
and contend." It is through such dynamic processes of engagement that
religion takes life.

The focus on lived religion thus proposes what I have called an empiricist orientation to religion. As anthropologist Michael Jackson has written, "to investigate beliefs or 'belief systems' apart from actual human
activity is absurd" because beliefs—even the most crucial—are "quiescent

most of the time, activated in crisis, but having no stable or intrinsic truth values that can be defined outside of contexts of use."[9] So Golden Rule Christians, according to Ammerman, are best characterized not by what they believe but by what they do. One of her sources told Ammerman that he had apprehended the truth of his Christianity by living it amid the crises and joys of everyday family life; this is how—and where—God became real to him. The authors of this volume point us to the creativity and improvisational power of theology as a component of lived experience, to the practice of *theologizing* in determinate circumstances.

Theologies are not made in a single venue only—in the streets or in the churches, at shrines or in people's living rooms; it would be unfortunate if the turn to lived religion meant simply changing the valence of the familiar dualities while preserving them, just substituting religious practices in the streets and workplaces for what goes on in churches. Likewise, although discrepancies of power in the domain of religion are real—there really are religious elites who claim and exercise real power over others, over their bodies and spirits, through their control of theological and moral discourse and worship protocols—theological practice cannot be gridded in any simple way along the axis of "elite" and "popular."[10] Nor is the relationship between theology and practice best conceptualized as that between mind and body, between an endeavor of the imagination and intellect, on the one hand, and the movements, disciplines, and gestures of the body, on the other. Rather, the focus on lived religion in this volume points us to religion as it is shaped and experienced in the interplay among venues of everyday experience (through the kinds of ties that the devout at St. Lucy's establish among their workplaces, homes, and the shrine itself in their prayers, for example, or by putting holy water in their radiators), in the necessary and mutually transforming exchanges between religious authorities and the broader communities of practitioners, by real men and women in situations and relationships they have made and that have made them.[11]

Religious men and women appear in this book as actors, *Homo religiosus* as *Homo faber*, in Jonathan Z. Smith's terms, the human at work on the world.[12] The material grounds for many of the improvisations and creations studied in this volume are the convulsive circumstances of American industrial capitalism, the ways in which the specific workings of the American economy have contributed to shaping human relations, self-understandings, and cosmological orientations in this country over the past century and a half. "The seemingly endless religious creativity of Americans" (as Stephen Prothero calls it) has not been anomalous to the development of modern capitalist culture in the United States (as the old secularization thesis maintained), but its inevitable dialectical counterpart. Americans have been compelled to make and remake their worlds and themselves endlessly, relentlessly, on constantly shifting grounds, in often brutal economic circumstances, and religion has been one of—if not *the*—primary media through which this work of making and remaking has proceeded. Some of the most characteristic idioms of American Christianity were crafted in response to the movements of masses of people from farms to cities, for example, or to the unexpected conditions of factory life they found there or to the particular realities of contemporary managerial culture. But such material circumstances have been largely hidden in the study of American religious history. We still talk about nineteenth- and twentieth-century revivalism, or the passion of contemporary fundamentalist Christians, or the astonishing creation of American Pentecostalism in terms of an "evangelical impulse" or the Puritan legacy, rather than as the creative working of real men and women—using inherited, improvised, contested, and contradictory religious idioms—with the actual circumstances of their lives. But Prothero tells us, for example, that cremation was proposed as a way for a mobile population to keep their dead nearby—the ashes of the dead could move from the country to the city too—and, as Ammerman writes, it is the hope of suburban Golden Rule Christians to "create a community in which mobile people can be rooted."

If appropriated and inherited religious idioms do not reflect or mirror the world but make it, then a historiography is required that does not look for religious windows onto wider social or cultural realities and does not treat religious creations as icons of history, but instead seeks to understand religious idioms dynamically, in place. The questions with which we approach religion should not concern frozen "meanings" but should instead query the complexities of lived religious practices. This volume's essays are not examples of microhistory. At issue is not finding "Puritanism" in a ritual but approaching religious behavior and understandings diachronically, to explore the unfolding interplay of religious idiom and immediate circumstance that constantly reconfigures both. This is how Rebecca Kneale Gould describes "homesteading": as an activity that changes over time, practiced by people who are transforming themselves as they work on the world and whose understandings of themselves and of homesteading are always shifting. Nothing is fixed here; there is no single, exemplary moment of meaning capable of being isolated and exegeted. Robert Coles has described religion as the "exploratory play of the mind"; the authors in this volume study that playfulness in action, as it does its transformative work on the self and the world.[13]

The practices of lived religion are not singular precisely because they exist in relation to what Schmidt calls the "densely textured level of everyday practice and lived experience." The orientation of this volume away from the orderliness and coherence of doctrine entails a historical hermeneutics attuned to "ambivalence and ironies," as Gould puts it, to the unexpressed and the contradictory. Gould tracks the interplay of impulses of freedom and control in the gardening theories of Helen and Scott Nearing, for example. Resisting the temptation to settle her analysis at either pole, she discerns instead "complex layers of meaning and motivation" that pull the Nearings in contradictory and inconsistent conceptual directions, often to their own bemusement. Schmidt refers to the "hybridity" and the "poisoned and contradictory nature" of gifts. He brings his analysis to a dialectical conclusion: "The tensile ways in which such tokens simultaneously bind together and ratify separation, concurrently evoke 'real' sentiments and commodify them, remain at the heart of the modern gift economy, its ritual dilemmas, and its market possibilities." The key words here are *tensile, hybridity, ambivalence, irony;* the central methodological commitment is to avoid conclusions that impose univocality on practices that are multifarious.

The hermeneutics of hybridity also requires that we abandon some cherished analytical categories in the study of religion. Prothero argues, for example, that the DePalm cremation ceremonies were neither "Christian" nor "secular." Our current critical vocabulary encodes such dualism, reifies discrete segments of experience, and erects boundaries that do not exist in the real world and that belie the protean nature of religious creativity. The discipline of religious studies—and within it, of American religious history—thus reflects and authorizes the broader understanding of "religion" current in the culture. But as Hall and Brown point out, the meaning and experience of "holiness" were not fixed for Puritans. "Holiness" was instead an "elastic category capable of accommodating very different goals." The analytical language of religious studies, organized as it still is around a series of fixed, mutually exclusive, and stable polar opposites, must be reconfigured in order to make sense of religion as lived experience. A new vocabulary is demanded to discuss such phenomena, a language as hybrid and tensile as the realities it seeks to describe.

I want to underscore how much the approach to lived religion in this volume diverges from orientations common within the academy and without. There is an almost irresistible impulse toward at least a casual functionalism in the way most people think about religion, an insistence that in religion the contradictions of social and domestic life, the tensions of history and psychology, find resolution. This is why religion is so often imagined entropically, a phenomenon of closure and stasis. This is also the politics of religious representation in the United States. In a nation in which religion has been so wildly creative and innovative, where there seems to be no end to the fecundity of religious imaginings or to their violent and disruptive consequences, the public discourse of "the religious" instead presents faith and practice in ameliorative and consensual terms. Nothing happens in the space of the sacred, nothing moves, nothing changes, nothing ever spins out of control, no one is ever destroyed there. Thus a respected journal of political opinion could refer recently to militant right-wing Christians as practicing "pseudo-religion" without any explanation by the editors of how they came to this normative assessment. They just assumed, evidently, that American readers would know that "authentic religion" promotes harmony, moral consensus, and healing.[14]

Consider, by way of further contrast, Chicago Catholicism as it appears in a recent study of that city's culture in the years following World War II.[15] For parishioners at St. Nicholas of Tolentine on the Southwest side, we are told, "there was no participation, no individuality, no choice" in religious practice; they "were simply spectators" at Mass. Hierarchy was taken for granted and no one would ever have thought of challenging the awesome authority of individual priests, however cruel or humiliating this was in its exercise. Catholic education was about discipline not learning, presided over by women who themselves led lives of extreme "restriction, . . . regimentation, . . . [and] subservience," always without resentment, dissent, or complaint. "You just went along," one sister is quoted in a reflection on her vocation that can stand for this whole portrait of a city's Catholicism. "That was the time, and you went along." Spiritual spectatorship, moral passivity, and religious subservience were deeply satisfying to midcentury Chicago Catholics, according to the author of this study, and anyone who doubts that this was so is simply revealing the anomic individualism and insipid mistrust of authority characteristic of post-1960s American culture.

But this is a funereal fantasy of Catholicism, without playground grottoes or relationships between humans and saints that drew on deep wells of desire and fear, without the array of vernacular religious idioms so diverse as to be, in fact, uncontrollable by authority. Is anyone ever "religious"—outside the imaginations of intellectuals—as these Chicago Catholics are said to have been? Are religious idioms ever so hermetic? But, again, this is not an idiosyncratic description of religion. Historians have long represented religious leaders and followers like this, setting them within religious contexts in which everyone does what he or she is supposed to do, in which authority is obeyed and ritual rubrics carefully followed. Yet no one has ever seen anything like this in the real world.

The explosive interrelationship of the religious and the social examined in this volume indicates instead the volatile and unpredictable nature of religious creation. The "sacred" as it appears in this collection is the space of activity, engagement, ambivalence, and doubleness. Those gathered around the Pennsylvania crematorium on December 6, 1876, for example, were all "advanced thinkers" and "thoroughly modern men," who imagined the event itself as "a strictly scientific and sanitary experiment," in the words of Col. Henry Steel Olcott. But whatever organizers may have intended or understood, a carnival developed around the burning body of Baron DePalm, a charivari at the hot juncture of life and death. Reporters indulged in macabre humor and treated their readers to fantasies about fertilizing the farmland of Mid-Atlantic potato fields with dead bodies. The mood of the day shifted again as the baron's body was rendered "transparent and luminous" by the furnace's heat, palm fronds placed at his side by Olcott raised themselves aloft, and the baron himself, betraying his own enlightened values, raised his left hand and pointed three fingers heavenward.

Religious creations are not stable. Like the baron's arm, they subvert the intentions of those who would manipulate them for their own ends. Griffith cautions observers of the Women's Aglow Fellowship not to assume that "submission," the word Aglow uses for the right attitude of women toward their husbands, especially in times of domestic crisis and marital doubt, means what it does in disciplinary sermons preached by men or even in the official public self-representation of the Aglow movement itself. As it is lived by the women of Aglow, "submission" reveals a different, more oppositional, valence. Likewise, Michael McNally writes that the deaths of Ojibwa by alcohol or violence "are deeply sedimented with a politics of history" and occasion a communal recognition of the cultural violence wrought by White oppression, what he calls the "politics of death." In the presence of these bodies destroyed, the Ojibwa Singers perform survival, hope, protest, and endurance. "Hymns do not only *stand for* an *anishinaabe* way of life," McNally tells us; "in ritualized performance they begin to effect it." Religious meanings are volatile; they do not conform simply to the expectations and dictates of power.

Underlying all the essays in this volume is a sense of the potentially explosive political import of religious practice or (in Coles' word again) of religious play, of its liberatory possibilities. Religious idioms can be appropriated for ends quite the opposite of those sought by power. Scholars who work on lived religion in the United States have become, as the evidence of this volume suggests, theorists of a relative cultural freedom. Religion, commonly seen as the binding element of American society, turns out to be one of its solvents; religious practices and imaginings constitute one of the primary sites of transgression in American history and culture. Fundamentalist Christian insistence on women's submission is reread as oppositional gender practice, for example, and the singing of Christian hymns by Native Americans and the buying of Easter cards by middle-class Protestant women as gestures of protest and refusal. The writers gathered here look for occasions of freedom and resistance constituted by the complexities of particular historical moments. They give us an ironic account of religious freedom: the space of freedom is made possible by breaks in culture, erupting in the fissures of contradiction, tension, and ambivalence of social life. Freedom, like religious creativity, lies not in the domain of the agent alone but in the space between the agent and his or her times, not transcendentally beyond history, but inevitably and ironically within it.

Historians of lived religion thus join a broader debate among contemporary intellectuals about the nature and limits of autonomy within the disciplinary confines of culture. There has been an increasingly refined awareness over the past two decades of the suppleness of social power. The disciplines of bourgeois society, which represents itself as the freest of social orders, are insidious, intimate, and pervasive, according to this critical orientation. Domination proceeds not necessarily through violence or overt coercion but through the very practices that constitute the modern self in its illusion of autonomy—its therapies, its techniques for self-understanding and self-representation, and the media that stimulate its desires and satisfy them.

Obviously, these reorientations of critical social thought have narrowed the range of choice, creativity, and autonomy. If "freedom" is in fact its opposite—if the discourse of "freedom" is one of the constituent disciplines of bourgeois psychology and sociology that masks, and makes for a lack of, freedom—then what are the possibilities for any kind of resistance to the authority of culture? How can one say no to power in its many guises? Some critical poststructuralists have located the ground of resistance in the supraindividual circulations of power itself. Judith Butler, for example, emphasizes the "generativity" of the incest taboo, arguing that "the law which prohibits . . . is the selfsame law that invites . . . and it is no longer possible to isolate the repressive from the productive function of the juridical incest taboo." The taboo produces "a variety of substitute desires and identities" as it forbids others.[16] Or as social theorist Goran Therborn has written, men and women are always simultaneously both subjects of and subject to their histories.[17] Others have located impulses of possible negation in what Michel Foucault called the "disorder of desire," or in the relentless, unquenchable yearning for what is lacking; still others have found it in the dark movement into the forbidden—into vice and consensual violence—or in the play of difference, or in Dionysian ecstasy and abandon, or in the "negative autonomy" of criminality.

The authors in this volume offer another response to the predicament of contemporary cultural theory in their accounts of the unstable, appropriational, and "tensile" nature of lived religion. Perhaps it was inevitable that the domain of relative freedom in the United States should turn out, among these scholars at least, to be religion. However present and necessary religion has been in the development of American capitalism, this has not always been a predictable partnership, as the many eruptions of religious anger and excitement in the nineteenth century indicate. Religious imaginings have generated compelling alternative visions to the authorized order, from the communal movements of the early industrial period to contemporary dissenting practices, like the Jehovah's Witnesses or the many African American religious improvisations of the Great Migration. The efficacy of religious idioms in resisting cultural discipline is emphasized in every essay in this volume, and so we can assume that some notion of resistance to power is central to the theory and phenomenology of lived religion. The sacred is reconceptualized as the place not simply where things happen, but where the circulations of power short-circuit. Danièle Hervieu-Léger talks about the Bible as being "active" with a "surplus of meaning": religious objects have an energy that subverts the powers possessed by the objectifications of the social order—for example, by gender, money, or status—a counter-fetishistic energy. Lived religion appears as the space of resistance par excellence in the United States since the colonial period, and so the approach to lived religion proposed in this book opens up a fundamental rethinking of the place of religion in the American experience, one that emphasizes dissent, subversion, and resistance, rather than harmony, consensus, and social legitimation.

In their impressive sympathy for and theoretical reflections on the religious improvisations of everyday life, however, some of the writers in this volume overlook religion's complicity in sustaining structures and patterns of alienation and domination. I want to contribute to the critical conversation this collection opens up with a dissent from what I see as the dominant political-religious orientation of the essays. Just as we have learned to understand the way power operates in the modern discourses and practices of freedom, so we might consider the ways that religious idioms, even those that appear oppositional to participants and to historians and ethnographers, are themselves deeply, subtly, but inevitably implicated in strategies of social and psychological discipline. It is not enough to speak of religious subversion and resistance unless one also speaks of how these movements of opposition may be at the same time idioms of discipline. Perhaps this collusion between religion and social discipline, between the sacred and the power of culture, is obscured by the way Western critical thought frames the relationship between freedom and domination, subversion and discipline, as oppositional. Hervieu-Léger points to a more dynamic possibility when she concludes her study of contemporary Catholic charismatic culture in France by noting how hierarchy and authority were reestablished in a religious idiom that proclaimed itself free in the Spirit. Language was controlled, leaders designated, desire and spiritual energy oriented, and experience coerced through what Hervieu-Léger calls a "dialectic between spontaneity and regulation." It is one of the challenges of the study of lived religion to examine how the inevitability of discipline coexists with the impulses of resistance and subversion emphasized by other scholars in this collection.

"Desire is inhibited less by 'reality' than by idiom," anthropologist Vincent Crapanzano writes in his study of devotion to the saints in Morocco.[18] Religious idioms make desire and imagination possible at the same time as they constrict and discipline desire and imagination; creating and disciplining are simultaneous processes, or, in Judith Butler's terms, one cannot separate the productive and the repressive functions of the taboo. Toward the end of his life, Sartre described freedom as "the small movement which makes a totally conditioned social being someone who does not render back completely what his conditioning has given him," a modest conception of cultural and psychological resistance that historian Richard Wolin glosses as "the everyday miracle of how an individual human life—isolated, idiosyncratic, and subject to the immense causality of historical conditioning—can nevertheless emerge in its irreducible singularity."[19] Wolin is right in suggesting this as miracle enough. Human beings at work on the world in the available religious idioms of their time and place are doing what they can with what they have at hand. Just as faith does not eliminate pain or death but renders them endurable (as Clifford Geertz put it), neither does religious practice obliterate social contradiction or liberate humans absolutely from their place in particular social, political, and domestic arrangements. Rather, religion enables them to do what they can in and through these realities, for while there are preconditions to our experience, our "*experience* of these preconditions is not entirely preconditioned," as Michael Jackson writes, and so we continually vacillate "between a sense of ourselves as subjects *and* as objects[,] . . . making us feel sometimes that we are world-makers, sometimes that we are merely made by the world."[20] So, too, just as religious idioms are not stable bearers of power or unambiguous intentionality—remember the baron's arm—so they are not completely reliable counterpoints to power either. Instead they offer, in Schmidt's words, "charged moments of encounter, exchange, practice, and relationship."

What is called for is an approach to religion and culture that embeds the religious person and community in history, that sees history and culture not as something that religious persons are "in" but as the media through which they fundamentally are, and that also understands the power of cultural structures and inherited idioms—what Pierre Bourdieu has named the "habitus"—both to shape and discipline thought and as well to give rise to religious creativity and improvisation.[21] What is called for, in other words, is the recognition that it is the historicized and encultured religious imagination that is also the imagination by means of which, in

Marx's famous expression, the frozen circumstances of our worlds are forced to dance by our singing to them their own melodies.

A final word about the existential or moral attitude assumed by the historians in this volume toward religious actors in the past. It is one of the hidden impulses of religious history to make our own experience safer by establishing secure boundaries between people doing religious things in the past and us today, a reflection within historiography of the broader impulse in the study of religions to secure the boundaries between us and them. But just as the otherness of the people we study is a construction, a disciplinary hedge against the recognition of any similarity between their imaginations, fears, needs, hatreds, and fantasies and ours, so the pastness of the past is a carefully erected and maintained barrier too. As Freud should have taught historians, the past is never dead, or even past; yet we persist in naturalizing this boundary, in believing, as one of my students once put it, "dead is dead." Indeed, the discovery of a resonance between our experiences in the present and those of people in the past is so fearsome to historians that they have branded it a heresy, and history departments strain to ensure that their neophytes are free of any taint of this notion. Thus it is assumed, for instance, that the lives and perspectives of contemporary Pentecostals have nothing to tell us about the motivations and desires of their counterparts at the beginning of the century, as if the intervening generations did not constitute a broader shared history linking present and past. Or as if these earlier believers were not human beings like ourselves.

The authors here breach this barrier. Their existential challenge may be the most disturbing and disorienting contribution of this collection to the field of religious history as it is constituted today. Gould establishes a link between the practices she studies and her own everyday concerns, for example. She understands that her intellectual curiosity is grounded in an existential impulse toward the other, a recognition—however implicit—of shared projects. Hall and Brown make us see that Puritan parenting was not alien to impulses we honor in ourselves. Cheryl Forbes' point of departure is the continuing popularity of Mrs. Cowman's devotionals today, and she sees the resonance of her own experience in the lives of women addressed by a text which itself is a dizzying transgression of temporal distinctions. Schmidt writes compassionately of the "mundaneness" of Easter cards that bespeaks the experience of getting and receiving such tokens from relatives, and valuing them. As it is practiced by these scholars, the study of lived religion entails scholarly restraint, compassion, and empathy. Historians often talk with distressing familiarity of the people they study in the past, with a special kind of arrogance rooted in the authority of possession. We are alive, they are dead; we have unreciprocated access to their secrets. But the authors of the essays in this collection that are concerned with the past resist passing judgment on the defenseless dead, and those whose work is concerned with living practitioners of religion know better than to make such judgments about the people they have been spending time with—they know that their sources can tell them just what they think of their academic pretensions.

I am always humbled by the lived complexity of experience, because I know from my own life the difficulty of responding gracefully and competently to unexpected challenges. Although Aglow member Jerry's decision to sacrifice her plans and control her anger and resentment in order to care for her alcoholic, emotionally distant father might be criticized from any number of perspectives as masochistic, inappropriately renunciatory, or submissive, because I have experienced similar dilemmas in my own life I find it as difficult as Griffith does to dissect this woman's choices in these ways. This is a moral as well as historiographic or ethnographic choice, a refusal to take intellectual refuge in the difference between us and them.

The study of lived religion risks the exposure of the researcher. His or her most deeply held existential orientations and moral values are on display with an obviousness not found in earlier ethnographic or, especially, historical accounts. Working on this intimate level, it is harder to avoid the question "so what do you think about all this *really*?" (as opposed to "what sense do you make of this historically?" or "how do you read this culture?"). The existential implication of the study of lived religion is this: we can no longer constitute the objects of our study as other. The authors in this volume propose what may be considered a postcolonial study of religion. To turn a last time to Sartre, whose spirit has hovered over my thinking about these essays, "research is a living relation between men [and women]" and "the relationship between them must be interpreted as a moment of history."[22] Lived religion refers not only to religion as lived by others but also to life as lived by those who approach others' everyday experience to learn about culture and history; it refers, in other words, to the conjuncture of two lived worlds in the study of religion.

NOTES

1. On Lourdes grottoes in the United States, see Colleen McDannell, *Material Christianity: Religion and Popular Culture in America* (New Haven, Conn.: Yale University Press, 1995); 155–62; on the practice of reproduction and imitation more generally in Catholic devotional culture, see the rich ethnographic and historical studies by Lawrence J. Taylor, *Occasions of Faith: An Anthropology of Irish Catholicism* (Philadelphia: University of Pennsylvania Press, 1995); William A. Christian Jr., *Person and God in a Spanish Valley* (New York: Academic

Press, 1972; Princeton, N.J.: Princeton University Press, 1989); and idem, *Local Religion in Sixteenth-Century Spain* (Princeton, N.J.: Princeton University Press, 1981).

2. Quoted in Frank A. S. Imperato, "The Sacred, Fenced In," paper prepared for my course on urban religion, Fordham University at Lincoln Center, December 1982. I am grateful to Imperato for allowing me to use this quotation. An undated pamphlet, "Souvenir from 'The Lourdes of America,'" records that "more than 5,000 persons contributed their labor and money" for the shrine's construction. My guess is that the pamphlet dates from the late 1950s.

3. On Lourdes, see Sandra L. Zimdars-Swartz, *Encountering Mary: From La-Salette to Medjugorje* (Princeton, N.J.: Princeton University Press, 1991); for an interesting recent account of a pilgrimage to the site, see Colm Tóibín, *The Sign of the Cross: Travels in Catholic Europe* (New York: Pantheon, 1994), 10–16.

4. Underlying the many distinctions of the discipline, such as true/false, natural/revealed, with books/without books, and magical/religious, Jonathan Z. Smith has written, lies the fundamental polarity, us/them. *Imagining Religion: From Babylon to Jonestown* (Chicago: University of Chicago Press, 1982), 6.

5. Students in this course read—and then ignore—Clifford Geertz's stricture that religious moods "range from exultation to melancholy, from self-confidence to self-pity, from an incorrigible playfulness to a bland listlessness—to say nothing of the erogenous power of so many of the world's myths and rituals. No more than there is a single sort of motivation one can call piety is there a single sort of mood one can call worshipful." *The Interpretation of Cultures* (New York: Basic Books, 1973), 97.

6. For a critical account of the limits of religious tolerance in the United States, see Stephen L. Carter, *The Culture of Disbelief: How American Law and Politics Trivialize Religious Devotion* (New York: Basic Books, 1993).

7. Jean-Paul Sartre, *Search for a Method*, trans. Hazel E. Barnes (New York: Vintage Books, 1968), 24.

8. Ibid., 28.

9. Michael Jackson, *Paths toward a Clearing: Radical Empiricism and Ethnographic Inquiry* (Bloomington: Indiana University Press, 1989), 65.

10. The relationship between—and possibly even the existence of—"official" and "unofficial" religion (or elite/popular, learned/unlearned, with texts/without texts, or some other like dualism) is a perennially vexed question in the study of "popular religion" (a term I cannot use without thinking of the comment by my friend, Gregory Schopen, an eminent Buddologist, that he will designate what he studies "popular religion" only if everyone else calls what they study "unpopular religion"). The work of Carlo Ginzburg, Emmanuel Le Roy Ladurie, and others in the 1970s and 1980s made it forever impossible (I thought) to understand cultural creativity as moving always from the top down, to think of elites as not implicated themselves in the values and orientation of their cultures, or to conceptualize popular religion as the distortion or misrepresentation of official religion; and the recent turn to "cultural studies" as a way of moving beyond the sterile dichotomy between intellectual and social history might also have been expected to contribute to resolving this nagging issue in religious studies. Yet the term "popular religion" persists, and with it the apparently unavoidable need to remind

ourselves anew with each study what we might be expected by now to know about the dynamics and organization of religious cultures. Many scholars of "popular religion" would agree—out of sheer desperation to conclude this conversation—with Leonard Primiano's exaggeration that "what scholars of religion have referred to as 'official' religion does not, in fact, exist" ("Vernacular Religion and the Search for Method in Religious Folklife," *Western Folklore* 54 [January 1995]: 37–56; the discussion of "official religion" is on pp. 45–47). Primiano, whose essay is an important contribution to the theoretical understanding of "vernacular" religion, immediately qualifies this forthright sentence, however, noting that "it may be possible to refer to various components within a religious body as emically 'official,' meaning authoritative only when used by empowered members within that religious tradition." The qualification of the qualification by the conditional "may be possible" is revealing: in an effort to mark out the authenticity, relative autonomy, and creative integrity of everyday religious practice, we seem to be in danger of losing sight of the centrality of issues of power, domination, discipline, and authority in religious contexts. It is now the defenders of popular, lived, or vernacular religion who seem to be in danger of obscuring the full complexity of religious culture.

The real problem ultimately seems to lie in the persistent ontology of religious studies: in what other discipline would Primiano have to insist that terms like "official" and "popular" have meaning only on a specific discursive field, in particular relations of social power, as opposed to denoting something somehow built into the very structure of reality? Without necessarily assenting to the entire postmodern project, surely we can agree that terms like "popular" and "elite" (and all their variations) are indeed meaningful, but only in particular discursive circumstances of meaning, thus freeing ourselves at last to study lived religion without having to defend it and without having to engage in torturous arguments to protect it from its implications in the circulations of power. For a superb recent example of how lived religion can be studied without apology, see William A. Christian Jr., *Visionaries: The Spanish Republic and the Reign of Christ* (Berkeley: University of California Press, 1996); for a sharp, anti-ontological critique of the discipline of religious studies, see Tomoko Masuzawa, *In Search of Dreamtime: The Quest for the Origin of Religion* (Chicago: University of Chicago Press, 1993).

11. I mean by this what phenomenological anthropologists call the "lifeworld," defined by Michael Jackson as "that domain of everyday, immediate social existence and practical activity, with all its habituality, its crises, its vernacular and idiomatic character, its biographical particularities, its decisive events and indecisive strategies, which theoretical knowledge addresses but does not determine, from which conceptual understanding arises but on which it does not primarily depend." Michael Jackson, ed., *Things as They Are: New Directions in Phenomenological Anthropology* (Bloomington: Indiana University Press, 1996), 7–8.

12. Smith, *Imagining Religion*, 89.

13. Robert Coles, *The Spiritual Life of Children* (Boston, Mass.: Houghton Mifflin, 1990), 7.

14. "Who Is Larry Pratt?" *The New Republic*, March 11, 1996, 9.

15. Alan Ehrenhalt, *The Lost City: Discovering the Forgotten Virtues of Community in the Chicago of the 1950s* (New York: Basic Books, 1995), 112, 132.

16. Judith Butler, *Gender Trouble: Feminism and the Subversion of Identity* (New York: Routledge, 1990), 76.

17. Göran Therborn, *The Ideology of Power and the Power of Ideology* (London: Verso, 1980), 16–17.

18. Vincent Crapanzano, *Tuhami: Portrait of a Moroccan* (Chicago: University of Chicago Press, 1980), 35.

19. Richard Wolin, *The Terms of Cultural Criticism: The Frankfurt School, Existentialism, Poststructuralism* (New York: Columbia University Press, 1992), 135; "The Itinerary of a Thought," in *Between Marxism and Existentialism* (New York: William Morrow, 1974), 35.

20. Jackson, "Introduction," in *Things as They Are*, 10, 21.

21. Pierre Bourdieu, *Outline of a Theory of Practice*, trans. Richard Nice (Cambridge: Cambridge University Press, 1977).

22. Sartre, *Search for a Method*, 72.

Chapter Two

"WHAT SCRIPTURE TELLS ME": SPONTANEITY AND REGULATION WITHIN THE CATHOLIC CHARISMATIC RENEWAL

Danièle Hervieu-Léger

Evolution in French Modes of Research: From the Sociology of Religious Practice to the Sociology of Belief

An ongoing concern of the sociology of religion has been to shed light on what religion really is. Beyond the norms fixed by religious institutions in matters of belief, practice, and behavior, how is religion "lived" by the faithful? What do they believe in? How do they manifest these beliefs in formal or informal practices? How do they organize their daily lives according to these beliefs? How does this "informal" religion reconcile itself with the "formal" religion, controlled by religious authority? Recognizing that compromises occur over time in the relationship between institutional orthodoxy and orthodopraxis, on the one hand, and the lived religion of the faithful, on the other, with what forms of religious sociability should we align these compromises? What are the religious practices, in the broadest sense of the term, in which the lived religiosity of a human group is manifested? These questions arise as soon as religion is treated as a social phenomenon in which is expressed, in a specific manner, the capacity of social actors to produce the meanings that direct their individual and collective experience. At the same time, however, it is necessary to emphasize the difficulty of identifying the several contexts, at once cultural, geographical, and historical, in which "lived" religion manifests itself, for this "lived" religion is, by definition, fluid, mobile, and incompletely structured.

Was it this difficulty that forced the sociology of "religious vitality" (so-called according to Gabriel Le Bras, who drafted the project early on) to concentrate on a quantitative study of Catholic practice?[1] Within this mode of sociology, the important task was to differentiate one group of Catholics from another on the basis of the frequency of religious acts or practices, a task predicated on the assumption that many Catholics did not conform to the rules prescribed by the institutional Church. It must be remembered that Le Bras, who aspired to know "how those millions of swineherds lived since the time of Reginon who demanded on behalf of their modest brotherhood the leisure of Sunday mass and how they visibly provided for the care of their souls,"[2] was well aware that "history acknowledges only kings." Moreover, he was a canonist whose interest in humanity was combined with the perspective of a lawyer. Such a scholar was instinctively prone to grant a privileged attention to the question of submission to the norm in the study of social behavior. Other factors in the making of this sociology also deserve consideration, of which the primary one is the objective importance of religious observance in the very fashioning of socioreligious identity, an identity all the more fraught with implications since, for centuries, the Roman Catholic Church occupied a position of quasi-absolute monopoly over the French religious scene.[3] Catholicism offered truths to believe in, rites to observe, an organization in which all believers could find their place and their law—in other words, a normative framework for all of religious life, individual and collective.

The idea that it is necessary to establish above all the manner in which this normative framework is actually applied within the community of Christians imposes itself that much more insofar as these requirements, particularly those concerning religious practice, are seen as inseparable from a "religious vitality" that animated the Christian masses, who sustained, evoked, or awakened it in different ways according to circumstances and the historical period. This theme, central to the design of Gabriel Le Bras, was also imposed on the generation of researchers that he united and formed, a generation marked, above all, by their observation of the measurable collapse of the world of observances within which the lived religion of the French had organized itself for centuries.[4] Furthermore, in view of the interpretive risks involved in the intuitive identification of the "lived" religion of the subjects, it is not surprising that these same researchers who, in the postwar years, were associated with having an authentically scientific status recognized for the sociology of religion, were moved to place greater importance on the incontestable objectivity which, in principle, characterizes the frequency of religious acts.[5] In its richest conception, this quantitative task of inventorying followers according to the practices they deem important (devotional, regular, seasonal, unconnected) has not only permitted the realization of a remarkably subtle cartography of observances as a whole.[6] It has also managed, by joining itself to the perspective of the regional history of evangelization, to reveal the existence of a plurality of "communities of followers" established over time within Catholicism as a whole.[7] Finally, this approach to the relationship of religious practice to prescribed religion remained linked to a problematic of the institutional regulation of such practices, a perspective that in the end left little place for the study of the meaning given to those practices by the followers themselves and took little account, a fortiori, of practices that could be instituted on the side, that is, outside that sphere of regulation.

This perspective experienced an initial significant shift at the end of the 1960s, at the same time that a debate arose among French historians of Catholicism over the ambiguities of the notion of "dechristianization" commonly associated with the reported decrease in regular observances in a France en route to rapid modernization. This inquiry could not fail to be stimulated by the work of historians who, like Georges Duby in regard to the fourteenth century,[8] showed that this historical period could be characterized, at one and the same time and without contradiction, by the subsiding of the influence of the ecclesiastical establishment and by progress in the diffusion of Christian values. At the same time that such work underscored the limits and flaws of institutional control over the lived religion of the masses, including the so-called Christian periods, it directed sociologists toward the unlimited field of those autonomous or semiautonomous practices over which the institution has had and still has only very little hold: local devotions, healing practices, local pilgrimages, domestic religious questions, and the like. The question of lived religion has thus appeared progressively in the French field of the sociology of religion in tandem with work on "popular" religion.

Certainly the problem was not unknown to classical sociology. Working relations were even established between certain researchers of the French school (notably Henri Hubert and Robert Hertz) and folklorists regarding those local practices that tapped popular fervor and of which the Church, which always presented itself as the guardian of true Christianity, was suspicious when not actually fighting them. The pioneers of this research, still following certain conventional ideas of theology that commonly linked "superstitions," "natural religion," and "paganism," regarded these phenomena as relics, evidence of an archaic or primitive era. Nevertheless, the discovery of the wide extent of these practices and the taking into account of their dynamics along with the always sensitive exchanges operating between the alleged "popular" religion and the dominant religion, began to modify this initial perspective. One was led toward the recognition of the multiplicity of phenomena encompassed under the heading of a single, and presumably uniform, religion, a recognition that opened interesting paths for the analysis of the varying autonomy of these several manifestations in relation to the dynamics of the entirety of a religious system.[9] In the Durkheimian school, Henri Hubert was particularly devoted to the study of such "unorganized popular beliefs and practices" and to emphasizing their local character. Studying a pilgrimage according to strict ethnological methods, Robert Hertz has shown that a dialectic begins to intrude between a local cult, quite possibly rooted in prehistory, and the ecclesiastical system that takes over and then popularizes to its own benefit themes from local tradition.[10] The direction taken by these examples of research was sharply different from a sociology of practice that favored institutional definitions of observance and hesitated to acknowledge any displays of religion by social groups acting "on their own behalf."[11]

Activated by the need to interpret the scope of reactions awakened at the heart of French Catholicism by the liturgical reforms implemented by the Second Vatican Council, reflection on popular religion was revived in the late 1960s. At first it was formed around the opposition between the religion of ordinary people and scholarly or learned religion: in this light, the reaction to the liturgical changes could be analyzed as the resistance of the masses to the action of a cultural elite that monopolizes the production and distribution of cultural and symbolic goods.[12] Beyond this somewhat shortsighted view of things, the question of popular religion crystalized a series of broader inquiries touching on lived religion and its relationship to institutional religion. When we speak of "popular" religion, are we opposing a primitive religion to an elaborate one? A fundamental religious need to a conscious faith? A spontaneous and self-determined religion to an erudite one? A religion of the underclasses to a bourgeois religion? An emotional religion to a rational one?

The diversity of possible approaches which were inscribed in this battery of oppositions suggested that the reality of popular or lived religion could be elucidated only by identifying the multiple scenarios—cultural, social, and institutional—which determine how the several types of "autonomous" practices are differentiated. Such a project would clarify the social logic of those divergences to which the established Church can respond with accommodation, repression, tolerance, or even, indeed, selective encouragement for purposes of more subtle control. The benefit of this procedure would be to decry the false unities constructed around the notion of popular religion and to permit the construction of a theory of the relative autonomy of "spontaneous" practices, the basis, according to François Andre Isambert (indisputably the great architect of this theoretical renewal), of a possible sociological approach to "religious forms neither classified nor qualified in advance by their content."[13]

This imperative lost some of its force when sociologists of religion found themselves mobilized in the late 1970s by the explosive development usually referred to as the "new religious movement," a development that provoked the reconsideration of the religious production occurring within modernity itself. The term "new religious movement" covers a highly composite ensemble of phenomena. In order to simplify, this renewal can be considered in three principal ways.

First, a spiritualizing facet, consisting of a nebula of groups and networks more or less informal and extremely mobile. These groups borrow their themes and principles liberally from different spiritual traditions of the East and West, combining them syncretistically and associating them when necessary with practices of a psychological kind (human relations techniques, transactional psychology, etc.). What is advanced in these groups and networks is the individual search for internal fulfillment; it is the perspective of personal development tied to a "heightening of consciousness."

Second, a conversionist facet, including Christian movements tied more specifically to the Church whose renewal they are seeking. These movements, illustrated in the Catholic context by the charismatic movement, are characterized by an insistence on internal change that can take place in every believer provided he or she abandons himself or herself to the gifts of the (Holy) Spirit. These gifts are made manifest in communities under the extraordinary forms of prophecy, healing, glossolalia, and so on. Enthusiastic from the start, from 1968 to 1973 these charismatic currents succeeded remarkably in their institutional acclimatization. This was particularly so in France, as will be seen later.

Third, a restitutionist facet characterized, in the Protestant camp as well as in the Catholic, by an active concern to reclaim for religious institutions the ability to influence society as supposedly they had done in the past. Certain fundamentalist Protestant currents that moved on to political activism in the early 1970s and certain integralist Catholic currents that created transnational networks from very active, often older national centers like Opus Dei in Spain or the Comunione e Liberazione movement in Italy[14] fall within this third entity.

Statistically speaking, it is clear that the development of these movements (the scope of which it is impossible to enumerate precisely, considering their fluidity of membership and the mobility of networks) has not overturned the religious landscape, neither in France nor in other Western countries. But the phenomenon has attracted the attention of researchers drawn to a much larger process, the proliferation of belief in modern societies nevertheless considered as rationally disenchanted.[15] This process requires us to reconsider the social and cultural significance of the rise of multiple "quests for meaning" unfulfilled by modernist ideologies of progress and the place of religion in the responses to these requests. In this way the issue of the relationship of modernity, marked by the economic crisis of the 1970s and becoming less and less sure of itself and its values, to religion and to different religious traditions returns to the forefront.

For the primary trait of this religious renewal is in fact to deploy itself in the very midst of modern society: having appeared on American campuses in the late 1960s as an offshoot of a current derived from the counterculture, it rapidly took shape in the heart of the educated White American middle class and spread to Western Europe by recruiting in a privileged (but not exclusive) way from the social strata of educators, social workers, and middle-ranking medical and cultural professionals of diverse types who had greatly invested in all the "new social movements" that were flourishing in the early 1970s.[16] These groups do not see (contrary to what the debates over popular religion would still suggest) any contradiction between a massively secularized modernity and a premodern religious culture that subsists marginally in regions and in social groups considered "behind" in relation to the general movement of society and culture. They allow us to view, in a particularly acute form, a tension internal to modernity itself. This tension concerns the conditions under which human individuals and groups can produce the systems of meaning that they need, in the absence of any code of meaning inherited from tradition, in order to situate themselves in a complex and continually changing universe.

If the study of these new religious movements has permitted a renewal of the classical perspective on the relationship between religion and modernity, it is because this approach keeps in view the complex unity of the phenomena of decreasing observances—those aspects that were emphasized for a long time by empirical studies of religious belief—and the phenomena of the reconstruction of beliefs that characterize modern society. Recent manifestations of "religious renewal" do not contradict all that was said in the past about the scope of secularization. They require a reconsideration of secularization in and of itself: not the process of the eradication of religion in a massively rationalized society, but one of the recomposition of the religious within a broader redistribution of beliefs in a society in which no institution can lay claim to a monopoly of meaning.

This process of the deregulation of institutional religion and of the autonomous proliferation of belief is leading sociologists of religion to pose the problem of lived religion in terms that make manifest the generalized expansion of the modern culture of the individual. Similarly, work is occurring on a question, long set aside, of the definition of religion and on a sociology of belief, considered theoretically.[17] But this effort of conceptualization makes sense only if it supports the reasoned description of observable phenomena. The case study presented here situates itself, very modestly, within that objective.[18]

A CASE STUDY

The Catholic charismatic movement appeared for the first time in American Catholic universities at the end of the 1960s. In the beginning, this devotional movement was strongly influenced by contacts its leaders had with the currents of revival taking place, during the same period, within Protestant denominations and particularly within the historically Pentecostal churches. Taking into account the importance of emotional expression within the earliest of the prayer groups, the practice of the gifts of the Spirit, the spectacular character of conversions, and the suddenness of change in the new converts' lives, the first observers of the Catholic charismatic renewal all emphasized its closeness to the various revival movements that were emerging in other Christian churches in the context of the new American spiritual culture of the 1970s. Since then, the movement has spread rapidly throughout North America and Europe. For twenty-five years, charismatic prayer groups have been mushrooming in European Catholic countries—and especially in France—where the Pentecostal revivalist traditions had practically no roots or influence.

In France, this religious movement, with its style of spontaneous religiosity, has both revealed and contributed to a profound evolution within "lived" Catholicism, an evolution that constitutes a new phase in the ongoing negotiations between modernity and the Catholic Church. It is possible to analyze some aspects of this evolution by focusing attention on a specific aspect of this new style of religiosity, that is, a way of reading and interpreting Scripture. More precisely, I introduce some reflections on the practice of spontaneous reading of Scripture that is spreading throughout these charismatic prayer groups. This case study is based on some of my observations concerning prayer groups in France and, to a lesser extent, in the United States. I must say that these observations were not driven by a particular interest in the practice of spontaneous reading of Scripture, as such. My principal interest was in the relationships among emotion, religion, and modernity and, more precisely, in the meaning and significance of the development of religious emotionalism in relation to traditional patterns of secularization. Is it, as some seem to think, a "return" phenomenon, exposing the limits of secularization in modern societies? Or is it a more complex process, involving a recomposition of religious activity in "rationally disenchanted" modern society?[19] I return briefly to this question at the close of this essay. Let me also note that the empirical observation of charismatic groups brought to my attention the more specific problem of the regulation of spontaneity within the movement. This process of regulation crystalizes, in some way, the ambivalent relationship that the new religious movements belonging to the Catholic domain have with the tradition of the Church and faith from which they spring. From this point of view, the question of the reading of Scripture appeared to be particularly relevant.

Before introducing some comments about this last point, it is probably useful to give a brief overview of the diversity of the prayer groups that are multiplying in all Catholic countries, and especially in France.[20] Their institutional status and their functioning are indeed very diverse: some of these groups have a formal bond with great charismatic communities such as l'Emmanuel, le Chemin Neuf, Le Lion de Juda, Le Pain de Vie, and Les Beatitudes, and, accordingly, are similar to religious orders. Many others are completely autonomous and self-regulating. Some groups are incorporated into the institutional device of a parish; they meet in a church and are open to believers on the same basis as any other parish activity. Still others, organized as informal networks, meet occasionally at the home of one of their members. Because of the variable style of their organization, the discretion these groups usually observe, and, above all, their mobility, it is particularly difficult to identify (and count) them. Depending most of the time on the initiative of lay men and women, they are created and dissolved according to the rhythm of the comings and goings of their members. This "fluidity" is a characteristic feature that in and of itself reveals them to be one of the most representative expressions of a religion of emotional community going hand in hand, in all highly developed societies of Western Europe and North America, with the increasing acclimatization of the modern culture of the individual within Catholic culture.

According to Max Weber's description, the religion of emotional communities refers to the community of disciplines gathered around a bearer of charisma. My own approach will be broader, for it includes within the religion of emotional communities those forms of religious communalization in which the expression of affect by individuals and the group is paramount and fundamental. The religion of emotional communities is first and foremost a religion of voluntary groups, implying personal commitment (or even conversion, in the revivalist sense) from each of its members. The testimony brought to the group by each convert and the recognition he or she receives in return create very close ties between the group and the individual. This bond of membership is particularly emotional when (as stressed by Weber) communities of disciples are grouped together around a charismatic figure. In all instances, however, repeated personal membership acts, involving every member of the group, tend to become the main aim of community gatherings. This intensification of the expressive dimension of religious life does not necessarily mean that this element is particularly effervescent. Groups in which song, dance, and glossolalia are used to bring participants to a state of trance-like collective excitement are relatively rare, and this kind of "hot" religiosity is seldom long-lived. However, all such emotional communities pay particular attention to bodily involvement in prayer (holding hands or shoulders and so on). The aesthetic and ecological need for an environment favorable to "emotional convergence" among the participants is also prominent, as is the widespread attention to nonverbal forms of religious expression. Moreover, there is a tight relationship between this recognition of the importance of the body and the senses in individual and collective religious life and the mistrust, whether explicit or not, of any kind of doctrinal or theological formulation of the convictions shared within the group.

This repulsion of "intellectual" religion is more than a mere expression of the rejection of any kind of specialized power, a rejection that usually characterizes self-regulating groups. It represents a conviction that the intellectualization of belief is unnecessary and even harmful to the community's purpose in that it allegedly destroys the singularity of personal commitments within the community. The primacy of individual experience over any kind of objectively controlled communal conformity explains the porosity of the borders established by emotional communities. One enters easily, but one leaves as easily, once emotional commitment to the community, its ideals, or its leader ceases. These flexible gatherings often come into existence through the condensation of wider and looser networks. They create possibilities for "making contact" or "keeping contact." They do not formally imply any permanent relationship among their members. Notions of obligation and permanence are, generally speaking, alien to the religion of emotional communities. Participation is normally a personal choice and lasts insofar as it brings satisfaction to the individual concerned. The fluidity of the emotional network corresponds to the mobility of individual intentions and of collective feelings within the group. It reveals the instability proper to emotional states taken as the gauge of intensity and authenticity in spiritual experience.

The notion of the religion of emotional communities is an ideal type: it describes, in an abstract way, a specific form of religious sociability. This type has been elaborated in order to identify certain trends that are also at work within religious institutions (parishes, movements, theology faculties, monasteries, and so on) that shape the religious behavior of individuals. But, from an empirical point of view, the features of the religion of emotional communities are most clearly attested to in the Catholic charismatic renewal, representing, in France, a mosaic of about two thousand groups bringing together five to one hundred members each. One characteristic of the renewal is its powerful attractiveness to youth. Ten thousand to fifteen thousand persons gather each year to participate in the summer meetings of the community "Emmanuel" at Paray-le-Monial. An estimated three hundred thousand persons are involved in the movement as a whole, either as members of regular prayer groups or as occasional participants in sessions and meetings. In different tones, all the currents of the charismatic movement insist with an equal strength on the internal change that can operate in each believer's life if he or she welcomes the gifts of the Spirit. These gifts often manifest themselves under the extraordinary forms of prophecy, healing, or glossolalia. Originally, the style of the communities was clearly influenced by a rather exuberant emotionalism akin to the style of the Protestant revivals. For about ten years, all of these prayer groups have become less extroverted. The leaders, often called "shepherds," now take the lead in regulating collective experience, including the reception of the gifts of the Spirit.

The progressive routinization of the fervency that was present at the beginning of the movement is congruent with the remarkable institutional acclimatization of the charismatic renewal within the Church, where it currently represents a sort of spiritual avant-garde. The official recognition presently granted to the charismatic renewal by Church authorities in France (as is also happening everywhere in Europe and North America) corresponds to a successful compromise between the interests of the movement (that attracts, in the context where it develops, only fervent Catholics in quest of a more intense spiritual life and allergic to any sectarian dissidence) and the interests of the religious institution. The latter hopes to benefit from a capacity for mobilization that appears to produce numerous (numerous in the French context!) priestly vocations.

I turn now to the spontaneous reading of Scripture that is an everyday practice in all Catholic charismatic prayer groups. The concrete functioning of the exercise is well known and often described: after an introductory prayer (invocation of the Holy Spirit, offering of the community, recapitulation of the members' spiritual expectations, and so on), one of the participants opens the Book. He or she generally chooses some verses at random and reads them in a loud voice. A time of silence generally follows the reading. Then, if they wish, the attendees speak in turn. Most often, each of them gives a personal comment: anybody is able to say what the passage inspires in him or her; he or she may indicate what the biblical episode means, according to personal experience; he or she may evoke how the text illuminates a choice about to be made or a way of behaving about to be adopted. More rarely, the one who speaks offers the group a theme for meditation and prayer. The address may be long or short. Sometimes, it is only a brief invocation: "Amen! Alleluia! Thank you, Lord!" The "collect" (a gathering of all these personal prayers) may sometimes introduce a common prayer of intercession or thanksgiving, but a collective debate about the meaning of the text is exceptional.

An initial principle concerns the typical informality of this communal relationship to Scripture: in principle, nothing is specified in advance except the "availability to the text" that is required of all participants. None of them is allowed to claim the right to tell how the text has to be listened to. I said: in principle. Actually—especially in long-lasting groups—collective and individual modes of spontaneity often meet their limitations. For example, the responsibility of opening the Book frequently falls to the shepherd, who determines the suitable moment to do it. Only at their beginning do groups plead for a completely free practice, which implies

that anybody, moved by a personal spiritual inspiration, has the authority
to invite the group to refer to Scripture at any moment. More often, the
practice of spontaneous reading is gradually integrated as an anticipated
moment in the schedule of the prayer meeting. A member of the group is
designated to recommend it.

One notices, however, that this practice has succeeded in keeping its
most spontaneous form more durably than have other, initially charismatic, practices. With the growing institutional integration of the movement, glossolalia and the baptism in the Spirit tend more and more to be
placed under ritual control. The rest in the Spirit, which inspired a major
distrust on the part of the Church at the beginning of the renewal, has
almost completely disappeared since then. In this context, the practice of
spontaneous reading seems to persist as a substitute for the most extraordinary manifestations of the effective presence of the Spirit in the group.
The personal free appropriation of Scripture is becoming the only ground
where "the unexpected" that is supposed to confirm the freedom of the
Spirit may demonstrate its effectiveness. Whatever the limitations that
curtail the spontaneity of the members, the point is that each believer is
entitled to appropriate the text personally and to communicate its meaning to the others.

In a Catholic context, the development of this practice establishes a
very distinct distance from the conventional rules concerning the reading
of Scripture. The random choice of the passage means, at first, a complete
independence with regard to the liturgical planning of readings defined by
the authorities of the Church. It excludes—since the commentary on the
text depends on the personal inspiration of any participant—the priest's
homily that usually accompanies the reading of the Bible. More generally,
it leaves aside any sort of official clerical commentary. For the same reason,
the scholarly commentaries emanating from experts in theology, exegesis,
or history are also set aside: anyone among the believers illuminated by the
Holy Spirit—man, woman, or child—is supposed to have something personal to say about the text according to one's own inspiration. This theme
of "inspiration" serves to justify spontaneous reading even if the practice
is indeed submitted to more complex regulation. It matches a clear rejection of any monopoly on interpretation, whatever the source. This rejection includes both the pretension of the institution to offer a unique "true
sense" of the text and the privilege of (religious or nonreligious) clerics
who employ a professional competence to impose an orthodox understanding of Scripture. Against this double pretension, charismatic prayer
groups oppose, with a flawless constancy, the evangelical reference: "This
has been hidden to sages and scholars, and revealed to the small." The
believer who leaves it up to the Spirit "has all the knowledge that is necessary to understand what the text tells."

Members of charismatic prayer groups constantly insist on the fact that the rejection of any monopoly on interpretation also includes the readings that use Scripture to legitimate the action of the group (and its members) in the world. This critique is aimed explicitly at the "base communities" mushrooming at the beginning of the 1970s, and referring themselves to the Latin American liberation theology (or to a European vision of liberation theology). The base communities also developed a sharp criticism of the official reading of Scripture. Their critical remarks were part of a political and religious protest against the functioning of the Church and its compromise with the authorities and the dominant classes. It pointed at first to the individualistic morality of official interpretations concerning the accomplishment of charity and justice and the construction of the Kingdom. It included the selection of liturgical texts that always tend—according to the same criticism—to water down the political and social strength of biblical assessments. The base communities wanted to produce an alternative reading of Scripture consistent with the political commitment of their members. This perspective was mostly effective in groups endeavoring to achieve a materialistic reading of the Bible inspired by the Marxist methodology developed by the Portuguese theologian Ferdinando Bolo: these groups planned to elaborate a revolutionary perusal of the gospel and wanted to demonstrate that communities fitted out with effective intellectual tools have the capacity to reveal and actualize the subversive power of the Bible. While doing so, they also wanted to reveal the social interests allegedly at stake in the Church's exclusive control of the "true" reading of Scripture.

Within charismatic prayer groups, the practice of spontaneous reading also means (at least implicitly) the rejection of clerical and institutional commentary on the text. But it is not supposed to produce an alternative reading, a new exclusive interpretation: it intends (at least ideally) to set free the plurality of individual perceptions, sensitivities, and expressions of the Word of God. This is exactly the point where the difference between the charismatic spontaneous reading of Scripture and fundamentalist practice comes into view. The fundamentalist reading rejects the idea of a regulating authority that stipulates an official interpretation of the text. In that sense, it includes a certain "anticlerical" tone. But this rejection has a completely different justification than that which occurs among Catholic charismatics. For the fundamentalists, it corresponds to the certainty that no human institution can claim the right to interpret the meaning of Scripture because the words of the Bible are, definitely, the Word of God. According to Jean Bauberot's distinctions, this perspective may come under a popular or a scholarly literalism, or may define itself as an inspirationism.[21] Whatever its variants, the Protestant fundamentalist tradition tends to postulate a perfect identity between the words of the sacred text (*le signifiant*) and their meaning (*le signifié*). Of course, one knows that—beyond the dogma of biblical inerrancy—a flexibility of interpretation can be reintroduced through sermons. But the absolute rejection of any relativization of the sacred words confers on the Bible an obvious significance that its reception by the community confirms: the text has only one meaning, and each believer is supposed to understand and accept it. In the prayer groups, on the contrary, the text is considered as a *signifié* that refers to a multitude of *signifiants*. Nobody—individual, community, institution—can claim to enclose them in a unique commentary.

I would like to illustrate this point with some quotations, selected from interviews:

> There is a complete unpredictability of the echo that the text arouses in the heart of the one who is faithfully listening to it.

> This unpredictability refers to "the unfathomable wealth of the Word of God, that completely overflows the very words of the text."

> There is always a surplus of meaning that is given to each believer. The one who refuses this overabundance opposes the action of the Spirit within each person who listens to the Word.

> The Text is not a mausoleum. The text is active. It is a divine Word as far as its meaning is revealed to the one who is listening to it in the Spirit.

All members of the prayer groups emphasize insistently the fact that each person, in the singularity of his or her individual path, is the addressee of a personally aimed Word.

"What I come to seek here, it is what the gospel tells me." This last quotation summarizes perfectly the dominant opinion among members of the charismatic prayer groups:

> Not what the Church tells that the gospel tells;
> Not what the text tells;
> But what the text tells me, "because it is written for me, and for each person around me."

It is not necessary to multiply quotations to stress the essential difference that exists between the two versions of spontaneous reading of Scripture. The fundamentalist practice attests the objective meaning of the text, beyond any institutional mediation. The charismatic practice is a way of asserting the primacy of individual subjectivity, even in religious matters. The fundamentalist principle of biblical inerrancy is a radical protest against all forms of transaction between the church and the mundane universe under the cloak of the interpretation of the text. The charismatic practice of spontaneous interpretation is—just as glossolalia and the quest for nonverbal forms of emotional communication between the believers are—an expression of protest against the stereotyped nature of the authorized religious language. The fundamentalist practice implies a complete heteronomy between the Word of God and the language of human beings (and, therefore, it calls for a rupture between religion and modernity); on the contrary, the charismatic practice is completely in tune with the modern culture of the individual, including the desire for self-fulfillment, the autonomous quest for one's own truth, and the improving of personal authenticity.

The question that comes to attention now is of course the one of the impact of this claim for subjectivity within Catholicism. Once again, we will see that the study of the charismatic practice of spontaneous reading of Scripture offers some interesting indications. One observes indeed that the controlled socialization of this practice within the charismatic movement allows the limited incorporation of some of the trends of the modern culture of the individual within Catholic culture. From this perspective, it is worthwhile examining the reasons why the prayer groups attach such great importance to the *collective* practice of spontaneous reading. If one admits, according to their own declarations, that each person has to discover, with the help of the Spirit, what meaning the text has as far as he or she is personally concerned, one can wonder why this person needs to share his or her personal reading and expression about the text within a group. When you ask members of such prayer groups, answers come very easily (I quote):

> It is not enough to simply set out our individual experiences with the text. We are not alone facing the text: it is the Spirit that understands and expresses itself through each of us.

> We testify mutually the lighting that the Spirit brings us.

> By listening to what everyone tells, we enrich our spiritual comprehension of the text.

> We discover a convergence that renews our awareness of the presence of the Spirit in the group.

Is the function of the community meeting only to create, from time to time, the opportunities for such accounts and mutual expressions to enrich and sustain the individual experience? This interpretation applies to a certain number of prayer groups that are closely related, from this point of view, to the ideal type of the mystic group described by Ernst Troeltsch. Such is the case of self-regulating groups, socially very homogeneous, and whose members possess (in Pierre Bourdieu's terminology) a high cultural capital. I have had the opportunity to verify this point while observing, for several months, an ecumenical group of students and scholars that referred explicitly to this particular model of religious association. Most of the time, however, the community practices of spontaneous reading appear to be the instrument of something like a "putting under control" of the subjective and direct access of individuals to Scripture. The persistent reference—illustrated by the quotations—to the presence of "the Spirit that listens to us and understands us" is essential from this point of view. If the presence of the Spirit justifies the recognition that anybody is allowed to speak according to his or her personal sensitivity to the text, then each of these personal expressions may become a marker for the experiences of the others. In this way, the space of legitimate readings, to which expressions of the individuals have to adjust themselves, gradually appears as the mutual adjustment of the various individual readings. This process needs time, and it varies according to the cultural and social background of the group. But all the groups, as effervescent as they are at their beginning, tend always to elaborate, in the course of their meetings, a common language that provides an unescapable stereotyping of the individual expressions within them.

This homogenizing regulation of individual expression within the group corresponds to a classic mode of group dynamics. But this dynamics is powerfully strengthened in many charismatic prayer groups where the affirmation of spontaneity is moderated by the imperative of the "discernment." In the Christian tradition, the "discernment of spirits" is a charisma of the Holy Spirit. This charisma is important especially because it has a close bond with the charisma of prophecy. According to the first epistle of Paul to the Christians of Corinth, those who are "taught by the Spirit" are characterized by their capacity for "discerning gifts of God" and "researching the best." The Spirit of God is supposed to join human intelligence to help it discover what comes from God and what does not come from God. In reference to the gifts of the Spirit, discernment has found a central place in the charismatic revival. But observation of a certain number of groups shows that the recognition of the presence of the "charisma of discernment" within a member and the affirmation that it is necessary to exert a "responsibility of discernment" in the group occur frequently at the same time. From the point of view of social control within the group, this convergence has obviously very direct implications. Responsibility for the discernment of spirits at first falls to each member of the group.

We cannot make the text tell anything.

There are always a lot of ambiguities in the spontaneous way we have of reading Scripture: we have to help ourselves mutually in order to distinguish between what the Spirit tells us and our illusion.

In this last domain, some members of the group whose "spiritual maturity" is recognized by the other members have a particular role to play. In principle, they get this recognition only from the quality of their personal testimony. Actually, other types of legitimate (and noncharismatic) authority (such as seniority in the group, being a priest, a monk, or a nun, the fact of having studied theology, etc.) are often restored through these means. Finally, the responsibility of discernment tends often to be formally allotted to the leader, the shepherd of the group. The charismatic practice of the discernment merges, in this case, with the official exercise of a power whose first task is the control of overflows of spontaneity and subjectivity in the whole life of the group, and particularly during the practice of the spontaneous reading of Scripture.

Does this regulating function of "community discernment" (variously exerted according to the internal structure of the group) reduce to nothingness the affirmation of the rights of religious subjectivity, which is at stake in the development of the practice of spontaneous reading within Catholicism? Actually, the dialectic between spontaneity and regulation is interesting because it illustrates perfectly the concrete situation of the charismatic movement within a Catholic universe. Charismatic groups do not want to drop out from their common Catholic home. Instead, they try to negotiate the conditions of a relative autonomy within the Catholic system. On the one hand, their involvement in free personal religious expression leads us to consider prayer groups as instruments of the acculturation of the modern culture of the individual within Catholic culture. On the other hand, the community formalization of these groups transforms them into instruments of the reinstatement of an individualistic and subjective protest, originating in this modern culture of the individual, within the Catholic tradition.

This ambiguity around the relationship to Scripture meets the more general ambivalence these emotional communities have about tradition. The religious spontaneity that characterizes the religion of emotional communities introduces elements of discontinuity with the sets of beliefs, doctrines, attainments, norms, and obligatory practices that the institution itself defines as the corpus of its tradition, of which it is the guardian and the mentor. As a "hot" phenomenon (opposed, according to a long-lasting Durkheimian tradition, to the "coldness" of institutional religion), collective emotion evacuates completely or partly, as far as the group is concerned, the need of referring to an authorized memory; that is to say, to a tradition. From this point of view, these phenomena may be regarded as contributing to the institutional deregulation that is coextensive with the general process of secularization. But the religion of emotional communities can be considered, at the same time, as a modern form of the socialization of individual experience within Catholic tradition. This is not only a consequence of the unescapable process of routinization that leads every lasting group to fix its own tradition. Empirical observation reveals, at the same time, that these socializations constitute, in the modern context of the dissemination of belief phenomena (the well-known "bricolage"), a favorable way for the aggregation of the "personal narratives" produced by individual believers, and for the ultimate merger of these narratives with the "Great Narrative"—the official tradition that the Church claims to preserve. In that sense, these observations concerning the practice of spontaneous reading of Scripture within charismatic prayer groups may open the way to a study of the process of cultural modernization within Catholicism and, as well, to a study of emotional socialization in accordance with dominant Catholic values and norms.

NOTES

1. Gabriel Le Bras never ceased urging that scholars of religion develop, notably, monographs on villages and kindred *petit pays*.

2. Gabriel Le Bras, *Etudes de sociologie religieuse* (Paris: Presses Universitaires de France, 1955), 352–53.

3. It is worth observing that, in spite of all the critiques made during the past thirty years of practices as too limited a criterion for evaluating the relationship between voting patterns and religion, the sociology of elections continues resolutely to consider the frequency of religious practice as a "synthetic indicator" (the more easily integrated into quantitative surveys, in any case) of the presence of religion.

4. This generation is marked by a recognition of the breadth of the loss of religious life linked to modernization, urbanization, and industrialization, a recognition of which the publication of Henri Godin and Yves Daniel's *France pays de mission?* (Paris: Editions de Minuit, 1943) is unquestionably the emblem.

5. For a particularly suggestive evocation of these debates about the scientific study of religion in France, see François A. Isambert, "Quarante ans déja," *Archives de sciences sociales des religions* 93(1996): 5–22.

6. See François A. Isambert and Jean Paul Terrenoire, *Atlas de la practique religieuse des catholiques en France* (Paris: Presses de la Fondation nationale des sciences politiques; Editions du CNRS, 1980).

7. See the important work of Fernand Boulard and Jean Remy, *Pratique religieuse urbaine et régions culturelles* (Paris: Editions Economic et Humanisme, les Editions Ouvrières, 1968).

8. Georges Duby, *Les Fondements d'un nouvel humanisme, 1280–1440* (Geneva: Droz, 1966).

9. "A religion," noted Durkheim, "is not necessarily contained within one sole and single idea, and does not proceed from one unique principle which, though varying according to the circumstances under which it is applied, is never-

theless at bottom always the same . . . but rather consists in a system of cults, each endowed with a certain autonomy. Also, this autonomy is variable. Sometimes they are arranged in a hierarchy, and subordinated to some predominating cult, into which they are finally absorbed; but sometimes, also, they are merely re-arranged and united. . . . At the same time, we find the explanation of how there can be groups of religious phenomena which do not belong to any special religion: it is because they have not been, or are no longer, a part of any religious system." Emile Durkheim, *The Elementary Forms of the Religious Life*, trans. Joseph W. Swain (New York: The Free Press, 1965), 56–57.

10. Robert Hertz, "Saint-Besse, étude d'un culte alpestre," *Revue de l'histoire des religions* 67 (1913): 115–80, repr. in *Mélanges de sociologie religieuse et de folklore* (Paris: Presses Universitaires de France, 1970). On popular religion as an approach within the French school of sociology, see Jacques Maitre, "La sociologie du catholicisme chez Cnarnowski, Halbwaches, Hertz et Van Gennep," *Archives de sociologie des religions* 11 (1966): 55–169.

11. Jacques Maitre, "Religion populaire," *Encyclopaedia universalis France* (Paris: Encyclopaedia Universalis, 1980), 14:25.

12. This problematic of elites and masses recurs, in the same epoch, among historians of religion, and especially among those who work on the institutionalizing of the Counter Reformation. See, e.g., Marc Venard, "Elites, masses, eglise: Modèles sociologiques et peuple de Dieu," *Recherches et débats* 71 (1971).

13. See François Isambert, *Le sens du sacré: Fête et religion populaire* (Paris: Editions de Minuit, 1982).

14. Cf. Salvatore Abbruzzese, *Comunione e Liberazione: Identite catholique et disqualification du monde* (Paris: Cerf, 1989).

15. Among the phenomena that witness to the proliferation of belief in modern societies there is, of course, the rising tide of belief in astrology, spiritualism, the parasciences, and the like. See D. Boy and G. Michelat, "Croyances aux parasciences: Dimensions sociales et culturelles," *Revue Française de Sociologie* 27 (1986): 175–204.

16. These social characteristics of the activists in the new religious movements are also found among the neo-oriental currents, in the renewal of Christianity, and in movements of Jewish renewal, all of which are occurring in both Europe and the United States.

17. In the sense which Michel de Certeau spoke of an anthropology of belief, taking account not only of beliefs but equally of practices.

18. A short version was presented in the Rennor Conference in New Religions and New Religiosity and the Twelfth Nordic Conference of the Sociology of Religion, August 1994 (forthcoming).

19. See Danièle Hervieu-Léger, "Present-Day Emotional Renewals: The End of Secularization or the End of Religion?," in *A Future for Religion? New Paradigms for Social Analysis*, ed. William H. Swatos (Newbury Park, Calif.: Sage, 1992), 129–48.

20. For one description of the charismatic movement in France (among many other possible references), see Monique Hébrard, *Les nouveaux disciples, dix ans*

après voyage a travers les communautés (Paris: Centurion, 1987). For a sociology of the acculturation of charismatic groups within institutional Catholicism, see Marline Cohen, "Vers de nouveaux rapports avec l'institution ecclesiastique: l'exemple du Renouveau Charismatique en France," *Archives de sciences sociales des religions* 62 (1986): 61–80.

21. J. Bauberot. "Integrisme religieux, essai comparatif," *Social Compass*, 32, no. 4 (1985).

Chapter Three

FAMILY STRATEGIES AND RELIGIOUS PRACTICE: BAPTISM AND THE LORD'S SUPPER IN EARLY NEW ENGLAND

Anne S. Brown and David D. Hall

"AND I WILL ESTABLISH my covenant between me and thee and thy seed after thee in their generations for an everlasting covenant, to be a God unto thee, and to thy seed after thee" (Genesis 17:7 KJV). Thus spoke the God of Genesis to Abraham, and thus came into being the covenantal relationship that enabled Abraham's long-barren wife, Sarah, to conceive (v. 15). To these new parents God promised the blessing of multitudes of descendants, all of whom would inherit the covenant and prosper under it (vv. 2–6, 16, 19). In this manner, and at the very outset of Scripture, the themes of covenant, fertility, and family continuity became intertwined.

This fusion of family and covenant was powerfully significant to the English Puritans who founded New England. These people understood themselves as heirs of the covenant of Genesis 17:7 and partakers of its benefits. "The same Covenant which God made with the Nationall Church of Israel and their Seed," John Cotton wrote in the early 1650s, "It is the very same (for substance) and none other which the Lord maketh with any Congregationall Church and our Seed." The main consequence of this ever-extending, ever-continuous covenant was that "Children that are born when their Parents are Church Members, are in Covenant with God even from their birth, *Gen.* 17:7–12 and their Baptisme did seale it to them." Eliding covenant, church, family, and infant baptism, the colonists celebrated a God who "promised to be a God to the Faithfull and their seed after them in their Generations, and taketh them to be his People."[1]

Yet the God of this all-encompassing covenant was also an exclusive God, dispensing saving grace to some and not to others. This exclusivity became manifest in the colonists' policy of church membership. Rejecting the inclusive parish system of the Church of England, with its almost-automatic access to church membership and the sacrament of baptism, the immigrants shifted to a model of voluntary or "gathered" churches based on a very different covenant, the covenant of grace, and open only to adults who could reliably be considered "visible saints."

Because it was the covenant of grace on which these gathered congregations were founded, the social bond within them was quite different from the social bond evoked by Genesis 17:7. Visible saints entered the church not as family members but as individuals. In this manner, the church on earth anticipated the rupturing of family bonds that would occur at the Last Judgment when Christ returned to earth. As imagined by the New England poet-minister Michael Wigglesworth, when the moment came for the elect and nonelect to go their separate ways, "The godly wife conceives no grief, nor can she shed a tear / For the sad state of her dear Mate, when she his doom doth hear." Mothers exhibited the same acceptance of separation in parting from children who were reprobate: "The tender Mother will own no other of all her numerous brood, / But such as stand at Christ's right hand acquitted through his Blood." Moving joyously into the Kingdom, saints transcended the emotions and expectations that ordinarily linked husbands and wives, parents and children. So had the archetypal "pilgrim" acted when, at the opening of Bunyan's *Pilgrim's Progress* (1678), he quit his wife and children to set out on the journey that led to Christ.[2]

Every culture encompasses contradictions, a rule that is amply demonstrated in the religious history of early New England. Our concern is with an overlapping series of contradictions rooted in the contrast between a covenant that signified family preservation and another that signified the rupturing consequences of a limited atonement. According to the covenant of Genesis 17:7, the church and the sacrament of baptism were agencies that enabled parents to incorporate their children within the protecting shelter of God's blessing. According to the new covenant, the church safeguarded the purity of visible saints, separating them from the unworthy, some of whom were spouses or children, and providing baptism only for the children of these saints. In the first situation, kinship and covenant coincided; in the second, they were probably at odds.

For more than a century—from the first moments of colonization in the 1630s to the Great Awakening of the 1740s—the church history of New England may be understood as a prolonged, contentious search for a means of holding together these two covenants. The synod that met in Cambridge in 1646 and 1648 wrestled with this issue, though the document the synod issued, familiarly known as the Cambridge Platform, left it unresolved. At two other gatherings of the clergy (in 1657 and 1662), the majority favored reshaping the scope of infant baptism to bring it in line with the covenant of Genesis 17:7—a decision forcefully protested by a minority. Both sides turned to the printing press in their attempts to gain popular support. Meanwhile, a wave of schisms or schism-like separations swept through local churches as ministers and congregants argued over the meaning of church membership. Near the turn of the century, Solomon Stoddard, the minister of Northampton between 1665 and 1729, proposed to open both sacraments to everyone who met certain moral standards, a solution that itself became controversial, with Cotton and Increase Mather as his main adversaries. During the revivals of the 1740s, the "New Lights" criticized all forms of compromise. So did Jonathan Edwards, who, after succeeding Stoddard in the ministry of Northampton, was expelled from the pulpit in 1750 when he sought to reverse the congregation's policies.[3]

It is not the purpose of this essay to retrace the history of these conflicts. Rather we are interested in how ordinary people worked their way through the contradictions that theology and Scripture framed for them. In actions taken and not taken lies the story we want to tell, a story of the choices people made in everyday life about when and whether they should affiliate with the church and participate in baptism, the Lord's Supper, and renewal of covenant. The rhythms of affiliation and participation marked out in everyday life constitute the basic structure of lived religion in early New England.

How people behaved can be addressed through quantitative data on affiliation and participation. But in seeking to understand why lay men and women acted as they did, we must turn to the meanings that invested church, sacraments, family, mothers, and inheritance.[4] It is equally important that we acknowledge the social field within which these meanings were appropriated and put to use. Why did parents want their children baptized? Why did wives commonly affiliate with the church before their husbands? And why did so many people refrain from participating in the Lord's Supper? Only when we unite the social and the theological can we fruitfully address these questions.

In saying that religious practices unfold in a social field, we have in mind a particular setting, the intergenerational family. Historical demography and social history have demonstrated that parents in early New England craved children. The data on patterns of inheritance indicate that these same parents pursued a "family strategy" of accumulating land, cattle, housing, and moveable goods to pass on to the next generation.[5] This strategy also had to address the intangible aspects of inheritance. How could parents ensure the physical health and moral well-being of their children? In a culture where sin and sickness were perceived as causally related and where God's justice and mercy were immediately sensible in the flow of daily life, the goal of family preservation could only be accomplished by gaining access to the benefits that resulted from participation in the church covenant. Yet how could families appropriate these benefits without setting in motion the divisive consequences of the covenant of grace? Was it possible to reconcile the nature of the gathered church with family-centered strategies of inheritance and incorporation?

The practices that hold the answer to this question drew on a rich array of meanings; it is with these meanings, as conveyed within the Puritan movement, that we begin.

THE GATHERED CHURCH: EXCLUSIVITY IN PRACTICE

Arising out of dissatisfaction with an English Reformation that, more for reasons of state than of theology, left much unchanged, the Puritan movement in the late sixteenth century pressed for a "thorough" remodeling of the national church. The major complaint of the reformers was that a policy of near-inclusive membership degraded what should have been an ethical community into a "mixt multitude" of the holy and the profane. Proposing that the church of the apostolic age serve as a normative model, Puritans argued that every church member should be a "living stone" shaped and hewn by the Holy Spirit to become a fit element of "God's house." Church membership was therefore not an automatic right but open only to persons who endeavored to pass from a state of sin to a state of holiness. Consistent with their understanding of the church as an ethical community, Puritans insisted that everyone within it engage individually and collectively in the process of sanctification.[6]

Long argued, yet long mired in frustration, the Puritan program was immediately put into action in New England. Many of the colonists (both clerical and lay) arrived in the New World preferring a particular variation on the original program. Instead of reestablishing a territorial parish system where, in some manner, each local church included everyone living within certain geographic boundaries, the colonists instituted voluntary congregations that drew selectively from the wider mass of people. They were able to establish this "Congregational Way," as it came to be called, because there was no parish system in place to dismantle and because, in the early years of immigration, feelings ran high against the corruptions of the Church of England. Some of the colonists also reasoned that a system of gathered, voluntary churches was a step toward accomplishing the return of Christ and the restoration of His Kingdom. Linking Congregationalism to the eschaton, they proposed to restore the purity of apostolic times even if, in accomplishing this purity, they had to unchurch persons who in England had been members of a parish. Thus it happened that, at one of the earliest church gatherings, a mere thirty persons of the more than two hundred present passed into membership.[7]

By the close of the 1630s, the colonists had taken a second and equally far-reaching step. Affirming that church members should be "visible saints," they instituted the procedure of a "relation" of the work of grace as the means by which adult candidates qualified for membership. These relations were narratives of spiritual experience, a telling of the journey from a despairing sense of utter worthlessness to joyous union with Christ. The theology that informed these narratives was authentically Reformed in assuming that salvation depended entirely on the will of God. In its "practical" dimensions, this theology transformed the mystery of election, for it postulated that the elect underwent a change of heart that was manifested in godly behavior, or sanctification. Presumably, therefore, anyone who could testify to having experienced such a change of heart, and whose behavior measured up, was of the elect. Through these series of assumptions, the test of a relation linked church membership to the divine economy of election to salvation.[8]

The image and idea of the church as a community of visible saints thus acquired a distinctive importance within the Congregational Way. The Cambridge Platform was emphatic: the members of "a visible church are *Saints* by calling." The Windsor, Connecticut church covenant of 1647 described the congregation as the "kingdom, and visible family and household of God"; twenty years later, the members of the church in Salem defined themselves as "true Believers being united unto Christ . . . [making] up one Misticall Church which is the Body of Christ, the members whereof having fellowship with the Father Son and holy-Ghost by Faith, and one with another in love."[9]

The same motifs were staples of New England sermons. In his ordination sermon of 1689, the newly chosen minister of Salem Village, Samuel Parris, referred to himself as charged with making a "difference between the clean, & unclean; so as to labour to cleanse & purge the one, & confirm & strengthen the other." Parris linked this work to the nature of the church: "By the Preaching of the word, Christ gathers a Church by separating of the Elect from the rest of mankind as his peculiar Flock. *15. John 19.* I have chosen you out of the world, i.e., I have separated you from the world." Half a century later, Jonathan Edwards imagined the church in the same manner, preaching that "Christ came into the world to engage in a war with God's enemies." In that war there was no middle ground: "The case admits of no neutrality . . . or a middle sort of persons." Hence the church must strictly limit itself to those persons who could credibly be accounted "gracious" or "real" Christians.[10]

The logic of this language worked against the inclusiveness of Genesis 17:7. John Davenport, the first minister of New Haven, made that logic explicit in arguing against family lineage as a basis for church membership. Declaring that the New Testament superseded the Old in this regard, Davenport insisted that membership was "not capable of being propagated and continued, in a lineal succession by natural generation." Similarly, the imagery of warfare was incompatible with notions of family incorporation. Samuel Parris did not shrink from the consequences of this symbolism: "hince it is," he told his congregation, that in the everyday lives of the saintly "not Seldom great hatred ariseth even from nearest Relations."[11] Parris thus echoed Wigglesworth's *Day of Doom*, which painted wives and mothers abandoning, without so much as a regretful tear, husbands and children who failed to qualify as visible saints.

The few and the many, the worthy and the unworthy: in this manner Puritanism in England and America continually evoked difference and separation. Within the walls of the church itself, this ethos was forcefully represented in the sacrament of the Lord's Supper, for as the Cambridge Platform put it, "holy things must not be given unto the unworthy" lest the "ordinances [be] defiled." To accomplish this purity the ministers wrote at extraordinary length about the necessity of adequate preparation before coming to the Lord's Table. No one should partake of the sacrament unless she or he had searched conscience, heart, and will for traces of unrepented sin. To approach the Lord's Table unprepared was to risk the horrific warning embodied in I Corinthians 11:27–29: "Whosoever shall eat of this bread, and drink this cup of the Lord, unworthily, shall be guilty of the body and blood of the Lord. . . . For he that eateth and drinketh unworthily, eateth and drinketh damnation to himself, not discerning the Lord's body." In sermon after sermon, the clergy cited these verses to enforce a fearsome taboo: come unworthily, and you will provoke the enduring wrath of God. In effect, therefore, the decision to participate in the sacrament was akin to the decision to seek church membership, for each depended on being able to affirm an identity as a visible saint.[12]

In the context of the great migration to New England in the 1630s, the image and idea of the church as holy place seemed persuasive. What else did the migration signify but a profound act of collective and individual cleansing, a literal and symbolic abandoning of the corruption that pervaded the Church of England? This way of thinking was, we know, compelling to ordinary people, who in town after town voted to establish gathered churches. Thereafter, it was woven into the myth of New England, a myth that the children and grandchildren of the immigrants continued to reiterate. A symbolism of holiness and purity persistently framed the decisions these people had to make about participating in church membership and the sacrament of the Lord's Supper.

Toward a "Middle Way"

As soon as the colonists created the Congregational pattern we have been describing, fellow Puritans in England began to denounce it, for two main reasons. First, because the new system replaced a parish structure with gathered, voluntary congregations, critics charged that the church as an institution no longer made the means of grace (preaching, discipline, and sacraments) available to all who were in need of the law and the gospel. Second, these critics insisted that the visible church could never really differentiate the elect from the profane because it had no certain rule by which to make that judgment. Arguing that the test of a relation fell far short of providing certainty, moderate Puritans urged the colonists to abandon the procedure and shift to a more comprehensive policy of church membership that would allow the visible church to serve as a "school" or "nursery" where the ignorant and the weak of heart could be taught and nurtured.[13]

Criticism from abroad was not the only reason most of the clergy began to have second thoughts about the Congregational Way. An early outbreak of radicalism, the Antinomian movement of 1636–38, was a frightening example of ideas about the discerning of visible saints carried to an extreme, for the Antinomians proposed that the indwelling of the Holy Spirit in the elect enabled them to discern who was truly worthy of church membership. Brushing aside any doubts about this capacity for spiritual discernment, Anne Hutchinson and her followers urged New England congregations to draw the strictest possible line between the holy and the profane.[14] At the other end of the spectrum, conservatives petitioned the ministers and magistrates to restore the inclusive parish system of the Church of England. These conservatives predicted that, in the long run, the rigor of the Congregational Way would bar an ever-increasing percentage of the colonists from church membership.[15]

Holding firm against either extreme, the ministers and a majority of the laity responded to criticism by moving in a direction that was already laid out for them by their understanding of the covenant of Genesis 17:7. Excepting a few Baptists, the colonists were in agreement from the outset that the children of visible saints should be admitted to baptism because they were encompassed within the covenant of their parents. (Adults who sought baptism for themselves were another matter, for they had to satisfy the test of a relation.) By the time of the drafting of the Cambridge Platform, the ministers were emphasizing the benefits of baptism, noting that infants who came into the church via this sacrament have many privileges which others (not church-members) have not: they are in covenant with God; have the seale thereof upon them, *viz.* Baptisme; & so if not regenerated, yet are in a more hopefull way of attayning regenerating grace, & all the spiritual blessings both of the covenant & seal.

The phrase "in a more hopefull way of attayning regenerating grace" implied an understanding of the church as school or nursery for children not yet fully within the covenant of grace, but headed that way if properly nurtured. Thomas Shepard, the first minister of Cambridge, made this understanding explicit in a sermon series defending infant baptism against the Baptists.[16]

The basis for this alternative understanding of the church was the intergenerational covenant of Genesis 17:7, to which children were admitted on the basis of their parents' membership. As we have noted, John Cotton was invoking Genesis 17:7 by the early 1650s. On the whole, his fellow clergy agreed with him that the covenant between God and Abraham remained in force among the colonists, though, like Cotton, they also reasoned that it had been supplemented by the covenant of grace. In explaining the nature of church membership, theological discourse in midcentury New England differentiated two kinds of covenants and two kinds of holiness: "federal holiness" and the "external covenant," on the one hand, and real holiness and the covenant of grace, on the other. Coexisting within the visible church, each of these forms validated a particular mode of church membership: the limited or "halfway" membership of children who were admitted to the sacrament of baptism and the "full" membership of adults who, qualifying in the discernment of their peers as among the redeemed, were admitted to all the privileges of membership, including participation in the Lord's Supper. This distinction between federal and internal holiness came into its own during debates in the 1650s and early 1660s about the basis of church membership. The key issue was the ambiguous status of the children of persons who, admitted to the church by virtue of their parents' covenant, seemed unable *as adults* to make a relation and qualify for "full" membership (meaning, most important, admission to the Lord's Supper) in the manner prescribed in the Cambridge Platform. Although a handful of ministers argued that the proper course of action was to expel these seemingly complacent adults from the church, the majority of ministers feared the consequences of so drastic a step. Moreover, the majority was persuaded that such adult "children of the church" were in some real sense incorporated within the covenant—albeit, the "external" covenant—and, accordingly, were entitled to bring their own offspring to the sacrament of baptism. Justifying this decision to allow the ongoing incorporation of children, the synod of 1662 repeatedly invoked the family-based covenant of Genesis 17:7 that conveyed God's "blessings" along the lines of intergenerational descent.[17]

Having in this manner departed from the vision of the church that lay at the heart of the Congregational Way, the synod of 1662 reclaimed that vision by insisting that access to the Lord's Supper continued to depend on satisfactory evidence of the work of grace. The thinking of the second-generation minister Jonathan Mitchel is indicative. Favoring the principle of external or federal membership, Mitchel complemented it with a vigorous defense of the "Holiness" of the gathered church, a holiness embodied in the practice of "Requiring further Degrees of preparation, in those that they received unto the Supper of the Lord." Citing I Corinthians 11:28–29, he argued that "Worthy Receivers" must "Examine themselves, and Discern the Lord's Body." Though he used the word "charity" four times in a single sentence, the thrust of the conditions Mitchel outlined was that "full" church members were obliged to manifest "a Work of Grace." Most first- and second-generation ministers agreed with him and wove this "middle way between extreames," as Mitchel termed it, into the fabric of the Congregational system.[18]

Among its several benefits, this middle way disposed of the specter that the gathered churches of New England would steadily diminish in size.[19] Yet the contradiction between the two covenants remained an ever-present reality. It was there for all to see in the institutional difference between two kinds of membership, a difference acted on each time the Lord's Supper was administered. It entered into the preaching of the ministers, who at one and the same time emphasized the "blessings" of the federal covenant and warned against presumptions of confidence on the part of those who were baptized but not, as yet, converted. A standard refrain in seventeenth-century evangelism, aimed in particular at "young people," was the theme of "now or never," as when Thomas Shepard of Cambridge warned the unconverted of his parish, some of whom were students at Harvard in their teens, that it would be "a wonder of wonders if ever God show . . . mercy" to them once they passed the age of twenty.[20] The fearful urgency of "now or never" was sharply at odds with the reassuring theme, being preached at the same time by the same ministers, of the benefits flowing from a covenant destined to endure for many generations. Always, therefore, the blessings of baptism were implicitly contradicted by the message of "now or never" and by the warning that baptized, halfway members who failed to "improve" themselves and advance to full membership were in jeopardy of God's wrath.[21] If baptism came at a price, so did participation in the Lord's Supper, for those in full communion or wanting to qualify for the sacrament were advised to ask themselves constantly whether they were worthy to participate in the sacrament. Thus it happened that the middle way much favored by the clergy after 1662 remained entangled with the distinction between who was saved and who was not.

FAMILIES, MOTHERS, AND THE SACRAMENTS

The lay men and women who filled the meetinghouses of New England each Sunday were fully aware of the complexities of this issue. The manner in which many of them dealt with these complexities is evident in certain patterns of decision making. When to affiliate with the church by renewing their baptismal covenant as adults, when to bring children to the ordinance of baptism, when or whether to participate in the Lord's Supper—in scores of congregations these questions were answered in a similar manner.

These patterns of decision making may be understood as an independent response to the contradictions embedded in the congregational system. Actors in their own right, the laity sometimes behaved in keeping with the recommendations of the clergy and sometimes went their own way. Always, their behavior reveals an insistence on aligning religious practice with family strategies of preservation and incorporation. Within the household, this task of aligning family and religion occurred in the context of certain expectations about parenting, gender, and the transmission of property to the next generation. Ordinary people—farmers, artisans, housewives—accomplished these expectations by drawing selectively on the complex symbolism of church, covenant, baptism, and Lord's Supper.

The social history of early New England reveals that lay men and women sought land and willingly changed towns or founded new ones in order to obtain enough property to sustain their children. This amassing of property was in keeping with a partible inheritance system. Parents wanted to provide each of their children a substantial measure of economic security—that is, enough land for each son to farm on his own and, in the case of daughters, the equivalent in goods. Another, perhaps more basic goal was for parents to pursue every possible means of ensuring the good health and survival of the next generation. In European family systems influenced by Catholicism, the kinship network extended beyond the nuclear family to include the beneficial protection of ancestors and godparents.[22] But for the colonists, the structure of the family was singularly focused on the parent–child relationship. Feeling a sense of urgency about having children, parents also worried about the many dangers that threatened family continuity. Children seemed extraordinarily vulnerable—to the malice of older women deemed "witches,"[23] to innumerable forms of sickness, to the uncertainties of a theology that divided the elect from the reprobate. What could be done to forestall—or, more realistically, to lessen—these dangers and promote family preservation? Was there another kind of goods that parents could pass on to their children, something even more valuable than land and cattle as a means of sustaining the continuity of generations?

It was in search of this other kind of inheritance that parents turned to the church. What it had to offer was a covenant that simultaneously performed two crucial functions: it linked parents and children through the sacrament of infant baptism, and it drew those children into a sacred community where blessings were more abundant than in the profane world. As had been promised in Genesis 17:7, the external covenant signified a privileged, beneficial connection between God and parents who, granted the great favor of fertility, wanted His protection for their children.

We can discern these expectations in statements made by men and women when they joined the church. Repeatedly, the candidates for membership in the gathered church of Cambridge alluded to the spiritual relationships within families. Some thanked their parents for being "godly" or, as Mary Angier recalled, for having "kept her from gross sins." Edward Collins was emphatic: "The Lord gave me that privilege to be brought up of godly parents." He ticked off the benefits: "Hence I received some restraint from them who, seeing an evil nature in me, were more careful to restrain me." Some candidates had to acknowledge that their families of origin had not been properly Christian: "For my education I was brought up in popery a good many years." Either way, a major theme of the Cambridge testimonies was the importance of family in the fostering of spiritual discipline. Absorbing this assumption, parents with young children were willing in the 1630s to risk the voyage to New England if doing so would enable them to bring their children up within a church that, unlike the corrupt Church of England, was founded on a true basis. It was this mode of reasoning that led "Mr. Crackbone's Wife," who wondered if her children would go to "hell . . . because I had not prayed for them," to decide to immigrate. So, too, Mary Sparhawk decided to participate in the perilous migration, "thinking," as she put it, "that her children might get good it would be worth my journey."[24]

"That her children might get good": this phrase serves as an apt transition to the expectations parents brought to the sacrament of infant baptism. Of the several practices that arose in and outside the church to ensure, symbolically, the preservation of the family, baptism was surely the most important. Before we turn to quantitative evidence that supports this claim, we need to look back on the institutional history of Congregationalism during the seventeenth century. Granting, as we must, a role to synods and second thoughts among the clergy in the elaborating of the halfway covenant of 1662, it is even more important to acknowledge the pressure that came from families who wanted the privilege of baptism for their children whether or not the parents had fully qualified for church membership. The first clear glimpse we catch of this pressure dates from 1634 when John Cotton, a minister in Boston, reported being asked by a grandfather if his status as a church member would entitle his grandchildren to be baptized. A decade later, in 1646, Robert Child failed to muster popular support for his motion to restore the parish system, undoubtedly because he went too far in proposing to reverse the Congregational Way.

But in the same year that Child was rebuffed, the Massachusetts government acknowledged in its call for a synod that "there be some [churches] who do baptize the children if the grandfather or grandmother be . . . members, though the immediate parents be not." More significant, the civil government reported the presence of "considerable persons in these churches who do thinke that the children [of persons who had been members of English parishes] also, upon some conditions and tearmes, may & ought to be baptized." Within another decade the deputies of the Connecticut General Assembly had signaled their support for a policy resembling the halfway covenant, and by the early 1660s the majority of the deputies in both Massachusetts and Connecticut—each of them voicing, presumably, the sentiment of most of the residents of their towns—had taken this stand. Another sign of popular expectations was the resignation in 1657 of Richard Blinman from the pulpit of the New London congregation after "some of the town manifested, that except he would practice" broader baptism, "the[y] would not paie his maintenance." To be sure, some church members were energetic in protecting the sacrament from what they deemed "corruption." But the tide in most congregations ran against them.[25]

Slowly but surely, the Congregational system accommodated itself to the nexus between family continuity and baptism. Despite the many variations at the local level, we can discern certain general patterns. Some churches began to keep a double set of books, differentiating "full" members, or adults who qualified by making a relation of spiritual experience, from those who entered on the basis of their parents' membership. By the end of the century, many congregations included a large fraction of the townspeople. Most of these people fell into the category of "children of the church," a term that encompassed both adults and children who had been admitted to membership by way of baptism. At a certain moment, many of these adult "children" participated in a ceremony of affiliation known as "renewal of covenant." Whatever the specifics, the "tribalism" (as one historian has termed it) that overtook the Congregational Way in the second half of the seventeenth century ensured that churches grew larger, not smaller, as second- and third-generation family members entered on the basis of a covenant that, although "external," was understood as a vehicle for God's blessings. If not a parish system in name or theory, a tribalistic Congregationalism was tending in that direction.[26]

The underlying connections between church membership and the family strategy of preservation emerge even more clearly from data that take account of gender. Wives acted to affirm church membership, either by renewal of covenant or by making a relation, more often than their husbands. In situations where both spouses became members, wives preceded husbands, on average, by a period of some years. Throughout the early history of the Congregational system, therefore, women *as wives* manifested a stronger interest in becoming church members than did their husbands.[27] Commonly, these women came forward to renew the covenant or to offer a relation at a particular moment in the life cycle, either when they were expecting a child (sometimes a second or third child) or shortly after getting married.[28] But of all the practices that arose to reconcile family preservation and church membership, none is more striking than the timing of the decision to bring children to be baptized. More often than not, parents carried a newborn child to the meetinghouse as promptly as possible, and this in spite of there being no basis for regarding baptism as efficacious—which it was, theologically, within Catholicism and the Church of England. A systematic study of the relation between date of birth and date of baptism for three early-eighteenth-century Essex County, Massachusetts towns reveals that, of the 2,850 children for whom baptism and birth records can be linked, 49 percent were baptized within the first week of life and another 10 percent within the next seven days.[29]

It was women, in the main, who brought children to the sacrament of baptism. Why they did so—why the rhythms of affiliation and participation on the part of women differed from the practices of men—bespeaks the assumption among these participants that mothers were especially responsible for the spiritual welfare of their children. This assumption pervaded the discourse of the clergy, as when Richard Mather, the minister of Dorchester, urged the women of his congregation in the 1650s to play the part of "faithfull Mothers" on the grounds that "Mothers . . . are more with [their] children whilest they are little ones, then their Fathers are." Evoking the birth experience—"you are at much paines with the bodyes of your children, and suffer not a little while you bear them in your wombs & when you bring them into the world"—Mather imagined mothers as "naturally of tender and dear affection for your children, and God mistakes it not that it be so." Accordingly, he reasoned that "the prayers and teares of a faithfull Mother may be the salvation of the childs soule."[30]

For real mothers in early New England, this reasoning was central to how they understood their role in the spiritual economy of the household. Actions can speak louder than words. On the eve of the synod that formulated the halfway covenant, the records of the gathered church in Dorchester contain this entry, among others, for 1660: "The wife of James Minott desired baptism for her children." This one example of a woman taking the initiative may stand for hundreds of such instances. Equally revealing of collective behavior, though again but a single episode, is the example of Jane Turell, a married woman and a church member living on the outskirts of Boston, who took her second child (the first had been stillborn) almost immediately to the meetinghouse to be baptized. The infant lived but eleven days. From Jane Turell's father came the following report of his daughter's response to this sad event: "all the family remember the many tears of Joy and thankfulness she shed at the presentation of this child to God in holy Baptism, and her more than common composure of mind and quietness at its death and funeral."[31]

Women may have been unusually interested in church membership for another reason. Knowing that the experience of childbirth put their lives at risk, they preferred to be within the covenant at the moment when they came face to face with the possibility of death. But the meaning of death (or of childbirth) was not limited to the stark dichotomy of "now or never." It was also a moment when expectant mothers thought about the next generation and what blessings they could pass on to their newborns. Within the social web of the family, to die well, in the assurance that any newborn would be in covenant, was to create a legacy of blessings for the living. As a minister early in the eighteenth century remarked, "God's covenant-people will prize God's Covenant-Mercy to their seed, as an inestimable blessing. Some when dying have express'd more comfort in this, than all else they could leave with them in the world."[32]

Though women felt a special sense of responsibility for the spiritual welfare of their children and arranged, accordingly, to affiliate with the church after being married or becoming mothers, their husbands often shared the same emotion. Together, husbands and wives regarded children, and especially pious children, as a great blessing. Yet these parents worried whether they had done enough for their children, for the other side of the coin was the curse of rearing unfaithful offspring whose very failings cast in doubt the sincerity of the parents and the security of the covenant of Genesis 17:7. The logic of that covenant was double-edged: conveying the benefits of the parents' membership, it could also convey unrepented sin, the price of which was borne by the next generation. Hence when children fell sick, it was common for parents to wonder if the cause was their own moral failings. Characteristically, a man whose four young children were suddenly "possessed" by the Devil blamed himself for their frightening condition; it was his own moral inadequacy, John Goodwin concluded, that allowed the Devil to afflict his offspring. Fifty years later, another father drew a similar connection between "the many sins of my youth and riper years" and the death of his young daughter, Tabitha.[33]

Contradictions thus reemerged within the framework of lived religion. Craving the protection of the covenant for their children, parents had to acknowledge that its benefits were contingent on their own spiritual condition. Moreover, parents who were versed in Reformed (Calvinist) theology knew that baptism was not sufficient as a means of grace. Something else—the deeper, more fully transforming mode of spiritual experience enacted by the Holy Spirit—had to occur within their children once they became adults. The most that parents could really do, therefore, was to position their children as best as possible, and hope that incorporation into full membership and the covenant of grace would occur down the road.

This mixture of feelings pervades the "Valedictory and Monitory Writing" written by Sarah (Whipple) Goodhue (1641–81), daughter of a pious father and married to a full church member in Ipswich. Sarah Goodhue began having children within ten months of her marriage and bore them regularly until dying in childbirth in 1681 after giving birth to twins. Writing about family, children, and covenant shortly before her death, she blessed the Lord for providing a husband who earnestly sought her own "eternal good" by taking notes on sermons she had to miss, being "necessarily often absent from the public worship of God." And she deeply appreciated the care her husband took for the spiritual benefit and blessing of their children: "be encouraged in this work," she wrote her children, because "your father hath put up many prayers with ardent desires and tears to God on behalf of you all." Yet she did not take for granted that her children would remain godly.

> My children be encouraged in this work, you are in the bond of the covenant, although you may be breakers of covenant, yet God is [a] merciful keeper of covenant. Endeavour as you grow up, to own and renew your covenant, and rest not if God give you life, but so labour to improve all the advantages that God is pleased to afford you.

Though it was her hope and expectation that parental and collective prayer would sustain the protection afforded by the covenant, she added the necessary qualification: only those children who "obey their parents" (and, by implication, God) would inherit "many blessings."[34]

Sarah Goodhue's uneasiness about the ongoing success of incorporation—would her children satisfy the conditions of the external covenant or forfeit its "advantages"?—was widely shared in the late seventeenth and early eighteenth centuries. As early as the 1650s, laments were being heard that the "rising generation" had thrown off the authority of parents and clergy. By the end of the century, there were further reasons for this concern about youth. In these years a handful of daughters and sons, most famously a daughter of the minister of Deerfield, passed over into Catholicism as a consequence of being taken captive in border raids from French Canada. These defections shook the confidence of everyone, whether ministers or parents, in the workings of a would-be tribal system. Meanwhile, the incessant movement of people into new settlements was carrying them beyond the reach of order, both familial and ecclesiastical. The rate of bastardy began to rise, possibly in response to what some historians have described as a growing imbalance between family size and the availability of land.[35]

Whatever the actual social history of these decades, the moral imagination of the colonists fastened on signs of behavior that seemed to betoken the breakdown of mechanisms—family order, family preservation—that were crucial to the well-being of the church. Much of the blame for this pending breakdown fell on parents, whom Cotton Mather accused (in rhetoric typical of this period) of leaving their children "very much Un-Catechised . . . and sadly Unconverted and Ungoverned as to the practices of Christianity."[36] As for "Young People," another minister complained in 1709 of "how Few are there comparatively, that when they are grown up do seriously Renew their Baptismal Covenant." It was troubling that young people seemed to feel no sense of urgency about affiliating with the church. "It is time eno' for me to be Religious: I am young, and have many years before me," one minister imagined them as thinking.[37]

As we listen to these complaints it is important to remember that, by the turn of the century, one mechanism of incorporation, the practice of infant baptism, was working relatively well. Yet some of these baptized "children of the church," and especially the men among them, postponed the practice of renewal of covenant. Many others hung back from experiencing the tumultuous work of grace that would entitle them to participate in the Lord's Supper. Indeed the most common pattern by the close of the seventeenth century among adult children of the church was for a substantial majority of the men, and perhaps even a majority of women, to refrain from the sacrament of Communion. In these years a minister suggested that the prevailing ratio of full to halfway members was 1:4, and church records bear him out. Again, the local variations were many, but the general situation seems clear: from one generation to the next, parents wanted baptism for their children but were much less eager to come, themselves, to the Lord's Table.[38]

Personal testimonies and the observations of the clergy suggest that scrupulosity was one source of this reluctance. The records of the Beverly,

Massachusetts First Church are laced with entries that reveal men and women postponing participation in the Lord's Supper even after joining the church as adults. In 1687, Mrs. Thorndike became a baptized member after "making profession publickly of her faith & repentance." "Not beeing clear in her own spirit," however, she "did not at present proceed to the Lords Supper." Six years later, Mary Ellenwood joined the church "upon a profession of her faith and repentance," yet "desired to wait a while before she comes to the Lords Supper."[39] Jane Turell, who *did* come to the Lord's Table, accomplished that step only after a long delay. "Her fears were great," her father recalled, "lest *coming unworthily she should eat and drink Judgment unto her Self* [I Corinthians 11:29]. She was often in Agony, that she might draw near to God with a true Heart, and in the full Assurance of Faith."[40] Samuel Sewall, who began to partake as a young adult (and as a husband about to become a father), had to overcome recurring waves of self-doubt before doing so. Together with other personal testimonies, these accounts suggest that lay men and women were deterred by the high expectations that surrounded the sacrament. It was especially the expectation of great danger should someone pollute the Lord's Table that stood in the way of wider participation. The laity "have drunk in an opinion," a minister observed in 1707, "that none but Converted Persons should come to that Ordinance, and so they neglect it."[41] Here was a case of listening too well to the clergy's message about spiritual preparation. Unable or unwilling to assert that they had experienced the new birth, lay people respected the purity of the sacrament rather than risk engaging in hypocrisy. Even in Stoddard's Northampton, people were reluctant to enact his program.

Scrupulous in this respect, yet eager to secure access to the sacrament of baptism, lay men and women made their way selectively through the possibilities for being religious. In explaining the choices they made, we must recognize that these people were trying to make sense of a religious system that presented them with a set of interlocking contradictions. What should they do about church membership when they were told that assurance of salvation was necessary for full membership and yet that infants were church members—to be sure, only in some partial respect—on the basis of their parents' covenant? What should they do when faced with a system that framed the sacraments of baptism and the Lord's Supper as inclusive and beneficial, but also as endangering to those who were unworthy? And how were they to accomplish the goal of family preservation when the very covenant the church offered for achieving this goal was so ambivalently represented?

Lived religion consisted of the practices that emerged in response to these questions. In refraining from the Lord's Supper, these people acknowledged the importance of holiness and reaffirmed the great myth of the church as set apart from the world. Ever concerned to assess the trade-off between benefits and danger, most of them reasoned that the sacrament of Communion posed too great a risk of bad consequences. Their thinking about baptism was different. Here the benefits outweighed the risk; here, participation was much to be desired as a means of ensuring family continuity. In this regard the thinking of the laity is revealed, above all, in the coincidence of marriage, pregnancy, and birth with decisions to renew the covenant or become a church member. That it was women who took the lead in making these decisions underscores the powerful nexus between family formation and church membership. Marking out a middle way of their own, lay men and women thus accommodated two very different realms of meaning, though always having to acknowledge that the inheritance of spiritual goods was far less certain than the inheritance of land and cattle.

INTO THE EIGHTEENTH CENTURY

How would these paradoxes play themselves out in everyday religious life after the turn of the century?

The increasing importance of renewal of covenant and of fast days directed at the "rising generation" are part of the answer. The earliest New England-wide fast day of this kind occurred in 1678; by 1700 or thereabouts, such fasts were becoming commonplace. From the late 1670s, clergy and people turned also to a practice that dated from the early years of settlement, but to which they gave a fresh significance: renewal of covenant. The practice came to have two forms. It was the rite of passage for "children of the church" who, as adults, wished to introduce *their* children into the covenant. A parent or person expecting parenthood re-affirmed his or her acceptance of the church covenant and the obligations that went with it. The second form was a community-wide ceremony, often linked to a fast (and, at a deeper level, to a perception of crisis) during which adults *and* youth jointly affirmed their commitment to the covenant.[42]

Thus on a March day in 1705, the townspeople of Taunton, Massachusetts, gathered in their meetinghouse for a ceremony of covenant renewal. "We gave Liberty to all Men and Women kind, from sixteen years old and upwards to act with us," the minister of the town reported, "and had three hundred Names given in to list under Christ." Remarkable for its size, encompassing as it did almost all of the town's adults, the ceremony also stirred up emotions of unusual intensity among a particular group; in the words of the same narrator, the scene included "Parents weeping for Joy, seeing their Children give their names to Christ."[43] May we interpret this outpouring of emotions as signaling the deep anxiety among these parents about the process of incorporation?

The response of lay people to the earthquake of 1727 provides another part of the answer. Believing that the trembling of the earth portended impending judgment, thousands of people hastily raised their practice of religion to a higher level. The messy bookkeeping in church records makes it difficult to distinguish new members from renewal of covenant and renewal from admission to the Lord's Supper. But it seems safe to suggest that, in a situation where "now or never" seemed suddenly compelling, many persons passed from halfway membership to full.

The revivals that broke out in 1740–42, together with a wave of religious excitement that had passed over the Connecticut River Valley in 1734–35, provide a clearer picture. In towns like Northampton, where nearly everyone was a baptized member in covenant, the three hundred persons Jonathan Edwards received into the church in 1734–35, and for whose conversion he vouched, almost certainly included a high number of persons who were already halfway members.[44] In such situations, the rush to experience the work of the Spirit fed on the undercurrent of fear that countless sermons had helped create. Revivals spoke to and resolved, at least for the time being, the long-existing disparity between two schemes of time and two levels of church membership by enabling scrupulous men and women to satisfy themselves that, at long last, they were worthy of the Lord's Supper. For others, perhaps less scrupulous, the revivals swept away any guilt about the performance of covenantal duties and allowed them to demonstrate an amazing array of "fruits."

Local descriptions accentuate another dimension of these events. It was widely reported that the "youth" of towns and congregations—youth being an elastic term that encompassed persons in their early twenties—were especially engaged.[45] This circumstance pleased the adults who wrote these reports because of what it signified for parents and families. In spite of all the ministers' complaints about "declension," these parents had been faithful in bringing up their children. Once again, the process of family incorporation was proving effective; what had not been adequately accomplished through ceremonies of covenant renewal was now being addressed through this new form of collective behavior.[46]

Some of the women and men of the Great Awakening who felt the sudden and relieving influx of the Holy Spirit were moved to rethink the nexus between family formation and church membership. Newly cleansed themselves, the "New Lights," as derisive contemporaries called them, began to demand that quasi-parish churches stop practicing the inclusive policies symbolized by the halfway covenant and resume the test of religious experience for membership. Like the Antinomians before them, some New Lights apparently suggested that the spiritually enlightened could intuitively discern the difference between saints and hypocrites. When churches, on the whole, rejected these proposals, a wave of schisms swept across New England as "Separates" hived off into purified congregations, some of which took a further step toward purification and repudiated infant baptism.[47]

In this manner a movement that seemed to promise family incorporation turned divisive, seeming to set families against families, wives against husbands, the young against the old. Within the terms of our story, these conflicts reveal the vulnerability of the practices and representations that linked family culture and the Congregational Way. All of a sudden, at least among the more radical New Lights, the multilayered meanings of covenant vanished, leaving only the covenant of grace and, as a consequence, personal holiness as the one criterion for access to the church and its sacraments. Looking back from the vantage of the Great Awakening, we realize that the vision of the church as holy space, though seemingly eclipsed by other attitudes in the decades since the 1660s, continued to resonate among the laity. Did the Awakening signify the overdue collapse of Mitchel's "middle way"? Did the New Light schisms bring to an end the possibility of combining both halves of the contradiction that lay at the heart of the Congregational Way?

The outcome of the controversy that erupted in Northampton in 1749 suggests, on the contrary, that the intertwining of covenant, family, and the life cycle remained persuasive. The cause of the controversy was Jonathan Edwards' repudiation of any and all practices—the halfway covenant, renewal of covenant, admission to the Lord's Supper—where the line between "real" saints and mere hypocrites (to use his terminology) had become blurred. Reaffirming the evangelical distinction between "real" and "outward," he pursued the logic of this distinction to the point of insisting that parents who "have no interest in the covenant of grace"— that is, parents admitted under the terms of the external covenant—could not introduce their children to the sacrament of baptism. Vigilant observer of lay behavior that he was, what especially angered Edwards was the timing of decisions by the men and women of Northampton to renew the covenant or advance to full membership, "it being visibly a prevailing custom for persons to neglect this, till they come to be married, and then to do it for their credit's sake, and that their children may be baptized." For Edwards this practice was tantamount to hypocrisy. And he was scornful of his congregation's expectations about inheritance: "may it not be suspected," he asked rhetorically, "that the way of baptizing the children of such as never make any proper profession of godliness, is an expedient originally invented for that very end, to give ease to ancestors with respect to their posterity?" But the congregation saw things differently.

Having, most of them, experienced some phases of the work of grace, and yet as parents feeling deeply the need of family preservation, they preferred the practices that their church had sanctioned for a half century. When push came to shove, the adult males in the congregation voted 200 to 20 to dismiss a minister who wanted to disrupt the bond between family incorporation and the sacraments.[48]

The stance of the laity in the Northampton controversy suggests that, notwithstanding underlying tensions and the ever-recurrent possibility of disruption, "covenant" remained an elastic category capable of accommodating very different goals. It also suggests that lay men and women continued to prefer a middle way that drew on two contrasting schemes of time, the evangelical framework of "now or never," and the strategy, linked to the moment of family formation in the life cycle, of ensuring continuity.

REUNITING THE SOCIAL AND THE RELIGIOUS

What are the implications of our narrative?

More than a half century ago, the literary historian Perry Miller argued that the whole of "the New England Mind" revolved around the concept and emblem of covenant. For Miller, the covenant was how the Puritans reconciled the contradiction between free will and determinism, human initiative and the sovereignty of an "arbitrary" God. In his version, social history entered only as a solvent of this synthesis. And in his narrative he relived the tension between hypocrisy and sincerity, linking measures like the halfway covenant to the first of these qualities and characterizing such changes in the Congregational Way as "declension."[49]

Passing by the adequacy of Miller's understanding of Reformed scholasticism, our goal has been to reunite what Miller sundered, the social and the religious; to represent the covenant theology in general and the halfway covenant in particular as a bridge between the two; and to interpret change over time not as the decline of religion and the advance of the social, but as an ongoing quest for practices that satisfied both the strategy of family preservation and the vision of the gathered church. "Declension" means something different to us than what it has meant to many other historians of early New England. In the context of the quest for strategies of incorporation and preservation, we may understand ordinary people who spoke of declension to be saying that their strategies for dealing with the next generation were not working quite as they had hoped. These worries, these signs of strain, do not signify that Puritanism was becoming ineffective. Rather, they illustrate the truism that no culture or family exerts thoroughgoing or complete control over the succeeding generation.

Almost a century ago, Max Weber proposed that Puritanism was in the forefront of modernization. Protestantism as a whole, but sectarian movements most especially, Puritanism among them, promoted a differentiation between the secular and the religious that Weber saw as leading to the "disenchantment" of the world. Emile Durkheim was similarly persuaded that, as Western culture approached modernity, religion had progressively withdrawn from the sphere of social life. We acknowledge the important forms of differentiation—notably the disassociating of economic, political, and legal systems from the church—that were well advanced in New England. Yet we also seek to reestablish the dynamic relation between the social and the religious that existed in early New England. The importance of debates about access to baptism is a sharp reminder of the "public" dimensions that a process such as family incorporation retained in the seventeenth century, in contrast to the privatized and sentimental family culture that became dominant by 1850.[50] The very tensions that our story reveals were rooted in part in a convergence of structures and expectations that, from the vantage of the 1990s, seems strikingly premodern, for present-day strategies for ensuring family preservation are no longer so bound up with the sacramental system.

The patterns that make up lived religion in any time and place reveal how ordinary men and women make their way through a set of choices, fashioning, as they do so, a mode of being religious that is responsive to needs that arise within social life. In representing lay people in seventeenth-century New England in this manner, we have insisted on the importance they attached to being within the church covenant for the sake of their children. Using the covenant to this end was fully in accord with the message of the ministers, though in distancing themselves from the Lord's Supper and refusing to go further than renewal of covenant, these people disappointed rigorists like Edwards. Above all, lay people valued the continuity of the "seed," and in turning to church membership to abet this continuity, affirmed the ongoing corporate role of families and churches, working together.

NOTES

1. John Cotton, *Certain Queries Tending to Accommodation . . . of Presbyterian & Congregationall Churches* (1654), quoted in Williston Walker, *The Creeds and Platforms of Congregationalism* (New York, 1893), 246 n. 1.

2. Michael Wigglesworth, *The Day of Doom* (1662), reprinted in Perry Miller and Thomas H. Johnson, *The Puritans* (New York: American Book Company, 1938), 601.

3. See, in general, Walker, *Creeds and Platforms*; David D. Hall, *The Faithful Shepherd: A History of the New England Ministry in the Seventeenth Century*

(Chapel Hill: University of North Carolina Press, 1972). For the purposes of this essay, we have passed by the colonists who never joined the church or who rejected the halfway covenant. By no means, therefore, does our interpretation take into account every kind of lay behavior in early New England.

4. Contrary to sound intellectual and cultural history, in this essay we do not indicate the longer trajectory of these meanings within Scripture, the Reformed tradition, and Elizabethan and Jacobean church history or how the problems we sketch intersected with the issue of "Separatism." E. Brooks Holifield, *The Covenant Sealed: The Development of Puritan Sacramental Theology in Old and New England, 1570–1720* (New Haven, Conn.: Yale University Press, 1974), is thorough and convincing on these matters, as are John S. Coolidge, *The Pauline Renaissance in England: Puritanism and the Bible* (Oxford: Oxford University Press, 1970), and Peter Lake, *Anglicans and Puritans? Presbyterianism and English Conformist Thought from Whitgift to Hooker* (Stanford, Calif.: Stanford University Press, 1988).

5. We take the term "family strategy" from Natalie Z. Davis, "Ghosts, Kin and Progeny," *Daedalus* 106 (Spring 1977): 64. Among the several studies of inheritance patterns in seventeenth-century New England, we have been influenced in particular by Philip Greven, *Four Generations: Population, Land, and Family in Colonial Andover, Massachusetts* (Ithaca, N.Y.: Cornell University Press, 1970), and by the comparative example of rural Ireland as described in Conrad M. Arensberg and Solon T. Kimball, *Family and Community in Ireland*, 2nd ed. (Cambridge, Mass.: Harvard University Press, 1968), esp. 131–32.

6. Coolidge, *Pauline Renaissance*, ch. 2; the pertinent New Testament verses are cited in the margins of ch. 4 of the Cambridge Platform (Walker, *Creeds and Platforms*, 207). See also Ernst Troeltsch, *The Social Teaching of the Christian Church*, trans. Olive Wyon, 2 vols. (London, 1931), 2:591–602.

7. On the general process of establishing churches, see Hall, *Faithful Shepherd*, ch. 5; and on the eschatological context and the broader "Separatist" impulse, see Stephen Brachlow, *The Communion of Saints: Radical Puritan and Separatist Ecclesiology 1570–1625* (Oxford: Oxford University Press, 1988).

8. Edmund S. Morgan, *Visible Saints: The History of a Puritan Idea* (New York: New York University Press, 1963), chs. 2–3.

9. Walker, *Creeds and Platforms*, 205, 155, 121.

10. *The Sermon Notebook of Samuel Parris 1689–1694*, ed. James P. Cooper Jr. and Kenneth P. Minkema, *Publications of the Colonial Society of Massachusetts* 66 (Boston, Mass.: Colonial Society, 1993), 49, 181, 184; *The Works of Jonathan Edwards*, vol. 12: *Ecclesiastical Writings*, ed. David D. Hall (New Haven, Conn.: Yale University Press, 1994), 220 (hereafter cited as *Ecclesiastical Writings*).

11. John Davenport, *Another Essay for Investigation of the Truth* (Cambridge, 1663), 6; *Notebook of Samuel Parris*, 184.

12. Walker, *Creeds and Platforms*, 223. A good example of such preaching is Samuel Parris's sermon series on these verses: *Notebook of Samuel Parris*, 272–308. The longer tradition is sketched in David D. Hall, *Worlds of Wonder, Days of Judgment: Popular Religious Belief in Early New England* (New York: Knopf, 1989), 156–60.

13. See, e.g, Richard Baxter, *Certain Disputations of right to Sacraments and the true nature of Visible Christianity* (London, 1658); the "preface" to the Cambridge Platform (Walker, *Creeds and Platforms*, 194–202); and, in general, Hall, *Faithful Shepherd*, ch. 5.

14. *The Antinomian Controversy, 1636–1638: A Documentary History*, ed. David D. Hall (Middletown, Conn.: Wesleyan University Press, 1968), 238, 232, 226.

15. Walker, *Creeds and Platforms*, 163–66.

16. Ibid., 224; Thomas Shepard, *The Church-Membership of Children, and Their Right to Baptisme* (Cambridge, 1663), 4, 6; and see also the *Result* of the synod of 1662, in Walker, *Creeds and Platforms*, 314. Pertinent to the larger story are other modifications the colonists made to ease the stringency of the initial procedures; the history of one of these is traced in Baird Tipson, "Invisible Saints: The 'Judgment of Charity' in Early New England Churches," *Church History* 44 (1975): 1–12.

17. Walker, *Creeds and Platforms*, 292, 296, 299, 305–6 (quoting John Cotton), 309, 315, 317, 318, 321, 326, 328, 329, 332. The bracketing of a parent's personal moral or spiritual abilities as a condition of the membership of children is evident in the documents Increase Mather assembled in *The First Principles of New-England* (Cambridge, 1675); see, e.g., John Cotton to an Englishman (dated 1648) accepting the possibility of baptizing children of parents who, although "ignorant or Carnal members of the parish," continued to be members of the church (pp. 5–6); and the citations from an unpublished treatise by Richard Mather, dated 1645, allowing parents to remain members as long as they had not behaved scandalously or renounced the covenant (p. 10). Responding to John Davenport and other critics of the synod of 1662, its defenders basically asserted that, unless persons already in the external covenant had been excommunicated, their membership remained valid and extended to their children.

18. Cotton Mather, *Magnalia Christi Americana* (London, 1702), bk. IV, pp. 176–80.

19. Hall, *Faithful Shepherd*, 201 n. 12.

20. *The Diary of Michael Wigglesworth*, ed. Edmund S. Morgan (New York: Harper Torchbooks, 1965), 119. Wigglesworth as a student and tutor at Harvard recorded a number of Shepard's and Mitchel's sermons.

21. A private statement is revealing. Joseph Green, a college student en route to becoming the minister of Danvers, wrote a sister in 1692, "You have been baptized and God has visibly owned you; but if you do not live up to your baptismal engagement then your baptism will rise up against you at the great day." *The Commonplace Book of Joseph Green*, ed. Samuel Eliot Morison, *Publications of the Colonial Society of Massachusetts* 34 (Boston, Mass.: Colonial Society, 1943), 226. See also the sermon series by Samuel Willard, *The Barren Fig Trees Doom* (Boston, 1690).

22. John Bossy, "Blood and Baptism: Kinship, Community and Christianity in Western Europe from the Fourteenth to the Seventeenth Centuries," in *Sanctity and Secularity: The Church and the World*, ed. Derek Baker, *Studies in Church History* 10 (Oxford: Ecclesiastical History Society, 1973), 129–43.

23. As John Putnam Demos has pointed out, a central theme of witch-hunting was the threat to young children posed by the women accused of being witches. *Entertaining Satan: Witchcraft and the Culture of Early New England* (New York: Oxford University Press, 1982), 170, 181, 198.

24. *The Confessions of Thomas Shepard*, ed. George Selement and Bruce C. Woolley, *Publications of the Colonial Society of Massachusetts* 57 (Boston, Mass.: Colonial Society, 1981), 65–67, 82, 115, 140.

25. Walker, *Creeds and Platforms*, 250, 169; Robert G. Pope, *The Half-Way Covenant* (New Haven, Conn.: Yale University Press, 1969), 31–32; see also 22, 25.

26. Edmund S. Morgan introduced the term "tribalism" in *The Puritan Family* (1944; rev. ed., New York: Harper Torchbooks, 1966). The essential corrective to Morgan, and an essay broadly supporting the arguments of this paragraph, is Gerald Moran, "Religious Renewal, Puritan Tribalism, and the Family in Seventeenth-Century Milford, Connecticut," *William and Mary Quarterly*, 3rd ser., no. 36 (1979): 36–54. Moran found that by the final quarter of the seventeenth century the Milford congregation embraced at least 46 percent of all families in the town. Had Moran taken into account the membership of *wives* in his calculation (his percentage is based on a comparison of adult *male* members with various lists of adult male inhabitants) the percentage would most likely be quite higher. In addition to this essay, quantitative, serial data on church membership pertinent to our argument are presented in the following works: Gerald F. Moran, " 'Sisters in Christ': Women and the Church in Seventeenth-Century New England," in *Women in American Religion*, ed. Janet Wilson James (Philadelphia: University of Pennsylvania Press, 1980), 46–65; idem, "The Puritan Saint: Religious Experience, Church Membership and Piety in Connecticut, 1636–1776" (Ph.D. diss., Rutgers University, 1974); Mary McManus Ramsbottom, "Religion, Society and the Family in Charlestown, Massachusetts, 1630–1740" (Ph.D. diss., Yale University, 1987), demonstrating that by 1677 nearly two-thirds of Charlestown households were churched; Laurel Ulrich, *Good Wives: Image and Reality in the Lives of Women in Northern New England, 1650–1750* (New York: Knopf, 1982), 216; Harry S. Stout and Catharine A. Breckus, "Declension, Gender, and the 'New Religious History,' " in *Belief and Behavior: Essays in the New Religious History*, ed. Philip R. Vandermere and Richard P. Swierenga (New Brunswick, N.J.: Rutgers University Press, 1991), 15–36; and Anne S. Brown, " 'Bound Up in a Bundle of Life': The Social Meaning of Religious Practice in Northeastern Massachusetts, 1700–1765" (Ph.D. diss., Boston University, 1995). Stephen R. Grossbart, "Seeking the Divine Favor: Conversion and Church Admission in Eastern Connecticut, 1711–1832," *William and Mary Quarterly*, 3rd ser., no. 66 (1989): 696–740, offers a different interpretation of church membership data.

27. Ramsbottom, "Religious Society and the Family," 105–25, 136–38; Moran, " 'Sisters in Christ.' " Ramsbottom's study of the Charlestown church shows that women took the lead as early as the late 1630s (the church was founded by an all-male group in 1630), and that the percentage of households relying solely on the membership of the wife increased from one in six in the first decade to one in two by 1660.

28. A close study of 340 households within the Beverly, Massachusetts First Church in the first half of the eighteenth century reveals that 57 percent of these households secured their ties to the church through one or both parents after the birth of the first child, but before the birth of the second. See Brown, "'Bound Up in a Bundle,'" 63, 245. Similarly, Moran demonstrates that in Connecticut "the mode" at the time of covenanting was one child, though during some decades in the eighteenth century the percentage of childless covenanters was greater than at others, particularly during the 1730–60 period, when congregations across New England experienced revivals. Notably, the most significant shifts toward childless covenantings occurred among *men*, as opposed to *women*, a fact that further underlines the link between motherhood and church membership. Moran, "Puritan Saint," 159–64, 308–11.

29. Brown, "'Bound Up in a Bundle,'" 69–70, 80–81; Ramsbottom, "Religious Society and the Family," 136–37; Hall, *Worlds of Wonder*, 155.

30. Richard Mather, *A Farewel-Exhortation to the church and people of Dorchester in New-England* (Cambridge, 1657), 12, 13. For another evocation of mothers as spiritual teachers and transmitters of "Rich Blessings," see Cotton Mather, *Awakening Thoughts on the Sleep of Death* (Boston, 1712), preface. See also Laurel Ulrich's discussion of the representation of women as mothers: *Good Wives*, chs. 8, 9, 12; Amanda Porterfield, *Female Piety in Puritan New England: The Emergence of Religious Humanism* (New York: Oxford University Press, 1988), esp. ch. 4. We do not find persuasive the political interpretation of women's membership that Mary M. Dunn argues in "Saints and Sisters: Congregational and Church Women in the Early Colonial Period," in *Women in American Religion*, ed. James, 27–46.

31. Pope, *Half-Way Covenant*, 34; Benjamin Colman, *Reliquiae Turellaie, et Lachrymae Paternae. Two Sermons Preach'd at Medford . . . The Lord's Day After the funeral of his beloved daughter Mrs. Jane Turell* (Boston, 1735), 101.

32. William Williams, *An Essay to prove The Interest of the Children of Believers in the Covenant* (Boston, 1727), 20–22. See the reference, below, to Sarah Goodhue's "Valedictory and Monitory Writing"; the poetry and meditations Anne Bradstreet addressed to her children provide further evidence of this point.

33. *Witch-hunting in Seventeenth-Century New England: A Documentary History, 1638–1692*, ed. David D. Hall (Boston, Mass.: Northeastern University Press, 1991), 275–79; Daniel King Diary, undated entry (probably between September 1, 1737, and September 1, 1738), Phillips Library, Peabody Essex Museum, Salem, Mass. The many instances of kin (sons, husbands, grandparents) dragged into the Salem witch-hunt of 1692 provide a telling glimpse of folk assumptions about continuities within families.

34. Sarah Goodhue, "A Valedictory and Monitory Writing," in Thomas F. Waters, *Ipswich in the Massachusetts Bay Colony*, 2 vols. (Ipswich, Mass.: Ipswich Historical Society, 1905), 1:519–24 (quoted material is from pp. 522, 523, 521). This brief history of Sarah Goodhue and her family was compiled from the following sources: Waters, *Ipswich*, 1:519; Henry Burdette Whipple, comp., *Matthew Whipple of Bocking, England and His Descendants* (Highpoint, N.C., 1965), 8; Jonathan E. Goodhue, comp., *History and Genealogy of the Goodhue Family in*

England and America to the Year 1890 (Rochester, N.Y., 1891), 5–14; Abraham Hammat, *The Hammat Papers: Early Inhabitants of Ipswich, Massachusetts, 1633–1700* (1880–99; repr., Baltimore, 1980), 405.

35. These processes of social change are described in John J. Waters, "Family, Inheritance, and Migration in Colonial New England: The Evidence from Guilford, Connecticut," *William and Mary Quarterly*, 3rd ser., no. 29 (1982): 78–85; idem, "Patrimony, Succession, and Social Stability: Guilford, Connecticut in the Eighteenth Century," *Perspectives in American History* 10 (1976). The presumed surge in the rate of bastardy is questioned by Roger Thompson, *Sex in Middlesex: Popular Mores in a Massachusetts County, 1649–1699* (Amherst: University of Massachusetts Press, 1986), 193.

36. Cotton Mather, *Addresses To Old Men, and Young Men, and Little Children* (Boston, 1690), 90.

37. Benjamin Colman, *The Nature of Early Piety*, included in [Cotton Mather, ed.], *A Course of Sermons on Early Piety* (Boston, 1721), second pagination, p. 27.

38. Solomon Stoddard, *The Inexcusableness of Neglecting the Worship of God Under a Pretence of being in an Unconverted Condition* (Boston, 1708), 21; see also *Ecclesiastical Writings*, ed. Hall, 36 n. 4. Here, when we speak of "halfway" members we include all children of the covenant, not just those who, as adults, affirmed or reaffirmed their covenant with the church.

39. Beverly First Church Records (MS. transcript, Peabody Essex Museum), 31, 35; see also, 34, 38, 47.

40. Colman, *Reliquiae*, 111.

41. *The Diary of Samuel Sewall*, ed. M. Halsey Thomas, 2 vols. (New York: Farrar, Straus, 1973), 1:35, 39–40; Stoddard, *Inexcusableness*, 18. The hypothesis of "scrupulosity" we owe to Edmund S. Morgan, "New England Puritanism: Another Approach," *William and Mary Quarterly*, 3rd ser., no. 18 (1961): 241–42.

42. Increase Mather, *The Duty of Parents to Pray for their Children* (1703; Boston, 1719), sig. A2 verso (recalling the fast of November 21, 1678 requested by the Commissioners of the United Colonies); William DeLoss Love, *The Fast and Thanksgiving Days of New England* (Boston, Mass.: Houghton Mifflin, 1895), ch. 15.

43. *Christian History for 1743*, 110–11.

44. *Works of Jonathan Edwards*, vol. 4: *The Great Awakening*, ed. C. C. Goen (New Haven, Conn.: Yale University Press, 1972), 157–58, 157 n. 3, 106, 121; *Ecclesiastical Writings*, ed. Hall, 52.

45. See, in general, David W. Kling, *A Field of Divine Wonders: The New Divinity and Village Revivals in Northwestern Connecticut 1792–1822* (University Park: Pennsylvania State University Press, 1993), ch. 6, for a summary of the scholarship on the First Great Awakening, during which the percentage of men rose and the age of converts fell. Afterwards, however, the patterns we have been describing reasserted themselves.

46. We base this statement on the many narratives of local revivals printed in *The Christian History* (1743–44).

47. C. C. Goen, *Revivalism and Separatism in New England* (New Haven, Conn.: Yale University Press, 1962), 130, 47–48.

48. The relevant documents, together with an introduction that elaborates on this interpretation of the controversy, may be found in *Ecclesiastical Writings*, ed. Hall (quotations from pp. 316, 213, 318).

49. See, in general, Perry Miller, *The New England Mind: The Seventeenth Century* (Cambridge, Mass.: Harvard University Press, 1939); idem, *The New England Mind: From Colony to Province* (Cambridge, Mass.: Harvard University Press, 1953).

50. See, e.g., Mary P. Ryan, *Cradle of the Middle Class: The Family in Oneida County, New York, 1790–1865* (New York: Cambridge University Press, 1981), a study that, in demonstrating anew the relationship between women as mothers and church membership, extends part of the argument we are making.

Chapter Four

PRACTICES OF EXCHANGE: FROM MARKET CULTURE TO GIFT ECONOMY IN THE INTERPRETATION OF AMERICAN RELIGION

LEIGH ERIC SCHMIDT

THE INTERPRETATION of gift cultures or gift economies, the circular process of gift and counter-gift, is a venerable interdisciplinary enterprise. Founded in large part on Marcel Mauss's classic, multidimensional *Essai sur le don* (1925), the twentieth-century discussion of the gift has spilled across the borders of anthropology, sociology, and comparative religion to engage scholars across the humanities and social sciences. Mauss saw the rituals of gift exchange, such as those of the potlatch, as involving a total social system—"religious, legal, moral, and economic." For Mauss, cultural patterns of offering, obligation, and reciprocity led interpreters into the heart of things: the graded structures of the social order, the nuances of honor and competition, the political and economic norms of the community, the aesthetics of a culture, the fetishistic power of goods, as well as the activities and expectations of the gods. To Mauss, gifts came alive as representations of social connection, as magical bearers of the "spirit" of the giver, as ritualized embodiments of attachment. He also did not hesitate to extend his conclusions into modern society: "Much of our everyday morality is concerned," he said, "with the question of obligation and spontaneity in the gift. . . . The theme of the gift, of freedom and obligation in the gift, of generosity and self-interest in giving, reappears in our own society like the resurrection of a dominant motif long forgotten." Amid the fragmentation and impersonality of a modern market society, "archaic" gift cultures allowed Mauss to conjure up a Romantic dream of primeval solidarity.[1]

For all the multidisciplinary discussion of gift economies, historians of American religion have rarely entered the fray, little concerning themselves with gifts, their complex moral and political economy, their polysemous rituals and symbols. Yet as both trope and practice, gifts bear further historical and ethnographic scrutiny from students of American religion and culture.[2] At the foundations of American culture are the canny exchanges among native peoples, Africans, and European colonists.

In these originating moments of circulation, gifts, with all their possibility for both tribute and subterfuge, condescension and deference, serve as a metonym for cross-cultural transaction, for the complicated meetings between peoples. Indicative of these colonial encounters was the dilemma of the wayfaring Quaker and antislavery radical John Woolman. When offered gifts in his travels from slaveholders, he confessed his quandary in his journal: "Receiving a gift, considered as a gift, brings the receiver under obligations to the benefactor, and has a natural tendency to draw the obliged into a party with the giver." Awkwardly, in a knot of tangled relations and tormented religious conscience, Woolman found himself trying to refuse the gifts or, failing that, going off to the slave quarters to make amends by dispensing "pieces of silver" to the Africans he met there. Through such gifts he tried to reposition himself in the social world from obliged subservience to independent benefactor. Even as he struggled to free himself from one hierarchic bond, he reinscribed another asymmetry.[3]

Gifts also stand out as a recurrent, almost indispensable accompaniment of rites of passage, the tangible embodiments of thresholds, the palpable souvenirs of transition: the mourning gifts that were part of the Puritan way of death, the increasingly elaborate gifts for weddings and birthdays among middle-class Victorians, and the varied presents for christenings, confirmations, first communions, or bar mitzvahs. Gifts are important markers of other temporal cycles as well, particularly in their prominence as tokens of the New Year or as signs of seasonal rebirth at Easter. They stand out, too, as a potential domain of the carnivalesque—the gift as practical joke, the deceptive gags of April fooling or the derisive shamings of mock valentines, both widespread customs in the nineteenth century. At the densely textured level of everyday practice and lived experience, the rituals of gift exchange offer rich interpretive possibilities.

Even if scholars of American religion were to keep their inquiry on more familiar terrain—the theologies, liturgies, pieties, and practices of American Protestants—the gift as a trope is pervasive. It is there in rituals of thanksgiving, in the solemn recognition of the divine bestowal of fecundity and earthly abundance. It informs the rhetoric and practice of benevolence, charity, almsgiving, and stewardship. It is present in the language and ritual of the Eucharist as recipients partake of the gifts of Christ's body and blood as well as in understandings of the Sabbath as a divine gift to weary humanity. It underpins Protestant soteriology, the "free gift" of salvation, righteousness, and eternal life, the atoning sacrifice of Christ that can never be balanced. As one contemporary evangelical woman wrote, "I wanted to give Jesus a gift. . . . But what did I have that I could give to the King?"[4] The trope also haunts the ceremonies of church weddings in the form of the bride as gift, the woman as object of male exchange: "Who giveth this woman to be married?" It shapes some of the basic presentations within the nineteenth-century Sunday school— for example, the little tokens given by teachers to students in recognition of such distinctly Protestant feats as perfect attendance or the prodigious memorization of Bible verses.

As scriptural precept and simple proverb, the gift works its way into the day-to-day wisdom of Protestant folks: "Freely ye have received, freely give"; "Give us this day our daily bread"; "One good turn deserves another"; "It is more blessed to give than to receive"; "Every good and every perfect gift is from above"; "The Lord loveth a cheerful giver." The image of heavenly gifts underpins the Victorian Protestant reappropria- tion of Christmas in numberless meditations on the gifts of the Magi or on the Father's "unspeakable gift" of His only begotten Son. At the end of the nineteenth century, there was no more important doctrine in the Holiness movement and in the roots of Pentecostalism than the gifts of the Holy Spirit. The pieties of the Holiness and Pentecostal movements were, at one level, an extended reflection on a divine gift economy—entire sanctification, Spirit baptism, healing, tongues, prophecy, discernment of spirits—gifts that were as much about new (or restored) ritual practices as novel theological ideas. Yet gifts were not only a matter of religious joy or ecstacy but also sometimes of rejection and taboo: in their austere regu- lation of the relations between the sexes, the Shakers, for example, sought to insure the boundaries of separation through the proscription of ex- change: "Brethren and sisters may not make presents to each other in a private manner."[5]

This opening litany of interpretive possibilities only hints at a bigger picture—the cultural history that could be written on the practices (and piety) of gift-giving and -receiving in American religious life. This broad- brush assemblage also suggests, though, a deeper series of questions: How might work within the field of American religious history be redi- rected in terms of the subtleties of a gift economy as opposed to the ascendant paradigm of the market culture in which growth, competi- tion, entrepreneurialism, and market share are foregrounded? The work of Roger Finke and Rodney Stark represents this free-market interpre- tive model in its most intrepid form: "Religious economies are like com- mercial economies in that they consist of a market made up of a set of current and potential customers and a set of firms seeking to serve that market. The fate of these firms will depend upon (1) aspects of their or- ganizational structures, (2) their sales representatives, (3) their product, and (4) their marketing techniques." For Finke and Stark, even religious sacrifices are turned into bargain investments, rational choices made to maximize benefits.[6]

Such economic assumptions, if in far more nuanced diction, shape much of the work currently being done in the field, whether on the rise of evangelicalism, the process of democratization in the early Republic, the proliferation of Bibles and tracts as commodities, or the burgeoning of megachurches. That the voluntaristic marketplace, along with its concomitant patterns of promotion and consumption, decisively shaped American religion is clear, but this supply-side model, focusing almost exclusively on the vending of faith and thus privileging the denominational winners in this free market, allows us to see finally only a small part of the complexity of American religious life. Since the supply-side construct concentrates largely on the cultural producers, on the dedicated entrepreneurs of faith from Whitefield to Asbury, from Finney to Bruce Barton, it has proven of limited use when it comes to the study of popular or lived religion, the everyday exercises of faith within congregations and families, at shrines or grottoes, or in the Sunday schools and on the streets. It may be of some help, I think, if we reflect more seriously upon religion in terms of practices of exchange—that is, in terms of a gift economy instead of a market culture.[7]

As an interpretive construct, a gift economy suggests the more complex motivations of religious actors as they meet, associate, sacrifice, struggle, jostle, and contend—with each other and with God. The practices and pieties surrounding gifts lead to charged moments of encounter, exchange, and relationship and away from an all-too rationalized, segmented, individualistic religious marketplace. The gift economy, far from pointing to a realm independent of the market or somehow above competition, encapsulates the tensile notions of rivalry and altruism, mass commodity and personal inventiveness, calculation and offering. Ministers and congregants, vendors and consumers, men and women, parents and children, as well as God and worshipers are embedded in intricate webs of relationship and exchange, give and take, bestowal and resistance, gratitude and resentment. Thinking of American religious life as a gift economy accents the small habits of faith, the tactility of memory, the vows of obedience, the promises of reward, the desperate deals struck with God, the performative gestures of acknowledgment, as well as the hierarchies of conferral and submission.[8] The construct of the open religious marketplace is not canceled by the gift economy, since competition, display, status, and rivalry are common parts of exchange, but the gift economy, unlike the market model, is not narrowly beholden to the values of salesmanship, growth, and market share. Gifts then, as with other religious practices, are supple and hybrid, positioned on the overlapping borders of self-interest and self-denial, festive play and strategic purpose, spirit and materiality, public and private, sacred and secular.

As a small gesture toward the reconfiguration of the "economy" of American religious historiography, this essay focuses on one crucial moment in the formation of these discourses and practices of gift exchange in American culture: Romantic constructions of gift-giving in the middle decades of the nineteenth century. In this essay, I dwell particularly on the ideas and experiences of two luminaries, Ralph Waldo Emerson and Caroline Kirkland. I do so in the belief that practices should not be separated from the ideas that inform them, nor should intellectuals, clergy, and theologians be treated as somehow outside the pale of lived religion. The notion of lived religion is itself intended to break down further the already crumbling oppositions between popular and elite, high and low, official and vernacular, the social and the religious, while preserving space for critical analysis of the issues of power, domination, and hierarchy (including the formative influence of the market revolution on the quotidian forms of modern religion). Seeing the equivocal piety of Emerson and Kirkland points us to essential tensions within the wider practices of exchange in the burgeoning consumer culture, then and afterward.

Romantic understandings of gifts were torn, ambivalent. Emerson, whose formulations were among the most renowned, was suspicious of gifts—their strategic possibilities, their obligating power, their seemingly inevitable compromise of individual autonomy and self-reliance. As the commercial revolution increasingly laid claim to the materials of gift-giving—from books to fruits and flowers to love tokens—Emerson expressed a familiar bewilderment over the confusions of market exchanges and gift exchanges, an alienation from the commodified and the shopworn. Despite all their Romantic potentiality, gifts seemed inescapably poisoned and contradictory, a theme carried through in this century in academic commentary from Mauss to Derrida.[9]

That poisoning is half of the story. The other half, indivisible from its complement, was a Romantic absorption in the promise and pleasure of gifts. Almost everywhere one turned, but especially if one turned within domestic and familial circles, gifts were proliferating in the nineteenth century, an expansion made possible by the ever-widening scope of the modern consumer culture and intellectually authorized by a host of domestic writers and novelists, including Sarah Josepha Hale, Mary Clarke, Louisa May Alcott, and Caroline M. Kirkland. These authors shared many of the same ambivalences with Emerson and other critics about the corruptibility of gifts, but they also managed consistently to redeem gifts, to sanctify them, to see in them near endless possibility for the strengthening of family, friendship, social intimacy, mutuality, and piety. The quite material domain of gifts, keepsakes, cards, souvenirs, and home-based festivals entailed a vision of human connection and community, a tangible theology of relationship that stood in sharp contrast to transcendentalist ideals of self-reliance as well as to market forms of individualism. The very creation of this expansive gift economy, a testimony both to the market's reach and to the cultural resistance to that power, suggests the need to consider the flourishing of religious alternatives to the open marketplace of competition.[10]

ROMANTIC ALIENATION: THE POISON IN GIFTS

Thou shalt take no gift: for the gift blindeth the wise,
and perverteth the words of the righteous.
—Exodus 23:8

Emerson, though deeply wary of modern gifts, hardly wanted to be taken for a Scrooge, a character who had made his appearance the year before the publication of Emerson's second series of *Essays* (1844) with its meditation on "Gifts." "I fear," Emerson hesitated, "to breathe any treason against the majesty of love, which is the genius and god of gifts, and to whom we must not affect to prescribe. . . . There are persons, from whom we always expect fairy tokens; let us not cease to expect them." But then he added in distinctly modern, market tones: "For the rest, I like to see that we cannot be bought and sold." "Injury and heart-burning," "shame and humiliation," cajolery and "degrading dependence," bribery and blackmail, seemed to lurk in the most basic exchanges between people. "It is not the office of a man to receive gifts," Emerson insisted in terms that were unintentionally though correctly gendered. "How dare you give them? We wish to be self-sustained. We do not quite forgive a giver." Concerned about maintaining an autonomous male reserve, Emerson even worried over the penetrating discernment implied in the glad gift: "If the gift pleases me overmuch, then I should be ashamed that the donor should read my heart."

Happy with ambiguity, inconsistency, and metamorphosis, Emerson left ample room in his essay (and in his family life) for the romanticization of "beautiful" gifts—for the "fairy tokens" of lovers as well as for the "rich argosies" and "wonder-box[es]" of domestic presents at Christmas and New Year's. Perhaps precisely because he found himself so inescapably drawn into these familial and sociable forms of gift-giving, Emerson dwelled with severity on the exacting obligations of bestowing, receiving, and reciprocating gifts. "How painful to give a gift," Emerson noted in a prefiguration in his journal in 1838. "It is next worse to receiving one. The new remembrance of either is a scorpion."[11]

Emerson's distrust of gifts was multilayered. For one thing, gift-giving was deeply ritualistic, hemmed in by elaborate social rubrics, which seemed little suited to transcendentalist ideals of intuition, inspiration, and spiritualized individualism. So much about the presentation of gifts was formalistic, routine, and obligatory, part of the outward garb of society that Emerson sought to transcend through the direct, private, and immediate experience of the Over-Soul. In the rather ethereal world of transcendentalist bonhommie, material tokens were worse than nothing when compared to the spirit. In friendships, Emerson said, one should in oneself stand as "a gift and a benediction. Shine with real light, & not with the borrowed reflection of gifts."[12] "Why insist on rash personal relations with your friend?" Emerson asked in his essay on friendship. "Why go to his house, or know his mother and brother and sisters? Why be visited by him at your own? Are these things material to our covenant? Leave this touching and clawing. Let him be to me a spirit. A message, a thought, a sincerity, a glance from him, I want but not news, nor pottage. . . . Should not the society of my friend be to me poetic, pure, universal, and great as nature itself?"[13]

In this meeting of souls, gifts dragged people back to the mundane, to social custom and obligation, to the humbly domestic. It returned Romantic individualists from lonely solitude, from Promethean independence and self-sufficiency to social games of flattery and magnanimity. As anthropologist Mary Douglas has aphorized, "The theory of the gift is a theory of human solidarity," and Emerson bristled at the corporate claims that gifts made on him, their invasion of his independence. "The height, the deity of man," he pronounced, "is to be self-sustained, to need no gift, no foreign force." "Let us even bid our dearest friends farewell," Emerson advised, "and defy them, saying, 'Who are you? Unhand me: I will be dependent no more.'"[14] Gifts thus suggested a social webbing in tension with many of the core Romantic notions of religion, friendship, inspiration, and art.

Among the most prominent dimensions of Emerson's alienation from modern gift giving was his estrangement from the calculation and confidence games of the marketplace. Emerson envisioned pure, creative, soul-imbued gifts—the poet's gift of a poem, the artist's offering of a painting, the young girl's present of a hand-embroidered handkerchief, but what he discerned all around him was something else. "Our tokens of compliment and love are for the most part barbarous," he averred. "Rings and other jewels are not gifts, but apologies for gifts. The only gift is a portion of thyself. Thou must bleed for me. . . . It is a cold, lifeless business when you go to the shops to buy me something, which does not represent your life and talent."

Despite his Christ-haunted and sacrifice-imbued rhetoric, Emerson turned not to Jesus but to nature to recover fitting, unsullied gifts. Flowers and fruits, plucked from nature itself, avoided the "false state" of the mart with its prosaic, all-too-convenient surrogates for self-expression and self-giving. As he noted somewhat innocently in his journal in 1866, when flowers were increasingly being commodified through the burgeoning industry of commercial floriculture, "Flowers grow in the garden to be given away." Emblems of "passion & sentiment," of "the frolic and interference of love and beauty," flowers were "a proud assertion that a ray of beauty outvalues all the utilities of the world." Though ornamental flowers and fruits were themselves becoming ensconced as shopworn merchandise right alongside the bibelots of the dry-goods store, Emerson still looked for "natural" gifts, artistic and material, that were somehow free of the market. Even more, he looked for those rare "true" gifts full of Christ-like self-giving, a "flowing of the giver unto me, correspondent to my flowing unto him." "Behold I do not give lectures or a little charity," Whitman affirmed in tones resonant with Emerson's "When I give, I give myself."[15]

Romantic concerns about the buying and selling of gifts were not solely an expression of a lofty, transcendentalist hauteur. The celebrants of domestic gift-giving also worried about the market's profanations. Sarah Hale, for example, thought that the "*printed* doggerel, bought in market and distributed through the penny post" for St. Valentine's Day, often carried "no more sentiment" than "patented recipes for colds, or notices of a new milliner's shop." (She suggested, with little sense of contradiction, that a more suitable token would be a subscription to her own *Godey's Lady's Book*.) Hale also wanted to spare the new familial fashion of a Christmas tree the contaminations of the market: decorate it with "loving gifts," she advised. "Do not load its green boughs with the *sugar candies now 'made to sell.'* You can adorn your Christmas-tree with the healthful gifts of Nature—apples, pears, grapes, nuts, and other fruits."[16] In a similar vein, one Methodist publication, the *Ladies' Repository*, in commenting on the growing fondness for lavish gifts for various festal occasions, particularly lamented "the jingle of gilded trinkets" for Christmas and the "glittering inventory of bridal presents" for the "modern fashionable wedding." "The *commercial* aspect of gift-making" was turning these modern rituals into a frivolous show of social status and acquisitiveness, transforming joyful giving into "a sharp, sordid, bargaining spirit." To the *Repository* essayist, presents for Christmas and weddings had come to be more about style, costliness, and display than "spontaneous loving impulse"; Christmas itself, the writer feared, was fast degenerating into "a hot-bed of stimulated gratification" for overly pampered children.[17]

Like Emerson and Hale, the writer for the *Ladies' Repository* also concerned herself with issues of the handmade and the ready-made in gift-giving. Enwrapped in the marketplace, festive presents were seen as becoming more and more about the duplicate articles of modern trade than the originals of painstaking handicraft. "Our whole code of gift-making needs revision," she announced. "Presents should be given and received more as the *symbols* of attachment," and this was to be accomplished through artless simplicity, not sumptuous expense:

> What costly article of *bijouterie*, fashioned by stranger hands, scrutinized by the greedy eye of trade, bandied from shop to shop, can have the beautiful significance of a wreath of skeleton ferns, an album of sea-weeds arranged on the spotless page, filament by filament, with gentle, dexterous skill, or a portfolio of pencil sketches in which our friend has wrought his heart and nature together in one twin volume?[18]

Such gift-making handicrafts, a particularly creative domain of women's work, were being usurped through commercial imitation and market expansion. In this struggle, the resistance of some women writers to the imperial extension of the market into the realm of gift-giving was deeper, more palpable than Emerson's more abstracted alienation.

Demarcating the authenticity of gift-giving in the face of the market was clearly a widely shared Romantic concern. As Caroline Kirkland worried in sweeping terms, presents, so filled with mystic possibility, were amidst this "bank-note world" in danger of losing "their sweet significance" and becoming "a meaner sort of merchandize." To remain beautiful and true, "a present," she concluded, "must be wholly pleasurable—voluntary—heartful—free—impulsive—without earthly alloy on either side."[19] Such Romantic anxieties over the profaning impact of commodification on gift-giving surfaced around various rituals—St. Valentine's Day, Christmas, New Year's, Easter, weddings, and birthdays—and Emerson's estrangement from the marketplace was rooted in these wider currents of alienation. His own intuitions on shopworn presents were apiece with broader cultural concerns about sincerity, innocence, spontaneity, simplicity, originality, and self-disclosure in gift-giving.[20]

Romantic worries about the lost purity of presents long haunted highbrow readings of modern gift practices, often impeding appreciation of the new rituals that had been so carefully crafted for home and family. This was particularly evident in the aesthetics of high modernism, which fed on the Romantic construction of the true gifts of art, creativity, and self. In their disdain for the schlock of a commodity culture, modernist aesthetes regularly scorned the banality of a consumerist gift culture of knickknacks, novelties, and cards. In *Kitsch: The World of Bad Taste*, Gillo Dorfles, teaming his work with that of Clement Greenberg and Theodor Adorno, fumed with familiar exasperation over the trivial, sentimentalized rituals of mass culture; whether Mother's Day or St. Valentine's Day, weddings or anniversaries, they were all celebrated with a flood of the tacky and the maudlin. "It is hard to believe that men have been able to wrap their most sacred relationships in such a thick veil of bad taste, dragging them down to the level of perverted rituals," Dorfles sniffed.[21] With the eclectic, democratized, messy aesthetics of postmodernism, such interpretive, hierarchic categories have been dramatically blurred, but the tone of despair over the ritual emptiness of the modern gift culture often persists. The Romantic elevation of gifts into a domain of artistic autonomy, cultural purity, and prophetic vision augured this modernist consignment of humbler gifts to the realm of the banal and the saccharine.

ROMANTIC ABSORPTION: THE PROMISE OF GIFTS

> Every man according as he purposeth in his heart, so
> let him give; not grudgingly, or of necessity: for
> God loveth a cheerful giver.
> —II Corinthians 9:7

The world of commodified gifts was never as trivial or empty as Emerson and his varied heirs feared. Historian T. J. Jackson Lears, in a postmodern turn at the end of his *Fables of Abundance*, celebrates "the transfiguration of the commonplace," artistic efforts "to reclaim the most forlorn, forgotten, and banal fragments of commodity civilization, . . . and resituate them in the architecture of the imagination, transforming them into numinous artifacts."[22] Lears tends to aestheticize this alchemy, turning to artists (such as Kurt Schwitters and Joseph Cornell) for the reanimation of quotidian materials, but it is a sacramental magic long evident on the other side of the Romantic view of gifts, alive in domestic rituals and curios. This other Romanticism resisted the highbrow view of art, religion, goods, and gifts, relishing the sentimental souvenir, transfiguring the token and keepsake in its redemption of the prosaic. In the home circle, with its varied red-letter days for gift-giving, women and children (and many men, too) discovered a "magician's wand with which to conjure marvelous surprises." As Caroline Kirkland praised gifts, the little "magic symbols of love," "The book that has been used and marked—the ring we have seen worn—the 'bent sixpence' of rustic lovers—the precious curl or braid set in simple guise—these, and a thousand other trifles that the ingenuity of affection easily devises when it would convey by some little token a notice of the stores within—have a value to be measured only by the wealth of the soul."[23]

Kirkland's "magic symbols" were the complement to Emersonian alienation and were suggestive of the concomitant Romantic absorption with the meanings of presents. Poet and essayist Charles Lamb, a writer for whom Emerson had little affection, was among the arch-sentimentalists of the gift. Gifts of all sorts he found "inexpressibly pleasant." "If presents be not the soul of friendship, they are the most spiritual part of the body of that intercourse," he said in terms that reversed the Emersonian economy of the soul. In a popular "Homily for the Fourteenth of February," Lamb gushed about the charm and expense of the "first valentine" he had received as a youth. "The Valentine was radiant,—all gold and gay colours, red, and yellow, and blue, and embossed, and glittering with devices, all of love. It was like a dream, so fine. I had never seen any thing like it. . . . I was satisfied,—delighted—what is the word? *enchanted*!" The dreamy beauty of new things, new commodities, new gifts inspired his imagination. One hears a popular echo of Lamb's glee in the letter from a Connecticut woman, Sophia Root, to her sister in 1861 about a valentine that the latter had sent to Sophia's young daughter Mary. "I cannot tell you how delighted Mary was with the valentine. . . . She jumped about and up and down in expression of joy. She has shown it to her schoolteacher and many other friends. It is a beautiful thing and she sends you many thanks for it."[24]

It was for folks like Mary Root, who carefully saved her valentine, that Lamb often wrote, penning verse after verse for dedications in the front of ladies' albums, those domestic repositories of keepsakes, mementoes, and souvenirs. Indeed, Lamb hallowed these little remembrances as he went. "An Album is," he rhymed,

> A Chapel, where mere ornamental things
> Are pure as crowns of saints, or angels' wings.
> A List of living friends; a holier Room
> For names of some since mouldering in the tomb,
> Whose blooming memories life's cold laws survive;
> And, dead elsewhere, they here yet speak and live.

"Mere ornamental things" were sanctified; they were made "holy" in the relational, intimate world of family and friends. Rather than protesting against the new gift economy, Lamb unabashedly celebrated it. For many, the new world of gifts and goods created little anxiety or alienation, instead only the bewitchment of memory and devotion.[25]

Lamb had plenty of company as a Romantic consecrator of gifts. Numbered in this fellowship was Caroline Kirkland, whose *Book for the Home Circle* (1853) included a substantial chapter on presents. In "a world of mixed motives," a market society of pretense and manipulation in which people seemed to have "faces and hearts made to order, of stone or ice," Kirkland looked back (as Mauss did in his turn) to a remote, precapitalist past—to "early and simple days," when gifts served as "the most natural expression of good-will and affection." To Kirkland, this impulse to give and to bind together was recoverable, alive among quixotic dreamers impervious to the disenchanting gaze of "the cold eye" of self-interest. When purified of the wrong motives, gifts emerged anew as a "magic art" of love, tenderness, and attachment. As Kirkland dreamed in a visionary passage on the fantastic, fetishistic possibilities of things,

> The essence of the present, properly so-called, consists in the sentiment of the thing. . . . O! the sweetness of the real "present!" What wealth of love may be enwrapped in it—what mystic meaning—what vows of truth—what rich memories of the past—what promise of the future! What a glory envelops the simplest object the moment it takes that sacred character.

In Kirkland's piety of keepsakes, gifts were about sentiments, feelings, affinities, connections, memories, and promises. The ability to share in them, to feel others in them and through them, to find presence in absence, was to Kirkland a sacramental sensibility. Giving in this revelatory and integrative sense, Kirkland theologized, "assimilates us nearer to God than any other" activity. As cheerful givers, "generous and confiding people" participated in a divine economy characterized, above all, by abounding grace, by freely bestowed love.[26]

What were some of the specific practices and characteristics of this consecrated, relational gift economy that Kirkland both embraced and helped construct? For one, gifts created a rippling circle of association—not only marked by counter-gifts, but also by notes and calling. Visits and acknowledgments were part of the etiquette of presents, so that exchanges for New Year's, Christmas, St. Valentine's Day, Easter, birthdays, weddings, or funerals regularly brought people together in quite direct ways and often well beyond the day of initial presentation. "The Mystery of Visiting," as Kirkland labeled it in her *Evening Book* on morals and manners, was the lustrous delight found in human company—a cheer, like gifts themselves, ideally shorn of a sense of duty and form. As one Massachusetts woman, Eliza Adams, effused over all the Christmas visitors who came by to celebrate in 1848, "We are all out at the house in a most noisy mood; some talking, others sewing, all most busy in the enjoyments of the day." Gifts and visits thus served as interrelated vehicles of attachment, affection, and exchange.[27]

These visits, notes, and calling cards were memorialized, as Lamb's poetry suggested, in women's scrapbooks and albums. Often themselves inscribed as gifts—"Millie Pickett Christmas Present from Papa 1877"—these scrapbooks were an embodiment of remembrance, a place to keep small forget-me-nots of friendship and kinship. The Winterthur Library and the Hallmark Historical Collection have amassed several dozen of these nineteenth-century albums, and in them one can see how cards and other small mementoes were prized. In saving and mounting these holiday greetings, women often wrote some identifying annotation underneath the missives—from cousin Elizabeth; Easter 1881; Helen's first valentine. In this way, a chronicle of friends, relatives, and important occasions could be maintained through albums filled with cards and keepsakes. Colorful and intricate Victorian cards for Christmas, Easter, and other events were cherished for the web of relationships, for the intimations of companionship, that they evoked. The little, formulaic, sentimental mottoes themselves consistently suggested this sense of lasting attachment: "Yours forever," "Think of me when far away," or "Fond remembrance." These goods were the materials of memory, lace-paper ties to living friends and scissor-and-paste shrines for recollecting the dead. Such albums formed a regular part of the ordinary devotions of middle-class Victorian women.[28]

Easter cards, which blossomed as a holiday vogue in the early 1880s, well illustrate the familial and pious dimensions of this circling gift culture. Not surprisingly, flowers, birds, and innocent little children were found in profusion, but more striking images were also to be found. In one set of cards, for example, the resurrected Lord was imagined as a cherub, reborn in the heavenly innocence of childhood, a blurring of Easter piety into Christmas devotion, the coddling love of the Baby Jesus. Also, angelic images of young girls were sometimes presented as embodying the resurrected Christ in what amounted to an apotheosis of the feminine. Jesus Himself often became an androgynous figure in these popular depictions; with flowing hair and delicate features, the risen Christ was almost invariably surrounded by flowers, cultural markings that decidedly feminized the Savior.

Since these cards, like those for other occasions, circulated mostly among female friends and relatives, these renderings of the divine were doubly important, embodying the domestic, woman-centered spirituality of the middle-class Christian home.[29] Easter cards were thus important in forming part of a female world of gift-giving rituals, ones in which the Savior Himself was often remade in the ideal image of middle-class Victorian women and their children—pure, tender, and comforting. Both in their familiar conventionality and in their reveries of resurrection, Easter cards effectively reimagined popular Christian piety, simply disregarding the terrifying, melancholiac dimensions of the Calvinist past as well as the medieval and early modern fascination with the pain and suffering of the crucified, bleeding Savior. As presents, they embodied the gentle, affective, hopeful, and sympathetic world of Victorian Protestantism.

Examples of the materials and practices of this domestic gift culture could be multiplied: the growing love of Christmas presents, the expanding cult of Santa Claus as the bearer of pure and unreciprocated gifts, the new joys of birthday parties and birthday cakes, the elaborateness of wedding presents that made tangible the triumph of romantic love, the recognition of anniversaries with an increasingly formalized system of gifts, the profusion of Easter knickknacks, or the staggering success of Mother's Day (and its associated gifts) after its founding in 1908. But perhaps it is more important, by way of conclusion, to return to the questions of community and relationship, market culture and gift economy: What were the implications of this expanding gift culture for constructions of social connection? Sociologist David Cheal argues that the modern gift economy, woman-led and family-centered, pits intimacy against community, that the contemporary gift culture is primarily about the "ritual construction of small social worlds" in which there are only limited opportunities to give expression to attachments beyond the family itself. Indeed, to Cheal, among the hallmarks of modern gift occasions is the birthday party with its "cult of the individual."

Sociologist Theodore Caplow in his revisiting of Middletown and its ritual cycles sees the familial dimensions of modern gift-giving in still sharper terms; contemporary exchanges focus overwhelmingly on close kin—a ritual response, Caplow sees, to the vulnerability of these "important but insecure relationships." "Every widely observed festival in Middletown now celebrates the family and the related ideas of home, mother and child, and feminine roles." From this perspective, the modern gift economy is highly insular and little engaged with civic life; it hardly constitutes a total system that embraces "the whole social life," as Mauss had envisioned archaic exchanges. From this angle of vision, the Romantic, familial gift culture, invented in the nineteenth century, finally tenders little more than another privatized ritual system reenforcing the dissolution of community and public forms of faith.[30]

But the Romantic gift culture of domestic writers offered an important alternative to the purer individualism of Emerson and other skeptics. The trust in gifts, in the tokens and trifles of friendship, was founded on reciprocity, commitment, remembrance, familiarity, sympathy, and enchantment. However circumscribed, that gift culture was far closer to Mauss's vision of hospitality and festivity than Emerson's often leery, empyrean musings. For all of Emerson's distancing from the marketplace, his own suspicions about gifts reproduced its logic: don't trust a giver; suspect ulterior motives; look for selfish designs; expect resentment; prize autonomy, freedom, and detachment over relationship; don't be bought and sold.[31] Hale, Kirkland, and others, though often just as wary of the marketplace, suggested a more expansive option rooted in a wider embrace of the materials of popular practice. And, again in recognition of Emerson's own ambivalence, he, too, in his warmer moments at home amid a "dancing roaring company," often redeemed the profusion of holiday gifts: "Aunt Adams had sent a wonderful tea-set; and Uncle George P Bradford books; & a clock was also set up, Lidian's gift; and Grandmamma added hers. It was a pelting shower of donations." Emerson was torn between his own intellectual musings on gifts and his lived experience of holiday festivity in which presents circulated with joyous abandon. At times, the gift economy managed to assuage even Emerson's market qualms and to check his individualistic propensities.[32]

If centered on the family, this gift culture, like the rituals of visiting, radiated outward into broader circles of kin and acquaintance. Ultimately based more on republican simplicity and bourgeois sincerity than genteel display and aristocratic hierarchy—presents of "small value" or of painstaking handicraft were consistently extolled—this Romantic gift culture embraced new commodities for the virtuous ends of attachment, fidelity, and affection.[33] "Let us not deceive ourselves," Paul Tournier preached on the significance of modern presents. "This great hunger for gifts is not so much a hunger for pleasure as for affection." The domestic gift economy, far more than the alienated individualism of transcendentalism or the marketplace, represented a social world closer to the Maori proverb that Mauss so favored: "Give as much as you receive and all is for the best."[34]

If that sounds too Romantic or quixotic—too much like I have figured out the moral of this story—let me tack back. The delicate frailty of many of the tokens of this gift culture—the lace-work cards or the fading flowers—suggests that these ritual forms of human connection were fragile, sometimes even flimsy, propositions. Often these gifts seemed, indeed, a confirmation of the peculiarly modern susceptibilities of social relationships to attenuation. As Joyce C. Hall remarked on the dramatic flourishing of his greeting-card empire, people simply did not have time anymore "to write long thoughtful letters," and cards were thus the right "social custom" for "our complex and mobile society." Presenting his product as a "true" purveyor of human feeling and connection, he boldly offered a ritual solution to these modern mobilities and fragmentations. His advertising slogan, with deep resonances in the gift culture of the nineteenth century, showed anew the inextricable alliances between the marketplace and Romantic sensibilities: "It's the Sentiment that Counts." Hall's cultural and commercial intuitions about modern rituals of gift-giving were clearly on target as Hallmark's $3.4 billion domestic market and its truly global dimensions suggest (the company's products reach into over one hundred countries). The contradictory ways in which such tokens simultaneously bind together and ratify separation, concurrently invoke "real" sentiments and commodify them, remain at the heart of the modern gift economy, its ritual dilemmas, and its market possibilities.[35]

Perhaps the most reliable moral to this story is found in the oscillation between Romantic alienation and absorption, the tug between the poison and promise of gifts. The Romantic gift economy (and all the home-based festivals that went with it) shuttled between home and marketplace, spontaneity and obligation, enchantment and disenchantment. Fathoming such ambivalence (as well as the common resolution of it) is an important part of interpreting lived religion in modern market societies. At Christmas, for example, only 28 percent say they enjoy Christmas shopping "a great deal"; only 36 percent report attending special Christmas Eve services; a whopping 78 percent send Christmas cards; fully 32 percent feel depressed at the holidays; and yet still 93 percent of Americans consider it their favorite celebration.

As one Michigan woman wrote to another woman on a Christmas card in 1966, "We are all . . . busy as bees trying to get thru the mobs in the stores, or maybe I should say join them. Such a rat race as its gotten to be. I'm afraid we've put the real meaning away. I get more disgusted each year." Both appalled and enthralled, she expresses her pious disillusionment on one of the quintessential commodities of the modern gift culture, a Christmas card (the envelope for which she has "personalized" with a stamp from the American Bible Society, showing a shepherd, the proclamation "Peace on Earth," and a Holy Bible). She fears that her ritual life has become a burden and an imposition, hurried and hollow. At the same time, she warmly embraces the holiday practices of the modern Christmas as vehicles of meaning, devotion, fancy, and exchange. Even as her experience of sacred and secular dimensions of the holiday blend together, she works with a sense of profanation and transgression—that is, boundaries of holiness, the blurring of which troubles her.[36]

For one more example of this wavering of experience, more pained and piercing, a look at a recent poem entitled "Gifts" by Maura Stanton is illuminating. She writes of Christmas shopping for a present for a dying aunt:

> But the many worldly objects
> I've fingered in a dozen shops—
> hand-blown glass, engagement books,
> tote bags stenciled with sleeping cats—
> seemed so wrong I stepped into
> this fragrance store for inspiration.

There she finds some sweet-smelling soap for a gift, and, paying for it with a credit card, "only money's ghost," she is suddenly reminded of devotional cards:

My thumb runs over the numbers
embossed on the slick front,
and with a tingle I remember
stroking my aunt's holy cards
enclosed with childhood birthday presents,
pictures of Mary dressed in blue
bending over the swaddled child, . . .
I'd stroke the textured halos
around the sacred heads, as if
sanctity might rub off on me,
absorbed through my human skin.

The alienation from the commodities of the marketplace, all those worldly goods that seem so wrong, is joined to other gifts, holy cards and birthday presents, made sacred through memories of childhood, family, and devotion. Stanton hopes, amid "devouring gloom," that the new gift of fragrant soap will somehow smell of "heavenly gardens," will become for her dying aunt a sacramental token of Christian transcendence.[37]

Insisting on the power of the market structures of consumer capitalism would be inadequate to capture such ambivalence nor would a scholarly celebration of these material practices as "popular" apprehend the ambiguities of such ritual engagement. The paradoxes of the gift economy hold onto the tensile dimensions of such experiences, these twin tales of Christmas ambivalence. Dancing back and forth between products and presents, shopping and devotion, anxiety and resolution, obligation and generosity, resentment and gratitude, alienation and affirmation, the gift economy as a construct allows for the tiny freedoms of imagination, the modest improvisations of lived practice, and the miniature refusals of the market's power. As Pierre Bourdieu observes of the "logic" of gift practices, "The most ordinary and even the seemingly most routine exchanges of ordinary life, like the 'little gifts' that 'bind friendship,' presuppose an improvisation, and therefore a constant uncertainty, which, as we say, make all their *charm*, and hence all their social efficacy."[38] Such an open-ended dialectic between necessity and possibility offers another way of thinking about the old division between popular culture and mass culture (and the allied construct of the culture industry). It effectively blurs such dichotomies (and the parallel ones in the study of religion, such as official and vernacular, elite and popular). Thinking of lived religion in terms of the gray areas of a gift economy foregrounds ambivalence—the attractions of modern ritual exchanges and their disenchantments, their freedoms and their inescapable conditions. Gift practices nudge us away from the supply-side, production-oriented model of the market into the negotiable reciprocities of exchange and the uneven graces of lived experience.

NOTES

1. Marcel Mauss, *The Gift: Forms and Functions of Exchange in Archaic Societies*, trans. Ian Cunnison (New York: Norton, 1967), 1, 63, 66. The academic literature on the gift is voluminous. For eight of the more important interpretations and commentaries elaborating on Mauss's work, see Raymond Firth, *Symbols: Public and Private* (Ithaca, N.Y.: Cornell University Press, 1973), 368–402; Claude Lévi-Strauss, *Introduction to the Work of Marcel Mauss*, trans. Felicity Baker (London: Routledge and Kegan Paul, 1987); Marshall Sahlins, *Stone Age Economics* (Chicago: Aldine Atherton, 1972), 149–83; Jacques Derrida, *Given Time: 1. Counterfeit Money*, trans. Peggy Kamuf (Chicago: University of Chicago Press, 1992); Annette B. Weiner, *Inalienable Possessions: The Paradox of Keeping-While-Giving* (Berkeley: University of California Press, 1992); James G. Carrier, *Gifts and Commodities: Exchange and Western Capitalism since 1700* (London: Routledge, 1995); Jonathan Parry, "*The Gift*, the Indian Gift, and the 'Indian Gift,'" *Man* 21 (1986): 453–73; Pierre Bourdieu, *The Logic of Practice*, trans. Richard Nice (Stanford, Calif.: Stanford University Press, 1990), esp. 98–111. The works of Carrier and Parry are the most relevant for theorizing the relationship between the gift economy and the modern market. Their studies point to the ideology of the pure gift as itself both offspring and legitimator of the market economy and social differentiation. But, as with Mauss's reflections on modern societies, the work of Parry and Carrier can be helpfully anchored through close historical consideration of the lived practices of the Romantic culture that generated the distinctions between gift and commodity that they seek to explain. Bourdieu's work is the most useful for theorizing gift exchange as a dialectical practice, both conditioned and improvisational.

2. Little work on gifts in the American context considers the topic from the specific perspective of religious history. Three recent works in cultural history are helpful, though Waits' study excludes religion from consideration: William B. Waits, *The Modern Christmas in America: A Cultural History of Gift Giving* (New York: New York University Press, 1993); Jenna Weissman Joselit, *The Wonders of America: Reinventing Jewish Culture, 1880–1950* (New York: Hill and Wang, 1994); and Andrew R. Heinze, *Adapting to Abundance: Jewish Immigrants, Mass Consumption, and the Search for American Identity* (New York: Columbia University Press, 1990), 71–79. Since books were a quintessential gift throughout the early modern and modern periods, cultural historians working on the history of the book have been especially attentive to gift-giving. See, e.g., Natalie Zemon Davis, "Beyond the Market: Books as Gifts in Sixteenth-Century France," *Transactions of the Royal Historical Society* 33 (1983): 69–88; David D. Hall, *Worlds of Wonder, Days of Judgment: Popular Religious Belief in Early New England* (New York: Knopf, 1989), 45–46, 218, 236–37, 266 n. 61; as well as the older work by Ralph Thompson, *American Literary Annuals and Gift Books, 1825–1865* (New York: Wilson, 1936). I have also explored holiday rituals of gift-giving in *Consumer Rites: The Buying and Selling of American Holidays* (Princeton, N.J.: Princeton University Press, 1995), and this more theoretical essay emerges out of that larger work and its more detailed historical and "ethnographic" descriptions.

3. John Woolman, *The Journal of John Woolman and a Plea for the Poor* (Secaucus, N.J.: Citadel, 1961), 50–52. For suggestive discussions of cultural encounter and exchange, see, e.g., Stephen Greenblatt, *Marvelous Possessions: The Wonder of the New World* (Chicago: University of Chicago Press, 1991); Richard White, *The Middle Ground: Indians, Empires, and Republics in the Great Lakes Region, 1650–1815* (Cambridge: Cambridge University Press, 1991). In a recent essay, Catherine Albanese has explored gift exchanges as a trope for religious encounter, borrowing, and conflict. See Catherine Albanese, "Exchanging Selves, Exchanging Souls: Contact, Combination, and American Religious History," in *Retelling U.S. Religious History*, ed. Thomas A. Tweed (Berkeley: University of California Press, 1997), 200–226.

4. Jane Kirby, "The Gift," *Aglow* 34 (May–June 1978): 9. I am indebted to R. Marie Griffith for bringing this article to my attention.

5. For Holiness and Pentecostal gifts, see, e.g., W. B. Godbey, *Spiritual Gifts and Graces* (Cincinnati: God's Revivalist Office, 1895); S. A. Keen, *Pentecostal Papers; Or, The Gift of the Holy Ghost* (Cincinnati: Cranston and Curts, 1895). For especially helpful secondary works, see Grant Wacker, "The Holy Spirit and the Spirit of the Age in American Protestantism, 1880–1910," *Journal of American History* 72 (1985): 45–62; Donald W. Dayton, *Theological Roots of Pentecostalism* (Metuchen, N.J.: Scarecrow, 1987). For the Shaker rules, see the *Millennial Laws, or Gospel Statutes and Ordinances* (1821), reprinted as an appendix in Edward Deming Andrews, *The People Called Shakers: A Search for the Perfect Society* (New York: Dover, 1953), 266. That the Shakers in practice often defied such injunctions is apparent from Sally Promey's study of their gift images from the 1830s and 1840s. See Sally M. Promey, *Spiritual Spectacles: Vision and Image in Mid-Nineteenth-Century Shakerism* (Bloomington: Indiana University Press, 1993).

6. Roger Finke and Rodney Stark, *The Churching of America, 1776–1990: Winners and Losers in Our Religious Economy* (New Brunswick, N.J.: Rutgers University Press, 1992), 17. To the extent that consumer responses figure into the account of Finke and Stark, they do so uniformly: religious shoppers, in this model, prefer strict doctrine.

7. For leading exemplars, see R. Laurence Moore, *Selling God: American Religion in the Marketplace of Culture* (New York: Oxford University Press, 1994); R. Stephen Warner, "Work in Progress toward a New Paradigm for the Sociological Study of Religion in the United States," *American Journal of Sociology* 98 (1993): 1044–93; Nathan O. Hatch, *The Democratization of American Christianity* (New Haven, Conn.: Yale University Press, 1989). For my part in *Consumer Rites*, I have tried to work with a clearly dialectical model of negotiation, focusing on both producers and consumers, ministers and congregants, buying and selling, the joyous religious embrace of the marketplace and the sour alienation from it, celebration and contestation. "Audience response" is seriously considered by some working within the market model. See Frank Lambert, *"Pedlar in Divinity": George Whitefield and the Transatlantic Revivals, 1737–1770* (Princeton, N.J.: Princeton University Press, 1994), 134–68.

8. Annette Weiner's *Inalienable Possessions* is especially astute on the maintenance of hierarchy and difference through exchange. "Things exchanged," she

argues, "are about things kept" (e.g., dynastic lands, sacred objects, and royal insignia), that is, the materials of power that are kept out of circulation (p. 10).

9. For historiographic references on the theory of the gift, see n. 1.

10. On the modern gift culture as distinctly feminized, see, e.g., Micaela Di Leonardo, "The Female World of Cards and Holidays: Women, Families, and the Work of Kinship," *Signs: Journal of Women in Culture and Society* 12 (1987): 440–53; Lewis Hyde, *The Gift: Imagination and the Erotic Life of Property* (New York: Random House, 1983), 102–8; David Cheal, *The Gift Economy* (London: Routledge, 1988), x, 5–8, 181–83.

11. Ralph Waldo Emerson, "Gifts," in *The Collected Works of Ralph Waldo Emerson*, vol. 3: *Essays: Second Series* (Cambridge, Mass.: Harvard University Press, 1983), 93–96; Merton M. Sealts, ed., *The Journals and Miscellaneous Notebooks of Ralph Waldo Emerson*, vol. 5: *1835–1838* (Cambridge, Mass.: Belknap Press of Harvard University Press, 1965), 489. For ways in which Emerson's suspicions about gifts migrated into the work of Nietzsche, see Gary Shapiro, *Alcyone: Nietzsche on Gifts, Noise, and Women* (Albany: State University of New York Press, 1991), 24–29. More traditional, Christian conceptualizations of gifts in terms of charity, benevolence, and community obligation are evident in Emerson's sermons from the early 1830s. See, e.g., Teresa Toulouse and Andrew Delbanco, eds., *The Complete Sermons of Ralph Waldo Emerson*, vol. 2 (Columbia: University of Missouri Press, 1990), 132–37, 196–200. As in his sermons, so also in his letters, Emerson showed clearer signs of affinity with the domestic gift culture. See, e.g., the descriptions of familial merriment surrounding Christmas and New Year's presents in Ralph L. Rusk, ed., *The Letters of Ralph Waldo Emerson*, 6 vols. (New York: Columbia University Press, 1939), 2:251; 3:365–66; 4:174; 5:49, 92–93, 129, 185–87 (the phrases "rich argosies" and "wonder-box" are from holiday letters to his brother William, 4:174 and 5:185).

12. Ralph Waldo Emerson, "Spiritual Laws," in *The Collected Works of Ralph Waldo Emerson*, vol. 2: *Essays: First Series* (Cambridge, Mass.: Harvard University Press, 1983), 93. For this passage, see also William H. Gilman and J. E. Parsons, eds., *The Journals and Miscellaneous Notebooks of Ralph Waldo Emerson*, vol. 7: *1835–1838* (Cambridge, Mass.: Belknap Press of Harvard University Press, 1965), 193.

13. Emerson, "Friendship," in *Collected Works*, 2:123.

14. Mary Douglas, "Foreword: No Free Gifts," in Marcel Mauss, *The Gift: The Form and Reason for Exchange in Archaic Societies*, trans. W. D. Halls (New York: Norton, 1990), x; Ralph Waldo Emerson, "The Transcendentalist," in *The Collected Works of Ralph Waldo Emerson*, vol. 1: *Nature, Addresses, and Lectures* (Cambridge, Mass.: Harvard University Press, 1983), 203–4; Emerson, "Friendship," in *Collected Works*, 2:126.

15. Emerson, "Gifts," in *Collected Works*, 3:93–94; Ronald A. Bosco and Glen M. Johnson, eds., *The Journals and Miscellaneous Notebooks of Ralph Waldo Emerson*, vol. 16: *1866–1882* (Cambridge, Mass.: Belknap Press of Harvard University Press, 1965), 34; Whitman quoted in Firth, *Symbols*, 375. On Emerson and the marketplace (and wider Romantic tensions with the commercial revolution), see Michael T. Gilmore, *American Romanticism and the Marketplace* (Chicago: University of Chicago Press, 1985), 18–34. For an especially important

discussion of the affinities of Romanticism with the consumer culture, see Colin Campbell, *The Romantic Ethic and the Spirit of Modern Consumerism* (Oxford: Basil Blackwell, 1987).

16. "A New Fashion for Valentines," *Godey's Magazine and Lady's Book* 38 (February 1849): 73–74; Sarah Josepha Hale, *Manners; Or, Happy Homes and Good Society All the Year Round* (Boston, Mass.: J. E. Tilton, 1868), 368.

17. Mrs. C. A. Halpert, "Festivals and Presents," *Ladies' Repository* 31 (January–June 1871): 43–46. For another critique of the growing "extravagance" of Christmas and wedding presents, see *Philadelphia Public Ledger*, December 22, 1856, 2.

18. Halpert, "Festivals," 43–46.

19. Caroline M. Kirkland, *A Book for the Home Circle* (New York: Scribner, 1853), 90, 99.

20. On these cultural themes, see esp. Karen Halttunen, *Confidence Men and Painted Women: A Study of Middle-Class Culture in America, 1830–1870* (New Haven, Conn.: Yale University Press, 1982).

21. Gillo Dorfles, *Kitsch: The World of Bad Taste* (New York: Universe Books, 1969), 129–30.

22. Jackson Lears, *Fables of Abundance: A Cultural History of Advertising in America* (New York: Basic Books, 1994), 402. In this wonderfully evocative work, Lears recognizes the alternative possibilities of transfiguration through gift exchange, craftsmanship, and collecting, but he little develops the point, concentrating his attention on the alchemy of artists (pp. 6–7).

23. Halpert, "Festivals," 45; Kirkland, *Book for the Home Circle*, 97–99.

24. Lamb on presents and friendship quoted in Kirkland, *Book for the Home Circle*, 94; Charles Lamb, "Valentine's Day: A Homily for the Fourteenth of February," from *Essays of Elia* reprinted in *The Republic of Letters; Republication of Standard Literature* 3 (1835): 88; Sophia Root to (unnamed) sister, February 21, 1861, box J4.14, Hallmark Historical Collection, Kansas City.

25. Charles Lamb, *The Complete Works and Letters of Charles Lamb* (New York: Modern Library, 1935), 548.

26. Kirkland, *Book for the Home Circle*, 90–91, 101. For two other consecrators of gifts, see Mary G. Clarke, *Home Garner; Or, the Intellectual and Moral Store House: Gathered for the Family Circle* (Philadelphia: Lippincott, 1856), 59–62, 98; Hale, *Manners*, 363–70. For a recent examination of Kirkland's work in relationship to a devout consumerism, see Lori Merish, "'The Hand of Refined Taste' in the Frontier Landscape: Caroline Kirkland's *A New Home, Who'll Follow?* and the Feminization of American Consumerism," *American Quarterly* 45 (1993): 485–523.

27. *American Ladies' Memorial: An Indispensable Home-Book for the Wife, Mother, Sister* (Boston, Mass.: Cornhill, 1849), 86; Caroline M. Kirkland, *The Evening Book: Or, Fireside Talk on Morals and Manners, with Sketches of Western Life* (New York: Scribner, 1853), 36–47; Eliza Adams quoted in Karen V. Hansen, *A Very Social Time: Crafting Community in Antebellum New England* (Berkeley: University of California Press, 1994), 82. Hansen offers an excellent discussion of visiting as an elaborate system of obligation, reciprocity, and community-building (pp. 79–113). Also, on visiting as a woman-led ritual, see

Carroll Smith-Rosenberg, "The Female World of Love and Ritual: Relations between Women in Nineteenth-Century America," in *Disorderly Conduct: Visions
of Gender in Victorian America* (New York: Oxford University Press, 1985), 61,
69–70.

28. See, e.g., Victorian Albums, L1.1, .7, .16, .19, .20, .34, Hallmark Historical Collection, Kansas City; the albums of Millie Pickett and Nellie Johnson,
Thelma Mendsen Collection, Winterthur Library, Wilmington, Del. See also
Dick's Original Album Verses and Acrostics (New York: Dick and Fitzgerald,
1879), 114–33. Most of the albums in the Hallmark and Winterthur collections
come from the 1870–1900 period, though several move back into the 1840–70
period.

29. For a critical and sharp-edged reading of this piety, see Ann Douglas, *The
Feminization of American Culture* (New York: Knopf, 1977). For more on Easter
gifts and knickknacks (including their visual illustration), see Schmidt, *Consumer
Rites*, ch. 4.

30. Cheal, *Gift Economy*, x, 16, 144–48, 154; Theodore Caplow, "Rule En-
forcement without Visible Means: Christmas Gift Giving in Middletown," *American Journal of Sociology* 89 (1984): 1306–23 (quotation from p. 1307); Theodore
Caplow et al., *Middletown Families: Fifty Years of Change and Continuity* (Minneapolis: University of Minnesota Press, 1982), 225–45 (quotation from p. 225);
Mauss, *Gift*, 25. Cheal's work is based on a Canadian survey from 1981–84, the
Winnipeg Ritual Cycle Study. For his part, Cheal is careful not to dichotomize the
public and private in modern gift rituals too sharply. Such terms are best dropped
from formulations about the gift economy altogether, since gifts constitute a crucial social practice that confounds such compartments and categories.

31. On Romantic ambivalence toward the market system (including Emerson's own), see Gilmore, *American Romanticism*, esp. 8–13.

32. *Letters*, 4:174, 3:365.

33. *American Ladies' Memorial*, 86. To stress simplicity over gentility is
problematic; this emphasis is certainly true at a prescriptive level in the work of
Kirkland, Hale, Halpert, Clarke, and others. At a practical level, gentility and simplicity, consumerist fashions and domestic handicrafts often merged in the new
gift culture. On the notion of "virtuous consumerism" in the middle decades of
this century, see Elaine Tyler May, *Homeward Bound: American Families in the
Cold War Era* (New York: Basic Books, 1988), 162–82 (quotation from p. 166).
On the continued privileging of handicrafts over machine-made commodities as
gifts, see Waits, *Modern Christmas*, 16–21. Waits places the cultural debate over
the transition to ready-made gifts as occurring between 1880 and 1920, which
misses its Romantic, antebellum roots, but his discussion of commercial strategies
to "decontaminate" commodities and to make them seem "pure" enough for gifts
is quite suggestive. Similarly helpful is Viviana A. Zelizer's discussion of the strategies for turning money into a gift—that is, the invention and demarcation of "gift
money" at the turn of the twentieth century—in *The Social Meaning of Money*
(New York: Basic Books, 1994), 71–118. The process of converting commodities
into gifts, the move from alienation to possession, is also central to James Carrier's
Gifts and Commodities.

34. Paul Tournier, *The Meaning of Gifts*, trans. John S. Gilmour (Richmond, Va.: John Knox, 1963), 56; Mauss, *Gift*, 69.

35. Joyce C. Hall (with Curtiss Anderson), *When You Care Enough* (Kansas City, Mo.: Hallmark Cards, 1979), 4–17, 25, 94; *My Hallmark Date Book* (n.p.: Hall Brothers, 1948), in "Stationery Scrapbooks," Bella C. Landauer Collection of Business and Advertising Art, New-York Historical Society. On Hall, see also Ellen Stern, *The Very Best from Hallmark: Greeting Cards through the Years* (New York: Harry N. Abrams, 1988); *A Centennial Tribute to the Memory of Joyce C. Hall* (Kansas City, Mo.: Hallmark Cards, [1991]). On these sorts of modern ritual tensions over dispersion and reconnection, see Gwen Kennedy Neville, *Kinship and Pilgrimage: Rituals of Reunion in American Protestant Culture* (New York: Oxford University Press, 1987).

36. Robert Bezilla, ed., *Religion in America, 1992–93* (Princeton, N.J.: Princeton Religion Research Center, 1993), 46–48; Frances Walls to Minnie Mattison, December 13, 1966, author's collection. On the importance of "ambivalence" as a category in the wider interpretation of popular religion, see Hall, *Worlds of Wonder*, esp. 3–4, 20.

37. Maura Stanton, "Gifts," *DoubleTake* (Winter 1996): 51.

38. Bourdieu, *Logic of Practice*, 99.

Chapter Five

LIVED RELIGION AND THE DEAD:
THE CREMATION MOVEMENT IN
GILDED AGE AMERICA

STEPHEN PROTHERO

ON DECEMBER 6, 1876, in the small town of Washington, Pennsylvania, the corpse of Austrian-born theosophist Baron Joseph Henry Louis Charles De Palm went up in flames in an event that was promoted as the first "modern" and "scientific" cremation in the United States.[1] It was a great triumph for the nascent cremation movement, which began in the United States in 1874, peaked in the mid-1880s, and was largely spent by the turn of the century, when cremation had earned, at least among many intellectuals, its current place as a legitimate though controversial alternative to burial.[2]

It is difficult to fix precisely the moment of origination of any movement, but there are ample reasons for dating the cremationist movement from 1874. Prompted by cremation discussions in Italy, Germany, and especially England,[3] American newspapers and magazines began in 1874 to cover the topic seriously. The *New York Times*, for example, published only one article on cremation in 1873 but no fewer than seventeen in 1874. In one of those seventeen pieces, the *Times* reported that support for cremation was growing "suddenly and spontaneously." A *Philadelphia Medical Times* editorial, also from 1874, noted "a great deal of discussion" on the subject, and speculated that "it seems as though the ceremony of burning the dead might actually be introduced among us." A *Harper's New Monthly Magazine* article from that year described "the sudden interest in cremation" as "one of the striking events of the time."[4] Although the cremation debate was carried forward largely by intellectuals, there is evidence that the broader public began, also in 1874, to consider cremation. In that year, both Pennsylvania and Georgia witnessed cremation hoaxes, a minstrel show called "Cremation" debuted in New York City, and the New York Cremation Society became the first voluntary association in the United States committed to the practice.[5] Clearly, cremation was touching a public chord.

Cremationists agitated for their cause in three of their own periodicals—*Columbarium*, *The Urn*, and *The Modern Crematist*—and in countless books, pamphlets, sermons, lectures, and articles. These sources multiplied so quickly that as early as 1875 the Boston Public Library thought it useful to publish a bibliography of cremation-related publications. During the last quarter of the nineteenth century, two forms of pro-cremation organizations sprang up in major metropolitan centers in New England, the Middle Atlantic States, the Midwest, and the Far West: reform societies devoted to preaching cremation to the American public and joint stock companies intent on raising money to build crematories and to conduct incinerations. The number of American crematories these pioneers produced grew slowly at first: from one in 1876 to only two in 1885. But by the turn of the century, there were twenty-four operating in fifteen states and the loved ones of over ten thousand Americans had chosen cremation over burial as the way to dispose of their dead.[6]

Despite the fact that the nineteenth-century cremation movement was widely covered in the American press, contemporary scholars have neglected it entirely. Historians of medieval and modern Europe have for decades expressed keen interest in studying death,[7] but writing about cremation remains something of a historiographic taboo in America.[8] There now seem to be good reasons to overturn this taboo.[9]

One reason is cremation's current popularity. Although cremation was performed relatively rarely in the nineteenth century, recently the practice has boomed. Liturgies have grown up around the practice, which is now accepted by the vast majority of Protestant denominations and a growing number of liberal Catholics and Reform Jews.[10] In 1994, nearly 21 percent of deaths in the United States were followed by cremation. That figure is up sharply from less than 7 percent in 1975.[11] In some states, moreover, cremation has already passed burial as the most common method for disposing of the dead.[12] Such figures lag far behind those from England, where cremation rates stand at approximately 70 percent nationwide, but they represent a significant overturning of what was until the late nineteenth century a virtual monopoly on earth burials in America.

Two Cremationist Arguments

To provide a sense of the contours of the early arguments advanced by cremation reformers, two pro-cremation orations from the key year of 1874 are described here:[13] a paper entitled "The Merits of Cremation," read by Persifor Frazer Jr. before the Social Science Association of Philadelphia on April 24, 1874; and a sermon on "The Disposal of the Dead," delivered in New York City less than two weeks later by the Rev. Octavius B. Frothingham. Together these texts demonstrate how cremationists utilized two disparate idioms: theology, the ancient queen of the sciences, and sanitary science, one of America's newest disciplines. In many respects, these arguments set the stage for over a century of cremationist claims to come.

Frazer began by noting that the aim of his social scientific paper was to determine which method of disposing of the corpse would serve "to make the dead harmless to the living." Drawing on the popular theory that diseases, especially urban epidemics such as cholera, were caused by "miasma," or gaseous emissions from organic matter decaying underground, Frazer claimed that burial failed miserably on hygienic grounds. Bodies buried in graves emitted "poisonous exhalations" that polluted both water and air and thus resulted in "injurious effects," including fever, diarrhea, and in some cases death. Cremation, on the other hand, was the "safest" of methods. It resulted in "no horrid exhumations and mangling of remains; no poisoning of wells; no generation of low fevers" and restored "to nature most expeditiously the little store of her materials held in trust for a few years."[14]

After advancing his pro-cremation argument on sanitary grounds, Frazer turned to religious considerations, especially the objection that cremation represented an affront to the resurrection of the body. Invoking a recent article by the bishop of Manchester, England, Frazer contended that God was as capable of raising a burned body as a buried one. Frazer concluded his argument regarding the resurrection by quoting the bishop:

> Could . . . it . . . be more impossible for God to raise up a body at the resurrection, if needs be, out of elementary particles which had been liberated by the burning, than it would be to raise up a body from dust, and from the elements of bodies which had passed into the structure of worms? The omnipotence of God is not limited, and He would raise the dead whether He had to raise our bodies out of church-yards, or whether He had to call our remains . . . out of an urn.[15]

The sermon favoring cremation given by the Rev. Octavius B. Frothingham at New York's Lyric Hall worked some of the same ground covered by Frazer ten days earlier, but it was delivered, not insignificantly, by a minister. In fact, "The Disposal of the Dead" may well have been the first pro-cremation sermon delivered in the United States. Although a number of prominent clerics would eventually lend their support to the movement for cremation reform, few spoke publicly on its behalf in the 1870s. Their reticence was no doubt informed by both custom and theology. Since the early Christians succeeded in overturning the Greek and Roman practice of cremation, burial had been virtually the only method for disposing of the Christian dead in the West.[16] Reinforcing this custom was the Christian belief in the resurrection of the body, a belief that for most Christians both supported the rite of burial and contravened the practice of cremation.

Resurrection theology and the tradition of burial dissuaded most Christian clerics in the United States from supporting the cremation cause early on, but the Rev. O. B. Frothingham was not like most Christian clerics. Though early in his career he had cast his lot with conservative Unitarianism and Christian transcendentalism, Frothingham had gradually moved beyond Christianity into the camp of free religion. He served as the first president of the Free Religious Association, which was founded in 1867 to provide self-proclaimed "scientific theists" with an organizational home, and the appearance of his *The Religion of Humanity* (1872) transformed him into the most visible American spokesperson for radical religion in the 1870s. The fact that Frothingham delivered this sermon both symbolized and solidified the link—a link that opponents of cremation would eagerly exploit—between the cremation movement and unorthodox religion.

In "The Disposal of the Dead," Frothingham argued against the custom of earth burial and for the innovation of cremation. His attack on burial began, like Frazer's effort, with an attempt to demythologize the sentiment of eternal sleep in the restful grave with arguments from the budding field of sanitary science. Deriding the sentiment of everlasting peace in the cemetery as an illusion, Frothingham argued that "Nature . . . seizes at once the cast-off body, and with occult chemistry and slow burning decomposes and consumes it."[17] This decomposition, he continued, disturbs not only the peace of the dead but also the health of the living. "The grave," he contended, is "a laboratory where are manufactured the poisons that waste the fair places of existence, and very likely smite to the heart their own lovers."[18]

Oddly, Frothingham attempted to divorce the cremation question from religious considerations—a curious tactic for a minister delivering a sermon. "There are many who feel that it is a case of religion against religion," he said, but "the practice of burning the dead can be reconciled with any creed." Though he argued that "the reform concerns us as men—not as believers in any particular dogma,"[19] Frothingham evidently was not persuaded by his own admonition, since he addressed numerous religious objections to cremation. In response to the claim (which would become a staple of anti-cremationists in years to come) that cremation was "a pagan custom" practiced in the "heathen" Orient, Frothingham ceded at least the facts of the matter. The ancient Greeks and Romans had practiced cremation, as did contemporary Hindus. But he insisted that these peoples were "as intelligent, refined, and worshipful" as any Americans and that their funerary practices were "associated with feelings of the noblest kind, with veneration and tenderness, and regard to moral obligations." He then added that while pagans burned, they also buried, "so that if there is any reproach in the paganism it must be shared by the custom of interment."[20]

To the prominent objection that cremation flew in the face of the Christian hope for the resurrection, Frothingham responded that the body eventually met the same end in both cremation and burial. The only substantial difference between the two methods was the time it took for the body to dissipate. Neither nature nor God discriminated between cremation and burial. "A moment's reflection suggests," Frothingham wrote, echoing Frazer, "[that] to recover a shape from a heap of ashes can be no more difficult than to recover it from a mound of dust."[21]

After dismissing these two main religious arguments against cremation, Frothingham argued for cremation on sanitary, economic, and aesthetic grounds. The sanitary and economic arguments were rather straightforward: cremation was simultaneously more hygienic and less expensive than burial. His aesthetic argument was more fully developed. The swiftness of the process of incineration was "a relief to the mind" when compared with "the slow and distressing" decay of inhumation, while "the graceful urn" was more beautiful than "the shapeless mound," and "white ashes" were preferable to "the mass of corruption" that lay in the grave. Frothingham, who apparently was not unduly attached to the custom of cemetery visitation, was also comforted by the fact that loved ones could keep the remains of the deceased in their homes or gardens and carry them along should circumstances call them away to other locations. Finally, Frothingham argued, cremation presented "a sweeter field of contemplation" for the Romantic mourner. "The thoughts instead of going downward into the damp, cold ground, go upwards towards the clear blue of the skies."[22]

The presentations of Frazer and Frothingham suggest a few general features of the nascent cremation movement. The first and most general is that the cremation movement was a reform movement. Cremationists were, more precisely, genteel reformers who were convinced that the widespread adoption of cremation would result in grandiose advances; it would uplift individuals, improve society, and thus contribute to the progress of "culture" and "civilization." Like other reform movements, the cremation cause was most popular among folks like Frazer and Frothingham: well educated, middle-class ladies and gentlemen from the Northeast. Physicians and sanitarians were well represented in the ranks, as were ministers, newspapermen, and university professors. Pro-cremation ministers typically came from liberal Protestant denominations such as Unitarianism, Congregationalism, and Episcopalianism, and from more radical religious groups such as free religion and ethical culture. Women's rights activists were also particularly active in the movement.[23]

Both Frothingham's and Frazer's presentations further reveal the synthesis of sanitary and theological concerns that was to become the stock cremationist thesis: that burial polluted whereas cremation purified. Cremation would, according to its advocates, make life in America's cities both more sanitary and more ritually pure. Given these overriding interests in both sanitary cleanliness and ritual purity—interests that are extremely difficult to disentangle—it is not surprising that cremationists carried out their crusade with religious fervor, referring to their cause as "the gospel of incineration" and their labor as "missionary work."[24] Dr. Hugo Erichsen, who would serve in the early twentieth century as the president of the Cremation Association of America, was most plain on this score: "Every cremationist must be a missionary for the cause and embrace every suitable occasion to spread its gospel, the glad tidings of a more sanitary and more aesthetic method of disposing of our beloved dead."[25]

Still, most early cremationists grounded their appeals, as did both Frothingham and Frazer, in reason, science, utility, and common sense. Toward the urban and immigrant masses who were a main target of their "disinterested benevolence," cremation reformers evinced an intriguing double-mindedness. On the one hand, they sneered at America's "unwashed" for continuing to bury, judging their refusal to cremate a defect not simply in reasoning but also in morals and, in some cases, spirituality. On the other hand, cremationists took it as a sacred duty to attempt to raise the masses up to a higher level of "culture" and "civilization." Many working-class Americans, they thought, would no doubt continue to follow religious superstition and uninformed sentiment, quite literally, to their graves, but reason and utility might sway some toward cremation.

The First Modern and Scientific Cremation

Despite the tremendous effort begun by reformers in 1874 to promote cremation as a purifying alternative to the polluting practice of burial, they did not arrange for an actual cremation until 1876. The reason for this delay was the lack of a suitable crematory. This shortcoming would not have presented a formidable obstacle if cremationists had been willing to engage in the ancient Greco-Roman and Oriental ritual of cremation in the open air, but despite their interests in restoring to America the grandeur that was Greece, Rome, and Asia, they were reformers to the core and, as such, were determined to find a better, more "modern," and more "scientific" way.

Cremationists went to great lengths in the nineteenth century to distinguish between ancient and modern cremation, preferring the latter over the former for three key reasons. First, while ancient cremation—and cremation in ostensibly "primitive" nineteenth-century India was included in this category—took place publicly in the open air, modern cremation took place privately in a state-of-the-art furnace. Modern witnesses were spared, therefore, many of the gory sights, sounds, and smells of the older procedure, which had the additional, decidedly un-American defect of taking far more time. Witnesses were also spared the noxious by-products of the affair, since the dangerous gases and liquids residing in the corpse were thoroughly destroyed by what many called the "purifying fire" of the furnace. Second, in ancient cremation the body was consumed by fire while in the modern procedure flames never touched the body, which was consumed by heat alone. Third, in modern cremation the ashes of the deceased were not mixed, as they were in the ancient rite, with what Frazer referred to as "foreign matter."[26] Together these three preferences demonstrate once again the preoccupation of modern American cremation advocates with both sanitation and ritual, cleanliness and purity. Modern cremation was seen as more sanitary, ritually satisfying, and aesthetically refined than its ancient, unscientific cousin.

Given the allegiances of nineteenth-century American cremationists to both ancient rite and modern technology, the depiction in the *New York Times* of cremation as "a form of burial at once ancient and modern" was apt.[27] The man who finally made possible cremation's migration to modern America was Dr. Francis Julius Le Moyne, who constructed the first bona fide New World crematory on his estate in Washington, Pennsylvania, a small town about thirty miles from Pittsburgh. The man who carried out the rite was Col. Henry Steel Olcott of New York City. And the man whose death made it all possible was the Baron De Palm. Like the Rev. O. B. Frothingham, Le Moyne, Olcott, and DePalm were all genteel reformers and "advanced thinkers," thoroughly modern men whose unorthodox religious ideas fueled the suspicion that cremation was an anti-Christian rite inextricably tied to Freemasonry, agnosticism, Theosophy, and other forms of religious eccentricity.

A wealthy and philanthropic physician of French Huguenot ancestry, Dr. Le Moyne was an advocate of both scientific farming and educational reform before he turned to the cause of cremation. He was also a committed abolitionist. He declined a nomination run for vice president of the United States as a Liberty Party candidate in 1840, but did run for governor of Pennsylvania on the abolitionist ticket in 1841, 1844, and 1847. Though he considered himself a Christian, he was reportedly "turned out of the Presbyterian Church for his political opinions."[28] Long before his estate was notorious for housing the first American crematory, it reportedly served as a stop on the Underground Railroad.[29]

Like Le Moyne, Olcott was a professional gentleman attracted to social reform movements and unorthodox religious ideas. Raised a Presbyterian, Olcott turned to spiritualism as a young man. He pursued careers in scientific farming and journalism before being admitted to the New York Bar in 1868. In 1875, he co-founded the Theosophical Society in New York City with Russian occultist Helena Petrovna Blavatsky. Eventually he moved to India and became the first American formally to convert to Buddhism on Asian soil.[30]

Among the early members of the Theosophical Society was Baron De Palm, an Austrian nobleman who according to a biting but prescient editor at the *New York Tribune* was destined to become "principally famous as a corpse."[31] Upon his arrival in New York in the winter of 1875, De Palm befriended both Olcott and Theosophy. He fell ill shortly thereafter, and died on May 20, 1876. Before his death, De Palm had instructed Olcott to arrange both a funeral and a disposition of his corpse befitting his unconventional faith. He had requested, more specifically, that his funeral be performed "in a fashion that would illustrate the Eastern notions of death and immortality," and that his corpse be cremated.[32] There is no record of why the baron wanted to be cremated, but he did express to Olcott "a horror of burial" informed by the fact that he had once known a woman who was buried alive.[33] In accordance with the baron's wishes, Olcott had the baron's body embalmed in an effort to preserve it until the necessary arrangements could be made. He also orchestrated what the media referred to as a "pagan funeral" on Sunday, May 28, 1876, at the Masonic Temple of none other than the Rev. O. B. Frothingham.[34]

The site Olcott finally found for the cremation was the newly constructed crematory in Washington. As it turned out, this was not the most auspicious place to stage cremation's coming out party. A town of four thousand to five thousand inhabitants, Washington was dominated, in the words of a *Times* newsman, by "old-fashioned Presbyterians, who regard the waltz as an invention of Satan and a game of cards as sure destruction." Though this description was no doubt intended to stroke the prejudices of cosmopolitan readers, Washington *was* both rural and provincial, decidedly lacking in the sorts of "advanced thinkers" who read the *Times* and walked Fifth Avenue. And so cremation was "rank heresy" in Washington. "No good church member within 1000 miles of Washington would give his body to be burned any sooner than he would sell his soul to Beelzebub."[35]

Dr. Le Moyne's crematory was a small, one-story, red brick building, approximately thirty feet by thirty feet. Conspicuously modest, it consisted of two rooms: a reception room for displaying the body before the cremation and the ashes after it; and a furnace room. The building rose atop a high knoll known by locals as "Gallows Hill"; it had previously served as a county site for executions by hanging. Though Le Moyne had constructed the crematory for his personal use, he agreed to allow Olcott to utilize it in De Palm's case in order to demonstrate both the legality and the practicality of modern cremation. Drawing on his legal training and his New York City social connections, Olcott investigated the laws relating to cremation, obtained the necessary permits, and arranged for a panel of theological, economic, hygienic, and technological experts to present the cremationist case to the press. He also gathered a slightly less committed cadre of scientists, clergymen, educators, and journalists to witness the spectacle to determine, in his words, "(a) Whether cremation was really a scientific method of sepulture; (b) Whether it was cheaper than burial; (c) Whether it offered any repugnant features; (d) How long it would take to incinerate a human body."[36]

The body of Baron De Palm was transferred by train in a rosewood coffin on December 5, 1876, from New York City to the Washington, Pennsylvania depot and into Col. Olcott's care. From there, it was taken by hearse to the Le Moyne estate, where it arrived around noon. At some point in the afternoon witnesses were gathered and De Palm's embalmed corpse was displayed in a plain coffin in the reception room. This viewing lasted only a few moments, however, since as soon as De Palm's torso was exposed to public view it was plain to all present "that the embalming process had not been so successful." Confronted with a body that "presented a painful and repulsive appearance," an aghast Col. Olcott commanded that the coffin be closed.[37] Later, in private and under cover of night, the corpse was taken out of the coffin, wrapped in white linen, slathered with aromatic herbs and spices, and placed onto an iron, cradle-shaped frame. This transfer from wood to iron was accomplished according to observers in order to prevent any untoward mixing of the sacred remains of the baron with the profane ashes of his coffin.

The cremation took place on December 6, 1876, and, thanks to Olcott's public relations efforts, was rather well attended. Journalists arrived from as far away as England, France, and Germany, and the health boards of Massachusetts, Pittsburgh, and Brooklyn sent official observers. Along with mourners and attendants, these officials brought the list of official invitees to about thirty eyewitnesses, who gathered decorously inside the crematory. But the publicity surrounding the event also attracted local residents staunchly opposed to incineration who, according to the *New York Times*, lent to the occasion the raucous air of a prizefight (or an execution).[38]

Inside the crematory, friends and relatives meditated on the life of the deceased while reporters jotted down notes. But the uninvited guests conducted themselves with less propriety, forming a "noisy, pushing crowd" outside. "They were," according to an evidently refined reporter, "coarse in their ideas and conduct, and many a brutal joke concerning the dead man went through the crowd, to the disgust of the more respectable visitors." The tableau outside, he determined, was repulsive. And there were, lamentably, no constables on hand to maintain order!

At least a few journalists assigned to the story took the event about as seriously as did the crowds. A reporter for New York City's *Daily Graphic*, for example, asked facetiously, "Why cremate when there is still so much waste land in which to bury? [Long Island] soil needs burials, especially of that practical race of people who, wishing to be of utility to mankind after their demise, are willing through decomposition and consequent enrichment of the soil to promote the growth of cauliflower and potatoes." The author even went so far as to suggest dynamiting the dead as "a more speedy method of getting rid of human remains"![39]

No one did much to discourage the levity of the reporters or the raucousness of the crowds, according to a clearly disappointed *Times* newsman, who complained that there were "no religious services, no addresses, no music, no climax, such as would have thrown great solemnity over the occasion. There was not one iota of ceremony. Everything was as business-like as possible." Neither Olcott nor Le Moyne would have been surprised by this assessment, since both men echoed Frazer and Frothingham in describing the cremation as a scientific and therefore utterly secular exercise. In fact, Le Moyne had written to Olcott that he "never intended or expected that our programme should include any kind of religious service, but should be a strictly scientific and sanitary experiment."[40] Nonetheless, the occasion lacked neither ritual activity nor spiritual significance.

After the coke-burning furnace was declared ready, invited guests had a last, abbreviated look at the body, or at least at its head. Someone pulled the sheet down a bit, exposing a face with a pained countenance, "utterly tenantless" eyes, and flesh "full of the virus of decomposition." After this final, grotesque viewing, the body was hastily carried across the center threshold of the two-room crematory to the furnace room. Olcott then placed over the corpse a white, alum-soaked sheet intended to prevent both the body's immediate blazing and any further public display of the baron's nakedness or his "painful and repulsive appearance." He also sprinkled the body with spices such as myrrh, frankincense, cassia, cinnamon, and cloves in an effort to lessen the unpleasant odor of burning flesh and hair and, one suspects, to bequeath to the occasion at least a vaguely Christian air. Finally, he placed on the corpse a collection of roses, smilax, primroses, palms, and evergreens "as an emblem," said the *Times*, "of immortality." Olcott and Le Moyne then debated whether it was more auspicious to slide the body into the furnace head- or feet-first. At approximately 8:30 A.M. they agreed on the former method. The baron's body was then lifted into the retort and the door was cemented shut to make the furnace airtight.

Immediately both the evergreens and the hair around the head were set afire and "the flames formed," according to the *Times* reporter, "a crown of glory for the dead man." At first witnesses were repelled by the distinctive smell of burning flesh, but eventually that unpleasantry abated as the aroma of flowers and spices filled the room. Witnesses who watched the goings-on through a peep hole in the side of the furnace noted that the aromatic flowers were almost miraculously reduced to ash without losing their "individual forms." About an hour into the proceedings a rose-colored mist enveloped the body. Later this rosy mist turned to gold. The body, meanwhile, became red hot and then transparent and luminous. All these effects lent to the retort "the appearance of a radient [sic] solar disk." After some time yet another symbol of immortality pressed itself on the witnesses—"the palm boughs . . . stood up as naturally as though they were living portions of a tree."[41] Then the left hand of the baron rose up and three of its fingers pointed skyward. The scientists present remarked that the latter incident was caused by involuntary muscular contractions, but less skeptical bystanders saw in it something of a spiritual phenomenon.

Following the cremation, which officially concluded at 11:12 A.M. with the formal pronouncement of Dr. Folsom, secretary of the Massachusetts Board of Health, that "incineration is complete beyond all question," interested parties gathered at Town Hall to listen to speeches advocating cremation. There they learned, among other things, that the fuel for the cremation had cost $7.04. On the following day, after the furnace had cooled, Col. Olcott collected the ashes. Later, at least according to his own recollections, he placed them in a Hindu urn and transported them to New York, presumably to Theosophical Society headquarters. A few years later, before departing for a new life in India, Olcott "scattered them over the waters of New York Harbour with an appropriate, yet simple, ceremony."[42] Apparently, however, not all the baron's remains made this pilgrimage. Some of his ashes and bones remained in a makeshift reliquary, a bottle in Dr. Le Moyne's office. Other bits of the baron were reportedly given away to gawkers as souvenirs.

Those who were unable to obtain these souvenirs, however, were not left empty-handed. Shortly after the cremation furnace cooled, Mr. James Wolfe, who had been invited to the cremation in his capacity as a fireman, fanned the flames of public opposition to cremation reform when he wrote, directed, and produced a play that climaxed with "the shoving in and blazing up of the body."[43] Wolf's production, which viewed the town's first cremation as an occasion for black comedy, testifies to the fact that the residents of Washington were both titillated and repulsed by cremation. The new death rite of Gallows Hill, while perhaps as entertaining as the hangings that previously haunted the place, was almost unanimously judged to possess far less redeeming social value. According to one estimate published shortly after the cremation, nine-tenths of the predominantly Presbyterian citizenry of Washington were opposed to the reform. Before Dr. Le Moyne's crematory was shut down, forty-one people would be cremated there, but Le Moyne would be the only Washington resident to make use of the facilities.

READING THE RITE

There is much to say about the social drama that was the first modern and scientific cremation in America, but I hazard only some brief observations here. To begin, the experiment was performed by and on behalf of middle-class reformers. Col. Olcott was a lawyer and Dr. Le Moyne, a physician. De Palm was, of course, a foreign-born baron and, if we are to believe *Frank Leslie's Illustrated Newspaper*, he was also a high-ranking Mason—"Grand Cross Commander of the Sovereign Order of the Holy Sepulchre at Jerusalem, Knight of St. John at Malta, Prince of the Roman Empire, late Chamberlain to His Majesty the King of Bavaria."[44] Each of these men was, like many other cremationists, a genteel reformer, committed to a myriad of "uplifting" reforms.

Though the De Palm cremation was associated, however vaguely, with a revival and restoration of Greco-Roman and Oriental death practices, it was designed as a modernist's reform of those rites. Even as cremationists conjured the glories of ancient Greco-Roman and Hindu civilizations to legitimate the practice of cremation in the modern West, they were determined to improve on those precedents, to adapt the practice to modern, scientific contingencies. Cremationists insisted, therefore, on incineration in a furnace rather than cremation in the open air, and they found numerous reasons to prefer the modern over the ancient practice. Even the Indophilic Olcott took great pride in the fact that the baron's cremation represented a vast improvement over Hindu burning rites. Because the body was disposed of in a closed furnace instead of an open pyre, Olcott later noted, "there could be none of that horror of roasting human flesh and bursting entrails which makes one shudder at an open-air pyre-burning . . . there was none of that unpleasant odour that sometimes sickens one who drives past an Indian burning-ghat."[45]

As scientific as this first modern American cremation may have been, it was also clearly associated with unorthodox religion. Later in the century, cremation's popularizers would attempt to distance their cause from religious dissent, but at least in its infancy, cremation was advocated largely by individuals with unorthodox religious views. Le Moyne, according to his friends, was nearly as radical in religious as he was in political matters. De Palm was, in Olcott's words, "a Voltairean with a gloss of Spiritualism." And Olcott was a Theosophist who, at best, saw Christianity as one of many true religions in the world and, at worst, dismissed the Christian church as the most intolerant and hateful of institutions.[46]

If De Palm's life was glossed with spiritualism, the events surrounding his death were infused with Asian spirituality. The funeral that Olcott had conducted months earlier for the deceased De Palm was as replete with references to Eastern religions as it was devoid of references to Christianity; and the cremation was attended, as reporters lamented, by nothing that resembled traditional Christian funerary rites. There was, moreover, a widespread awareness among early cremationists that their beloved rite was an Asian import. Less committed witnesses to De Palm's cremation also clearly associated the practice with the "heathen," but exactly which "heathen" isn't clear. While one *New York Times* report echoed Olcott in describing the receptacle for the baron's ashes as a "Hindoo cremation urn . . . decorated with Hindoo characters and devices," another story from the same paper indicated that the urn was designed "after the manner practiced by the ancient Greeks and Romans."[47] This confusion is telling, since nineteenth-century American cremationists associated cremation with what they saw as the great civilizations of Greece, Rome, *and* India, and since Americans in general were not yet well educated about the differences among the traditions they lumped together under the banners of "paganism" and "heathenism." Still, despite the confusion, witnesses agreed that cremation was a foreign import.

This may be one reason why attempts to modernize cremation did little to sway the American populace, who like the citizens of Washington continued strongly to prefer burial, largely on religious grounds. Cremation, traditionalists argued, was a heathen, pagan, and therefore anti-Christian rite that had been practiced by ancient Greeks and Romans and continued to be performed by Hindus; it overturned nearly two thousand years of the Christian custom of burial; it demonstrated a lack of respect for the sanctity of the body, which is "the temple of the Holy Ghost"; and it flew in the face of the Christian doctrine of the resurrection of the body. Many cremationists, moreover, were publicly associated with unbelief and agnosticism. For all of these reasons, cremation was officially opposed not only by Washington, Pennsylvania churchgoers but also by the Catholic Church (in a number of edicts issued by Pope Leo XIII in 1886).[48]

Despite the connection between cremation and "heathenism" and notwithstanding the laments of newspapermen, the events surrounding De Palm's incineration were in no way utterly desacralized. In fact, what we seem to have here is a classic case where "dechristianization" is mistaken for "secularization."[49] Clearly the De Palm cremation ceremonies were not recognizably Christian. But they were hardly secular either. On the contrary, virtually every step in the process was wrapped in the sacred. No cremationist involved in the De Palm incineration believed that his corpse was simply profane material to be dispensed of this way or that. All, in fact, were convinced that there was a right way and a wrong way to perform the new rite they were in the business of constructing. Like the baron's Masonic Temple funeral, which was, no doubt, post-Christian, but aimed nonetheless to "illustrate the Eastern notions of death and immortality" via hymns, creeds, prayers, and a myriad of evidently religious symbols,[50] the cremation demonstrated dechristianization without secularization. The same *Times* reporter who lamented that "there were no religious services . . . not one iota of ceremony" also reported that Olcott and his fellow cremationists evinced "all proper respect for the dead," that the corpse had been "lovingly showered" with flowers and evergreens "as an emblem of immortality," that the flames of the burning evergreen formed "a crown of glory for the dead man," and that some witnesses saw the gradual uplifting of the left hand and the pointing upward of three of its fingers as a miraculous message of sorts. The reporter (who compared the rite with "the fiery ordeal through which Shadrach, Meshach, and Abed-nego passed" in the Hebrew Bible) also noted that officiants preoccupied themselves with a myriad of details, which together indicate that Olcott and his charges saw themselves as priests of sorts conducting a solemn ritual. They had the body drained of fluids in order to prevent an unseemly explosion, wrapped the corpse in pure white cloth, draped it in an alum-soaked sheet in an effort to prevent any display of nakedness, and after some debate purposefully placed the body into the furnace headfirst. They took pains to take the baron out of his coffin prior to the cremation in order to avoid mixing his ashes with foreign remains and thus confusing sacred relics with profane fuel. In short, it would not have been the least bit out of character if at the conclusion of this pioneering cremation rite Olcott and the other officiants at De Palm's incineration had prayed, as the *Times* newsman apparently did, "peace to his ashes."[51]

Finally, just as this cremation evinced the association between cremation and similar Asian death rituals, it made plain the connection between cremation and the modern Western sciences of hygiene and public health. Earlier in the century, reformers concerned about the health hazards that urban graveyards posed to city dwellers had launched a movement to construct cemeteries outside cities.[52] By the last quarter of the nineteenth century, however, European immigration was swelling cities well beyond their earlier boundaries and swallowing up these new, formerly suburban, cemeteries. Those who saw cremation as a solution to this public health problem received a boost from Louis Pasteur's germ theory, which posited that the contagious diseases that had recently ravaged cities in both Europe and the United States were spread through microorganisms (rather than through "miasma," as previously believed). As this new theory was disseminated, the American public gradually adopted a host of hygienic and sanitary reforms touted by American practitioners of sanitary science as surefire ways to prevent the spread of disease in what appeared to be an increasingly dangerous urban environment.[53] Those who organized the first modern cremation in America attempted to capitalize on this growing concern by describing fire as a "great purifier" and championing cremation as the "germ destroyer" and "the greatest of all disinfectants."[54]

THE CREMATION MOVEMENT AFTER DE PALM

Following the cremation of Baron De Palm the cremation movement moved ahead markedly if unspectacularly. On July 31, 1877, Dr. C. F. Winslow, formerly of Boston, Massachusetts, became the second person to be cremated in modern America when his corpse was reduced to ashes in a furnace in Salt Lake City, Utah.[55] Mr. Julius Kircher, a German American Lutheran, raised a ruckus in New York City in November 1877 when he resolved a dispute with his Jewish wife about whether their deceased eight-day-old son should be interred in a Lutheran or a Jewish cemetery by cremating the infant in a furnace in his paint factory on East 15th Street.[56] Mrs. Jane Pitman of Cincinnati became on February 15, 1878 the first woman to be cremated in modern America and the second person to make use of the facilities at Dr. Le Moyne's crematory.[57]

Massachusetts passed a groundbreaking law on May 26, 1885, specifically permitting cremations. Seven years later, the *Washington Post* reported that "cremation is making steady if not rapid progress" in the United States and *The Urn* announced that cremation, which was being eagerly discussed "from Maine to California," had "come to stay, and . . . taken perennial root."[58] Such successes prompted one cremationist to liken the cremation movement to "a snow-ball rolling down a snow clad hill [that] grows as it progresses" and another to prophesy that "in the very near future, [cremation] is to be the most common, if not the only mode of disposal of the dead."[59]

More sanguine observers admitted that the movement made little statistical headway in the nineteenth century. "Despite the recent effort to popularize cremation . . . the public are as much, if not more inclined to old-fashioned burial than ever," one wrote,[60] and *Chamber's Encyclopedia* reported that the cremation movement found "little favour in the United States."[61] But this skeptical side, too, had its hyperbole. The *New York Times* entitled one clearly premature article on the subject "The End of Cremation."[62] And in a separate piece on a later cremation at Le Moyne's crematory, that same paper wrote, "Cremation in the United States has labored under heavy disadvantages; and so numerous have these disadvantages shown themselves to be, that it will be surprising if it does not give way under them and disappear."[63]

Somewhere between these disparate assessments lay the truth of the matter. Statistically, the nineteenth-century cremation movement was an exceedingly modest success. The main triumph of the cremationists was their ability to transform cremation from a practice nearly universally condemned as barbarous and pagan into a legitimate albeit controversial alternative to burial. This modest achievement is hinted at in a *New York Times* editorial written at the peak of the cremationists' efforts. "The disposal of the dead by cremation has lost its novelty," the writer noted in 1885, "and those who direct that their bodies shall be burned are no longer regarded as demented, or even as eccentric."[64]

The trek of the diagnosis of the cremationists' ills from dementia to eccentricity and beyond points to a number of facets of lived religion in Gilded Age America. Perhaps the most important is that while the era was saturated in the sorts of refined religious ideas that fueled the debates over evolution, biblical criticism, and the rise of comparative religion—factors that have been widely analyzed by historians of the period—it was also steeped in the more commonplace religious metaphors, narratives, and practices that are the stuff of lived religion.[65] The citizens of Washington who vigorously opposed cremation were committed not only to traditional Christian doctrines but also to metaphors such as the image of death as sleep, to practices such as the tending of familial graveyards, and to narratives regarding, for example, the arising of sleeping bones at the end of times, the reunion of each set of bones with its departed soul, and the subsequent divine judgment of these reconstituted psychosomatic persons. But the cremationists were also religiously committed, albeit to alternative practices, metaphors, and narratives.

There is no denying that cremationists responded to metaphors such as the image of death as sleep with a strategy of demythologization. In fact, cremationists relished describing in excruciating detail exactly how and why time spent underground in a coffin was anything but restful. Peruse the cremationist literature even casually and you will learn that worms and snakes regularly feast on corpses (excreting what they don't digest), that bodies are routinely snatched by grave robbers, and that unsuspecting loved ones are buried alive at alarming rates. Cremationists, in short, responded to the popular notion that, like Lazarus, the dead are not really dead but only sleeping by arguing that the buried coffin was a site not of eternal rest but of ceaseless and gruesome activity. Poets who say that the grave promotes rest and sleep, free religionist Felix Adler argued, are "throwing a false glamour over the hideous reality."[66] The buried coffin was a place not of peaceful stasis but of unsettling change, a site of decomposition, decay, and putrefaction and thus a breeding ground for "miasma" and/or germs. It just wasn't true that buried bodies rested peacefully.

If the cremationists had stopped here, they might rightly have been labeled secularizers. But they did not. Accompanying their demythologization of Christian stories and images was a thorough remythologization. The slowly unfolding drama of the sleeping corpse awaiting its resurrection was clearly rejected. But in its stead came the fast-paced drama of the fiery separation of pure soul from impure body and the freeing of that soul from earthly restraints. The author of an article in the spiritualist periodical, *Banner of Light*, contended that cremation sped up the necessary postmortem process of freeing the spirit (the essential self) from the inessential, "irksome" body. "Whatever tends to separate the particles and atoms of the physical, and to hasten the disintegration of the organic structure, such as the process of cremation will do, only assists in the work of more speedily releasing the spirit from its irksome contact with senseless clay."[67] Theosophically inclined cremationists advanced similar arguments, albeit in more occult language. "It is a convenient and expeditious way of letting loose the astral body," contended one theosophist, who admitted that she was attracted to rather then repelled by the fact that Hindus practiced the rite.[68] Another Theosophist testified as follows:

> There is a certain magnetic connection between the soul and the body, which persists until the latter is entirely disintegrated. . . and the soul is more or less held in an earth-bound . . . condition until the body is thoroughly decomposed. Fire, the great purifier, releases all such magnetic conditions instantly, painlessly, and thoroughly, and is unquestionably the proper method for disposing of dead bodies from an occult standpoint.[69]

Although this line of argument was expecially popular among "advanced thinkers" like spiritualists and Theosophists, at least some Christian cremationists joined in the chorus. One wrote that Christians will be raised not in their "physical" but in their "spiritual" bodies. "Nobody now believes in the resurrection from the grave of the very matter, the gross flesh and bones of the body that we burn . . . [The] spiritual body will come up out of the grave . . . [and] we will be free from the grossness of matter."[70]

That the cremationists were remythologizing as they demythologized is also evident in their practices. While on the one hand many early cremationists aimed to put an end to the practice of visiting your loved one at the family's graveyard, they supplanted that time-honored rite with the arguably more intimate practice of communing with that loved one at home. For cremationists practicing what Catherine L. Albanese has termed "nature religion,"[71] this communion might take place at the family's prize rose bush (a favorite spot for the scattering of ashes), where it could be accompanied not by thoughts of sin, redemption, and resurrection but by memories of a life well lived, images of natural rebirth, and narratives of the cycles of the seasons. For cremationists participating in the new cult of the home, this communion might take place near the fireplace mantle, where ashes could be displayed alongside other Victorian souvenirs (hair wreaths, for example) reminding loved ones of the dearly departed.[72]

All these shifts involved dechristianization rather than secularization. It was not religion itself that was being replaced, but traditional Christian ways of thinking, feeling, and acting. The displacement of the remains of the deceased from the graveyard to the home represented not a rejection of religion but a resituation of it (in this case, from the public sphere to the private). The shift from the traditional Christian self (as a mysterious concatenation of spirit and matter) to the cremationists' self (as a restless spirit seeking not to be housed in "the Temple of the Holy Ghost" but to escape its "gross" materiality) represented merely an alternative spiritual vision. So too the cremation of Baron de Palm was not by any stretch of the imagination a wholly secular affair; it can be seen properly only as an alternative religious ritual carried out by an new cadre of quasi-priests. The early history of the cremation movement thus makes plain once again the seemingly endless religious creativity of Americans. By attempting to "uplift" what they saw as the vulgar religious rite of burial into the more sanitary and more spiritual practice of cremation, the genteel reformers who spearheaded the movement contributed to the rapidly proceeding pluralization of lived religion in America.

NOTES

1. Though billed by its organizers as revolutionary, this occasion was not the first cremation in America. Many American Indian peoples burned their dead in the open air long before Columbus, and at least two American Blacks, both accused of capital crimes, were reportedly sentenced to death by public burning in the colonial period. Also cremated before Baron De Palm was Colonel Henry Laurens of Charleston, South Carolina, a wealthy merchant and an ex-president of the Continental Congress who was apparently convinced that "his body was too good to be eaten by worms" (*New York Times*, December 4, 1876, 8). In 1792, he became the first European American to be cremated in the United States. See James R. Chadwick, *The Cremation of the Dead* (Boston, Mass.: Geo. H. Ellis Co., Printers, 1905).

2. This estimation of the course of the cremation movement is based largely on published sources, which take off in 1874, peak in the mid-1880s, and decline to close to zero at the century's end. Michel Ragon notes in *The Space of Death: A Study of Funerary Architecture, Decoration, and Urbanism*, trans. Alan Sheridan (Charlottesville: University of Virginia Press, 1983) that the catalogue at Paris's Bibliothèque National "cites a great many works on cremation published between

1882 and 1894; that no such works are mentioned for the period from 1936 to 1959 . . . and that since 1960 only German works on the subject are referred to" (p. 314). I suspect that I will find a similar publication curve in the Library of Congress catalogue, albeit with an earlier peak. I further suspect that Ragon's thesis that cremation publishing declined in the twentieth century because "the idea has gained acceptance and the time for polemics has ended" (p. 314) can be applied not only to France but also to the United States.

3. Particularly influential in the United States was Sir Henry Thompson, "Cremation: Treatment of the Body After Death," *Contemporary Review* 23, no. 2 (January 1874): 319–28.

4. "Cremation: Proposed Incorporation of the New Society," *New York Times*, April 25, 1874, 2; "Cremation," *Philadelphia Medical Times*, April 25, 1874, 473; "Editor's Easy Chair," *Harper's New Monthly Magazine* 49, no. 290 (July 1874): 283.

5. Philadelphia's *Sunday Press* produced a spoof about a physician who cremated his deceased son in a furnace in the cellar of his home. Though intended for publication on April Fool's Day, it actually appeared weeks later. See "Cremation in Philadelphia," *New York Times*, April 20, 1874, 1; and "The Philadelphia Cremation Story a Hoax," *New York Times*, April 22, 1874, 1. A newspaper in Georgia also published an apocryphal account of a pro-cremation meeting. See "Cremation: The Stupid Philadelphia Hoax Imitated in Georgia," *New York Times*, April 28, 1874, 8. The play, which debuted on Broadway on October 12, 1874, was later published as *Cremation: An Ethiopian Sketch* (New York: Robert M. De Witt, 1875).

6. John Storer Cobb lists cremation statistics by crematory in his *A Quarter Century of Cremation in North America* (Boston, Mass.: Knight and Millet, 1901), 117. Cobb reported 10,867 cremations in nineteenth-century America.

7. Particularly influential are *Western Attitudes toward Death: From the Middle Ages to the Present*, trans. Patricia M. Ranum (Baltimore, Md.: Johns Hopkins University Press, 1974), and *The Hour of Our Death*, trans. Helen Weaver (New York: Knopf, 1981), both by Philippe Ariès. See also Richard Etlin, *The Architecture of Death—The Transformation of the Cemetery in Eighteenth-Century Paris* (Cambridge, Mass.: MIT, 1984); Thomas A. Kselman, *Death and the Afterlife in Modern France* (Princeton, N.J.: Princeton University Press, 1993); Emmanuel Le Roy Ladurie, *Love, Death and Money in the Pays d'Oc* (New York: Penguin, 1984); John McManners, *Death and the Enlightenment* (New York: Oxford University Press, 1981); Ragon, *The Space of Death*; Michel Vovelle, *Piété baroque et déchristianisation en Provence au XVIIIe siècle* (Paris: Seuil, 1978); Michael Wheeler, *Death and the Future Life in Victorian Literature and Theology* (Cambridge: Cambridge University Press, 1990); Paul Barber, *Vampires, Burial, and Death: Folklore and Reality* (New Haven, Conn.: Yale University Press, 1988).

8. There are some useful studies of death in America, including James Farrell's *Inventing the American Way of Death, 1830–1920* (Philadelphia, Pa.: Temple University Press, 1980), and David E. Stannard's *The Puritan Way of Death—A Study in Religion, Culture, and Social Change* (New York: Oxford University Press, 1977). *Death in America* (Philadelphia: University of Pennsylvania Press, 1974), a volume edited by Stannard that originally appeared in *American Quar-*

terly, also contains a number of helpful essays. The only sustained scholarly study of cremation in America is sociologist Robert W. Habenstein's "A Sociological Study of the Cremation Movement in the United States" (Ph.D. diss., University of Chicago, 1949).

9. The cremation movement promises to tell us something significant about the history of the body and thus open up new questions in American religious history and chart fresh avenues of approach to traditional ones. The history of the body, which is a more powerful presence in the European than in the American historiography, is founded in my view on two key assumptions. The first is that the body is a historical, cultural, and social construct rather than a natural object. As such, it has been experienced, symbolized, and understood differently in different times and places. The second assumption is that the body is both a producer of culture and society and a symbol that historians can read for evidence of cultural and societal change. Or, in the words of Katharine Young in *Bodylore* (Knoxville: University of Tennessee Press, 1993), "Culture is inscribed on the body . . . [and] at the same time fabricated out of the body" (p. xvii). See, e.g., Mikhail Bakhtin, *Rabelais and His World*, trans. Hélène Iswolsky (Bloomington: Indiana University Press, 1984); Peter Brown, *The Body and Society: Men, Women and Sexual Renunciation in Early Christianity* (New York: Columbia University Press, 1988); Caroline W. Bynum, *The Resurrection of the Body in Western Christianity, 200–1336* (New York: Columbia University Press, 1995); Michel Feher et al., eds., *Fragments for a History of the Human Body*, 3 vols. (Cambridge, Mass.: MIT, 1989); and Catherine Gallagher and Thomas Laquer, *The Making of the Modern Body* (Berkeley: University of California Press, 1987). Work on the history of the body has been influenced by developments in fields outside history and religious studies, most notably in phenomenology and anthropology. Perhaps the most influential anthropological work is Mary Douglas's *Natural Symbols: Explorations in Cosmology* (New York: Vintage Books, 1973). The sociology of the body is less developed. See, e.g., Bryan Turner's *The Body and Society: Explorations in Social Theory* (New York: Basil Blackwell, 1984).

10. See, e.g., Louis Cassels, "Christians Accepting Practice of Cremation," *Northeast Funeral Director* 21, no. 7 (1972): 15.

11. Cremation Association of North America, "Cremation Figures from 1876 to Present."

12. Ibid. The ratio of cremation to deaths in 1991 was 60 percent in Nevada and 55 percent in Hawaii.

13. These are not the only two such texts from 1874. See also George Bayles, "Disposal of the Dead," *Sanitarian* 2, no. 3 (June 1874): 97–105; Fannie Roper Feudge, "Burning and Burying in the East," *Lippincott's Magazine* 13, no. 33 (May 1874): 593–603; and George Bayles, "Cremation and Its Alternatives," *Popular Science Monthly* (June 1874): 225–28.

14. Persifor Frazer Jr., *Social Science Association of Philadelphia, Papers of 1874: The Merits of Cremation* (n.p: n.p., n.d.) 7, 8, 12. This paper was originally published in the *Penn Monthly* in June 1874.

15. Ibid., 13.

16. See Alfred Darby Nock, "Cremation and Burial in the Roman Empire," *Harvard Theological Review* 25, no. 3 (July 1932): 321–59.

17. Octavius B. Frothingham, *The Disposal of Our Dead* (New York: D. G. Francis, 1874), 11.

18. Ibid., 13.

19. Ibid., 13, 27–28.

20. Ibid., 18.

21. Ibid., 20.

22. Ibid., 22–24.

23. The fact that cremationists were reformers is incontrovertible, yet historians of reform in the United States have not typically taken the cremationists into consideration. Among the most prominent Gilded Age figures who aligned themselves with the cause were abolitionist Cassius M. Clay, newspaper editor Charles A. Dana, educator Elizabeth P. Peabody, author Mark Twain, Senator Charles Sumner, Buddhist sympathizer Moncure Conway, and ethical culturist Felix Adler. A number of prominent men of wealth and society—capitalist-philanthropist Andrew Carnegie and Harvard President Charles Eliot, for example—also supported cremation, as did a group of influential liberal Protestant ministers, including Unitarians Jenkin Lloyd Jones and Edward Everett Hale, Congregationalist Henry Ward Beecher, and the Episcopalian Bishop of Massachusetts Phillips Brooks. As if to affix the official seal of "REFORM" on the movement, Thomas Wentworth Higginson, perhaps the most universal of all universal reformers, also pronounced himself a cremationist. Robert W. Habenstein argued in "A Sociological Study of the Cremation Movement in the United States" that the cremationists were reformers and claims that the "vast majority" of women's rights activists were pro-cremation (p. 127). Among the women's rights agitators Habenstein linked with the movement were Julia Ward Howe, Margaret Fuller, Kate Field, Margaret Deland, Lucy Stone, Elizabeth Cady Stanton, Grace Greenwood, and Frances Willard. Still there is evidence that women as a whole were far less active in the cremation movement than men. A number of pro-cremation articles lament women's involvement in the cause—see, e.g., Louis Lange, *Church, Woman and Cremation* (New York: United States Cremation Company, 1903)—and statistics seem to bear this lamentation out. Women were cremated only about one-half as frequently as men in nineteenth-century America.

24. *Scrapbook on Cremation*, 73; New England Cremation Society, *Information Regarding Cremation* (Boston, Mass.: New England Cremation Society, 1899), 17.

25. "The First National Cremation Convention" (excerpt from *Sunnyside* ca. 1913), in *Pamphlets on Cremation* in John Crerar Library, University of Chicago, Chicago, Ill.

26. Frazer, *The Merits of Cremation*, 15.

27. "De Palm's Incineration," *New York Times*, December 7, 1876, 6.

28. "Dr. LeMoyne's Furnace," *New York Times*, February 19, 1878, 2.

29. For Le Moyne on cremation, see F. Julius Le Moyne, M.D., *Cremation: An Argument to Prove that Cremation is Preferable to Inhumation of Dead Bodies* (Pittsburgh, Pa.: E. W. Lightner, 1878).

30. On Olcott, see Stephen Prothero, *The White Buddhist: The Asian Odyssey of Henry Steel Olcott* (Bloomington: Indiana University Press, 1996).

31. Quoted in Henry S. Olcott, *Old Diary Leaves: The History of the Theosophical Society* (Adyar, India: Theosophical Publishing House, 1974), 1:172.

32. Ibid., 150.

33. Ibid.

34. I discuss this funeral at length in my book, *The White Buddhist*. For more contemporaneous accounts, consult Olcott, *Old Diary Leaves*, 1:147–84; "A Theosophical Funeral," *New York Times*, May 29, 1876, 1; "'Theosophical' Obsequies," *New York Tribune*, May 29, 1876, 4; "Baron de Palm's Funeral," *New York Tribune*, May 29, 1876, 5; and "A Rosicrucian in New-York," *New York Tribune*, May 26, 1876, 4.

35. "Dr. LeMoyne's Furnace," *New York Times*, February 19, 1878, 2.

36. Olcott, *Old Diary Leaves*, 1:170.

37. "Baron De Palm's Cremation," *New York Times*, December 6, 1876, 10.

38. "De Palm's Incineration," *New York Times*, December 7, 1876, 6.

39. "The Baron's Cremation," *New York Daily Graphic*, December 6, 1876, 2.

40. Quoted in Olcott, *Old Diary Leaves*, 1:170.

41. "Cremation of the Remains of the Late Baron De Palm," *Frank Leslie's Illustrated Newspaper*, December 23, 1876, 259.

42. Olcott, *Old Diary Leaves*, 1:183. One newsman claimed De Palm's ashes were thrown into the ocean off Coney Island! ("The End of Cremation," *New York Times*, October 17, 1879, 4).

43. "An Unceremonious Rite," *New York Times*, February 16, 1878, 5.

44. "Cremation of the Remains of the Late Baron De Palm," *Frank Leslie's Illustrated Newspaper*, December 23, 1876, 268.

45. Olcott, *Old Diary Leaves*, 1:176.

46. Ibid., 149.

47. "Baron De Palm's Remains," *New York Times*, December 5, 1876, 8; "Baron De Palm's Request," *New York Times*, December 4, 1876, 8.

48. These edicts, which were informed by the perception that cremationists, especially in Italy, were rabidly anticlerical and sharply inclined toward Freemasonry, forbade Roman Catholics to join cremation societies or to request cremation. Catholics who refused to honor them were to be denied church burial. Church officials were careful to note, however, that their opposition to cremation was circumstantial. Thus the way was open for revisions to Catholic canon law by Pope Paul VI in 1963 that effectively lifted the ban on cremation. For a discussion of changing Catholic attitudes toward cremation, see "Cremation," in *The Catholic Encyclopedia*, ed. Charles G. Herberman et al. (New York: Appleton, 1907–14), 4:481–82; "Cremation: Permissible," *Time*, June 12, 1964, 85; Paul E. Irion, *Cremation* (Philadelphia, Pa.: Fortress, 1968), 73–84; and John F. McDonald, "A Decade of Cremation in the Roman Catholic Church," *Pharos* 42, no. 1 (February 1976): 35–40. Catholic views on the cremation question are also expressed in James P. Murphy, "The Cremation Movement is Anti-Catholic," *Catholic World* 73, no. 436 (July 1901): 453–62; and Bertrand L. Conway, "The Ethics and History of Cremation," *Catholic World* 117, no. 702 (September 1923): 721–35.

49. The literature on "secularization" is vast, in both the historical and the sociological arenas, and I will not reprise it here, except to note that the term is as polysemous as it is controversial, referring in one textual incarnation to rationalization and in another to differentiation, laicization, privatization, disenchantment, etc. On "dechristianization," which I see as a more readily definable and useful construct, I have been influenced especially by Michel Vovelle, *Piété baroque et déchristianisation en Provence au XVIIIe siècle* (Paris: Plon, 1973).

50. Olcott, *Old Diary Leaves*, 1:150.

51. "De Palm's Incineration," *New York Times*, December 7, 1876, 6.

52. Stanley French, "The Cemetery as Cultural Institution: The Establishment of Mount Auburn and the 'Rural Cemetery' Movement," in *Death in America*, ed. Stannard, 69–91.

53. The nineteenth-century sanitary movement is only beginning to be studied by historians. General treatments include John Duffy, *The Sanitarians* (Urbana: University of Illinois Press, 1990); Phyllis Palmer, *Domesticity and Dirt* (Philadelphia, Pa.: Temple University Press, 1989); and Claudia and Richard Bushman, "The Early History of Cleanliness in America," *Journal of American History* 74 (1988): 1213–38. Broader in scope but nonetheless extremely provocative is Richard L. Bushman, *The Refinement of America: Persons, Houses, Cities* (New York: Knopf, 1992).

54. Jerome A. Anderson, quoted in Massachusetts Cremation Society, *Cremation* (Boston: Massachusetts Cremation Society, 1920), 47; "Homeopathists Favor Cremation," *The Urn* 1, no. 9 (October 1892): 6; "Cremation and Sanitation," in *Scrapbook on Cremation*, 33.

55. "Cremation of a Boston Physician," *New York Times*, July 18, 1877, 2; "The Cremation of Dr. Winslow," *New York Times*, August 5, 1877, 5; "The Salt Lake Cremation," *New York Times*, August 9, 1877, 3.

56. "Cremation of a Baby," *New York Times*, November 20, 1877, 8; "The Kircher Cremation Case," *New York Times*, November 21, 1877, 8; "No Objection to Cremating," *New York Times*, December 5, 1877, 8.

57. "An Ohio Lady To Be Cremated," *New York Times*, February 13, 1878, 1; "The Cremation of Mrs. Pitman," *New York Times*, February 14, 1878, 5; "An Unceremonious Rite," *New York Times*, February 16, 1878, 5; "Dr. LeMoyne's Furnace," *New York Times*, February 19, 1878, 2.

58. "His Ashes Under a Rosebush," *The Urn* 1, no. 4 (May 25, 1892): 4; "The Progress of Cremation in the United States," *The Urn* 1, no. 11 (December 25, 1892): 1.

59. "More About Incineration," in *Scrapbook on Cremation*, 17; "Cremation at Detroit," *The Urn* 1, no. 10 (November 25, 1892): 6.

60. "Cremation as a Science," *The Medical Record* 11 (December 16, 1876): 816.

61. "Cremation," in *Chamber's Encyclopedia* (Philadelphia, Pa.: Lippincott, 1897), 3:556.

62. "The End of Cremation," *New York Times*, October 17, 1879, 4.

63. "Dr. LeMoyne's Furnace," *New York Times*, February 19, 1878, 2.

64. Untitled editorial, *New York Times*, November 17, 1885, 4.

65. See Paul A. Carter, *The Spiritual Crisis of the Gilded Age* (Dekalb: Northern Illinois University Press, 1971); and Arthur M. Schlesinger, *A Critical Period in American Religion, 1875–1900* (1932; repr. Philadelphia, Pa.: Fortress, 1967).

66. Quoted in "The New Crematory Temple," *New York Times*, November 20, 1884, n.p.

67. Reprinted in "Spiritualism and Cremation," *The Urn* 1, no. 7 (August 1892): 3.

68. *The Urn* 1, no. 9 (October 1892): 11.

69. Jerome A. Anderson, quoted in Massachusetts Cremation Society, *Cremation* (Boston: Massachusetts Cremation Society, 1920), 47.

70. C. E. B., quoted in "Resurrection," *The Urn* 1, no. 7 (August 1892): 2.

71. Catherine L. Albanese, *Nature Religion in America: From the Algonkian Indians to the New Age* (Chicago: University of Chicago Press, 1990).

72. Historians of American religion have observed a shift of the site of religious practices and feelings from the public sphere of the church to the private sphere of the home in this period. See Colleen McDannell, *The Christian Home in Victorian America, 1840–1900* (Bloomington: Indiana University Press, 1986); Ann Douglas, *The Feminization of American Culture* (New York: Avon, 1977); and A. Gregory Schneider, *The Way of the Cross Leads Home: The Domestication of American Methodism* (Bloomington: Indiana University Press, 1993).

Chapter Six

COFFEE, MRS. COWMAN, AND THE DEVOTIONAL LIFE OF WOMEN READING IN THE DESERT

CHERYL FORBES

A DEVOTIONAL BOOK, unlike a sermon, is homespun, ordinary, and serviceable, something to read over coffee in the morning, something to think about while waiting for the laundry to finish or the pasta to cook; it does not pretend to the learned discourse of theology. Of all the devotional writers and devotional books that one might name, in the United States and in this century, the names that spring to mind first and foremost are those of Mrs. Charles E. Cowman and her master work, *Streams in the Desert*,[1] first published in 1925 and never out of print since. For a book so unknown outside a certain religious circle and yet so intimately known within that circle, it has had a remarkable publishing history: it has sold in the millions, it has been translated into numerous languages, and a copy was buried with Chiang Kai-Shek.

Yet what is even more remarkable than its history is its continued popularity, even today. *Streams* would seem to be an anachronism, rightfully belonging to an older time and a different cultural landscape than our own. Paradoxically, Mrs. Cowman's book continues to be read in an age that would seem to be the antithesis of everything she represented—even among women in conservative Christian circles who, like other women, have joined the workforce, have children in day care, and live in a culture so aptly characterized by Stephen Carter as one of disbelief.[2] Their actual deserts, then, are not the same deserts that concerned Mrs. Cowman, but their metaphorical deserts may not be so different. And so her books remain popular because, as I hope to demonstrate, she wrote as a woman for women in daily search of a spiritual life—women embarked on a popular spiritual quest in search of meaning in the context of daily living.

But Mrs. Cowman's continued popularity is not the only paradox we face when we open both the original *Streams* and its sequel, *Streams in the Desert 2*.[3] Although she lived and worked in the twentieth century and has roots in the literature of spiritual ecstasy and the Protestant Reformation, Mrs. Cowman nevertheless seems Victorian in her sensibilities, her sentimental rhetoric, her prose rhythms, and her unexpected spiritual affinities. For instance, she advocates hard work and sacrifice to gain spirituality, the opposite of the Reformation theology of grace. She is far more likely to cite a Victorian like the broad churchman and Episcopal bishop Phillips Brooks (1835–93), who advocated making chapel attendance voluntary at Harvard University,[4] than to cite a Puritan. Although we find repeated references to Brooks, we find only an occasional excerpt from *Pilgrim's Progress*, one citation from Richard Hooker,[5] a couple from Jonathan Edwards[6] and Matthew Henry.[7] Theodore Parker[8] and Ralph Waldo Emerson appear, as does Margaret Sangster, a turn-of-the-century advocate of women's independence and columnist for *Collier's*.[9]

Yet Mrs. Cowman was a missionary and co-founder with her husband of the Oriental Missionary Society.[10] She believed in and practiced what the gospel songwriter called "that old-time religion"; she was a dispensationalist, what journalists now call the religious right—an adherent of born-again popular religion. When Mrs. Cowman published *Streams* in the mid-1920s, fundamentalism was reaching the height of its reaction to the social gospel, university professors, and the controversies over evolution. Recall that 1925 was also the year of the Scopes trial.

Although Mrs. Cowman accepted the literal interpretation of the Bible and fundamentalist theology, she nevertheless exercised considerable latitude in her own biblical interpretation. In her choice of texts she seems unconcerned about theological purity, as the partial list of authors mentioned above shows. In fact, conventional categories of religious history and theology do not apply when it comes to understanding *Streams*. We cannot assume that Mrs. Cowman interprets certain passages or terms the way theologians even of her tradition would do or that she was much concerned about a writer's theological bona fides. Recently, her publisher, Zondervan, received a letter about this very issue. The letter writer claimed that someone must have altered Mrs. Cowman's text to include the highly suspect Phillips Brooks, who was, insisted the writer, a believer in evolution and so not a Christian. Of course, no one had altered the text. What mattered to Mrs. Cowman, apparently, was the use to which she could put Phillips Brooks, not whether he held evolutionist views. And Brooks is not the only "suspect" Christian to be found in *Streams*. Readers can also find writers quoted whom no one would put into a Christian camp, not even the broadest and most inclusive camp we might imagine.

Whether or not Mrs. Cowman's readers would admit it, Mrs. Cowman's vision is fraught with contradictions, twists, reversals, paradoxes, and theological conundrums. It is personal and impersonal; triumphant and tragic; hierarchical and egalitarian. Still, it offers a way for readers, women in particular, to make sense of the inescapable, inevitable, essential, daily hardships of life. Not in spite of, but because of her contradictions, paradoxes, and indifference to theological niceties, Mrs. Cowman gives readers hope. Moreover, her own practice of reading, which she records in *Streams* and allows readers to duplicate for themselves day by day and year after year, makes her a writer of great significance in the lived experience of women's spirituality in twentieth-century America.

What follows in this essay is a look at a few key meditations that reveal the themes of suffering, despair, and isolation that concerned Mrs. Cowman. These themes structured her own reading, and so structure *Streams in the Desert*, making the book a primary example of twentieth-century popular piety unmediated by minister or theologian. The themes suggest why Mrs. Cowman has had and continues to have such a profound and loyal following among Christian women. Although we cannot ever know for certain what a reader takes from a text—even when we ourselves are the readers—nevertheless the place to begin to answer why *Streams* appeals to women is with the text itself, the text and its creator. And so in searching the text, we will inevitably be in search of Mrs. Cowman herself.

A PATCHWORK TEXT

To understand *Streams in the Desert*, we must first understand the basic form of the daily devotional. First comes a Bible verse, then a brief meditation, usually a page or less, followed by a prayer, poem, or brief concluding comment. In many ways, the devotional appropriates the form of printed sermons from seventeenth-century America, which also began with a biblical text, followed by a sermon on the text that incorporated numerous references without attribution (or, as David D. Hall puts it in his story of popular religion in seventeenth-century New England, "by patchwork quoting"[11]). Mrs. Cowman's text, though, does not purport to be a full discourse on the Bible verse quoted; however, the meditations have the force of popular hermeneutics, and thus her role is analogous to that of a minister.

Several important assumptions about spiritual life underlie the genre and Mrs. Cowman's work in particular. A believer needs time during the day for meditation, every day of the year. Such meditation should consist of reading a Bible passage, thinking about its meaning and possible personal significance, and praying. Popular religious books aid believers in their devotional life. This has always been their purpose, and the belief that a true Christian sets aside daily time for Bible reading and meditation goes back at least to the Puritans.

Mrs. Cowman expected her readers to read and reread her devotional year after year after year. Her text is not, in Stanley Fish's words, a self-consuming artifact; it is not dialectical.[12] By definition, the genre *ought* to be self-consuming; readers ought to use it up and move on, if they heed her advice. However, Mrs. Cowman offers advice not to change her readers, the role of a dialectician as Fish defines it, but to encourage readers to do what they already know they ought to do. Thus, Mrs. Cowman uses language, metaphors, stories, and experiences familiar enough to her readers to offer them daily spiritual sustenance—the same sustenance she had received from her own devotional life.

In fact, Mrs. Cowman's texts *are* the texts she herself studied. That is, she did not write most of the meditations but culled them from her library of devotional books. Some of the books she once had ended up in Zondervan Publishing House. They show the eclectic nature of her reading—everything from Oswald Chambers to Robert Browning. Most striking, however, are the numerous daily devotionals from the late nineteenth and early twentieth centuries, compiled by women and long out of print: *Daily Suggestions for Workers: Many Thoughts Borrowed from Many Minds,* by Ellen Dyer and published by Harper in 1898, and *A Daily Staff for Life's Pathway,* by Mrs. C. S. DeRose from 1895 and published by Fredrick M. Stokes. Each such book, and there are many of them, contains notes and comments not only in the margins of the texts but on scraps of paper and old envelopes. Some of the notes read "used, January 12" or consist of a list of dates with a brief word next to it, as if the scraps of paper were Mrs. Cowman's way of organizing her own devotional life, the way she lived her religion. The most thoroughly read, as evidenced by its worn appearance and the rubber band holding it together, is *Daily Strength for Daily Needs,* selected by Mary W. Tileston, the thirteenth edition published in 1907 by Methuen. On the flyleaf we find the words written in her husband Charles Cowman's hand, "To my darling Lettie, January 1917, Tokyo, Japan, From Charlie."

Streams, then, is pieced and patched together—a hybrid text, an appropriated text—though it is easy for a reader to forget this, so compelling is the force of the person creating the text. The mind of Mrs. Cowman becomes the thread, stitching Bible verse, daily routine, season, and religious attitudes together: her connections, her responses, her readings of women like Mary Tileston and other late-Victorian devotionalists whom she marked and copied onto scraps of paper, old envelopes, bills—detritus to devotion.

For a woman who does not have a library, does not know many religious writers, or lacks the time to invent her own meditations, a daily devotional, especially dated from January 1 to December 31, fills the gaps—a package deal including Bible, wise thoughts, prayer. Impersonal, true, but paradoxically personal as you or I put ourselves into the text. Mrs. Cowman even includes an entry devoted to the subject of daily devotions (September 29). Because the entry is interesting from several perspectives, I return to it later. Here let me point out that the entry asserts that a great Christian is never in a "religious hurry" in his or her devotions but spends much time "in his closet," the reference being to Jesus' metaphor about prayer (Matthew 6:6 KJV).

So we find in a daily devotional of short entries a dismissal of the very genre. We find in a daily devotional that supposedly puts the Bible at the heart of its discourse only brief Bible passages, used problematically, as we shall see. Is *Streams* food for the spiritual life, or a symptom of someone starving spiritually? Is *Streams* an appetizer, or the whole meal? Whether Mrs. Cowman intended this, in practice women use her devotional to fulfill the need for and requirement of daily meditation without their expending much time or effort—"daily devotions," a ritual in a religious tradition that rejects ritual as emphatically as it knows how.

HILLS AND VALLEYS

Mrs. Cowman chose a compelling and fitting title for her text, for several reasons. First, it conjures up images of Old Testament prophets, John the Baptist, and Jesus and His forty days in the wilderness. Second, it echoes certain Bible passages, like the one prophesying John's construction job: to make a straight highway in the desert. And third, it is, of course, a quote from Isaiah 35:6: "in the wilderness shall waters break out, and streams in the desert."

This passage follows the famous section used by Handel in the *Messiah* about deaf ears unstopped, blind eyes opened, and lame limbs leaping like a deer. The desert is a metaphor for the sinner whom God redeems, transformed into a land of crocuses, cedar trees, grass and papyrus, and pools of bubbling springs. In short, the desert is no longer a desert once God gets His hands on it, and a sinner is no longer a sinner. But Mrs. Cowman does not use the metaphor in this way. Rather, life remains a desert with an occasional stream to wet the parched throat. God gives us just a little water so that we do not die of thirst in this weary and wicked and inhospitable land. He gives us just a foretaste of what is to come, but never the thing itself. All else must wait until the other side of death. On this view of life hangs Mrs. Cowman's view of the spiritual life. We are never out of the slough of despond, to use Bunyan's image; we are never out of the desert.

This leads us to the fourth reason Mrs. Cowman's title is compelling. It presents both desert and stream, thirst and water, barrenness and fecundity. It captures the continuum of life, even if her spiritual bent is to lean toward dust rather than loam. A stream often disappears, or goes underground, only to reappear hours or miles later; a metaphorical or religious stream behaves no differently.

Mrs. Cowman begins with "A Personal Word," which instructs us how to read her text and what to expect from it and from God:

In the pathway of faith we come to learn that the Lord's thoughts are not our thoughts, nor His ways our ways. Both in the physical and spiritual realm, *great pressure means great power!* Although circumstances may bring us into the place of death, that need not spell disaster—for if we trust in the Lord and wait patiently, that simply provides the occasion for the display of His almighty power. "Remember his marvellous works that he hath done; his wonders, and the judgments of his mouth" (Ps. 105:5).

And then follows the controlling verse from Isaiah: "in the wilderness shall waters break out, and streams in the desert."[13] The stream has been present all along, merely invisible. Just so with God, she implies, who doesn't always make sense to us; we must wait and watch and trust, no matter how irrational or barren life may seem. These instructions also apply as we read Mrs. Cowman's own text, which does not always seem to make sense. But if we wait, watch, and trust her, Mrs. Cowman will pull the pattern together. The way she works mirrors the way she sees God work.

Mrs. Cowman also claims a kind of spiritual oneupmanship on behalf of her readers. Not only is life hard, but life is hard in order to make us harder, or hardier, than it. She advises us to embrace hardship when it comes; at times she comes close to recommending that we seek hardship. For when judged by the life of the spirit, people with hard lives receive great benefits and more power than those who slide through life—indeed, they receive the greatest power. In hinting that we should seek difficulties to increase our patience, fortitude, and hardiness, Mrs. Cowman offers us the quickest way to increase our spiritual capital.

Mrs. Cowman captures an ancient Christian theme about the paradoxical relationship between powerlessness and power, which is particularly significant for women, who have long been encouraged to embrace powerlessness as the means to ultimate power.[14] Women who are denied worldly power can have something better: spiritual power. Mrs. Cowman's devotional offers a way out for women who feel powerless and trapped by their circumstances. In addition, Mrs. Cowman suggests that she herself understands her readers' feelings of powerlessness, the daily struggle to survive, an irony when we realize that her income from *Streams* allowed her to wield great power in her missionary organization.

Let us consider, then, the entry for January 1, which begins with a quotation from Deuteronomy after which Mrs. Cowman in a rare, direct address to her readers, says: "Today, dear friends, we stand upon the verge of the unknown. There lies before us the new year and we are going forth to possess it. Who can tell what we shall find?"[15] Her direct address to us, her "dear friends," indicates a relationship, an intimacy, between writer and reader. We could dismiss it as Victorian affectation, or we could regard it as Mrs. Cowman's feeling for and understanding of her audience, a conclusion warranted by her work as a missionary with the numerous deputations, talks, speeches, and ladies aid meetings she undoubtedly attended. She knew her readers.

The opening address functions on another level as well; it makes writer and reader equals, sharing the same fears, uncertainties, and concerns. Mrs. Cowman lays her hand on the arm of her reader—a gesture of concern, warmth, and mutuality. Unlike an authority, a male preacher, for instance, Mrs. Cowman closes the distance between herself and her audience. Her reader never feels preached at or looked down upon from some high spiritual point. Mrs. Cowman assumes a relationship with her reader that from the beginning is nonhierarchical, despite her overarching hierarchical view of reality. Woman to woman and writer to reader is different than wife to husband, us to God, citizens to rulers, and so forth. In Mrs. Cowman we find a woman able to convey contradictions without seeming to contradict. She was able to make the contradictions fit into a meaningful pattern, which was a large part of her appeal.

The verses Mrs. Cowman quotes from Deuteronomy refer to the Israelites entering and possessing the land of Canaan, a beautiful, lush land, evocative of all that is bountiful in God's creation. By association and analogy, important characteristics of her devotional writing as well as much religious literature written by and for women, Mrs. Cowman connects Canaan with the unknown new year. But notice what happens under Mrs. Cowman's hand. The good land of Canaan, about as un-desert-like as a land could be described, becomes a land of terror, pain, and desolation. She turns golden sand into burial mounds, Mediterranean warmth into a land blighted by winds and desolate of tree and fruit. The hills, a word that conjures up images of gentle, rolling, friendly land and that Isaiah couples with valleys, rain, and fecundity, is interpreted this way by Mrs. Cowman:

> The land is a land of *hills* and *valleys*. It is not all smooth nor all downhill. If life were all one dead level of dull sameness it would oppress us; we want the hills and the valleys. The hills collect the rain for a hundred fruitful valleys. Ah, so it is with us! It is the hill *difficulty* that drives us to the throne of grace and brings down the shower of blessing; the hills, *the bleak hills of life* that we wonder at and perhaps grumble at, bring down the showers . . . how many would have been killed . . . but for the hill—*stern, hard, rugged, so steep to climb*. God's hills are a gracious protection for His people against their foes![16]

Notice the progression in this passage, addressed, again, directly to the reader. Her intimacy with us allows her to address us in the prior paragraph as "anxious one." She knows that, appearances notwithstanding, we are troubled.

So despite the joyful, rich, exultant image of Canaan, and despite the joyful opening to her meditation, by the second paragraph the anxious reader enters Mrs. Cowman's thoughts and encounters life's troubling hills. At first, the hills appear for variety (to break up that "one dead level of dull sameness," the bane of too many women's lives) and out of environmental necessity ("the hills collect the rain"). But soon the hills become difficult, then bleak, then stern, hard, rugged, and steep to climb. They have metamorphosed into a terrifying land, not a land of milk and honey, just as the anxious reader expected. The good times were too good to last. And after Mrs. Cowman overturns the image of hills, after she moves us on the first day of the year from fecundity to desolation, she adds a coda. These wretched hills are God's "gracious protection." Clearly, Mrs. Cowman consistently presents a dualistic vision of life, good and bad, joyful and fraught with trials. In short, she offers a vision of life as most of us experience it. The strength of her devotional is that she confronts the desert with more than grim determination—and she confronts it on behalf of her readers. See, she says. I know how quickly the storm clouds gather, how easily a quarrel develops, how a split second of bad judgment can wreck a day, a week, even a life. And then what? she asks. Then what? When it all seems so hopeless, so meaningless, so random, then what?

Just put one foot in front of the other, Mrs. Cowman counsels, and keep climbing. Before you know it you have reached the top of whatever hill lies in your way. Mrs. Cowman offers hope to the victimized, marginalized, and disenfranchised, though she would never have used those words about herself or the other women she knew. They were not on the margins; they were in the center of the action, known to be so by the depth of their trouble. God loves those He chastises, she might have said.

ALL ALONE

Let us return to that strange entry for September 29, where Mrs. Cowman directly confronts the nature of the devotional life, for the entry relates not only to the genre and her view of vernacular religion, but also to the question of audience. Two themes emerge: solitude and passivity, and the relationship between them.

Mrs. Cowman chose the latter part of Psalm 109:4 as her text, "I give myself unto prayer," or as the NIV phrases it, "I am a man of prayer." The complete verse reads, "In return for my friendship they accuse me, but I am a man of prayer." The word "but" makes no sense unless we know what the first three verses say (and the latter half makes no sense without the first half). Someone or some group has been slandering David, who is giving God the details, intending later to catalogue a list of curses that he would like God to bring off—such as causing his slanderer to face bankruptcy proceedings and die young, thereby sending his wife and children to the poorhouse. In advocating his cause David says, "*but* I am a man of prayer." In other words, "I'm not what people say because I pray." David is his own character witness and defense attorney in a spiritual trial; this is legal language.

This is the context we need before reading the entry for September 29. To declare prayer as your persona acts as a rationalization, a reason, a justification, and a defense for the harsh sentence David asks God to hand out. The accompanying meditation, chosen from "The Still Hour," begins with several rhetorical questions, paramount among them, "Who ever knew an eminently holy man who did *not* spend much of his time in prayer?" And then follows a story about George Whitefield and his claims to have spent "whole days and weeks" praying. "It has been said," the passage continues, "that no great work in literature or science was ever wrought by a man who did not love solitude."[17]

The context of David's claim to prayer and the assertion that greatness comes only to men who spend much time alone—"an elemental principle of religion," the entry claims—leaves most women out on at least two counts: gender and time. How many women have the luxury of days and weeks to spend praying? Or even hours? (Most men may not have such luxury, either, but the possibility of it is greater.) The point is that true spirituality comes from effort, thus adding another price to be paid for the commodity that is true religion. Although the roots of Mrs. Cowman's devotional are buried in the Reformation doctrine of "by faith alone," and although much of her text recommends forbearance, long-suffering, patience—the sacrificial responses of the religious life—in this entry she advocates hard work and striving for a religious life. How are we to reconcile passages that recommend effort with those that insist that "straining, driving effort does not accomplish the work God gives man to do"?[18]

Let us look more closely at solitude versus community (so implied) and action versus inaction. Although Mrs. Cowman would never have explicitly said that the practice of true religion comes through time alone rather than church attendance, her text effectively says this for her. The Christian life is a solitary life; time alone (a euphemism for time with God) is the sine qua non of a true Christian. The above entry provides one example of this; we find another for October 2: "And he took them, and went aside privately into a desert place" (Luke 9:10). The first lines of the meditation read, "In order to grow in grace, we must be much alone. It is not in society that the soul grows most vigorously. In one single quiet hour of prayer it will often make more progress than in days of company with others. It is in the desert that the dew falls freshest and the air is purest."[19]

Hall argues that, although popular religion in seventeenth-century New England was an every-person-for-herself religion, "the everyday meaning of religion . . . involved the social experience of withdrawing from one kind of community and uniting with another."[20] By the time Mrs. Cowman writes, the social experience, the community of believers, has shrunk to a community of two—the Christian and God. Practical piety is private; indeed, it *must* be for good Christians who want to become great Christians. Daily devotions thus become the singular mark of a true Christian, which was not the case in seventeenth-century New England (Hall points out that Puritans thought of daily prayer, Bible reading, and meditation as duties of a Christian, but not the practices that defined people *as* Christians [21]). It is hard to find a meditation in Mrs. Cowman's work that talks about the communal nature of the Christian life, of the church. In the October 2 entry on solitude, we find yet again an irony in the juxtaposition of this meditation with the passage from Luke. Jesus did not go alone but with His disciples, and when the crowds followed Him He turned and talked to them.

The theme of isolation merges with that of passivity. A few examples will demonstrate this. In the entry for April 5 (II Kings 4:4) we find:

> They were to be alone with God, for they were not dealing with the laws of nature, nor human government, nor the church . . . but they must needs be isolated from all creatures. . . . There are times and places where God will form a mysterious wall around us, and cut away all props . . . and shut us up to something divine, which is utterly new and unexpected. . . . Most religious people live in a sort of treadmill life . . . but the souls that God leads out into immediate and special dealings, He shuts in where all they know is that God has hold of them, and is dealing with them, and their expectation is from Him alone.[22]

A few metaphors are worth noting. References to the wall and to the props knocked out from under us suggest the drama of a suffering Christian (the props, the mystery, the new and unexpected), as contrasted with a boring, uneventful life. Mrs. Cowman expected the unexpected, God's miraculous intervention in life's pain as well as in its mundane aspects. She seems to disdain the "treadmill life" of most religious people. And yet many of us live a treadmill existence, and it is as strong and legitimate an image as that of life as broken, trouble-filled, dramatic. Mrs. Cowman may prefer stage metaphors to that of the treadmill, yet she nevertheless fully recognizes how many people are trapped by the treadmill.

The April 7 devotion talks about waiting and watching, and the following one asserts that "in order really to know God, *inward stillness* is absolutely necessary. . . . I composed my body to perfect stillness, and I constrained my troubled spirit into quietness, and looked up and waited; and then I did 'know' that it was God. . . . There is a perfect passivity which is not indolence."[23] Ted Leeson in *The Habit of Rivers* provides an apt metaphor for the kind of passivity without indolence that Mrs. Cowman is advocating. Leeson writes:

> Where the river runs swiftly over shallow bedrock, a line of standing waves will develop. If they are spaced just right, you can trap the boat [a driftboat] in a trough between two crests. Though the water rolls and wells on all sides, the waveform remains stationary, and the boat sits calmly amid the turbulence in apparent defiance of some law. You occupy a place within a place, holding in the flux, anchored by the water itself.[24]

We are the boat, sitting calmly, occupying "a place within a place," despite the turbulent waters around—and at the same time, the water is the anchor. Just so, in Mrs. Cowman's text God causes the turbulence and is also the anchor that prevents our foundering.

In order to practice passivity, stillness, and silence, in order to "wait" for God, a Christian needs to be alone. Solitude becomes the prerequisite for passivity and if, as in the April 5 entry, a believer does not separate herself, then God does it with His "mysterious wall."[25] Or, as the October 7 entry explains with a different metaphor, God immerses a believer "in times of darkness. . . . The sky is overcast with clouds. The clear light of heaven does not shine. . . . One feels as if he were groping his way in darkness. . . . What shall the believer do? . . . The first thing to do is do nothing."[26]

Isolation. Passivity. And, over and over, the promise that a Christian's trials come from God and successful isolation and passivity will result in greatness: "Where showers fall most, the grass is greenest" (October 9);[27] "It is by being cast down and not destroyed; it is by being shaken to pieces, and the pieces torn to shreds, that men become men of might" (October 11);[28] "Difficulty is the very atmosphere of miracle—it is a miracle in its first stage" (October 14);[29] "God uses most for His glory those people and things which are most perfectly broken" (October 15);[30] and "An assured part of God's pledged blessing to us is delay and suffering" (October 18).[31]

Mrs. Cowman may offer such contrary and problematic views because of the hybrid, patchwork nature of her text—a bricolage. Not only does she cull passages seemingly at random from throughout the Bible (though preferring the Old Testament to the New and sometimes misquoting)—

from Isaiah 24:15 to Colossians 2:15, to II Kings 6:17, to Habakkuk 2:1—but she also snips sections from the publications of familiar preachers, theologians, and writers. Taken together, they often clash, jarring each other and the reader, creating disconnections and contradictions. She appropriates C. H. Spurgeon, Hannah Whitall Smith, George Mueller, Frances Ridley Havergal, Henry Van Dyke, Henry Ward Beecher, Harriet Beecher Stowe, and Johnathan [sic] Edwards. Such familiar names may comfort readers because their stability, trustworthiness, and authority attach to Mrs. Cowman. But if we consider their religious positions, particularly when juxtaposed with such writers as John Ruskin, Christina Rossetti, William Wadsworth Longfellow, and Francis De Sales, they make strange companions, as motley a crew as Chaucer's Canterbury pilgrims.

Take Harriet Beecher Stowe, for instance. George Marsden comments that "Beecher's church . . . had the attraction of not demanding exact beliefs"[32] and claims that Harriet Beecher Stowe not only excoriated Calvinism "but any teachings that tied eternal salvation to correct theological belief"; instead "the essence of Christianity was moral character."[33] Had such ideas been suggested to Mrs. Cowman she would have been horrified. Yet in her text such quasi-religious, high-toned Victorian moralists sit hard by fundamentalists like A. B. Simpson, George Whitefield, and Andrew Murray. We also find people like Margaret Bottome, Annie Johnson Flint, Miss Ophelia G. Browning, Adelaide Proctor, Elizabeth Cheney, and Katherine Lee Bates, to list only a few of the unfamiliar, long-forgotten women, Canadian and American (Flint, at least, was Canadian) often appended to a few lines of rhymed verse. Or we find entries with initials only, or the words "from a tract," or "selected," which appear repeatedly. Such are the mental scraps out of which Mrs. Cowman pieces her devotional.

Theology is of far less consequence, obviously, than the emphasis on overcoming trials and tribulations from God (and not, note, from the Devil) and on rejecting despondency, worry, and anxiety (which would be natural feelings for someone whose life was one trial after another tribulation). Mrs. Cowman may have believed that life is a desert, but she wanted readers to be inspired to joy in the desert path because it leads to a great destination.

At the same time, the cumulative Christian narrative Mrs. Cowman tells inevitably means contradiction. Because God loves us, He sends us trials and tribulations that through His love He enables us to overcome. The more we suffer the more we know God loves us because we know that ultimately He is the source of our suffering as He is the source of our surcease. Undoubtedly life is a spiritual desert—or a treadmill—but just as undoubtedly life is infused with miracle, with deliverance. Although we cannot bring miracles into our life just by willing them, the daily practice of devotions, the daily determination to suffer joyfully, even with anticipation, ensures that we are prepared to recognize, if not accept, the miracles when they come. As well-tilled but parched soil can soak up rain when it falls, so can we, well-tilled through our devotional life, find miraculous refreshment.

"WHAT SHALL WE FIND?"

Streams in the Desert opens with a question that indicates Mrs. Cowman's narrative structure, that of the spiritual quest: "Who can tell what we shall find?" It refers to the new year as well as to life itself. Those words might also serve as an epigraph to the book. "We stand upon the verge of the unknown. . . . Who can tell what we shall find?" Or, to rephrase the question, Who can tell *whom* we shall find?

Despite her intimate opening address, Mrs. Cowman remains an enigmatic, shadowy figure in her own text. Her apparent absence is a key to the appeal *Streams* has for readers. In a text that is in so many ways prescribed—one that claims to give answers to a Christian's every despair—we find discourse so open that each reader can imagine the author as her own friend, a woman called Mrs. Charles E. Cowman. She does not give us autobiographical particulars. And yet, in a way, she *does* tell us. Just look in the mirror. Or into your own heart and soul. What her audience is, she is.

As I said earlier, what holds the whole of *Streams* together is the mind of Mrs. Cowman. The selections, so decontextualized and recontextualized by Mrs. Cowman, make it so. What is important in *Streams* is not who "David" is, a name we find on June 20. Or who wrote her late husband's favorite poem, which we find in the August 26 entry. Or what kind of person Annie Johnson Flint was. It does not matter what they believed or what the context of their belief was. It only matters that their words inspire the reader to infuse them with personal significance. Christina Rossetti, Harriet Beecher Stowe, and Ralph Waldo Emerson might not have been fundamentalists or orthodox (as many of Mrs. Cowman's readers would define those terms), but their words are uplifting. They helped Mrs. Cowman receive God's grace, and she believed that they would help others as well.

Curiously, only when we turn to *Streams in the Desert 2* do we find Mrs. Cowman named not only as compiler but as author of numerous meditations. Comparing the two volumes reveals that the central themes of the original are indeed the themes and concerns of Mrs. Cowman's own life:

"Sorrows are too precious to be wasted" (February 26);[34] "We must know how to put occupation aside. In an inaction which is meditative, the wrinkles of the soul are smoothed away" (March 27);[35] "It takes a real faith to trace the rainbow through the rain" (April 2);[36] "A shattered and broken personality releases the fragrance of Christ" (June 6);[37] "What should be the attitude of a Christian when placed in a difficult and trying situation— a place of severe testing? . . . A refusal to look *at* the difficult circumstance, but *above* it" (June 9).[38] Here is evidence that Mrs. Cowman offers women a way of *being* that focuses on the inner life of the spirit and so transcends—if not provides a way to ignore—the inescapable, inevitable, essential, daily hardships of life. Once we have read Mrs. Cowman's meditations in volume 2 we can return to volume 1 and hear her voice in those meditations that are unnamed, as in this telling entry: "Left alone! . . . If His followers spent more time alone with Him, we should have spiritual giants again. . . . Covet to get alone with God . . . it must mean more depth and power."[39] The two volumes consistently narrate the themes of suffering, worry, active passivity, and passive activity—themes expressed as often in the versifying of numerous unknown women as in the prose meditations. Because these verses are a central part of the discourse (almost every entry includes at least a few lines of verse), we need to consider an example before we close.

In volume 1, the entry for March 9 is almost entirely a poem by Miss Mary Butterfield. The final stanza captures all of Mrs. Cowman's most deep-felt themes:

> Oh, paradox of Heaven. The load
> We think will crush was sent to lift us
> Up to God! Then, soul of mine,
> Climb up! for naught can e'er be crushed
> Save what is underneath the weight.
> How may we climb! By what ascent
> Shall we surmount the carping cares
> Of Life! Within His word is found
> The key which opens His secret stairs;
> Alone with Christ, secluded there,
> We mount our loads, and rest in Him.[40]

With language reflecting *Little Women* and *Pilgrim's Progress*, Miss Butterfield reinforces the paradoxical narrative Mrs. Cowman has told. God sends us trials, we climb up (recall the metaphor in the first entry) by resting "within His word," to reach our secluded community, "alone with Christ." And Annie Johnson Flint, who must have been Mrs. Cowman's favorite versifier, reaches out to all readers, no matter how great or small

their problems: "His grace is great enough to meet the great things— . . .
His grace is great enough to meet the small things" (February 26).[41] From
"crashing waves" to "insect worries" and "squeaking wheels," God covers
them all, His private contract with each believing reader.

A HOME

Mrs. Cowman appeals to women, and has remained in print, a perennial
best-seller of popular piety, because she pierces women's sense of isolation
and alleviates their burden of daily trials, confusions, and contradictions. In
short, she assures women that their suffering *counts* and that their lives have
meaning; they are significant to the one who counts the most, to God.

People hunger for meaning; we want to know where our suffering orig-
inates and why it comes, as well as how to overcome it. We also need to
know that someone shares in our grief. Mrs. Cowman's devotional books
give readers what they seek. Somehow, in some way, she makes readers
her intimate friends, her fellow sufferers, her companions on the most
important adventure of life—the daily, necessary, spiritual quest for God.
Streams fulfills the promise of its title by providing every day, year after
year, the spiritual water readers need in the desert of life.

Mrs. Cowman knows us; we know her. We are neighbors, friends,
back-fence gossips who commiserate with one another as we hang our
clothes on the line. We find companionship and identity in her text. We
also find a place to belong, a home. Mrs. Cowman conveys community,
her book populated by unbelievers and believers, by fence-sitters, sinners,
and saints.

Women's lives and work have long gone unrecognized and ultimately
unvalued, as Mrs. Cowman knew. She knew, too, that while most women
never expect reward or gratitude, they do expect hardship, sorrow, and
sickness. They need to know that their pain matters and that, as deep as
the pain may be, there is even deeper comfort. As the entry for August 9
says, "comfort does not come to the lighthearted and merry. We must go
down into 'depths' if we would experience this most precious of God's
gifts."[42] The more burdensome a life, the more God's gift of comfort
women experience. A central way to experience this comfort is through a
specific practice, that of daily devotional reading.

Readers of *Streams in the Desert* identify with its creator. Reader, creator, and text fuse to become, in the words of the June 9 entry, "the eagle
that soars in the upper air, [which] does not worry itself as to how it is to
cross rivers."[43] Mrs. Cowman knows that women can become eagles; she
knows that women can soar above their troubles, as turbulent as they
might be. Helping women find and strengthen their wings defines the role
of her devotional literature.

NOTES

1. Mrs. Charles E. Cowman, *Streams in the Desert 1* (Grand Rapids, Mich.: Zondervan, 1965). When the Zondervan Publishing House bought Cowman Publishing in 1965, *Streams in the Desert* already had sold more than two million copies.

2. Stephen L. Carter, *The Culture of Disbelief: How American Law and Politics Trivialize Religious Devotion* (New York: Basic Books, 1993).

3. Mrs. Charles E. Cowman, *Streams in the Desert 2* (Grand Rapids, Mich.: Zondervan, 1966).

4. George W. Marsden, *The Soul of the American University: From Protestant Establishment to Established Nonbelief* (New York: Oxford University Press, 1994).

5. Richard Hooker (1554?–1600), English writer and theologian, is best known for his *Laws of Ecclesiastical Polity* (1594), which helped determine Anglican theology.

6. Jonathan Edwards (1703–1758), American preacher, theologian, and writer, helped precipitate the Great Awakening.

7. Matthew Henry (1662–1714), an English Nonconformist minister, is best known today for his elegantly written devotional commentary, originally called *Exposition of the Old and New Testaments* (1708–10). Because of his sudden death, his commentary ends with the New Testament book of Acts but was later finished by numerous other ministers and the whole book was edited by G. Burder and John Hughes in 1811.

8. Theodore Parker (1810–60), Unitarian minister and lecturer, is best known for his work as an abolitionist. Strongly influenced by Ralph Waldo Emerson's transcendentalism, while in seminary Parker came to doubt the infallibility of the Bible and the exclusive claims of Christianity, which caused him to be shunned by other Unitarians.

9. John R. Stilgoe, *Alongshore* (New Haven, Conn.: Yale University Press, 1994).

10. The Oriental Missionary Society, founded by the Cowmans in 1901, originally worked primarily in Japan and China. Around the time missionaries were kicked out of China, the organization became the Overseas Missionary Society, and it is now called OMS, International.

The Cowmans served overseas from 1901 to 1917, when Charles Cowman's ill health forced them to return to the United States. During the next six years Mrs. Cowman nursed her husband until his death. She then became a frequent speaker at the Winona Lake Bible Conference, Winona Lake, in north-central Indiana, as well as during weeklong summer missionary meetings sponsored by the OMS. The organization owned a home at the Bible conference center, where Mrs. Cowman lived during the summer. Winona Lake, with theological affinities to the Keswick movement, became well known as a center for Bible teachers and devotional speakers like Mrs. Cowman. Billy Sunday was its most famous speaker.

11. David D. Hall, *Worlds of Wonder, Days of Judgment* (New York: Knopf, 1989), 27–28.

12. Stanley E. Fish, *Self-Consuming Artifacts: The Experience of Seventeenth-Century Literature* (Berkeley: University of California Press, 1972).

13. Cowman, *Streams 1*, 6.

14. The chapter in this volume by R. Marie Griffith on prayer and healing in the Women's Aglow Fellowship (itself having affinities with the Holiness and Keswick movements, as did Mrs. Cowman's missionary organization) is another example of the paradoxical relationship between power and powerlessness.

15. Cowman, *Streams 1*, 7.

16. Ibid., All but the initial italics have been added.

17. Ibid., 301.

18. Ibid., entry for September 3, 275.

19. Ibid., 304. However, even in this theme Mrs. Cowman contradicts herself. In a later entry based on Exodus 3:1–2, the meditation reads in part that "the vision came in the midst of common toil, and that is where the Lord delights to give His revelations. He seeks a man who is on the ordinary road" (p. 325). "Common toil" and "the ordinary road" presuppose society.

20. Hall, *Worlds of Wonder*, 118.

21. Nevertheless, it is true that the Reformation directed Christians toward intense individual piety.

22. Cowman, *Streams 1*, 116.

23. Ibid., 118.

24. Ted Leeson, *The Habit of Rivers: Reflections on Trout Streams and Fly Fishing* (New York: Lyons and Burford, 1994), 25.

25. Cowman, *Streams 1*, 116.

26. Ibid., 309.

27. Ibid., 311.

28. Ibid., 314.

29. Ibid., 317.

30. Ibid.

31. Ibid., 321.

32. Marsden, *The Soul of the American University*, 161.

33. Ibid., 79.

34. Mrs. Charles E. Cowman, *Streams in the Desert 2* (Grand Rapids, Mich.: Zondervan, 1966), 61.

35. Ibid., 91.

36. Ibid., 98.

37. Ibid., 161.

38. Ibid., 164.

39. Cowman, *Streams 1*, 73.

40. Ibid., 86.

41. Ibid., 73.

42. Ibid., 249.

43. Ibid., 185.

Chapter Seven

THE USES OF OJIBWA HYMN-SINGING AT WHITE EARTH: TOWARD A HISTORY OF PRACTICE

Michael McNally

Introduction: Missionary Uses of Hymn-Singing

Beginning in the 1830s, Protestant missionaries promoted translations of their favorite hymns as part of a fervent campaign to Christianize and assimilate the Ojibwa, or *anishinaabe*, people of northern Minnesota.[1] They shared hymn music as a cherished expression of worship. They also thought of the hymn as a sharp tool for rooting out the indianness of native people in the work of cultural revolution.

The revolution never came—at least not fully enough to allay missionaries' deep frustrations in their more honest moments. But whenever they heard those old familiar tunes sung in the native tongue, they held on to the moment as if it were a precious jewel. Missionaries understood hymn-singing as nothing short of the sound of civilization, a harbinger of days to come. "I am always deeply touched with their singing," wrote the Episcopalian Bishop Henry Whipple while on a visit to northern Minnesota's White Earth Indian Reservation in 1881:

> The *wild* Indian voice is harsh. [N]othing could be more discordant than their wild yell and hideous war song. The religion of Christ softened this; their voices became plaintive, and as they sing from the heart their hymns are full of emotion. All sing, and you are taken afar to think of the multitude no man could number.[2]

Whipple was right. Hymn-singing seemed to capture native people's imaginations, and missionaries did what they could to harness the energy to their own ends. But in the ongoing struggle to survive, Ojibwa people put the singing to different uses than these missionaries had in mind. It is that story that I wish to tell. I focus on two moments of hymn-singing at White Earth: first in the 1880s, when singing began to take shape as an organized practice, and then a century later, when a group of concerned elders at White Earth rekindled the tradition. Indeed, for many at White Earth today, the songs have become powerful emblems of who they are as a people.[3]

Because the story of Ojibwa hymn-singing as a musical form corresponds to the violence of disease and dispossession experienced by *anishinaabe* people at the hands of colonialism, I want first to ask how singing
Christian hymns could come to serve as a spiritual resource for so many of
them today. Ultimately, the story of hymnody among the Ojibwa is a
larger story of renegotiating identity, a story in which religious practices
play a leading role.[4] Following Antonio Gramsci and Pierre Bourdieu,
who moved the study of domination and resistance away from overt
shows of political or military force to the more subtle ways that these
social dynamics play out in symbolic life, we can see practices like music-
making as much more than the cultural trappings of deeper processes:
they are the bread and butter of colonizing power and resistance.[5] To
quote Ojibwa singer Erma Vizenor, "We sing in order to survive."[6]

Second, I want to distinguish the different uses to which music-making
has been put in order to suggest, as Catherine Bell has done in a more
theoretical context, that ritual is not sui generis activity, wholly other than
the social, economic, and political practices of survival. Like these other
forms of social action, ritual is strategic action, embroiled in the shifting
demands of history and dependent on the capacity of ritual actors to draw
on its resources in response to those shifting demands. Ojibwa religion,
like any religious complex, is no monolith that is merely *acted on* by forces
of change; the very tradition is a matter of bricolage. By discussing hymn-
singing in terms of practices, Ojibwa religiousness can be understood not
as some airtight symbol system placed on the world by "the Ojibwa
mind," but as itself a product of practices—idiosyncrasy as much as idea-
tion, making do as much as making meaning.[7]

But first to the music itself. While prose can elicit neither the sound of
sung hymns nor the fuller texture of their performance, perhaps I can
suggest something of what makes Ojibwa hymnody distinct from other
Anglo-Protestant hymnody. Imagine a small church guild hall crowded
with folding tables and chairs set up for an all-night wake. A blue haze of
cigarette smoke, backlit by harsh fluorescent lights, disabuses one of any
expectations for the exotic in this Native American ceremony. Painful realities are present in the room as mourners come to terms with what was
likely an untimely, often violent, death. The Ojibwa singers, men and
women in their sixties, seventies, and eighties, file in and sit at the center
table as the forty-odd people who have gathered gradually settle down to
listen. Coffee percolates on the serving counter; an occasional clinking of
pots and pans emerges from the adjacent kitchen as women prepare the
potluck dishes for the feast that follows.

At some unheralded moment, the voice of the lead singer emerges with
the first notes of "Number Twenty-Five." He sings deeply, with his eyes
closed to focus the intensity. Soon voices of the other singers join in, and

the room hushes to hear the hymn with which this singing group customarily begins each performance. Because the singers know each syllable of this song so well, few need look for direction from the worn Ojibwa hymnals. The text of hymn "Number Twenty-Five," a translation of Isaac Watts's "Come Holy Spirit, Heavenly Dove," reads as follows in the Episcopalian Diocese of Minnesota's 1910 *Ojibwa Hymnal*:

> Ondashan, Kichi Ochichag,
> Widokawishinam,
> Atoniu sagiiwewin
> Ima nindeinang
>
> 'Na eji-gotugiziyang
> Oma aking ayayang;
> Nin kichi bejiwimin su
> Ishpiming wi-jayang.
>
> Anawi nindinend amin
> Nagumotagoyun;
> Nind anamiawininan
> Nonde ko takisin.
>
> Ondashan, Kichi Ochichag,
> Widokawishinam,
> Moshkinaton nindeinang
> Iu sagiiwewin.

In a sense, the text as such is beside the point: performance extends the shape of each syllable of Ojibwa to make the hymn sound more like a chant than a sung poem. Because the pace is five to ten times slower than that of conventional hymn-singing of Anglo-Protestant worship, it takes some time to make out the contours of a familiar melody. The singers continue their meditative pace through fifteen or more songs, pausing every third hymn or so in order that a singer might stand to lend some words of condolence or witness or prayer. At some appropriate point, the lead singer announces by number the next hymn to be sung, and the other singers listen carefully to the first notes of the lead singer's chosen tune prior to joining in.

Singing at wakes has become a formalized practice in a number of ways. On heightened occasions like wakes, only certain people at White Earth do the singing—a group of a dozen men and women seniors who call themselves the White Earth Ojibwa Singers.[8] Widely respected as leading elders of the community, this group will travel up to several hours when asked to perform at a wake, with no compensation save gas money and a hot meal.[9] Sometimes, the singers do not even know the mourning families for whom they sing, yet they pride themselves on freely sharing their music with any who ask.

Sometimes, the hymns sound like little more than background music for the other activities at the wake. Relatives visit, friends offer tobacco and prayers near the body, children drink Kool-aid and get wound up. At other times, the singing seems to fit the mood just right and the room becomes still; nothing in the world seems to move except for the chanted syllables as they rise, linger, and fall.

In either case, the music is always slow and solemn, sung a cappella, with neither harmony nor ornament. If a singer sounds off-pitch according to conventional standards, that does not seem to matter. To the White Earth Singers, "sounding good" has more to do with the spiritual tenor of the gathering, the state of mind of the singers, and the sincerity of their spiritual commitment, which, like wisdom, is hard-earned after many years of unsung struggle.

Sharing food in a potluck feast is as much a part of a proper wake as is sharing music. Some are certain to bring foods of the land—wild rice, fish, deer meat, swamp tea, and fry bread. Others are bound to bring the other staples of contemporary life—variations on USDA commodity cheese and macaroni hot dish, brownies, and Minnesota Jello salad.[10]

While it is tempting to proceed to interpret these and other details of performance, I wish to call attention to what stands *behind* each performance of Ojibwa hymns, that is, the shared values of community that the White Earth Singers try to call forth in their songs. As Thomas Turino observes in his study of the complex social world of Andean panpipe music, "the sound object may not be the most important thing about music and it cannot be abstracted from the ethics, processes and occasions of communal life."[11] To explore the social frame of reference surrounding hymn-singing is, I believe, to find what makes the music so compelling. We ought to look then, at the historical context that gave rise to the tradition, beginning with the uses for which evangelical missionaries intended the translated hymn.

MUSIC AS MISSIONARY TOOL: THE DIDACTIC USES OF THE HYMN

Nineteenth-century Protestant evangelicals regarded hymns as ideal resources in an otherwise difficult mission project. Missionaries were frustrated by what they saw as a constitutional Ojibwa indifference to religious instruction, an indifference they construed as childish. "I can liken these In[dian]s to nothing more aptly than stubborn peevish children," one missionary among the Ojibwas declared, "who have to be gratified in all their wishes & are obstinate and refractory if refused."[12]

In the task of reforming the manners of children, hymnody seemed to many Protestants a promising means for disciplining impressionable young minds into the Christian life. Hymns set forth each element of evangelical Christian piety—submission, sobriety, thrift, industry, and self-examination—in an accessible, if not pedantic, manner.[13] Witness the text of "Awake My Soul, and with the Sun," translations of which appeared as a morning hymn in a number of Ojibwa hymnals:

> Awake my soul, and with the sun
> The daily stage of duty run,
> Shake off dull sloth, and joyful rise
> To pay thy morning sacrifice.
>
> Redeem thy mis-spent time that's past,
> And live this day as if thy last;
> Improve thy talent with due care,
> For the great day thyself prepare.
>
> Let all thy converse be sincere
> Thy conscience as the noon-day clear;
> Think how all-seeing God thy ways
> And all thy secret thoughts surveys.

Hymnody was believed effective in this didactic task because it was affective, uniquely equipped to smooth children's rough edges and to awaken their passion to learn. In the words of an evangelical teachers' manual used extensively at American Board of Commissioners for Foreign Missions (ABCFM) missions to the Ojibwas:

> Singing is admirably calculated to harmonize the feelings of the children, and cement attachment to each other. It seems to tranquilize and soften the more obdurate tempers. It also acts as a magnet of attraction to the volatile. It tends to soothe the impatient. By singing the hymns the infant mind is enriched with pure and important sentiments, which it is believed will not fail in some degree to direct the future conduct of all.[14]

Just as hymns were believed strategic for raising children, so evangelicals believed them ideal resources in the mission field for raising up the entire peoples looked upon as children, and they worked tirelessly to prepare, publish, and reissue Ojibwa hymnbooks. Missionaries deployed the little books in worship, schools, and daily interchanges as phonetic bridges to the oral world of *anishinaabe* communities.

The region's first printed Ojibwa hymns appeared as appendixes to spelling books and Scripture tracts, though missionaries also possessed a few precious copies of the large collection of hymns translated by Peter Jones of Ontario in 1829.[15] A child of an Ojibwa mother and a Welsh father, Jones underwent conversion in a camp meeting, became a Methodist preacher in the vicinity of Toronto, and made numerous translations of hymns and Scripture. Though subsequent hymnals owed much to variations in dialect, orthography, and the idiosyncracies of performance in the oral tradition, Jones' translations provided the basis on which ensuing versions rested. ABCFM missionaries reprinted five hundred copies of Jones' hymnbook in their own orthography in 1836. By the 1870s, versions of his translations with additional hymns had gone through another eight editions under the Methodists and the American Board.

Regardless of their position in denominational debates between evangelical and High Church wings, Episcopalian missionaries to the Ojibwas relied heavily on the music of the hymn in their efforts and drew on Jones' early translations as well.[16] Frederick O'Meara's prayer book of 1853 contained an appendix of twenty-five pages of hymns, a number that grew in four subsequent editions. An 1886 revision of the prayer book by J. A. Gilfillan and others at White Earth led to the subsequent Ojibwa hymnal that shaped and was, in turn, shaped by the performance traditions discussed below.[17]

By 1870, an estimated five thousand copies of books containing Ojibwa hymns were circulating in the western Lake Superior and Mississippi headwaters region. Yet because these printed hymn texts remained largely phonetic documents of a practice that was rooted in the oral tradition, the question of their actual impact begs further inquiry.[18]

Music as Negotiation: The Uses of Hymn-Singing in the 1880s

From the outset, *anishinaabe* people sang hymns with enthusiasm. Documents of the 1830s, 1840s, and 1850s make frequent reference to the fervor with which Ojibwa people incorporated hymns into their repertory of song, and missionaries did what they could to discipline the singing.[19] Yet a formalized tradition of hymn-singing did not appear until the late 1870s and early 1880s, two decades that brought radically changed circumstances to the newly created White Earth reservation. Examining how hymn-singing practice emerged in response to these new circumstances takes us to the heart of the matter.

In the first third of the nineteenth century, when a still viable fur trade hinged on native cooperation, and when extended Ojibwa families could move relatively freely about the land for their seasonal subsistence, Ojibwa communities were notably able to set the terms of their cultural exchange with missionaries.[20] In this climate, hymns took their place rather casually in the larger musical repertory. The sharing and learning of new songs, after all, had long been a currency of Ojibwa social relations with other peoples.[21]

Beginning in the 1850s, though, the final collapse of the fur trade and a series of treaties shifted the balance between natives and Ojibwas decisively.[22] In 1867, a new reservation was created in what had been a no-man's land between the Ojibwa and their Dakota neighbors. Because White Earth was rich in timber, lakes, and prairie, it was touted as a show-case for the assimilation programs of U.S. Indian reform policy.[23] Education, land policy, treaty payments, almsgiving, even naming practices were all orchestrated at White Earth to dismember the communal structures of *anishinaabe* life and to reengineer a society on the basis of individual responsibility, private property, and agriculture.

Life at White Earth disoriented the thousands who moved there. As speculators and timber interests steadily seized the land base out from under them, *anishinaabe* were cornered into a precarious reliance on treaty annuities. Material want put the people at the mercy of outside interests. Previously independent bands were squeezed into one political unit. A more pronounced class system emerged, as existing social distinctions of age, kin, region, and ethnicity became of greater consequence in the competition for survival and favor.[24] Meanwhile, Indian agents, businessmen, and missionaries capitalized on these distinctions, playing one group off another in their own competition for *anishinaabe* land, timber, and souls. Much of the dispossession of these years was brokered from within, by those who oriented themselves quickly to the values of the market and the accumulation of wealth.[25]

After ten short years, optimism for the White Earth experiment crashed on the rocks of alcoholism, epidemic tuberculosis, smallpox, and violence. Missionary correspondence from these early years at White Earth bespoke the unrelenting presence of death. In 1880, the superintendent of Episcopalian missions observed that the native village of White Earth had buried hundreds of its own in six years while the neighboring White community of Richwood had not endured a single death.[26] Against the backdrop of this chaos, missionaries began to remark on a more formal tradition of Ojibwa hymn-singing at White Earth. Here, at what added up to a large-scale refugee camp, hymn-singing developed from a casual practice into something that seemed to do important cultural work.

By the early 1870s, the Episcopalian mission under Bishop Whipple succeeded in bringing nine young White Earth men into the ministry as deacons. Unlike previous mission efforts, this native leadership attracted many *anishinaabeg* at White Earth to participate in the life of a growing community of *anamiajig*, "those who pray." With the deacons as their backbone, the Episcopalian *anamiajig* came to exercise considerable autonomy in their own affairs.[27] While they took part in the public activities of the mission, it is clear that the community came most fully to life beyond the circle of mission influence, in gatherings held almost nightly in the one-room shacks of their own people. Along with prayers, speeches of mutual encouragement, and the sharing of food and re- sources, the singing of Ojibwa hymns is what the *anamiajig* did in these candle-lit gatherings.[28]

A more formalized practice of hymn-singing at White Earth appears to have grown around two key elders, a woman named Suzanna Roy and a man named Shay-day-ence. Shay-day-ence had been a respected leader of the *midéwiwin* ceremonial complex, a keeper of medicinal knowledge, oral tribal history, and hundreds of songs that brought the more powerful forces of life to bear on the affairs of the people. At Gull Lake, Shay-day- ence reportedly led the opposition to the mission. Once removed to White Earth, though, Shay-day-ence evidently spent some years drinking, and later followed his son, one of the deacons, into the *anamiajig* com- munity.[29] In the eleven years before his death, Shay-day-ence distin- guished himself as a full-time Christian holy man, "the real, recognized leader of the Christian community as he had before been of the hea- then."[30] Shay-day-ence was so "thoroughly saturated" with religion, Archdeacon J. A. Gilfillan remarked, that his "whole talk and [his] whole thought is about [it]."[31]

Shay-day-ence led a group of thirty young men from "house to house," "singing Chippewa hymns, and praying and exhorting each other" in the Christian life.[32] This visiting became a kind of vocation for them as they sang three or more nights each week. They also took their songs to the sickbeds, deathbeds, and gravesites of the community, often singing until dawn.[33] At about the same time, a group of women gathered around Suzanna Roy, one of the first native women baptized Episcopalian at Gull Lake. They met weekly to "do crafts, encourage one another in good works, to watch over the young and . . . to make their homes like Chris- tian homes."[34] By 1875, a number of these bands of women had come under the "spiritual charge" of several native women.[35] As was true for the young men, hymns set the tone for each of these activities.

By the mid-1880s, the practice of singing had become noticeably uni- form in the devotional meetings led by those so-called Singing and Pray- ing Bands, or guilds. According to one account,

> In all these meetings the method of procedure is the same; meet about nightfall, begin with singing a Chippewa hymn, then prayer, then another hymn, then the leader names the one who is to speak after he or she sits down—another hymn, then another speaker is named and so on until nine or ten o'clock. The singers are appointed who shall select and start the

hymns, generally young people. The speakers are nearly all middle aged or elderly men or women. There is never any excitement nor extravagance . . . but solemnity. . . . In these meetings they seem to find most of their joy—they have not other parties nor meetings but only those connected with religion.[36]

Men and women of the guilds were committed to adapting *anishinaabe* ways to the growing sphere of American society. They brought to other *anishinaabe* communities their message of contained social change, enough to respond to changing circumstances of survival without compromising basic *anishinaabe* values. They provided crucial support to nascent mission churches on the Red Lake and Leech Lake reservations. Bishop Whipple observed that Shay-day-ence's well-dressed singers had "done much to break up old heathen dances and gambling." Of course, their music itself was a significant departure from cultural precedent. Conspicuously absent from the hymns was the beat of the drum, deeply resonant with collective identity and spiritual power in Ojibwa thought.[37] Neither did hymn-singing involve dancing, another practice integral to much ceremonial music-making. Though hymns did not lie entirely outside the Ojibwa semantic field attached to the power of music, they were distinguishable in function from certain dream songs and *midéwiwin* songs, which were believed to effect direct change in the world of experience.[38] Hymn tunes were largely of European origin, though transformed in Ojibwa performance. The hymn's textuality stood in marked contrast to *anishinaabe* songs, which stressed repetition, brevity, and haiku-like allusions to powerful dreams.[39]

To be sure, the changes brought by these guilds and the music they sang generated tensions between Singing and Praying Bands and other White Earth *anishinaabeg*.[40] Indeed, many at White Earth chose active, even militant, resistance to all incursions of Christian teachings, songs, and practices as part of their own strategy for survival.[41] Nevertheless, amidst the chaos of the 1880s, the life of the *anamiajig* can be understood as a resourceful attempt to forge a new kind of community around the more fundamental of *anishinaabe* values. The hymn-singing that set the tone at every significant moment in the life of the *anamiajig* collective can be understood as the musical medium through which the paradoxes and possibilities of their new life were articulated and negotiated. To explain, allow me to return our attention to accounts of devotional meetings. Again, the social frame of reference is as important as the details of performance, if not more so.

Those who rose to talk in the pauses between hymns had the right to speak their mind about anything. "Recit[ing] their experiences . . . and their struggles, trials, falls and risings up again," the *anamiajig* spoke as often about temporal matters as spiritual ones.[42] One might have needed to borrow the deacon's ox to plow his vegetable garden; another might have needed an elder to look after an ill child while she went off to set nets for fish. A feast during each meeting provided the entire community with at least one meal per day, and resources were pooled for the use of all.[43] Out of scant treaty annuities, the singers raised a fund to "assist those in distress," or at least to guarantee a decent burial for those who could not endure.[44] While some at White Earth were getting ahead by adopting market-oriented values and looking out for their own, the *anamiajig* reaffirmed their allegiance to the well-being of the collective.[45]

Hymn-singing also set the tone for a pronounced effort on the part of the *anamiajig* to move beyond the factionalism that crippled White Earth. In 1881, for example, the Young Men's Singing and Praying Band told Bishop Whipple it had tried with some success to bring feuding chiefs together in order to "have one mind."[46] If single-mindedness or consensus had underwritten *anishinaabe* survival for millennia, it was the singers who seemed most intent on continuing to bring such consensus about.[47] And while the extensive travels of these Singing and Praying Bands to other *anishinaabe* communities on the Red Lake and Leech Lake reservations appeared to missionaries as driven by raw evangelical zeal, the details suggest that the *anamiajig* had insight into the mechanisms tearing their communities asunder. Spreading a not unfamiliar gospel of collective survival, their message and music emphasized the Christian and *anishinaabe* values of peace-making, self-sacrifice, generosity, and mutual nurture.

As a seasonal subsistence off the land became less viable, as disease and relocation radically undermined whatever social stability had been secured in the late years of the fur trade, the *anamiajig* of the evening guild meetings were picking up the pieces and fashioning a new life at White Earth. Hymns were the music that accompanied this new life, that set its tone and established its rhythms. When hymns were raised, if the singers were of one mind, the music itself realized in sound the communal values for which they struggled. As Thomas Turino observed in the slums of Lima, "During special moments, culturally specific rhythms and forms of movement are not merely semiotic expressions of community and identity . . . they become their actual realization."[48]

Like other students of the place of art in culture, Turino has observed that music has a curious ability to communicate that which exhausts other forms of expression. Where everyday speech breaks down, Turino writes, music is capable of articulating "the complexity and tensions of history and of life itself."[49] For the *anamiajig* of the 1880s, the music of the hymns was perhaps alone capable of this "symbolic work," making room for a viable life that preserved some of the core values of a people.

MUSIC AS REMEMBERING THE DISMEMBERED: CONTEMPORARY USES OF HYMN-SINGING

A century later, the context of life at White Earth is very different, and consequently, the uses to which hymn singing has been put are different as well.[50] After a hundred years of dispossession, the native community at White Earth today owns fewer than 7 percent of the reservation's land base, and three-fifths of the enrollees have sought a living elsewhere. Despite optimistic projections of casino income, landlessness, unemployment, and poverty are still the norm. White Earth still endures deep internal divisions—a factionalism supporting and supported by larger structures of U.S. economic and political oppression. Sadly, untimely death also remains a part of life at White Earth.[51] Whether caused by suicide, homicide, alcohol, diabetes, or cancer, most deaths are deeply sedimented with a politics of history. Indeed, one could justly call each a death by dismemberment, since land theft, policies of assimilation, subversion of indigenous social structures, and the loss of a loved one are widely experienced as different faces of the same protean reality of colonization.[52]

Displayed on the kitchen walls of several Ojibwa homes I visited is a xeroxed transcript of a message delivered by a respected spiritual man, who diagnosed the social ills this way:

> We need to realize who we are and what we stand for. . . . We need to be as one again! We need to work again for the common good of all of us! We the *anishinaabeg* are the human beings of this land. . . . We are the keepers of that which the Great Spirit has given to us. . . . If it is to be destroyed, only we can do it, by turning our backs on our language, our culture, our traditional drums and our religion. Never allow them to forget the injustices. . . . And, always my friends, remember the suffering of our *anishinaabeg*.[53]

Though the White Earth Ojibwa Singers might view "the traditional" in slightly broader terms, they share this elder's diagnosis: the community suffers from dismemberment understood both in social terms ("we need to be as one again") and in spiritual terms of alienation from its true identity as *anishinaabe* ("we need to realize who we are and what we stand for . . . the *anishinaabeg* are the human beings of this land"). For the White Earth Singers, survival against the odds hinges on a remembering of language, culture, and identity. The story of their formation as a singing group in the first place testifies to their commitment to help White Earth remember.

Beginning in 1983, a handful of concerned elders gathered Thursday evenings to bring hymn-singing back to their community. While the elders could recall hymns performed at the wakes and prayer meetings of their youth, and while singing groups were operative in other reservation communities, there had been no organized singing at White Earth village for some time. Importantly, they did not simply start singing. Most had to learn the songs anew, with the aid of a cassette recording of singers from a nearby reservation. Within a few years, seventeen gathered regularly. Some still spoke Ojibwa fluently. Others had grown up with the language but were schooled and shamed out of its daily use. Some had lived their entire lives on the reservation. Others had spent years away, serving in the armed forces, working on railroads and in timber camps, or making ends meet in the cities. Wherever they had been, at this juncture, these women and men were coming into their roles as elders of a needy community. Singing hymns became a rallying point around which a core group of elders would coalesce to assume local leadership, albeit unofficial, in White Earth village. When they thought it was time to take a stand against a proposed casino, a number of these elders were twice arrested for civil disobedience at the construction site. With time, they came to perform at a variety of occasions, including graduations, protest meetings, and events of cultural sharing, but their songs are most powerfully encountered as a music of mourning, a prominent presence in many if not most of White Earth's wakes.[54]

One man has counted the memorial cards from over two hundred wakes he has performed with the White Earth Singers since 1983. For those who bury someone every other week, no one wake stands alone, but takes place along a continuum of wakes held that month and that year. With so many wakes, so many moments of potential forgetting, the White Earth Singers are keenly aware of the high stakes of their work. They sing to help a family remember a lost loved one. They also sing to help the people as a whole remember who they are, to reflect on where they come from, and to take stock of where they are going as a community. For this reason, wakes are among the most public events at White Earth.

Ojibwa hymn-singing recollects the lives of previous generations of singers and their capacity to endure the contradictions of life under colonialism.[55] Ojibwa poet Larry Cloud Morgan likens hymn-singers to a chorus of Greek drama, entering the scene at watershed moments to lift onlookers above the absurdity of the moment to view the larger contexts of suffering. Cloud Morgan also likens the hymns to a shroud, tucked around the dead regardless of merit or life circumstances, and taking up the fragments of their brokenness into the enduring dignity of being *anishinaabeg*, a dignity earned through the suffering and survival of the *anishinaabeg* of centuries past.[56]

While hymn-singing helps remember a powerful past, it is also a re-membering, oriented toward future survival, transforming relationships in the present and working toward social change. The hymns accomplish this not so much through *what* they remember as through *how* they remember, for hymns do not function in experience as ordinary texts. In fact, because so few people speak the language fluently, the texts are beyond the lexical comprehension of most who attend the wakes.[57] The no less powerful meanings emerge more subtly from the language itself and the values associated with its sounds. Precisely because Ojibwa hymns say nothing in particular, they are all the better equipped to prompt a host of varied, even conflicting, associations of an *anishinaabe* past. This way, they can integrate different ways of imagining identity in the common experience of singing, listening, and remembering.[58]

Ojibwa hymns can do this symbolic work because fundamentally they are *music*. Though I will not explore the musical terrain in detail here, I do want to point out that music, more than other forms of expression, is capable of holding the contradictions of life in suspension.[59] Moreover, as music, hymns do not simply stand for an idealized *anishinaabe* way of life. When ritualized in performance, they begin to effect that ideal. Aesthetics of performance intone the ethical priorities of the community, among them humility and the priority of community well-being over self-interest. Unalloyed human voices chant the syllables in common. No virtuoso voice stands out to command attention. Indeed, what singers might lack in terms of virtuosity makes little difference to those who hear the moral example of the singers' lives as much as they hear the sounds of the singers' voices.

Paul Connerton has observed that communities tend to remember their most cherished values in ritual practices—things done rather than things said. He argues that embodied ritual action, such as gestures, dance, music-making, and liturgical settings of texts, help societies remember because these forms of expression, being more diffuse, "contain a measure of insurance against the process of cumulative questioning" prompted by more propositional, more discursive forms of expression.[60] The musicality and liturgical operation of language enable Ojibwa hymn-singing to articulate a workable agreement on what constitutes the collective past without establishing any particular interpretation of that past as normative. In this act of remembering, conventional boundaries that distinguish, for example, Christians from ardent non-Christians, are shown to be quite permeable.

Of course, there is a doubleness to this process, for memory is also an arena where meanings are contested. For some, the memories evoked by the hymns are unequivocally those of the colonization of land and mind. For example, when one Ojibwa man heard the White Earth elders sing hymns at a ceremony honoring a new drum, he whispered to me, "That's just not right." He thought the presence of such "Christian" music was disrespectful to the drum, a symbol resonant with spiritual identity. Hymns were simply inconsistent with his own evolving *anish-*

inaabe identity.[61] On the other end of the spectrum, some exclusively Christian Ojibwa people oppose any mingling of hymnody with unchristian elements. In 1993 the bishop's committee and priest of White Earth's Episcopal parish affirmed hymn singing in Ojibwa, but ruled out any ceremonial practices associated with the *midéwiwin* tradition at wakes using the church building.[62] For the White Earth Singers (most of whom are life-long members of that parish), however, the incense of smoldering sage, quiet offerings of tobacco, pipe ceremonies, and other music in the repertory set to the drum are entirely consistent with, if not constitutive of, the life of singing hymns.

Hymns serve to articulate social boundaries even as they attempt to bridge them. But it is important to remember that the lines along which contention builds are complicated and shifting—more elusive than might be dispensed with in such blunt categories as Christian and traditional, young and old, or urban and rural. Many of those Ojibwas who stake out their identity in opposition to Christianity nonetheless maintain deep respect for the Ojibwa singers and their music. As was true for the guilds of a century ago, hymn-singing today is not just about the sound object. But the symbolic work that contemporary hymn-singing performs is that of musically and ritually generating a shared experience of an agreed-upon Ojibwa past.

CONCLUSION: TOWARD A LOGIC OF HYMN-SINGING PRACTICE

How it is that hymnody, intended as it was to root out the indianness of native peoples, has become an emblem of distinctiveness and the stuff of survival for so many Ojibwa people today? Of course, to consider this a puzzling question at all is to assume a deep-seated myth that deems native peoples authentically *Indian* only to the extent that they exhibit precontact, non-Christian, "traditional" culture.[63] Nonetheless, posing the question can be illuminating if framed in terms of Bourdieu's understanding of the distinctive "logic of practice." Even as we strive to make sense of a practice, we must recognize that practices are immersed in life's shifting demands and oriented toward practical concerns of survival. In practice, as Bourdieu observes, "no more logic is mobilized than is required by the needs of practice."[64] Indeed, Bourdieu thinks this illogical logic is why practice can do what it does. Analysts may find their interpretations frustrated by this logic, but people get by in this world precisely because, to quote Bourdieu again, "practice exists on the hitherside of discourse." Perhaps it is appropriate that one of my field journal entries reads, "Long live the difficulties of my project!"

So how might we characterize a logic of hymn-singing practice? What distinguishes the logic of hymn-singing in the 1880s from that of its revitalization in the 1980s? First recall that the initial years at White Earth posed unprecedented social and ecological demands on those forced to settle there in close proximity. Survival had always involved "making do," but the early years at White Earth pushed *anishinaabe* resourcefulness to its limits. For food, clothing, and shelter, many simply had to seek the protection of the well-connected Episcopalian mission. And at least some figures like Shay-day-ence came to the conclusion that new forms, both social and spiritual, were needed to ensure that more fundamental *anishinaabe* values remained viable.

But the singers of the 1880s did not simply adopt the hymns that missionaries promoted. In practice, they transformed evangelical hymns into something wholly other. This may seem a commonplace observation, but it appears in its fuller complexity in light of Catherine Bell's use of the term ritualization. By thinking in terms of a process of ritualization rather than ritual, Bell is able to get at the strategic ways in which ritual agents take otherwise mundane activities, set them apart through schemes of ritualized time and space, and suffuse them with a surplus of meanings such that what is established within the ritualized frame can "order, rectify or transform" other "nonritualized situations to render them more coherent with the values of the ritualizing schemes."[65] And while few of the singers would think of their performances as being of the same order as a pipe ceremony or the Eucharist, Bell's notion of ritualization opens up interpretive language to span the "more or lessness" of the hymns' ritual intensity in different performance contexts.

Bell's work on ritualization is particularly helpful for the light it sheds on how practices promoted in colonial contexts can function, paradoxically, as redemptive for dominated groups even while they effectively bring unequal power relations into being.[66] After Kenelm Burridge, Bell calls this "redemptive hegemony" in an attempt to show the intersection between accommodation and resistance, between structure and agency in ritual practices.

Bell's understanding of ritualized practice here relies on Bourdieu's idea of the *habitus* as the set of dispositions or "regulated improvisation" by which a structured and structuring process occurs. "Objectively regulated and regular without being in any way the product of obedience to rules," the practices of the *habitus* can be seen as "collectively orchestrated without being the product of the organizing action of the conductor."[67] The conjunctural site of the *habitus* does not represent the internalization of structures that are in any real sense "out there," but rather accounts for the play within the momentum of historical and social regulation in which human agents can effectively improvise on their world. Bourdieu continues: "this infinite yet strictly limited generative capacity is difficult to understand only so long as one remains locked in the usual antinomies . . . of determinism and freedom, conditioning and creativity, consciousness and the unconscious, or the individual and society."[68] One could add accommodation and resistance to the list of antinomies that fade in the logic of practice. It is the analyst, equipped with the writing, recording, and abundant time necessary to practice theory, who "wins the privilege of totalization" by which accommodation and resistance might be made separable.[69]

The social conditions of the difficult early years at White Earth were such that symbolic accommodation was tantamount to survival. Amid the poverty, social chaos, and dispossession of land, missionaries and agency officials succeeded in discouraging many *anishinaabeg* from the drumming, dancing, and feasting that were such central practices of communal identity. In terms of structure, the new music of hymn-singing worked its way more thoroughly into Ojibwa lives than had been the case prior to the reservation period. Wittingly or not, those who sang hymns were playing into this devaluation of Ojibwa tradition.[70] They participated, with varying levels of commitment, in the public life of the mission, singing Ojibwa hymns in church on Sunday morning. But neither missionaries nor the *anamiajig* would say that hymns were simply forced on a victimized people.

In terms of agency, the *anamiajig* did not simply accommodate to the hymn. The *anamiajig* stylized performance so as to make the hymns their own. They took the hymn outside the mission's circle of influence, ritualizing singing in the autonomous spaces of the people's tar paper shacks. Ritualized singing came to be associated with particular groups of singers and their way of life; it also became associated with particular occasions—devotional meetings and wakes—and associated with particular sequences and aesthetics of performance. Viewed from above, singing hymns involved both accommodation and resistance. But at eye level, on the complex cultural field of practice, hymn-singing so to speak involved neither.

I do not mean to imply that this ritualization happened entirely at the level of conscious intent. Such a line of thought underestimates the depth of religious experience and overlooks the distinctive logic of practice. As an alternative, we might entertain Bell's and Bourdieu's notions that humans are socially equipped with a set of senses beyond the standard five, including a sense of ritual or a sense of the sacred. In a logic of practice, this sense of the sacred, like the sense of direction, does not operate circuitously in the intellect. It acts more directly, seizing opportunities where they are to be had in the interest of making do.

It seems to me that an acute "sense of the sacred" was what brought the *anamiajig* to invest themselves so deeply in the music of the hymn. Imbued with Ojibwa understandings of the concept and function of music, hymn-singing in the 1880s became a viable way to evoke the more deeply felt *anishinaabe* values in sound and to engender in evening hymn-sings the solidarity necessary for survival. Under strained circumstances, survival may have depended on such spiritual boundary crossings. While this represents only one among various spiritual alternatives chosen in response to colonization, for those who did embrace the hymns, the practice of singing and the practice of community—musical sound and social unity—were part and parcel of one another.

A century later, in the little guild halls that bear the names of early singers, another group of White Earth elders have found power and purpose in the hymns. Again, in light of Bell's stress on the agency of ritualization, these elders may be understood as more than mere mouthpieces for some "Ojibwa Mind" and its timeless traditions. They are historically situated people diagnosing community needs and equipped to draw on resources of ritual to address them. At the wakes, hymn-singing has evolved to become generative of power when despair would otherwise reign.

Central to the effect of ritualization is how meanings are played off one another. The singers' ritualization of memory ensures that memory is not simply a product of recall but a process of evaluating what is worth remembering. Rather than simply recollecting the dispossession of missions history, the singers call forth the integrity of those past generations of Ojibwa singers who made meaning and made do amid the structures of dispossession. The discernment of their ritualized memory is spatially evident in the example of a wake for a young man who had been shot in the chest at a wedding reception in Minneapolis, the victim of a gang hit. The second night of his wake was held at White Earth, in the Rock Memorial Guild Hall, a small building adjacent to Breck Memorial Episcopal Church. It is named for Reuben Rock, a lay church leader of this century, and for the guilds that I have characterized as the social matrices within which Ojibwa singing developed. More than one hundred people of all religious stripes, including the White Earth Singers, gathered for the young man's wake and attended the last viewing of the body on the morning of the burial. But when the bell rang next door for the funeral service, at most thirty-five people actually went into the church. Most mourners, including some of the close relatives, stood outside and visited together quietly as they awaited the procession to the cemetery. No more than ten yards apart, the guild hall and the church, the wake and the funeral, might as well have been separated by miles in terms of their associations.[71] Though the wake and funeral shared the same Ojibwa hymnal, the songs at the morning funeral did not carry the resonance they did when sung by the elders the previous night, a testimony to the power of ritualization.

Landlessness, disease, and division still tax the community's capacity to make a living. But survival at White Earth today hinges not so much on spiritual boundary crossing as on a discerning process of remembering: invoking the language, values, and cultural ballast necessary to negotiate the modern world. While Ojibwa singing has worked its ministry differently in the 1880s and a century later, in both cases the practice has been about survival.

I wish to conclude with a story that I think appropriately reflects on the practice of studying practices. On a number of long drives in northern Minnesota, I have had a chance to visit at length with one of the original White Earth Singers. As I have found to be the case with other elders, the man has seemed taken aback whenever I pose direct questions about hymn-singing as such. Any questions I aim toward the meanings or recent history of hymn-singing have been redirected to other topics—in part, no doubt, as an expression of resistance to my line of inquiry. Yet because we speak rather frankly about my research agenda and because he seems to have taken my education under his wing, I don't think his measured responses are solely a function of mistrust.

I think it has something to do with the nature of hymn-singing. Talk about hymns can, at any moment, flow into talk about the high number of wakes in the past month, the young neighbor who shot herself, or the young man whose head was struck with a tire iron after a party. Talk may just as easily pass over to stories of throwing prickly wild cucumbers at other kids in the early days, or of where on the reservation the maple sap has started to run.

Such connections speak to a web of life in which practices, hymn-singing being but one, are inextricably related in lived experience. These connections remind those of us in the business of theorizing that our inquiries place boundaries around phenomena that are otherwise seamlessly woven into all of life. When we study practices like Ojibwa hymn-singing, we consequently must not overlook the wild cucumbers.

NOTES

I would like to thank the following people at White Earth: Charlie Aiken, Marge and Lowell Bellanger, Josephine Degroat, Sylvia Gale, Charles Hanks Jr., Margaret Hanks, Juanita Jackson, Dan Kier, Marge MacDonald, Jack Potter, and Ethelbert Vanwert. Larry Cloud Morgan and Erma Vizenor in particular have set high standards for responsible teaching and scholarship. If I have anything right, it is because of their patient instruction and support. I am also deeply indebted to my academic teachers, David Hall, Bill Hutchison, Inés Talamantez, and Christopher Vecsey. Comments on previous drafts by Ann Braude, Rebecca Kneale Gould, R. Marie Griffith, Larry Gross, Steve Holmes, Joel Martin, James Treat, and members of Harvard's New World Colloquium have been helpful, as has the generous assistance of Minnesota Historical Society staff. Each has taken a risk on me, though none save myself is responsible for any errors or oversights that remain. Field research and writing were made possible through the generous support of the Mellon Foundation, the Roothbert Fund, and the Louisville Institute for the Study of Protestantism and American Culture.

1. The Ojibwa (pronounced Ojibway, also Chippewa or *anishinaabe*) nation was historically a loose congeries of bands pursuing a seasonal subsistence in the Upper Great Lakes region. A common language, ritual complex, and clan system linked the seasonally migrating bands. According to the 1990 census, there are 106,000 Ojibwa people in the United States. Seven Ojibwa reservations are found in the woods, lakes, bogs, and prairies of northern Minnesota, but roughly half the enrolled population lives off the reservation.

2. Henry Benjamin Whipple, in *Minnesota Missionary* 4, no. 10 (July 1881): 5.

3. In addition to this particular tradition of hymnody, which has historic ties to the Episcopalian mission, a distinctively Catholic hymnody obtained at White Earth until about a generation ago. There is also some singing in Ojibwa at area Missionary Alliance, Lutheran, and Pentecostal congregations, though to a quite different effect.

4. Because it has been dismissed as a music of acculturation, native hymnody has attracted little research. When pioneering ethnomusicologist Frances Densmore issued her multivolume *Chippewa Music* early in this century, she omitted mention of hymns altogether, even though she acknowledged the crucial encouragement of two native Episcopalian clergymen, Charles Wright and Edward Kah-O-Sed, the latter having compiled the *Ojibwa Hymnal* in use to this day. The idea of Christian hymns, whatever the language, seemed merely to suggest acculturated Ojibwa life. I am nonetheless indebted to a number of studies of native hymnody. See esp. Beverley Cavanagh, "The Transmission of Algonkian Indian Hymns: Between Orality and Literacy," in *Musical Canada: Words and Music Honouring Helmut Kallmann*, ed. John Beckwith and Frederick Hall (Toronto: University of Toronto Press, 1988); Gertrude Kurath, "Catholic Hymns of Michigan Indians," *Anthropological Quarterly* 30 (April 1957): 31–44; Richard J. Preston, "Transformations musicales et culturelles chez les cris de l'est," *Recherches Amérindiennes au Québec* 4 (1985): 19–29; Lynn Whidden, "Ethnic Series: Cree Hymnody as Traditional Song," *The Hymn* 40 (July 1989): 21–25. For discussions of native hymn texts, see David E. Draper, "*Abba isht tuluwa*: The Christian Hymns of the Mississippi Choctaw," *American Indian Culture and Research Journal* 6 (1982): 43–61; J. Vincent Higginson, "Hymnody in the American Indian Missions," *Papers of the Hymn Society* 18 (New York, 1954); Thomas McElwain, "Rainbow Will Carry Me: The Language of Seneca Iroquois Christianity as Reflected in Hymns," in *Religion in Native North America*, ed. Christopher Vecsey (Moscow: University of Idaho Press, 1990), 83–103; and Willard Rhodes, "The Christian Hymnology of the North American Indians," in *Men and Cultures: Selected Papers of the Fifth International Congress of Anthropological and Ethnological Sciences*, ed. Anthony F. C. Wallace (Philadelphia: University of Pennsylvania Press, 1960), 324–31.

5. For Pierre Bourdieu, see esp. *Language and Symbolic Power*, trans. Gino Raymond and Matthew Adamson (Cambridge, Mass.: Harvard University Press,

1991). Given the fragmentary record of his intellectual life as a political prisoner, Gramsci's contribution is more difficult to isolate. See, e.g., *An Antonio Gramsci Reader: Selected Writings 1916–1935*, ed. David Forgacs (New York: Schocken, 1988). I have benefited greatly from two applications of this theoretical framework. See John and Jean Comaroff, *Of Revelation and Revolution: Christianity, Colonialism, and Consciousness in South Africa*, vol. 1 (Chicago: University of Chicago Press, 1991); and Thomas Turino, *Moving away from Silence* (Chicago: University of Chicago Press, 1993).

6. Erma Vizenor, conversation, July 1994.

7. By speaking of the tradition as bricolage, I do not want to water down the violence involved in Ojibwa culture change under colonization and missionization. My perspective draws on a number of rather unrelated sources: Wilfred Cantwell Smith's understanding of religious traditions in *The Meaning and End of Religion* (Minneapolis, Minn.: Fortress, 1962), Pierre Bourdieu's *Outline of a Theory of Practice*, trans. Richard Nice (New York: Cambridge University Press, 1990 [1977]), and Michel de Certeau's *The Practice of Everyday Life*, trans. Stephen Rendall (Berkeley: University of California Press, 1984).

8. The women and men who comprise the White Earth Singers today number from seven to fourteen. Several younger singers in their thirties and forties accompany them and provide transportation—a valuable resource in a rural community with few reliable cars and licensed drivers. Most of the White Earth Singers were raised as Episcopalians, though several are Roman Catholic. Each would consider himself or herself to be a "traditional person" who values the spiritual life and who tries to put into practice a communal ethic of simple living, generosity, and respect for the land. Most, but not all, grew up with Ojibwa as either their first or second language. Many were students at government boarding schools, where Ojibwa was discouraged, if not prohibited.

9. The term "elder" is not so much a designation of biological age as one of social stature. In *anishinaabe* tradition, authority has been widely dispersed among circles of elders, whose collective wisdom guaranteed prudent direction for the community. As participants in wider American society and as subjects of "quasi-sovereign" tribal governments constituted under act of Congress, contemporary Ojibwa communities experience considerable tension between the more centralized structures of official decision making and the diffuse leadership of elders.

10. I ought to add here as a methodological note that my time "in the field," like Thoreau's year at Walden, was often graced with my mother's generous cooking and laundering. Because going "to the field" for me meant simultaneously "coming home" to Minnesota, my investments and allegiances in this project are complicated in generative ways.

11. Turino, *Moving away from Silence*, 241.

12. William Boutwell to Samuel Pond, March 22, 1839, Grace Lee Nute Manuscripts Relating to Northwest Missions, box 6, Minnesota Historical Society (henceforth MHS).

13. See Susan Tamke, *Make a Joyful Noise unto the Lord: Hymns as a Reflection of Victorian Social Attitudes* (Athens: Ohio University Press, 1978).

14. Mrs. Howland, *The Infant School Manual*, 8th ed. (Worcester, Mass., 1835), 25.

15. Peter Jones, *Nahkahnoonun kanahnahkahmoowaudt ekewh ahueshenah-paigk anahmeahchik* . . . (New York, 1829). Jones' first printed translations appeared two years earlier in the back of a Mohawk hymnal, entitled *A Collection of Hymns* (New York, 1827). For a detailed biography, see Donald B. Smith, *Sacred Feathers: The Reverend Peter Jones Kahkewaquonaby and the Mississauga Indians* (Toronto: University of Toronto Press, 1987).

16. On evangelical Episcopalians, see Diana Hochstedt Butler, *Standing against the Whirlwind: Evangelical Episcopalians in Nineteenth-Century America* (New York: Oxford University Press, 1995).

17. For the publication history of nineteenth-century Ojibwa texts, see James Constantine Pilling, *Bibliography of the Algonquian Languages* (Washington, D.C.: U.S. Government Printing Office, 1891). Catholic Ojibwa hymns first appeared in print in 1837, translated by a Slovenian priest named Frederic Baraga. Baraga's popular hymns were expanded and reissued several times throughout the century.

18. For an excellent discussion of how native hymnody bridged the gap between spoken and written word, see Beverley Cavanagh, "The Transmission of Algonkian Indian Hymns: Between Orality and Literacy," in *Musical Canada: Words and Music Honouring Helmut Kallmann*, ed. John Beckwith and Frederick Hall (Toronto, 1988).

19. Mission outposts recruited musically trained teachers to organize choirs and to accompany the hymns with organ and piano. An Oberlin College-based mission even started a "singing school" in the 1840s, as part of a movement to use simplified musical notation to train undisciplined singing into more uniform, regular hymnody.

20. For a good discussion of the nature of symbolic exchange, see Richard White, *The Middle Ground: Indians, Empires, and Republics in the Great Lakes Region 1650–1815* (New York: Cambridge University Press, 1991).

21. "If an Indian visits another reservation," Densmore observed in 1910, "one of the first questions asked on his return is: 'what new songs did you learn?' " Frances Densmore, *Chippewa Music II*, Bureau of American Ethnology, Bulletin 53 (1913): 2. The sharing of songs was also a currency of ceremonial exchange and innovation. When the spiritual and military movement led by Tecumseh and his brother, the Shawnee Prophet, was brought to the Lake Superior Ojibwas, new songs and dances were integral parts of the message. See William W. Warren, *History of the Ojibway People* (St. Paul: Minnesota Historical Society Press, 1984 [1885]), 321–22. See also Gregory Evans Dowd, *A Spirited Resistance: The North American Indian Struggle for Unity, 1745–1815* (Baltimore, Md.: Johns Hopkins University Press, 1992).

22. Treaties of 1837, 1842, and 1847 ceded the northern third of Wisconsin and central Minnesota. Treaties of 1854, 1855, 1863, and 1866 ceded the northern half of Minnesota. See Elizabeth Ebbott, *Indians in Minnesota*, 4th ed. (Minneapolis: University of Minnesota Press, 1985 [1971]).

23. On U.S. assimilation policy, see Francis Prucha, *American Indian Policy in*

Crisis: Christian Reformers and the Indian, 1865–1900 (Norman: University of Oklahoma Press, 1976); and Robert Mardock, *The Reformers and the American Indian* (Columbia: University of Missouri Press, 1971).

24. For an insightful study of these social processes in the Muskogeean context, see Joel Martin, *Sacred Revolt: The Muskogees' Struggle for a New World* (Boston: Beacon, 1991).

25. See Melissa Meyer's detailed treatment of ethnicity and dispossession in *The White Earth Tragedy* (Lincoln: University of Nebraska Press, 1994).

26. J. A. Gilfillan, untitled typescript, 1880, J. A. Gilfillan Papers, MHS.

27. Enough anyway to fluster the White archdeacon in charge of the station. Joseph A. Gilfillan considered it his duty to safeguard the theological integrity and discipline of "his" native deacons. Tensions came to a head in 1882, when Gilfillan found the native clergy had met in council and launched a strike, refusing to hold services until he be removed from his position as superintendent and they receive a living wage. Gilfillan remained in office, but the deacons tripled their wages. Again, in 1886, Enmegabowh and the native deacons issued "a call to throw overboard all white people connected with the [Episcopal] mission." J. A. Gilfillan, "Indian Notes," *Minnesota Missionary* 1, no. 12 (September 1878); J. A. Gilfillan to H. B. Whipple, July 19, 1886, Whipple Papers, box 15, MHS.

28. The white Episcopalian priest at nearby Leech Lake, also a target of the 1882 strike, voiced concern that nightly Ojibwa prayer meetings were eclipsing public "Prayerbook worship" in importance. Edwin Benedict to H. B. Whipple, September 26, 1881, Whipple Papers, box 15, MHS.

29. J. A. Gilfillan noted that Shay-day-ence, while still an active *midéwiwin* leader in the 1850s, wished his son to be "learned in all the learning of the Egyptians" that he might have "all the knowledge of the Whites, as well as of the Indian." J. A. Gilfillan, "Some Indians I have Known," *The Red Man* (December, n.d.): 152–55.

30. Henry B. Whipple, "Indian Notes," *Minnesota Missionary* 10, no. 1 (January 1886).

31. J. A. Gilfillan to H. B. Whipple, n.d., Whipple Papers, box 1, MHS.

32. Shay-day-ence via J. A. Gilfillan to H. B. Whipple, November 23, 1875, Whipple Papers, box 11, MHS.

33. "Indian Notes," *Minnesota Missionary* 3, no. 7 (April 1880): 2; "Indian Notes," *Minnesota Missionary* 4, no. 9 (June 1881).

34. H. B. Whipple, in *Minnesota Missionary* 4, no. 10 (July 1881): 5. In the 1880s, an Episcopalian missionary named Sybil Carter established an extensive lace-making industry around the women's guilds. For an account, see Pauline Colby, *Reminiscences*, MHS.

35. J. A. Gilfillan to H. B. Whipple, December 3, 1875, Whipple Papers, box 11, MHS. The names of the spiritual leaders, "Cornelia Boardman, Mrs. Alex Roy, Mrs. Maendjiwena, Kakabishigwe, [and] Emma Whitefisher," interestingly encompass both English, Anglicized Ojibwa, and Ojibwa baptismal names. These gatherings of song, prayer, worship, and collective craft-making developed into a tradition of women's auxiliary that became central to communities. "Our women look forward to these gatherings," observed a missionary to the neighboring Leech Lake reservation, "as the chief social event of the week. . . . Frequently

some women will rise and make an address and this always has the respectful attention of the other women." Pauline Colby, *Reminiscences* (1891), MHS.

36. J. A. Gilfillan, "Indian Notes," *Minnesota Missionary* 10, no. 5 (May
1886). Another visitor remarked, "one present at their meetings would think that
John Wesley or his followers had been there." "Notes from the Indian Field,"
Minnesota Missionary 6, no. 6 (March 1881).

At nearby Onigum on Leech Lake, a similar devotional movement under lay
leadership met every evening except Tuesday for "singing, prayer, and mutual
encouragement in the Christian life." Here, all assembled, both women and men,
took part under the "spiritual charge" of two lay elders, Kegiosh and Susan
Bongo, the children of an Ojibwa mother and a runaway African slave who lived
as an *anishinaabe* and became a prominent trader. The male leader, Kegiosh, always spoke first to the gatherings where congregants "confess[ed] sins to one
another and are healed." "Notes from the Indian Field," *Minnesota Missionary* 4,
no. 6 (March 1881).

37. It is not enough to think of the drum as secondary accompaniment to
song. The Ojibwa language distinguishes grammatically between animate and in-
animate objects, and genders *dewe'igan*, or drum, as animate. A drum is not so
much an object as a subject, a powerful "person" deserving of an elaborate code
of respect. See Thomas Vennum Jr., *Ojibwa Dance Drum: Its History and Construction* (Washington, D.C.: Smithsonian Institution Press, 1982).

38. On Ojibwa music, see Frances Densmore, *Chippewa Music*, Smithsonian
Bureau of American Ethnology, Bulletins 45, 53 (1910, 1913); Thomas Vennum
Jr., "A History of Ojibwa Song Form," in Charlotte Heth, *Selected Reports in
Ethnomusicology* 3, no. 2 (1980): 43–75; Beverley Diamond, M. Sam Cronk,
and Franziska von Rosen, *Visions of Sound: Musical Instruments of First Nations
Communities in Northeastern America* (Chicago: University of Chicago Press,
1994).

39. While it is plausible that nineteenth-century Ojibwas set hymns to indigenous tunes, Minnesota missionaries wrote of no unfamiliar tunes in the historical
record. Frederick Burton, who visited Ontario's Garden River Ojibwa community
in the first decade of this century, offers the first ethnomusicologically inclined
account of Ojibwa hymnody. Burton wrote that while he first thought he heard
"Christian words to an ancient Ojibway tune," he later realized that the singers'
performance had "cover[ed] and disguise[d]" a "civilized melody" with the
"mannerisms . . . characteristic of ancient Ojibwa song." See Frederick Burton,
American Primitive Music, with especial attention to the Songs of the Ojibways
(New York: Moffat, Yard, and Co., 1909). Today's singers do, however, speak
about some hymns having been set to certain "old Indian tunes."

Despite their textuality, Ojibwa hymns do embrace many of the language conventions of other Ojibwa music. While translations follow the basic contours of
the Christian originals, they are markedly understated, relying like other Ojibwa
songs on brevity, allusion, and word-pictures to articulate the unspeakable myster-
ies they saw in, for example, the narratives of Jesus' suffering and passion.

40. In August 1879, fewer than one-fourth of the "full blood" population
were communicants in the Episcopalian Church. "A Work among the Indians,"
Spirit of Missions (August 1879).

41. For a survey of Ojibwa resistance to Christianity, see Christopher Vecsey, *Traditional Ojibwa Religion and Its Historical Changes* (Philadelphia, Pa.: American Philosophical Society, 1983), 45ff. Taking resistance as the baseline, Vecsey attributes the growth of an Ojibwa Christian community to the fact that White Earth was "controlled territory, subject to the autocratic rule of missionaries." "The Ojibwas," continues Vecsey, "were a defeated, captive audience to the Christian message." Ibid., 50.

42. "Notes from the Indian Field," *Minnesota Missionary* 4, no. 6 (March 1881).

43. Note that feasting and giveaways were common practices targeted by assimilation policy as pillars of communal values to be discouraged and even declared illegal.

44. Taycumigizhig via J. A. Gilfillan to H. B. Whipple, June 23, 1884, Whipple Papers, box 16, MHS.

45. Again, I refer to Melissa Meyer's *The White Earth Tragedy*, in which she discusses ethnicity at White Earth in terms of economic orientation. She charts the basic differences between those oriented toward collective subsistence off the land and those oriented toward the market and interested in the accumulation of wealth. This seems to me a very useful starting point for understanding social distinctions, far more accurate in the White Earth case than blunter determinants of ethnicity such as blood, language, culture, or even religion.

46. "What We Did in this Year," unsigned fragment, June 6, 1881, Whipple Papers, box 15, MHS.

47. The young men's guild also took it upon itself to chart a new course for the entire community. "We would be very glad if you could tell us the ways and rules of your White Society," they asked Whipple. "Let them write us about what we ought to do that our society may be in better order." Committee of Majigizhig via Henry Selkrig to H. B. Whipple, August 14, 1881, Whipple Papers, box 15, MHS. Of course, the *anamiajig* were not free of divisions in their own ranks. But the few correspondences that document their affairs often ring with calls for Bishop Whipple's involvement to settle the differences, "so that we can work in harmony for the prosperity of the church." Majigizhig "for and by desire of the young men's association" to H. B. Whipple, Whipple Papers, box 16, MHS.

48. Turino, *Moving away from Silence*, p. 111.

49. Ibid., 99.

50. By passing over a century, I don't mean to imply that hymn-singing at White Earth had died out completely. Prayer meetings and hymn-singing remained staple practices of community survival, though commanding little attention in written sources. As Indian policy following World War II promoted the migration of native people away to available jobs in cities like Minneapolis and Chicago, Episcopalian officials lamented the loss of the more active members of the mission parishes. "Annual Report on Indian Mission Work for 1956," Protestant Episcopal Church, Diocese of Minnesota Papers, box 70, MHS.

51. In the early 1980s, more than a third of deaths in Native America took people before they reached their mid-forties, compared to 12 percent among the population as a whole. Data for 1980–1982, U.S. Congress, Office of Technology

Assessment, *Indian Health Care*, OTA-H-290 (Washington, D.C.: U.S. Government Printing Office, April 1986), 19.

52. Even when the wake is for someone who lived to a ripe old age, the community's capacity to remember is challenged by the politics of history, for such elders are likely to be among the few who held the privilege of Ojibwa as a first language, who told the stories, and who knew firsthand how "the old people did things."

53. "Words of Wisdom," ca. 1985.

54. In each case, according to Erma Vizenor, the music they make is really a different thing altogether, depending on the context and spirit of the gathering.

55. A number of different contradictions seem to present themselves at contemporary wakes. People speak of belonging to the land and yet the land no longer belongs to them. They speak of a strong commitment to standing up for the land and are yet frustrated by a lack of political and economic power to do so. They maintain a deep respect for life and are yet faced with frequent reminders of how life can be wasted.

56. Larry Cloud Morgan, conversations, January 1993, July 1991. Concerning memory, the hymns' overt Christian content cannot be overlooked. For those fluent in the language, or who nevertheless understand the Ojibwa Christian emphasis on the theme of sacrifice, the hymn texts remember the powerful stories of Jesus' paradigmatic suffering, stories that in their own right confer a larger meaning on struggle and pain in the present day. Consider, for example, that the word used for "salvation," *bimaadjiiwewin*, is closely related to *bimaadiziwin*, an Ojibwa term loosely translated as "life" but rich in associations with the circularity of all existence, implying an aesthetic beauty and basic goodness to the perpetual motion of natural cycles and a moral virtue to that activity that contributes to the fullness of that circulating life. This is in marked contrast to the manifest content of the evangelical texts, which call for a radical conversion from a state of nature to a state of grace. For a discussion of such translation issues in missions history, see Lamin Sanneh, *Translating the Message* (Maryknoll, N.Y.: Orbis Books, 1992). On the Ojibwa language, see John D. Nichols and Early Nyholm, *A Concise Dictionary of Minnesota Ojibwe* (Minneapolis: University of Minnesota Press, 1995); and Frederic Baraga, *A Dictionary of the Ojibway Language* (St. Paul: Minnesota Historical Society Press, 1992 [1878]).

57. According to one study, fewer than thirty Ojibwa people in Minnesota, aged thirty-five and under, speak the language fluently. See White Earth Land Recovery Project, Occasional Report, 1994.

58. There is a politics to the sound of this language. In light of the concerted effort to stamp out the language and culture—or of the more subtle effort to "folklorize" them—the spoken word is resistance. Larry Cloud Morgan observes that to think or speak in Ojibwa is to enter a wholly different way of organizing experience and valuing people and land. For those who share his fluency, engaging that worldview can be subversive to the drift of modern American values. A single word can evoke deep-seated allegiances to the land and the people of the land that transcend civil laws and compel political action even against slim odds.

59. Turino observes that music "combines many signs with varied and even conflicting significance . . . into a unified whole." Where everyday speech breaks

down, music is capable of articulating "the complexity and tensions of history and of life itself." Turino, *Moving away from Silence*, 111.

60. Paul Connerton, *How Societies Remember* (New York: Cambridge University Press, 1991), 102.

61. Ironically, the ceremony was a presentation of the drum in question to the safekeeping and discretionary use of the White Earth Ojibwa Singers. They certainly do not confuse the repertories of the hymns and drum songs, but the fact that they do keep a drum is instructive of how these musics traverse conventional boundaries.

62. Episcopal Church Newsletter, June 1993.

63. See James Treat's introduction to *Native and Christian: Indigenous Voices on Religious Identity in the U.S. and Canada*, ed. James Treat (New York: Routledge, 1995).

64. Bourdieu, *Outline of a Theory of Practice*, 109.

65. Bell, *Ritual Theory, Ritual Practice*, 107–8. Roland Delattre's distinction between articulation and expression in regards to ritual is extremely useful. "To speak of ritual as an expression . . . tends artificially to separate form and content. It is to look for the meaning . . . in something else which it expresses. . . . Ritual does not merely express a humanity and reality otherwise constituted, but is itself creative and constitutive of humanity and of wider realities insofar as we are engaged with them." Roland Delattre, "Ritual Resourcefulness and Cultural Pluralism," *Soundings* 61 (1978): 285.

66. Bourdieu elaborates on the structured and structuring *habitus* as a "bodily hexis," an embodied site, where structure and agency conspire, in several books. See *Outline of a Theory of Practice*, 78–95; *The Logic of Practice*, trans. Richard Nice (Palo Alto, Calif.: Stanford University Press, 1990 [1980]), 52–65. Talal Asad reminds us that it was not Bourdieu who termed this bodily province the *habitus*, but Marcel Mauss in an essay entitled "Techniques of the Body." See Asad, *Genealogies of Religion* (Baltimore, Md.: Johns Hopkins University Press, 1993), 75.

67. Bourdieu, *The Logic of Practice*, 53. Bourdieu refers to the *habitus* as "embodied history," since what appears as objective reality is the inherited field of possibilities that history and social relations places on human agency. The structures do not exist outside culture and history, but are structured in time through the dispositions of the *habitus*.

68. Ibid., 55.

69. Bourdieu, *Outline of a Theory of Practice*, 106.

70. Interestingly, however, missionaries were often deeply frustrated with what they viewed as the frequent "backsliding" among their Ojibwa converts.

71. The wake itself is a field of action charged with a politics of missions history. While missionaries often protested the social causes of death (Indian Office corruption and greedy whiskey traders), they seldom hesitated to make hay of untimely deaths as their most "teachable moments." A Red Lake Ojibwa man put it well: "When we come [to the mission], we are often told that we are within a step of the grave. This is not pleasant to us." Sela Wright to American Missionary Association, March 6, 1854, in *American Missionary* 8 (1854): 59.

Likewise, missionaries struggled perennially to set the terms of their participation in the funerals of Ojibwa people, trying to contain what they saw as inappropriate excesses in Ojibwa mourning custom (wailing, dancing, drumming, and feasting). Even as late as the 1950s, issues surrounding wakes arose often enough to occupy the regional staff meetings of Episcopalian clergy, some of whom were themselves native. The clergy resolved to take more time "to instruct people on the Church's teaching and custom concerning funerals," again centering around issues of "excess." They expressed concern about the implications of open caskets given a statute outlawing the serving of food in proximity to dead bodies. Also problematic was the continued practice of giving lengthy burial addresses, which the clergy agreed to condone only "if short and to the point." At the extreme, a Catholic priest serving Pine Point village in the 1960s refused to allow wakes in his parish altogether. "Digests of Indian Field Staff Meetings," July 20, 1953, September 23, 1958, February 16, 1960, Protestant Episcopal Church, Diocese of Minnesota Papers, box 70, MHS.

SUBMISSIVE WIVES, WOUNDED DAUGHTERS, AND FEMALE SOLDIERS: PRAYER AND CHRISTIAN WOMANHOOD IN WOMEN'S AGLOW FELLOWSHIP

R. MARIE GRIFFITH

DOROTHY was a young wife and the mother of two preschool boys in 1965, when she found herself wishing that her husband Elmer "could be someone different." "Overnight, by some quirk in my mental osmosis," she later wrote, "I became obsessed with the thought that my healthy, happy, needed-to-be-changed-in-my-sight husband was going to die." Believing her vision represented "a revelation from God," Dorothy began spending most of her time alone, brooding over her husband's imminent death. She "withdrew" from all social activities, "making excuses against participating in any endeavor that would take me from the house." She closed the drapes in her home to avoid visits from neighbors and was in bed by nine every night "to dwell undisturbed in my other world." She went so far in her preoccupation as to plan the details of Elmer's funeral service, "even to the hymns that would be sung." Yet she concealed her thoughts so well that Elmer "had no idea anything was wrong with me." Later describing this time as one of great illness in which she "subconsciously" wished for her husband to die, Dorothy noted emphatically, "Oh, God, how sick I was!"

Eventually, Dorothy broke her long isolation by confiding in a friend, who told her that her thoughts represented a delusion from Satan. Realizing that she "had been deceived" and that "God would [n]ever work in this way," Dorothy prayed. "As I prayed," Dorothy explained, "I realized the depth of that deception. The truth was, I wanted my husband more than I wanted anything else, whether he changed or not." She "gladly . . . renounced Satan and his lies and his hold on my life," then confessed everything to Elmer. Elmer's response to Dorothy's confession affirmed the rightness of her decision, for he became "a man I had never seen before. He had every right to slap me in the face but instead he took me in his arms. With tears streaming down his face he whispered, 'Honey, all I care about is that you get well.'" Dorothy began to recuperate from what she later called her "mental illness" by returning to the Bible and praying regularly for healing from her fear and guilt. After a few weeks, she felt Jesus speak to her the words of Luke 8:48: "Daughter, be of good comfort: thy faith hath made thee whole; go in peace." Surrendering herself to those words, she experienced release from the guilt and pain that had plagued her for so long.

Ten years later, Dorothy testified in print to the changes that occurred in her life following her confession and surrender:

> My life has been so utterly transformed that I can't find words to express it. My husband, who showed me his real strength the night he forgave me, became the man I had always longed for when I began to appreciate him. I had longed for a husband who would be my spiritual head; I have him. I had longed for a man who would counsel me spiritually rather than I, him; I've been blessed with one. I had longed for a husband who could pray down the power of God with believing prayer; I stand amazed now when I see Elmer's faith.

Finally in total submission both to God and to her husband, Dorothy felt herself to be healed from her terrible sickness and to be living a new life of joyous certainty and peace. In 1975, when her story was published in *Aglow* magazine, Dorothy was praying "constantly," thanking God for her "wonderful man" and for the friend who was "bold enough" to confront her with the fact of her delusion.[1]

Jerry grew up with an alcoholic, emotionally distant father. According to her account, printed in *Aglow* in 1974, she felt hostile toward him from a very young age and continued to resent him throughout much of her adult life, as his drinking worsened considerably. In 1971, when Jerry learned her father had cancer, she and her husband postponed their long-awaited vacation to visit him just prior to his major surgery; as she later testified, however, "I went to him, not from love, but because he was old, alone, and it was my duty." Seeing the care he would need following surgery, Jerry reluctantly moved her father close to her home and resigned as youth director at her church. Throughout his radiation therapy, he continued to drink every day, while Jerry bitterly contemplated the sacrifices she had made in her life for this man she did not love.

As her unhappiness increased, Jerry discussed the situation with her doctor and then her pastor, who told her she must rid herself of the hostilities in her life so that she "could be the effective Christian God wanted [her] to be." The minister prayed with her but she still felt despondent and burdened, not knowing "where to leave those hostilities." She began to pray daily that God would remove her bitterness toward her father and give her "a clean heart." She asked forgiveness for her disgust with her father's drunkenness and pleaded with God to help her love him as he was. On the fifth day of praying these forlorn prayers, she began to feel "totally immersed in God's love from the head to toe"; suddenly, "cleansing tears" flowed down her cheeks as she "began to laugh and praise the Lord." Surrendering herself to this unexpected, consoling experience of "such peace and love," she felt freed from her anger, "able to love freely and reach out for love."

From that time on, Jerry wrote, her obligation to her father became "a joy." As he lost strength, she "grew to love him so much." Shortly before he died, her father took her hand and for the first time said to her the words she had longed for all her life: "Jerry, honey, I love you." She told him she loved him too and, released from her anger and the suffering it had brought her, Jerry reportedly continued to feel the joyous inner peace that came to her during prayer. Jerry concluded her story: "It was a gift from God that I will always treasure, but a gift He could only give after He had taken away the hostilities in my heart."[2]

Dorothy and Jerry crafted their narratives for an audience consisting of participants in Women's Aglow Fellowship International, an organization that emerged out of the Full Gospel Business Men's Fellowship in 1967 as an interdenominational group "where those coming into the charismatic renewal could meet to pray, fellowship, and listen to the testimonies of other Christian women."[3] Known first as the Full Gospel Women's Fellowship, the group adhered to a twofold purpose, combining evangelization of non-Christian women with encouragement for Christian women perceived as starving from the so-called deadness of American mainline churches.[4] Although Aglow was originally a small, local fellowship based in Seattle, Washington, it grew quickly and steadily into an extensive national organization. In 1969, the group's leaders began publishing a newsletter, *Aglow*, which would eventually turn into a glossy magazine with over 75,000 subscribers. The magazine's growth, in turn, stimulated the global expansion of the fellowship itself, which has continued to spread across the United States and throughout much of the world into the 1990s.[5]

In the early days, as now, testimony and prayer were central devotional practices within the Aglow organization, enacted at local gatherings and worship services as well as transmitted in stories published in *Aglow* magazine and other printed texts. Whether experienced in public settings as oral communication or privately as written literature, both testimony and prayer provided women with means for sharing their everyday experiences—the sorrows as well as the successes—and for learning coping strategies from one another. Both in magazine articles and in local monthly fellowship meetings, Aglow members described their trials as wives and mothers, testifying to the misery of a life without Jesus and to the joy and peace received through prayer and complete surrender to God's will. Such stories were not simply or primarily confessional; rather, they were told in hopes that other women would find relief and truth in them, by feeling their own needs expressed in another woman's narrative and envisioning solutions to their own crises based on the lessons of the victorious narrator.

The stories of Dorothy and Jerry provide a useful point of departure for examining Aglow narratives and the devotional practices such narratives describe. Like so many other women in Aglow, these authors had experienced crises within their families and were struggling to love in the face of intense disappointment, frustration, and anger. In each case, the woman was challenged by other Christians to pray for release, and through prayer experienced, first, a change in her own attitude and, second, a change in her circumstances that eradicated the suffering. Surrendering to God, these stories proclaim, leads to freedom from depression, guilt, and hostility; submission brings victory.

Such stories begin to illuminate the complex meanings embedded in notions of "home" and "family" and the ways in which evangelical women who participate in Aglow have used prayer to alleviate the conflicts and contradictions that arise within their households. Incorporating powerful themes both from the broader evangelical culture and from contemporary therapeutic idioms, narratives like those of Dorothy and Jerry explicitly counsel their female audience to surrender their wills to God and to submit themselves to God's hierarchy of earthly representatives, particularly clergymen and husbands. According to narrative conventions, domestic unhappiness stems largely from stubborn willfulness, so that healing can only occur when the wife pliantly consents to obey her husband and allows him to reign as the leader of the home. While further analysis of the stories reveals multiple possibilities for reinterpreting and even subverting the doctrine of submission to women's own ends, it remains the case that most stories in this genre prescribe an exceptionally conservative model of traditional gender roles.

Examined over a much longer range and trajectory of narratives, however, these stories also open to us a medium for perceiving significant shifts over time in Aglow's teachings about women, submission, and power. Stories like that of Dorothy in particular recall other stories from Aglow texts printed in the 1970s, yet they differ in substantial ways from many stories printed from the mid-1980s on, when a perceptibly wider range of options around female submission and power gradually emerged. In order to unfold these shifting notions of Christian womanhood, this essay explores the range of meanings that Aglow women attach to female submission and surrender, historical changes in these meanings along with challenges to former attitudes, and the strategic uses of such meanings in reworking family relationships and responsibilities. Prayer, the turning point in Aglow stories, marks the moment when all attempts to assert control over the conditions in one's family life are willingly dissolved in favor of sacrificial obedience. In this way, prayer works as a kind of axis for the fashioning of practical Christian womanhood, enabling religious identity to be formed and reformed even as domestic life is presumably transformed as well.

"The Man I'd Always Longed For"

Many Aglow stories invoke the theme of marital disappointment, describing in explicit detail the authors' frustrations as wives. Like the women interviewed in studies conducted by sociologists Mirra Komarovsky and Lillian Rubin, and the survey respondents in the Kelly Longitudinal Study analyzed by historian Elaine Tyler May, women in Aglow have often expressed dissatisfaction with their husbands and have spent much time and effort sharing advice for dealing with difficult home lives.[6] Aglow magazines and books are filled with stories from women articulating lives of domestic pain, described variously in terms of abuse, neglect, lack of love, or simply boredom. Fantasies of suicide and divorce abound and are richly elaborated, as the authors tell of falling into bleak despair and of longing to escape through death. Only after reaching this final point of grim desperation is the path to healing revealed, a path that begins with a prayer of surrender and ends with a joyful commitment to wifely submission.[7]

While few evangelical women express fantasies about their husbands' deaths in terms as explicit as Dorothy's, her story is typical in the meanings she draws from her situation and in the messages she conveys about coping with an unhappy home life. Like Dorothy, writers typically describe domestic misery in terms of both sickness and sin, construing their despair as caused by Satan but deepened by their own acquiescence to it. Their lives feel isolated and they fail at their wifely roles because they wish for their husbands to be, in Dorothy's words, "someone different." In order to be healed, then, they must repent of their error and realize the "deception" behind it, taking full responsibility for their unhappiness and accepting their husbands without expecting them to change. Giving up all hopes or expectations of marital satisfaction and simply accepting the duties bestowed by their supposedly God-given role of wife as helpmeet, these women describe the pleasant surprise of discovering the greater happiness that is the reward for this sacrificial obedience, some finding their husbands to be "the man I had always longed for." Two more stories will help illustrate this process as it is typically described in Aglow literature.

Mary, deeply disappointed in her marriage, was planning a divorce from her unappreciative husband, Cal, who frequently snapped at her with such cutting remarks as "Can't you ever be happy?" and "Just once I'd like to have a meal on time." Miserable and near despair, Mary asked Jesus to come into her heart, forgive her sins, and be the master of her life. Grimly, she prayed: "If you don't do it there's no point in going on with life. You aren't getting any bargain, but if you can use me, here I am." Shortly afterward she was baptized in the Holy Spirit and seemingly miraculous changes began occurring in all areas of her life, most significantly in her marriage:

> A few weeks later when again Cal said, "Where's lunch?" I began screaming and then stopped midway and prayed, "Jesus, I'm losing my temper, I'm sorry. Forgive me and help me." Once again Cal came in at noon and said, "Where's lunch?" I felt the old anger starting to rise in my body. I clenched my jaws shut so I wouldn't cry out. I prayed, "I'm losing it again, Jesus. Forgive me and help me." No bitter words came out and the anger backed down and disappeared. I was able to say later, "Cal, I've irritated you by not having your lunch ready. I'm sorry." He was amazed. From that time on we began to grow in love for each other and for Jesus until now, five years later, we are able to minister to others.

As Mary learned to surrender her anger to Jesus and submit herself lovingly to her husband, she writes, her misery dissolved and, without any apparent changes in Cal, her bleak marriage was transformed. As she felt herself filled to overflowing with the loving warmth and comfort of the Holy Spirit, the domestic tasks that once made her life feel like drudgery became "a joy."[8]

Donna, who once felt lost and disconsolate in her marriage, recalled that earlier period as her own "state of rebellion." Her bitter conclusion at the time, however, was that she "had married the wrong man. At least that was a good excuse for my being in such a mess." Resentful of her husband's constant changes in career plans, she began criticizing Doug and telling him what to do. "I felt my ministry was to constantly let my husband know how backslidden he was, how unspiritually-minded he was, and that I was doing all I could to hang on in the hope that some day he would wake up and see the light." From Doug's point of view, she later realized, she was not being "a help-meet for his needs": "Unaware of my position as a wife I thought God had made me a leader and that my husband was not making a very good follower."

Finally, after God reprimanded her, Donna says she realized that she needed to surrender to Jesus. When she did, she later wrote, "it seemed a lot of the blame I had put on my husband for things just disappeared. God completed the healing he had begun in our marriage." Her lesson for her readers is to follow her example in submitting themselves to God and husband:

> You may never be able to change your circumstances. If you have five children, you have five children. If your husband is a doctor, your husband is a doctor. If your husband works as a plumber, that is his job. Quit saying, "If my circumstances were only different, then I know God could use me." But begin to pray, "Jesus, help me to allow You to use me in the circumstances in which You have seen fit to place me."

Accepting the circumstances of one's life, even the aspects that seem least appealing, and then striving to fulfill one's God-given roles within those circumstances: these steps constitute the presumed recipe for a happy life, supplying the means for achieving contentment in the midst of daily struggles.[9]

The stories of Mary and Donna, like that of Dorothy, assure their readers that good results will follow a wife's willing acquiescence: once women's attitudes are transformed and they accept their submissive role, their husbands also become happier and more benevolent, reflecting the benevolence of God. Importantly, such stories are indicative of the ways personal power may be encoded in the doctrine of submission, as the women center their narratives on their own capacity to initiate personal healing and cultivate domestic harmony. While not viewed as essential to the woman's healing, changes in a husband's behavior furnish added confirmation that such a healing has indeed taken place. For instance, the fact that Dorothy's husband actually wept when she told him of her illness is highly significant to her story. Rather than slapping her in the face, as she says he had "every right" to do, Elmer embraced her lovingly and expressed his concern that she be healed. Likewise, Mary's husband, Cal, responded to her newfound submission with love and appreciation, and Donna's husband, Doug, was transformed even as she was. Such changes, these writers assert, occurred in large part as the result of the decisive actions of the wives.

These narratives are meant to convince *Aglow* readers of the sincerity of the husbands' love for their wives and the assurance of their manly protection; as Dorothy writes of Elmer, he "showed me his real strength the night he forgave me." Such husbands represent the ideal Christian man, upholding the image of a loving Father God: strong yet gentle, a dynamic leader who is unafraid to express tender feeling, stern and rugged in his righteousness yet willing to forgive and to respond in benevolence. Dorothy, Mary, and Donna are in submission to their husbands' authority, but that authority, like Jesus', is depicted as compassionate and wise, never dominating or cruelly oppressive. Submit to your husband, the authors instruct their readers, and you, too, will discover the man you've always longed for, his seeming harshness softened by your willing obedience to his demands.

This message may be reassuring to women whose husbands are Spirit-filled Christian men, holding a similarly benevolent perspective on male authority, but for women whose husbands are "unsaved" or "backslidden," as is often the case, exhortations to wifely submission may be more ambivalently received. This problem has been repeatedly addressed in the Aglow literature as a common dilemma. In 1974, an anonymous writer, her own "heart ach[ing]" as the wife of an "unbeliever," offered this somewhat gloomy advice:

> Sometimes a Christian wife is under bondage in her home. It is not her own to do with as she pleases. In God's divine order, the wife is placed under the authority and direction of the husband whether he is saved or not. If he does not wish her to accept visits from her minister or have church meetings there, then according to Scripture, she should abide by his wishes. . . . At times you may feel that you can't bear another week, another month—and you will be right; you can't. However, you can live for today and this is all that you are asked to do.

Urging her readers to do all they can to love and serve their husbands, she concludes with great hopefulness that "[T]he Christian wife, by her trust, her prayers, her life and her love, can loose the Holy Spirit and the grace of God to do a special work in her husband's life."[10]

This lesson of submitting to one's non-Christian husband, in hopes that he will eventually be saved through the good example of his wife, is extended frequently in Aglow literature into a lesson on surrendering more fully to God. Another anonymous wife of an unsaved husband articulated this dynamic in poignant terms: "Each time Ralph has failed me, I have grown closer to the Lord and have learned to love my husband more." Over the years, she says, she has learned to be patient and to await God's plan for her husband, who—she is certain—will someday be saved.

> At first I prayed for my husband's salvation; now I simply and gratefully thank God for it. . . . Often I get specific in my prayers concerning events I want my husband to attend, things I'd like him to read, facts I want him to hear. But I have learned not to be disappointed if these prayers are not answered the way I want them to be. God knows more about it than I do.

Acknowledging the continuing temptation to despair, she notes:

> Sometimes even now circumstances seem so bad that I can't pray. During these times, the Lord has taught me to say, "Lord, I don't understand. I'm weary, but Your Word says You'll never fail me or forsake me, so it's up to You, Father." As soon as I start to pray in this way in difficult times, peace comes over me. I know He understands and I can wait for Ralph's salvation with the assurance that everything is under control.

The only option for dealing with an unsaved husband in these Aglow stories is cheerful submission to his will in mundane things, construed as an act of surrender to God's will. When the will of God and the will of the husband conflict, as they inevitably do, the wife must simply trust that her necessary obedience to her husband enables God to deal directly and swiftly with him.[11] In other words, as a male fundamentalist minister put it, "[S]ubmission is the wife learning to duck, so God can hit the husband."[12]

Informing these doctrines of male authority and female submission, as Dorothy and other Aglow women describe them, are meanings attached to the ideals of home and family, meanings formed out of desire for the pleasure and security that these ideals so invitingly promise. The significance of the family in American evangelical culture, long analyzed by historians of American religion, has been helpfully illuminated in anthropologist Carol Greenhouse's description of one community's understanding of the family as representing not simply "a set of relationships (as anthropologists might see the family, for example)" but rather "a set of interlocking roles, or identities."[13] The essential goal for individuals holding this view of family life is to perfect the various roles expected of them—wife, mother, daughter, sister, husband, father, son, brother—and then to feel those roles as authentic and natural. She concludes that "family life, while all-important as a model for society itself, is also crucial to the cultural formation of individuals by isolating them within relationships over which they believe they have no control."[14]

What such a conceptualization of the family means, as Greenhouse observes, is that family harmony hinges on the expectation that each member will perform his or her God-ordained role properly, accepting and following the prescriptions that each role carries within it. When conflict arises, the purported solution is the restoration of proper, rule-governed behavior. Like other groups rooted historically and socially in Pentecostal, fundamentalist, or evangelical culture, Women's Aglow has always idealized the family and, like Greenhouse's community, has taught that the antidote to family disharmony is renewed clarification of precisely defined roles.[15] Thus, even as Aglow stories and prayers have been filled with references to the pain of marriage, motherhood, and domestic life generally, they emphasize how such pain may be healed through a submissive and disciplined commitment to what is perceived as true Christian womanhood. The stories recounted here suggest a context in which women describe neglectful parents, distant husbands, and delinquent children, but whose relationships are eventually transformed and made whole because of a woman's submissive behavior. Yet it is evident from these accounts that the family continues to be a source of great suffering; no family manages fully to live up to the expectations and ideals promoted by the popular idealization of the "Christian home."

In her important study of evangelical family life, sociologist Judith Stacey examines the complexities and often unacknowledged contradictions within the "widespread nostalgia for eroding family forms" currently prominent in many varieties of political and religious conservatism. Her research, which uncovers the ordinariness and frequency of divorce behind the rhetoric upholding the "traditional family," is suggestive of the negotiations made by those whose own family patterns clash with their religious ideals.[16] As with Stacey's families, the hope of Aglow women and their sisters of creating a perfect family inevitably remains at least partially unrealized. In cases where even moderate domestic happiness seems impossible, an alternative family may be constructed, taking the place of the disappointingly real family at home. Where no loving father is present, there is a protective, nurturing Father in heaven; for those whose husbands are uncommunicative and generally inadequate, God or Jesus may act as the romantic lover-husband, ever faithful and solicitous of His beloved's needs. Books published by Aglow Publications confirm these possibilities, encouraging readers to "experience the nurturing side of God's character" and to become the "chosen bride" of Jesus.[17]

Several Aglow writers have fruitfully utilized a passage from the book of Isaiah: "For your Maker is your husband—the Lord Almighty is his name."[18] Jo Anne, a single mother of two, appeals to her readers' desires for a perfect husband when she writes, "How would you like to be married to a husband who is always faithful, ever concerned for your welfare, who wants only the best for you and who will love you no matter what you do?" Quoting Isaiah, she responds to her own question: "Surprise! The Bible says we've already got exactly that kind of husband. The God of the Universe my Husband! What a mind-blowing idea." Recounting various stories of learning gratefully to accept this notion and to submit to God as her husband, Jo Anne offers other unmarried women the "opportunity" to "take [God] seriously" and to receive Him as the perfect husband.[19]

Another woman, widowed only three weeks at the time she wrote her story, tells of receiving a dozen long-stemmed roses, with a card saying they are from friends.

I hold them in my arms and smell their sweetness. As I lift my face from them, I know without any hesitation or doubt that despite the card, these roses have come from Jesus. He knew I needed such a gift at this precious moment: the type of gift that a man sends a woman, a husband gives a wife. It is just one more way that Jesus has become my husband, one more way He is saying, "I love you."[20]

Having God as a husband does not necessarily preclude having an earthly husband as well, however; as another widow writes after her remarriage: "God said that He would be my husband, revealing Himself to me as the Lord of Hosts, the powerful present One in the time of need . . . but on top of that He sent me a flesh-and-blood husband, Andy."[21] Whether a woman is widowed or divorced, married or remarried, God acts as the perfect husband for her, wisely guiding and protecting her in a perfectly ordered "love relationship."

The characterizations of God as perfect husband closely resemble the heroes of contemporary romance literature analyzed by literary critic Janice Radway in *Reading the Romance*. "Strong and masculine" yet "equally capable of unusual tenderness, gentleness, and concern for [the heroine's] pleasure," the ideal romantic hero for the Smithton readers interviewed by Radway is one who recognizes "deep feelings" of love for the heroine and who realizes that "he could not live without her." Like Radway's readers, who want their hero to be both protector of the heroine and dependent on her love, Aglow women desire their divine hero-husband both to lead and look after them and to be nurtured by the mutually gratifying relationship between them. Following God's commands, doing everything He asks of them and more, flattering Him continually by "just telling Him how wonderful He is and how much we love Him," Aglow women fulfill their visions of perfect love relationships, satisfying their unfulfilled needs for affection, protection, and self-esteem through a perceived marital relationship with God.[22]

In addition to the alternative "marriage" provided by a relationship with God, the Aglow community, acting as "a network of caring women" (the organization's slogan), becomes a kind of surrogate family for the women who participate, at least ideally. Members frequently refer to each other as "my sisters," a common enough appellation in evangelical circles but one with distinctive meanings in the Aglow context. For women who have experienced painful estrangement from their own families, and who have perhaps failed to find fulfillment in recovery groups, a local Aglow fellowship may provide a satisfying form of intimacy, although, as I have observed elsewhere, such closeness may carry the cost of lost privacy or undesired reinterpretation of one's story.[23] More specifically, the organization may allow for the reinvention of one's personal identity, as one joins in a collective process of narrative construction. The relatively recent creation of Aglow "support groups," advertised as providing "safe places" for hurting women, contributes to the sense of Aglow as a refuge within which women share their feelings of pain and frustration and find love.[24] Feeling herself to be in relationship with God, a woman may come to feel a part of the Aglow "family," her felt need for love potentially nourished within the sisterhood offered there.

As women come to feel closely bonded with other Aglow members, conflict may arise in the home. Many women speak of conflicts between their religious lives and their family lives, describing husbands jealous and resentful of the time their wives devote to Aglow activities as well as their new devotion directed toward God and time spent on religious practices such as daily Bible reading and prayer. Women teach each other how to deal with those kinds of pressures: by attending to one's husband more willingly, for instance, and trying to include him and other family members in daily devotions without "forcing" anything on them; or, as one Aglow speaker recommended to her listeners, by staying home from church and "lying in bed" with one's husband on occasional Sunday mornings, making sure he feels cared for and loved.[25] Predictably, however, tensions in this area are not easily resolved. The doctrine of submission, which applies equally whether one's husband is a "Spirit-filled Christian" or not, may in fact increase these tensions, as already suspicious husbands mistrust the motives behind their wives' new and seemingly inexplicable behavior. As Aglow women share strategies with one another, they address these and related concerns about balancing domestic duties with spiritual responsibilities, committing themselves fully to both as they believe God requires.

Praying together helps Aglow women create alternative families and ease the conflicts that may occur when such alternatives supplant one's earthly family at home. Praying aloud before an audience that includes many others dealing with similarly conflicted situations allows the women both to articulate the felt crises of their lives—and perhaps gain sympathy and support from the other women who hear their stories—and to begin to resolve these crises by surrendering their own will and asking God to take control. Perhaps the most important role prayer plays is to turn Aglow women toward accepting the limitations of the family and the need to work unceasingly at improving their capacities as wives and homemakers. Through an intricate and highly ritualized process, guilt and anger are reportedly transformed into surrender and acceptance, and possibilities for redemptive healing emerge.[26]

The Power of Submission

Surrendering one's will to an authority is a vital meaning of submission, but this is not its sole meaning for evangelical women; in fact, submission is in no way a transparent, unidimensional, or static concept but is rather a doctrine with a discernible, fluid history, even in the relatively short time period examined here. Far from being a fixed entity churning out traditional teachings on gender roles, evangelical theology has always been varied, so that even a group as apparently conservative as Aglow contains a broad repertoire of choices and mutable scripts around such ideals as female submission to male authority. While many outsiders might readily assume that conservative Christian women such as those who belong to Aglow are merely participating in their own victimization, internalizing patriarchal ideas about female submission that confirm and increase their sense of personal inferiority, the women themselves claim that the doctrine of submission leads both to freedom and to transformation, as God rewards His obedient daughters by healing their sorrows and easing their pain. Thus interpreted, the doctrine of submission becomes a means of having power over bad situations, including circumstances over which they otherwise may have no control. As close attention to both oral and written narratives suggests, the apparent simplicity of the ideology of submission masks a rich variety of meanings that, once enacted in devotional practice, prove to be more intricate and subtle than they initially seem.

One text that illuminates these intricacies and complicates the notion of submission as passivity or meek subordination is a kind of evangelical self-help book for women, written by Darien B. Cooper, entitled *You Can Be the Wife of a Happy Husband*. First published in 1974, this book is still in print and is used and revered by Aglow women to this day. While teaching submission as "God's role for you as a woman and a wife," Cooper assures her female readers that in becoming submissive wives they will also see changes in their husbands, and that they will find the greatest happiness possible fulfilling their role:

> I believe the role of the wife in the marital relationship is the choice role. . . . Submission never means that your personality, abilities, talents, or individuality are buried, but that they will be channeled to operate to the maximum. . . . Submission never imprisons you. It liberates you, giving you the freedom to be creative under the protection of divinely appointed authority.[27]

Cooper supports this perspective by insisting on women's need for "protection" in a dangerous world, claiming that within this protected sphere women may enjoy the flourishing of their God-given creativity.

According to Cooper, a woman's marital dissatisfaction stems from "preconceived ideas of how her husband should act." She writes, "When he fails to live up to your expectations, you may be hurt, irritated, and disappointed. You and your husband will only be contented and free when you quit setting goals and stop expecting him to be who he is not." Cooper tells women to display pride in their husbands rather than shame, to accept them as they are rather than "ridiculing" or "belittling" them. Instead of trying to manipulate a husband, she advises, "Respond to his leadership in a relaxed manner, and you will find that your husband usually wants to please you." She recounts story after story of women whose wifely submission improved their marriages by bringing their husbands closer to Jesus. The husband will respond lovingly to a submissive attitude, Cooper asserts: "As God's Word fills and controls your heart, you will gain the praise of your man. Wait for it; do not demand it." Throughout her book Cooper enjoins women to "Accept him as he is!"[28]

In Cooper's view, then, submission brings benefits not only or even primarily to the husband, but also and equally to the wife. Submission is not about grimly resigning oneself to a subordinate position but rather is about "freedom." She addresses women's concerns about submission: "Many women are afraid that they will lose their individuality if they subject themselves to their husbands. . . . Paradoxically, only when you submit to God—in any area—do you know the fullest freedom and power."[29] Submission may be about dependency and compliance, but it is not about helplessness, according to Cooper. Of course, the very fact that she feels compelled to make submission seem more palatable for women evidences conflict over the notion, a point to which I will return.

Cooper's book, as I have noted, is widely used among Aglow women, and she continues to speak to Aglow groups around the country on how to have "happy husbands." Her claim—that the doctrine of submission is ultimately beneficial to women—gets added energy from the belief that men's natural passions need to be domesticated and contained; left unchecked, these passions will rage out of control and may cause injury to women. According to Cooper, men's sexual appetites must be satisfied lest they revert to savagery or adultery. She advises her readers to satisfy their husbands sexually and warns, "If you do not fulfill your husband's sexual needs, you may be a stumbling block in his life and cause him to be led away from spiritual truths instead of toward God." She concludes this section: "Your husband will be the happy man you want him to be when he feels that you accept him as he is, admire him for his masculinity, and put him first and foremost (after God) in your life. He will feel needed at home because he knows he is respected as the family leader, provider, and protector."[30] The wife's influence is also her responsibility; it is up to her to see that her man is kept satisfied as well as contained, assuring him of his worth by admiring his virility.[31]

Such advice has long been articulated by antifeminist women, among others, to diverse ends. In *The Power of the Positive Woman*, for instance, antifeminist activist Phyllis Schlafly writes: "A wife must appreciate and admire her husband," observing that the marriage will fail unless "she is willing to give him the appreciation and admiration his manhood craves." Feminist writer Barbara Ehrenreich rightly notes that Schlafly's analysis, here and throughout her spoken and written pronouncements on similar matters, betrays a deeply distrustful and contemptuous image of men as variously weak or monstrous in contrast to women viewed as active and loving.[32] From this perspective, wifely submission is good for wives as well as husbands because it works as a strategy of containment. It is what men need to bolster their fragile egos, and women should ostensibly comply in order to maintain domestic harmony as well as their own security. If done properly, all parties benefit. Thus the author of a 1976 Aglow booklet, *Quiz for Christian Wives*, tells of the healing that took place in her unhappy marriage when she realized the importance of openly admiring the "good qualities" in her husband, Arthur: that is, the qualities for which *he* wanted to be admired, such as his "broad shoulders" and his "big strong hands." "Such a simple little thing," she remarks, was the turning point in their relationship and the beginning of her new life of love and joy.[33]

Nancy, a local Aglow leader whom I asked about wifely submission, repeatedly declared that she was a "former feminist" who had finally learned "to move beyond all that" into God's true purpose for her life. Having realized that feminism was "bad for [her] marriage," Nancy gave up trying to "compete" against her husband and learned to follow the "marriage principles" of wifely submission to male authority. When I pressed her to explain, Nancy brought up the Hollywood movie, *War of the Roses*, as an example of what happens when men and women do not obey God's prescribed roles and persist in doing things their own way: they hate, hurt, and ultimately destroy each other. Nancy's own marriage, in contrast, was allegedly saved when she committed herself to submitting to her husband, a commitment which, she admitted with a chuckle, she did not always manage to keep. In any case, Nancy assured me that her husband had in fact stopped drinking along the way and now made a conscientious effort to ensure that she felt happy and loved, a transformation that she attributed in great part to her obedience to the principle of wifely submission to the husband's authority.[34]

Related to this tactical notion of submission as a means for turning men into happy husbands who then want to please their wives is the notion of what may be termed "sacred housework," wherein surrendering to one's ordained tasks is seen as an act of worship that also leads to greater happiness in the home. This idea is frequently articulated in Aglow literature, as in *Aglow in the Kitchen*, a cookbook for Christian wives. The author of that book writes of being "stunned" when her husband taught her that "cooking and homemaking are ministries *to the Lord*." Recalling the kinds of "homey tasks" that Jesus had performed during His time on earth, she tells of getting the lettuce from the refrigerator, tearing it up for salad, and "talk[ing] to the Lord": "Jesus, thank You for showing me that housework is sacred. Help me to realize while I am cooking and cleaning that I am doing them for You because You are living here and my husband is Your representative." In this way, what was once drudgery is ostensibly transformed into worship, service, and domestic happiness.[35]

When housework is perceived as sacred, it may also become an important source of self-esteem. As a young housewife and mother whose husband was a traveling evangelist, Betty found herself "very dissatisfied" and "depressed." Finally, she was healed from her misery when Jesus gave her a "vision" of her "role in the home as a happy wife and mother." She began to see that if she were happy, her husband and her children would also be happy, a notion that allowed her to begin to see herself as "the 'hub' of the wheel," around which "everything revolves." She notes, "I began to see myself as VERY IMPORTANT to the members of my family." Her concluding words suggest the continuing ambivalence she feels toward this state, along with her hopeful determination to feel good about herself as a housewife: "I know from experience that I will not always be staying at home, but I also know that with God's help I can have that real contentment WHEREVER I AM."[36]

Here again the lesson disseminated is that surrendering to the roles of housewife and mother brings joy to everyone, most significantly to the submissive woman herself. As Betty tells her readers, women find joy and learn that they are "VERY IMPORTANT" when they simply yield to God's expectations of them, transforming housework from a source of boredom and depression into a wellspring of joy and self-esteem. The frequent admissions by Aglow authors that they find such work as cooking and cleaning and running errands mind-numbingly dull show that such a transformation is anything but easy. Still, in their description of submission and surrender as "natural" and in the reminder that other members of the family could not get along without them, the women of Aglow formulate what they perceive as a workable solution to a persistent dilemma, achieving a kind of pride and self-respect in the most mundane tasks.

Once again, the meanings of submission and surrender for these evangelical women prove to represent far more than simple passivity. They are

central notions around which the women of Aglow rework their identities, creatively balancing compliance with strength as they transform
themselves into ideal Christian women. At the same time, submission
holds instrumental value, by containing husbands and thereby regulating
the home, and is capable of being subtly modified or subverted, so that
the women retain a kind of mediated agency through their reliance on the
omnipotent God. Out of a doctrine that could seem to leave them helpless, evangelical women have generated a variety of substantial yet flexible
meanings through which they experience some degree of control, however deflected it may often appear.

The story does not end here, however, as a mere tale of creative acceptance of the doctrine of wifely submission. Since the mid-1980s, discussions of the subject have significantly dropped off in Aglow literature,
more or less quietly. While wifely submission continues to receive scat-
tered mention, the general message has perceptibly shifted toward a notion of modified or "mutual submission." Writers often emphasize that
while the Bible clearly dictates female submission to male authority,
earthly men have not infrequently abused that doctrine to their own selfish ends, rather than accepting their own authority as the kind of Christ-
like responsibility intended by God. The chronological shift in meanings
around wifely submission is most clearly seen in the popular Aglow Bible
study, *God's Daughter*. Written by Aglow staff member Eadie Goodboy
and first published in 1974, this booklet has been widely used by Aglow
participants; by 1991, it had gone through fourteen printings. The tenth
chapter of this text comprises the most comprehensive and sustained examination in Aglow literature of the biblical doctrine of submission, and
the important changes that have taken place in this chapter over time indicate shifting notions of Christian womanhood in Aglow, as in American
evangelicalism at large.[37]

In 1974, this chapter began by emphasizing the difficulty women face
in accepting the doctrine of submission: "The area of submission in the
Christian walk has been widely neglected and ignored. To many women
it may carry threatening overtones. We visualize Jesus as our Shepherd
and ourselves as sheep under His loving care, and we find it easier to
yield to His Lordship spiritually than physically to people in authority
over us." The passage goes on to observe that "our natural tendency is
to confuse submission with servitude, and picture one who is submissive
as downtrodden and abused, a 'doormat.'" Yet, the writer suggests,
the opposite is the case. Just as the sacrifice made by Jesus on the cross
was a "willing" act for the benefit of others, so too should the marriage relationship reflect that same willing self-sacrifice. Thus, "Submis-
siveness is not an outward form or a role of foolish servitude, but an
attitude of the heart."

In this view, woman's particular vulnerability requires protection from man, which is why God places her under the headship of her husband (or, in the case of an unmarried woman, her father). The result is not imprisonment but just the opposite: "Since everything which comes to us from God is meant for our good, we find that coming into an attitude of submission produces freedom. A train is created to run on a track. As long as the train stays on its track, it is free to fulfill that for which it was made. When it jumps the track, chaos results." Rather than participating in the "role-reversal so common in society today," the author concludes, women are to find the vast "service and creativity in our God-ordained roles" as wives, mothers, and homemakers.

In 1985, this chapter was substantially altered. Now, rather than suggesting that teaching submission is like giving medicine to an unwilling child, the author places the idea of submission in the context of previous lessons about the joy of following God's will: "The emphasis of these lessons has been on the subject of yieldedness: letting or allowing the Lordship of Jesus to have total expression through our lives. We have been renewing our minds, unlearning old behavior patterns, tuning in to hear what the Father is saying, studying what He desires, becoming sensitive to sin and to the joy of obedience." She invites readers to "look again at this area of ministry of submission" which, though "often misunderstood or questioned," is the "root of all things spiritual, because it alone takes the proper attitude before God and others." Now, in place of the biblical passages emphasized in the earlier edition, verses are noted in which Jesus spoke of His own total submission to God; rather than turning this immediately into a lesson about wifely submission, moreover, the author points to Jesus' relationship with God as "the pattern for *us* to follow in our personal relationship with God." The chapter then moves into a detailed discussion of humility and of the choice entailed in making this commitment to God, a choice that seemingly has nothing to do with gender but is required of all people, men and women, as children of God.

Finally, the last third of the chapter turns to Ephesians 5:22, the passage about wifely submission that was the centerpiece for the earlier edition of this booklet. The author notes, "This may seem to be a difficult position for some of us who are married women to joyfully agree with, especially in an age when misunderstanding of this verse may have caused some abuse. We need to understand, however, what God desires and how He perceives it." Placing this verse in the context of the larger passage from which it is taken, the author notes that there are various scriptural "counterbalance(s)" to the notion of wifely submission and argues: "[S]ubmission to our husbands does *not* make us 'second class citizens' or those who are ranked 'lower on the totem pole' as lesser beings than the husband. As viewed by God, we have a side-by-side relationship. He looks at us as equally important, but each is designed to function for His glory, in his or her role." Urging a far more limited version of wifely submission to male authority than that earlier affirmed, the chapter ends by asserting that "The entire Christian life is to be a submitted life." Though still affirming gender role differences, this passage has excised the stress on female vulnerability, rebellion, and rigidly defined female roles so central to the original study.

What these different versions suggest is a range of variable notions pertaining to "power" and thus also to "surrender," a range that is confirmed by analysis of the larger literature of Aglow. There is, first, the most immediately apparent meaning of a surrender to God as a way of releasing divine power, enacted in (and only in) prayer; second, complete submission to the husband as God's representative and leader of the home; third, a more carefully nuanced form of the latter, which accepts the husband *as he is* while retaining some room for private critique of his behavior; and fourth, what I have termed "containment," that is, submitting more in word than in deed and celebrating the power to influence—or, in less flattering terms, manipulate—a husband to one's own ends.[38] Although Aglow writers often jumble together these assorted meanings, the categories hold very different implications for thinking about the resources one has at hand for dealing with familial relationships, and for thinking about one's own capabilities in the larger world. As teachings on proper gender roles have fluctuated over time, the strictest of these interpretations has gradually given way to those that are more lenient, flexible, and centered on women's capacity to release divine power and effect change.

Both submission and surrender, then, turn out to be far more slippery concepts than they first appear. Out of the hodgepodge of meanings embedded within them may emerge diverse and even contradictory attitudes toward the peculiar obligations and freedoms bestowed on women by an omnipotent God. While the repressive potential is unmistakable, the possibility also exists for what feminist theologian Sarah Coakley has approvingly termed "power in vulnerability," that is, "the willed effacement to a gentle omnipotence which, far from 'complementing' masculinism, acts as its undoing."[39] In between these two options is the more commonly stated objective, that submission is most valuable for wives, that by means of willing and joyous submission, a man may be domesticated, his will to power contained and transformed into loving protection of his wife. In the latter case, submission provides a strategy for getting what a woman wants, which in these cases appears to be the taming of men's naturally monstrous urges into gentleness, appreciation, and affection and the creation of ideal Christian families. In this sense, submission may work as a tactic of the relatively powerless to recover their power and to create a space within which they may feel both fulfilled and free.[40]

"UNABLE TO LIKE AND YET COMPELLED TO LOVE":
FROM WIFELY SUBMISSION TO DAUGHTERLY ANGER

The disillusionment and disappointment Aglow women have felt toward their own families is repeatedly apparent in Aglow narratives from the 1970s to the 1990s, as is the desire to replace disappointment with happiness and bring greater familial harmony into their homes. The homes women increasingly seek to correct are, however, not only the ones they find themselves in at the moment but also the ones they recall experiencing as children. An examination of Aglow literature shows that growing numbers of women since the 1970s have described the families they grew up in as debilitating for them when they later tried to form families of their own. Stories are filled with accounts of abusive, alcoholic parents who did not attend lovingly to their children and whose violent methods of coping with their own misery wounded those around them. Like Jerry, whose story I recounted at the beginning of this essay, countless women tell about wretchedly unhappy childhoods in which they were bereft of nurturing and grew up unaware or mistrustful of parental love.[41]

Becky, writing in 1985, told of her parents' divorcing when she was two years old. By her senior year in high school, she had seen her father only once. "It was obvious he didn't care about pursuing a relationship with me or my younger sister. I tried not to dwell on it, but whenever I found myself in an uncomfortable position . . . I would fall to pieces."[42] Jessica, writing her testimony for *Aglow* magazine in 1990, recounted her pain at being the daughter of a severely alcoholic mother and her longing for a "shared-love relationship with Mom" that was not to be. When her rage, "a too-long-dormant volcano," finally erupted at her mother, Jessica was tormented by guilt and fear until she begged God to help her heal and understand her mother's own pain. Even now, she writes, "the tears begin to fall again. But now tears of release mix with those of pain; release for what might have been, but is not; for the devastation alcoholism has caused; and for my mom—the woman I am unable to like and yet compelled to love."[43]

Accounts such as these have spawned an outpouring of self-help books published by Aglow since the mid-1980s, all centered on healing from the childhood traumas of neglect and abuse. In *Daddy, Where Were You?: Healing for the Father-Deprived Daughter*, the author writes vividly of her own pain when her father deserted her at a young age, and of the healing she received from learning that God is her true Father.[44] Another, *When Love Is Not Perfect: Discover God's Re-Parenting Process*, discusses issues surrounding child abuse—emotional, physical, and sexual—and provides "a biblical framework to help victims experience God's re-parenting."[45] Others, such as *Healing the Angry Heart: A Strategy for Confident Moth-*

ering, further describe the "tragic cycle" of child abuse and low self-esteem, offering help for those who have been caught in this cycle as children and, later, as mothers.[46] All authors advocate prayer for healing and counsel their readers to ask God to help them forgive and love their abusive parents, as difficult as such an act may seem. In practicing this kind of forgiveness, readers are told, victims of abuse will in turn be free to love their own children more fully. It is not a forgiveness easily achieved, writers agree, but rather one that must be sought with determination and, once attained, carefully guarded. As one Aglow author urges, "Pledge to pray for your parents every day."[47]

Childhood shame, rooted in emotional, physical, or sexual abuse, continues to be of great concern to Aglow women today. Glenda, a local Aglow officer, angrily recounted during our interview the ways in which her mother constantly made her feel like a "bad girl" as a child by incessantly criticizing her behavior, mocking her blemished complexion and frizzy hair, and ridiculing her awkwardness in front of other people. Glenda observed that her main problem throughout her life has been low self-esteem, noting, "I felt like I never measured up." Only when a woman prayed with her at an Aglow meeting did she begin to realize, in her words, "the idiocy of everything I had pointed out [about myself]—none of us are worthy. That's why Jesus died on the cross!" After a long and painful process, Glenda says her relationship with her mother has been healed, yet throughout our conversations she constantly lambasted herself for being "a terrible mother" and always spoke in self-deprecating terms about herself. The persistent effects of Glenda's childhood shame were all too evident.[48]

This theme of looking at one's childhood for the causes of adult frustrations and unhappiness, then learning to forgive one's parents as the first step in healing, is repeatedly echoed by popular speakers at Aglow events. An example is Quin Sherrer, a longtime member of Aglow's international board, prolific writer of books and articles on prayer, and popular speaker at Aglow conferences, who publicly speaks about being deserted by her father at the age of twelve. At the time her father left, she says, she "closed off" her heart to him and vowed silently, "I'll never forgive him." Years of bitterness and "stuffing" her feelings of anger and hurt down inside herself changed after she was told by a minister to repent of her anger against her father and to forgive him. She was then able to go to her father and experience the restoration of their relationship. Quin's story has become paradigmatic for many women in Aglow dealing with similar feelings of hatred, as they struggle to follow her example and hope for similarly miraculous results.[49]

As common as accounts of abandonment and abuse are in Aglow narratives, it would be incorrect to identify Aglow as composed only of women who were abused as children or whose primary concern is healing from parental neglect. Many narratives, in fact, do not directly address such issues, while some women praise their parents as models of love and virtue. Still, vast energy among Aglow women is given to teaching each other to pray for and forgive parents for their shortcomings and to work through the anger caused by their mistakes. The introduction of Aglow "support groups" in 1989 and their explosion since that time give evidence of this theme, illustrated in the following passage describing women in pain:

> They live next door, they jog past you in the park, brush against you in the express elevator of the downtown office building, and hand you your prescription from the pharmacy. The cumulative effects of dysfunctional homes, divorces, abuse, addictions, compulsions, financial stress, and multiple role expectations have gripped the lives of countless millions of women, imprisoning them in hopelessness, isolation, shame, depression, and fear.[50]

Whatever the extent of actual abuse in these women's lives, it is evident that one function of the narratives recounted in *Aglow* magazines and at their meetings, and of the prayers described in these narratives, is to bring about healing from the pain and anger of perceived mistreatment at the hands of parents and husbands.

Two points bear emphasis. First, Aglow narratives have from the beginning contained seemingly endless permutations on a common theme: the pain of family life. While a shift in emphasis from marital problems to childhood traumas—and thus from the sin of wifely disobedience to the pain of daughterly victimization—has apparently taken place, that shift should not obscure the fact that both narrative scripts have been present from the beginning and continue to be articulated today, as women struggle to cope with various forms of domestic unhappiness. Second, within the Aglow organization, there is a certain cachet (as well as pathos) to having a bad family life. Expressions of sorrow are not simply allowed but are in fact encouraged and take on scripted forms within the narrative context. Like the recovery movement to which it is so intricately connected, Aglow fosters a certain kind of victimology in which women's suffering is attributed to the family—often construed today as "dysfunctional"—yet becomes meaningful for Aglow women when domestic crises are identified as opportunities for personal atonement and growth. In this way, the meaning of "bad parents" or a "bad husband" changes when women leave their homes and enter Aglow: while living in an unhappy home might well be a terrible experience, Aglow offers women the chance to reinterpret family crises in ways that replace the burden of guilt and shame with redemption and hope for healing.

Although the notion of victimization and the conviction that one's "sickness" is one's own burden of sin apparently contradict one another, these beliefs are held together through an avowal of the need for prayer and surrender. In all the narratives, the key to restoration of the family is a prayer in which one confesses one's total impotence and begs for help from God. Relinquishing her desire to control the circumstances of her life, the woman surrenders her will to that of God and may submit to her husband or begin to work through her anger at her parents. The result, which can occur only after the woman accepts responsibility for her situation, expresses repentance, and forgives her husband and any others toward whom she has felt anger, is a presumably transformed home life. Her surrender enables the woman to believe her sins have been forgiven, but it also works to rid her of her earlier sense of injustice and victimhood, bringing her out of bitter disappointment and depression into a sense of her own responsible agency. She is, according to the narrative formula, no longer victim but victor.

"BEAUTIFUL BOLDNESS": WOMEN CALLED
TO SPIRITUAL WARFARE

In 1980, Aglow President Jane Hansen heard a message from God, saying, "Aglow will be a network of praying, warring, interceding women, covering the face of the earth."[51] Since that time, spiritual warfare has occupied an increasingly important role in Aglow, as leaders and members have intensified their engagement in the putative battle being waged between God and Satan, as interpreted within the "third wave" movement of the Spirit to which Aglow is intimately connected.[52] Hansen is an active member of the Spiritual Warfare Network, a group "specializing in intercession specifically directed to weaken the territorial spirits or principalities and powers which obstruct the spread of the Gospel."[53] Most of Aglow's International Advisors and Advisors-at-Large are also members of the Spiritual Warfare Network, including David (formerly Paul) Yonggi Cho, leader of the world's largest church; George Otis Jr., author of several books on spiritual warfare and "spiritual mapping" and a leader in the A.D. 2000 and Beyond movement; John Dawson, director of Youth with a Mission and author of *Taking Our Cities for God*; Dick Eastman, member of the Spiritual Warfare Network; Cindy Jacobs, president of Generals of Intercession and member of the executive council of the National Prayer Embassy; and C. Peter Wagner, professor of church growth at Fuller Theological Seminary and coordinator of the Spiritual Warfare Network. All are active participants in the "third wave of the Holy Spirit," a term Wagner describes in his 1983 book by the same name. Having already sent the "first wave" as Pentecostalism and the "second wave" in the form of the charismatic movement, Wagner writes, God has now sent an even more powerful "third wave" of spiritual work, distinguished by a new emphasis on healing, spiritual warfare, and what John Wimber has termed "power evangelism," as well as a persistently premillennial theology.[54]

Under Jane Hansen's leadership, Aglow has increasingly moved in this direction, an intensification of its long adherence to the belief that we are living in the "end times" or "last days" and that Christ's return to earth to usher in the Kingdom of God is imminent. From its leaders, Aglow has also adopted some rather controversial spiritual warfare strategies in the form of "spiritual mapping," in which warfare prayers are made over maps—particularly the "10/40 Window," a rectangle between 10° and 40° latitude in which over 90 percent of the world's unsaved population is supposedly located—of areas across the earth where evil spirits and "strongholds" are believed to exert force against the gospel. Throughout these spiritual warfare networks, particularly in Aglow, women are seen as having a crucial role, called by God not only to evangelize in traditional ways but also to "do battle" against the evil forces thought to be at work in the world. Even as they insist that they are merely "ordinary women," then, they have found for themselves a role with extraordinary implications.[55]

Notions pertaining to spiritual warfare have a long history in millennial theology and evangelicalism and are rooted in scriptural passages such as the following: "Put on the full armor of God so that you can take your stand against the devil's schemes. For our struggle is not against flesh and blood, but against the rulers, against the authorities, against the powers of this dark world and against the spiritual forces of evil in the heavenly realms" (Ephesians 6:11–12 NIV).[56] Aglow's emphasis on women's important roles in this battle, a seemingly sharp contrast to the stress on submissive femininity and loving nurture, requires some explanation. Here, unlike actual military war, men are not perceived as the primary combat soldiers, with women at the sidelines cheering them on. Nor are men and women envisioned as precisely equal in either responsibility or power. Rather, Aglow teaches that women must be at the frontlines of the war, with a role that sometimes appears more central than that of Christian men.[57]

Two women affiliated with Aglow, Quin Sherrer and Ruthanne Garlock, have co-authored a prescriptive book, published in 1991, entitled *A Woman's Guide to Spiritual Warfare*. After describing the battle against "discouragement, fear, harassment, and other ploys of the evil one," they defend women's role in the spiritual war: "Sure, men are also called to duty, but women have a special interest in this battle." Admonishing their female readers who perceive themselves as weak and helpless, the authors note, "Why is it that we are so influential? Perhaps because women often feel things deeply. We are readily moved with compassion." Moreover: "Quin's theory is that because women were created to give birth in the natural realm, we know more about travailing to give birth in the spiritual realm. We have a high tolerance for pain. We have the tenacity to stick it out until the birthing is done and our loved ones are brought from darkness into the light of Jesus." The lesson resounds: Christian women, not despite but actually because of their "feminine" emotionalism, are called to a position of great responsibility, in which they must fight against evil by enlisting as loyal and vigorous soldiers in God's army.[58]

As Aglow women describe and practice it, spiritual warfare involves "intercession," mediating between God and the person one is praying for, as well as standing between that person and Satan to "restrict satanic forces." This is a process of "binding" Satan by forbidding him, in the name of Jesus, to tempt or destroy human beings who rightfully belong to God. As performed in Aglow groups, spiritual warfare is a loud and vigorous process, involving shouting—in tongues and in English—and dramatic bodily gestures that indicate combat with unseen yet powerful forces. By fighting against Satan and constantly praying to God for assistance, Satan's evil power can be blocked and ultimately conquered: "The enemy's attempt to draw us into sin causes our inner conflict. But if we choose to obey God, he gives us success in these skirmishes. Then we are empowered to battle outwardly, dispelling the powers of darkness and setting other captives free."[59] This passage reveals once again the doctrine of surrender connected to implications of power. In choosing to obey God's will rather than give in to Satan's temptations, women are rewarded with the God-given authority to banish Satan and to render him virtually powerless.

Satan's attacks on women include destroying their marriages and bringing misery into their homes, and Aglow literature contains frequent illustrations explaining how spiritual warfare may be waged against the sinful actions of children and husbands. Alicia, whose husband, Carl, appeared to be having an extramarital affair, sought advice from her Aglow friend, Ruthanne, who recounted the story in print:

> I told Alicia that I felt Satan was using this woman's attention as a snare to ruin her husband's testimony and his marriage. I advised her to renounce her hurt and anger, then forgive both of them. Alicia prayed and forgave Carl and the woman involved. Then we bound the spirits of deception, pride, and lust in both of them. We declared in the name of Jesus that all ties of sexual attraction between Carl and this woman, or any other woman he had lusted after, were broken. We asked the Holy Spirit to reveal truth to him, to expose the enemy's snare, and to bring Carl to repentance.

Afterward, Ruthanne told Alicia that she should no longer argue with her husband about the situation; instead, she advised, "Just ask the Lord to help you express love to him." That very night Ruthanne saw a "radiant" Alicia, who exclaimed, "I can't believe the change in Carl! . . . The Lord must have dealt with him . . . , because he . . . apologized to me for his involvement with that woman and for hurting me. I told him I forgave him. His whole attitude has changed, and I know the Lord will help us work everything out."[60]

While not directly challenging the doctrine of wifely submission, Alicia subverts it through a legitimate means; rather than confronting Carl with her pain and anger at his infidelity, she went straight to the authority of God, who, in her view, took control of the situation and transformed Carl's heart. The story of Alicia represents a rather different alternative from that taken by Dorothy; whereas Dorothy took responsibility for her marital unhappiness upon herself, Alicia perceives the problem as her husband's acquiescence to the power of Satan. This difference in the two stories, printed sixteen years apart, represents a similar shift in emphasis as that described previously: a growing willingness to articulate the sins of the husbands (and parents) rather than taking the full burden of blame upon oneself.

Also intriguing are the ways that the language of spiritual warfare may work to undercut the claim to have surrendered fully to the will of God. Certainly God is believed to be the source of women's power, and yet it sometimes appears as if God takes a backseat while the women themselves do battle against the demonic forces in the world. While prayers of assistance are incorporated into the practice of warring against Satan, for instance, the women take matters into their own hands by fighting him themselves as they "command" him to yield to their will. In their surrender, they do not limit their actions to praying for God to take charge of the situation but rather "come against" the enemy as soldiers waging war. Although the battle is always fought "in Jesus' name," the women's insistence on their own agency is apparent. As I heard one Aglow leader exclaim at a spiritual warfare workshop in 1993, "I just want to be a prayer warrior, and I'm going to pray until I win! Because our God is a winning God, and we are winning women!"[61]

Besides forces tearing apart families, there are various other "strongholds" or "spirits" that Aglow women attack by means of spiritual warfare. These include witchcraft, Freemasonry, and "occult" phenomena that are believed to lurk menacingly in the world and to induce people to act immorally. Such forces are believed to seep into one's life and home even without one's knowing it, as when one woman recounted discovering a book she had purchased secondhand was tainted by witchcraft because of the sins of its previous owner.[62] By fighting these spirits through practices of spiritual warfare, Aglow women believe that they play not only a significant role but a truly necessary one in the lives of their families, their neighborhoods, and the nation as a whole, protecting the safety of innocent people who may well be unaware that such spirits exist. More visible targets of spiritual warfare may include illegal drugs, homosexuality, and abortion, all of which are believed to be forces of Satan that are contributing to a precipitous moral decay in American society. Sending prayers to God about these issues is considered at least as important—and in some ways more so—than doing actual political work against them, for the women believe that their prayers may help change people's hearts and cleanse society from even the most threatening forms of evil. Here and elsewhere, Aglow women assume that their prayers are powerful religious, social, and even political weapons and that they as Christian women have a tremendous responsibility to make warfare prayers and be loyal soldiers of the cross.

The discourse of spiritual warfare prayer is distinct from that of submission, emphasizing female power and authority rather than meek surrender and extending women's realm of activism beyond home and church into the broader society. Like evangelical members of the Woman's Christian Temperance Union at the end of the nineteenth century, whose commitment to "Home Protection" impelled them to broaden the female sphere and revise the ideal of the True Woman, many evangelical women at the end of the twentieth century have seemingly undergone what historian Carolyn DeSwarte Gifford has termed "re-conversion," a renewed conviction of God's great expectations for women to be prayer warriors in the public sphere. Called to be Deborahs and Esthers, both groups of women gradually reimagined Christian womanhood as involving the God-given authority to fight the principalities and powers of the world.[63] As Aglow women frequently declare, they aspire to the "beautiful boldness" to which they avow God has called them.

REINVENTING CHRISTIAN WOMANHOOD

For the women of Aglow, there is power in prayer, and its reach is not confined to the home but spreads outward into "the world." Through acts of surrender as well as through the tactics of spiritual warfare, these women believe that they may contain enemy forces—the lust of a husband, perhaps, or even such perceived evils as certain social and political policies affecting the "traditional family." These "warfare" strategies also provide a means by which female submission may be subverted and transformed into a tool of authority. Understanding how this process works may lead to greater understanding of the meanings of healing, transformation, and liberation that are so deeply a part of their faith and piety and may also challenge the flat interpretation made by some observers (including many feminists) that female submission is no more than "a delicately balanced commingling of resourcefulness and lack of self-respect."[64] What Aglow women feel (or say they feel) to be liberation or even "empowerment" may, of course, look like something very different to those whose experiences of power bear little resemblance to those of the women I have described here. The task is to bring these perspectives together—hearing the women's narratives on many levels or, in Janice Radway's terms, viewing them from multiple lenses—so as to create a richer account of religion as it is lived by the women of Aglow.

This discussion of the family, prayer, and notions of submission and surrender in Aglow indicates the complex and varied meanings of Christian womanhood for evangelical women. Being a Christian woman involves compliance to male authority, but it also demands the strength and stamina to do battle against Satan. To be a Christian wife is to be privileged with God's choicest role, in the words of Darien Cooper: a role enacted by holding the family together as a stable, happy unit. The ideal of Christian womanhood that charismatic women create and maintain is constructed between a kind of timid passivity, on the one hand, and "unfeminine" assertiveness, on the other. This ideal is articulated by Aglow President Jane Hansen, who warns against a facile interpretation of total submission to an authoritarian husband even as she rejects "the banner of women's lib, ERA and NOW": "I love being a housewife, a mother and all that goes with that. . . . That's part of who God created me to be. But he also created me to be more than that."[65] Repeatedly criticizing "the women's movement" for rejecting the notion that men should be heads of the household and for stirring up distrust and dissent between men and women, still Aglow participants continue to emphasize women's power to do great things in the world and, in very recent years, seem perceptibly to be moving toward egalitarianism. Admitting that the emphasis on female submission has changed a lot within Aglow, many women, including Hansen, now speak of "mutual submission" between husbands and wives as the ideal, an ideal long distorted, in their view, by church leaders but presently coming into its own.[66]

Historian Margaret Bendroth's observation about fundamentalism, that its "continuing attraction for women ensured that gender questions would arise over and over," remains true in the modern world, and not only for fundamentalism but for other forms of conservative or "traditional" religion as well.[67] In the case of Aglow, older ideals have gradually mixed with modern realities to produce collage-like results. By the mid-1990s, Aglow publications not only recognized that a high percentage of their readership was comprised of women who worked at jobs outside the home, but authors actually provided models for career women, in that few of them described themselves as full-time homemakers (as earlier writers almost inevitably had). Thus, a passage from the Aglow Bible study *God's Daughter* that originally read, "Because we, as women, are the homemakers, we have the blessing of opening our homes to God's people," was revised in 1985 to read more simply, "We, women, have the blessing of opening our homes to God's people."[68] Evangelical ideals of Christian womanhood, then, while always containing multiple possibilities for revision and even subversion, perceptibly shifted after the mid-1980s, as notions of submission were modified by other notions of female occupation as well as female power.

Over time, as increasing numbers of charismatic women have become divorced, single mothers, the older ideal of the happy, submissive wife has given way to newer models of women warriors battling the forces of Satan and helping each other surmount the apparent wreckage of their lives. Admissions of childhood abuse and alcohol-drenched marriages have tempered any remaining optimism about squeaky clean and happy families, yet the tone of victory still resounds as the women create alternative family relationships with God and with their evangelical sisters. Unlike most of the earliest stories published in *Aglow* magazine, written by women who assumed their audience to be mostly, like them, housewives with children, the Aglow literature produced in the 1990s assumes little about their readers' domestic status except that their lives are probably full of grief and confusion over their roles as Christian women, a condition reputedly connected to women's enduring quest for self-esteem. Changing ideals of Christian womanhood in Aglow literature are thus intricately connected to changing social patterns in American marriage and family life since the 1960s, and the array of such ideals reflects choice as well as confusion about dissolving gender role boundaries.

Religious practices provide further insight into the processes of negotiation that occur as Aglow participants reshape and refine their identities as Christian women. Such practices create moments of active engagement with beliefs and assumptions that may conflict in unseen ways. Prayer is a particularly illuminating practice in the case of Aglow because of the doubleness of its operation, serving simultaneously as a means of articulating the pain and frustration felt in daily life and as a tool for solving these crises. As a mode of both direct and indirect communication, prayer brings to light all kinds of conflicts and contradictions that could otherwise remain hidden in Aglow women's lives and illuminates how really very difficult submission, surrender, and forgiveness can be. Yet the women persevere, struggling to practice these ideals and hoping that in this case, practice can make perfect.

Central to this study, as in other analyses of lived religion, are questions about how particular religious practices actually work for those who enact them, the relation of such practices to broader social matrices, and the impact of such practices on ordinary life. By highlighting the workings of power in the Aglow organization, I have aimed at discerning whether practices such as prayer and storytelling about prayer effectively oppose or conserve norms of discipline and authority. Do, that is, such apparently conventional rituals hold potential for resistance or do they, tangibly as well as covertly, merely replicate the hierarchical status quo and ultimately perpetuate female subordination?[69] My own reading of these materials suggests that these practices work in double ways so as both to conserve particular meanings and to oppose others, upholding various power arrangements and even instilling them in newcomers while allowing other arrangements to be challenged and possibly reshaped.

This analysis may offer some insights for reconsidering the practical effects of activities such as prayer; it may prompt, in other words, a strategy for avoiding the either/or dilemma in which practices are viewed as *either* opposing *or* conserving certain meanings and values in grand terms. One way of articulating such a strategy might be to think in metaphoric terms of "making room." What practices such as prayer and, even more, telling stories about prayer do for the women of Aglow is to open up space in areas that once were tightly bounded, limited, constrained. By "making room" for new ways of imagining their situations, prayer makes those boundaries appear wider and less constraining than before. Dorothy opens up the drapes in her living room and imagines her world expanding. Darien Cooper's readers discover that they have the power to make their husbands happy and thereby enhance or ameliorate conditions at home. Alicia, doing battle against the "powers of darkness" that have attacked her husband, receives assurance that her marriage has been healed. Although problems may well persist and other hardships are sure to transpire, there is always room for hope, opening up new space within which one's sense of self may be transformed. What emerge into view are not simply glib or superficial solutions to life's perduring trials but spaces of calm assurance, expectation, and possibility.

The boundaries are not demolished, however. They shift, tightening in spots that are not always immediately evident. The capacity for active protest and dissent shrinks drastically; the sanctions against "rebellion"—including rebellion against conventions strictly upheld within Aglow—are great. Dissatisfaction and unhappiness with one's life may only be voiced as a way of illuminating one's own weaknesses and recognizing the responsibility to surrender and accept whatever comes. The potential abdication of personal will and desire is not only individually stifling but also, and perhaps more ominously, politically immobilizing. Surrendering one's will in Aglow all too often seems to include the surrender of one's willingness to think independently and of the capacity to protect oneself, a capacity that these women cannot afford to lose.

In the end, then, the room these women make for themselves may be negated by the room they lose; nevertheless, the notions of submission and surrender, enacted through prayer, through narrative, and through changed behavior in everyday life, provide Aglow women with a means of reinventing themselves, of "making room" for themselves within a familial or larger social context that they also believe to be transformed. The larger political implications of this process are unclear, but at the very least, the willful determination these women manifest in reworking their lives seems to suggest possibilities for further changes in the future. Aglow prayer narratives hinge on moments when new possibilities for identity are realized, and it is in the surrender to such possibilities that new selves may be born.

NOTES

1. "My Husband's Going to Die," *Aglow* 22 (Summer 1975): 9–11.

2. "Daddy Never Said, 'I Love You!'" *Aglow* 16 (Winter 1974): 24–26.

3. "Reflections on Aglow's twenty-year ministry to women around the world" (brochure printed by Aglow Publications, 1987, 4). Historical studies of the charismatic movement include David Edwin Harrell Jr., *All Things Are Possible: The Healing and Charismatic Revivals in Modern America* (Bloomington: Indiana University Press, 1975); and Richard Quebedeaux, *The New Charismatics* (New York: Doubleday, 1976), completely revised and published as *The New Charismatics II: How a Christian Renewal Movement Became Part of the American Religious Mainstream* (San Francisco: Harper and Row, 1983). On the Full Gospel Businessmen's Fellowship, see Vinson Synan, *Under His Banner: History of Full Gospel Business Men's Fellowship International* (Costa Mesa, Calif.: Gift Publications, 1992).

4. Today local meetings attract up to one hundred women. Individual chapters are interdenominational and convene monthly for prayer and worship, often in church sanctuaries, civic centers, or public auditoriums. Each chapter is part of a larger regional group with its own board of officers, who together oversee the meetings and the chapter leaders. At one time Aglow claimed to serve over a half million women in the United States; however, in September 1993, their membership was down to 19,717 women in the United States, with supposedly thousands more throughout the world. The organization discontinued publication of *Aglow* magazine in 1991, but has continued to publish a variety of newsletters, Bible studies, and Christian self-help books since that time.

5. I have outlined the history and current configuration of Women's Aglow elsewhere; see Griffith, *God's Daughters: Evangelical Women and the Power of Submission* (Berkeley: University of California Press, 1997), esp. ch.1.

6. Mirra Komarovsky with Jane H. Philips, *Blue-Collar Marriage* (New Haven, Conn.: Yale University Press, 10th printing, 1987); Lillian Breslow Rubin, *Worlds of Pain: Life in the Working-Class Family* (New York: Basic Books, 1976); Elaine Tyler May, *Homeward Bound: American Families in the Cold War Era* (New York: Basic Books, 1988). See also Brett Harvey, *The Fifties: A Woman's Oral History* (New York: HarperCollins, 1993); William Chafe, *The American Woman: Her Changing Social, Economic and Political Role, 1920–1970* (New York: Oxford University Press, 1972); Carl Degler, *At Odds: Women and the Family in America from the Revolution to the Present* (New York: Oxford University Press, 1980); Benita Eisler, *Private Lives: Men and Women of the Fifties* (New York: Franklin Watts, 1986); Eugenia Kaledin, *Mothers and More: American Women in the 1950s* (Boston, Mass.: Twayne, 1984); and Leila Rupp and Verta Taylor, *Survival in the Doldrums: The American Women's Rights Movement, 1945 to the 1960s* (New York: Oxford University Press, 1987).

7. Sociologist Susan D. Rose, writing about similar narrative scripts among charismatic women, observes that whereas feminists would interpret the illnesses of Dorothy and other women as encoding both surrender and rebellion against their prescribed female roles, the women themselves perceive such illnesses as warning signs that they stepped out of their proper place. See Rose, "Women Warriors: The Negotiation of Gender in a Charismatic Community," *Sociological Analysis* 48, no. 3 (1987): 245–58.

8. "Master of My Life," *Aglow* 13 (Spring 1973): 20–23.

9. "Pieces of the Puzzle," *Aglow* 11 (Fall 1972): 20–23, 27.

10. "The Wife of the Unbeliever," *Aglow* 19 (Fall 1974): 29–31.

11. "My Non-Christian Husband," *Aglow* 29 (Spring 1977): 20–23. See also "Glad You Asked That," *Aglow* 15 (Winter 1974): 17. For success stories of converting a previously unsaved husband, see "He Gave Me Love," *Aglow* 28 (Winter 1977): 3–6; and "We've Made It," *Aglow* 35 (July–August 1978): 12–14.

12. Ed Hindson, "The Total Family," *Faith Aflame* 4, no. 1 (January–February 1979): 12; cited in Joan Jacobs Brumberg, *Mission for Life: The Story of the Family of Adoniram Judson, the Dramatic Events of the First American Foreign Mission, and the Course of Evangelical Religion in the Nineteenth Century* (New York: The Free Press, 1980), 222.

13. Carol Greenhouse, *Praying for Justice: Faith, Order, and Community in an American Town* (Ithaca, N.Y.: Cornell University Press, 1986), 48.

14. Ibid., 49.

15. Particularly since World War II, this religious concern for family life has taken on an increasingly anxious tone among conservative evangelicals and fundamentalists. David Harrington Watt and Margaret Lamberts Bendroth have separately argued that there was a shift after the war from the earlier fundamentalist preoccupation with apocalyptic speculation to increased attention on "practical issues of moral conduct." In particular, the new emphasis turned, often quite fiercely, to the issue of the Christian home. Bendroth describes this shift as initiated by "a desire within fundamentalism for more uniform standards of feminine conduct and a movement toward greater structure in gender relationships." The new emphasis on female submission to masculine headship reshaped notions of

hierarchy and had a significant impact on evangelical ideals of family life. See Bendroth, *Fundamentalism and Gender, 1875 to the Present* (New Haven, Conn.: Yale University Press, 1993), 98–99; Watt, *A Transforming Faith: Explorations of Twentieth-Century American Evangelicalism* (New Brunswick, N.J.: Rutgers University Press, 1991), 84–91.

16. Judith Stacey, *Brave New Families: Stories of Domestic Upheaval in Late Twentieth Century America* (New York: Basic Books, 1991).

17. Sontag, *When Love Is Not Perfect*, 78; Newbrough, *Support Group Leader's Guide*, 36.

18. Isaiah 54:5 (NIV).

19. "A Christian Road Map for Women Traveling Alone," *Aglow* 20 (Winter 1975): 8–11, 15.

20. "'I Shall Not Fear,'" *Aglow* 31 (Fall 1977): 16.

21. "Testimony: A Story of God's Care," *Aglow* 33 (March–April 1978): 21–23.

22. Janice Radway, *Reading the Romance: Women, Patriarchy, and Popular Literature* (Chapel Hill: University of North Carolina Press, 1991), 81; "A Christian Road Map," 10.

23. Griffith, *God's Daughters*.

24. See Newbrough, *Support Group Leader's Guide*, 7.

25. February 1994. The speaker made the recommendation during a conference workshop for women with non-Christian husbands.

26. Nancy T. Ammerman has discussed this process in *Bible Believers: Fundamentalists in the Modern World* (New Brunswick, N.J.: Rutgers University Press, 1987), esp. 134–46. See also Stacey, *Brave New Families*, 113–46.

27. Cooper, *You Can Be the Wife of a Happy Husband: By Discovering the Key to Marital Success* (Wheaton, Ill.: Victor Books, 1974), 17.

28. Ibid., 30, 78, 119, 138.

29. Ibid., 139.

30. Ibid., 153.

31. This image of men as naturally out of control and so needing constraint is common in contemporary evangelical teachings on the family, as in the following passage from Christian family guru James Dobson: "The single male is often a threat to society. His aggressive tendencies are largely unbridled and potentially destructive. . . . When a man falls in love with a woman, dedicating himself to care for her, protect her, and support her, he suddenly becomes the mainstay of the social order. Instead of using his energies to pursue his own lusts and desires, he sweats to build a home, save for the future, and seek the best job available. His selfish impulses are inhibited. His sexual passions are channeled. He discovers a sense of pride—yes, masculine pride—because he is needed by his wife and children. Everyone benefits from the relationship." "A New Look at Masculinity and Femininity," *Moody Monthly* 82 (June 1982): 54.

32. Schlafly, *The Power of the Positive Woman* (New Rochelle, N.Y.: Arlington House, 1977), 54–55; cited in Ehrenreich, *The Hearts of Men: American Dreams and the Flight from Commitment* (New York: Anchor Press/Doubleday, 1986), 163.

33. Mae Erickson, *Quiz for Christian Wives* (Lynnwood, Wash.: Aglow Publications, 1976), 6–8.

33. Interview, January 27, 1994.

35. *Aglow in the Kitchen*, ed. Agnes Lawless and Ann Thomas (Lynnwood, Wash.: Aglow Publications, 1976), 7. Another author, in a prayer printed for "my son's partner," writes: "If housework ever seems to be a monotonous chore to her, help her realize that whatever she does in word or deed, she should do it with all her heart as working for You" (Quin Sherrer, *How to Pray for Your Children*, [Lynnwood, Wash. Aglow Publications, 1986], 34).

36. "My Home: My Ministry," *Aglow* 11 (Fall 1972): 25–26.

37. For this discussion, I compared three versions of this booklet by Eadie V. Goodboy: the original (*God's Daughter: A Study of Practical Christian Living for Women*, 1974); a version slightly revised in 1976 and reprinted in 1981 (*God's Daughter: Practical Aspects of a Christian Woman's Life*); and a version revised in 1985 and reprinted in 1991.

38. I am indebted to theologian Sarah Coakley for helping me distinguish between these forms of power and surrender.

39. Coakley, "*Kenosis* and Subversion: On the Repression of 'Vulnerability' in Christian Feminist Writing," in *Swallowing a Fishbone?: Feminist Theologians Debate Christianity*, ed. Daphne Hampson (London: SPCK, 1996), 110.

40. Michel de Certeau, *The Practice of Everyday Life* (Berkeley: University of California Press, 1984), esp. xviii–xx, 24–28, 29–42.

41. Shirley Dobson, wife of well-known evangelical psychologist James C. Dobson, has described her own childhood in an alcoholic home and its after-effects. See, for instance, "Shirley Dobson: From Shaky Childhood to Secure Womanhood," in Helen Hoosier Kooiman, *Living Cameos* (Old Tappan, N.J.: Revell, 1971), 30–38.

42. "The Best Choice," *Aglow* 76 (May–June 1985): 7.

43. "Mom's an Alcoholic!" *Aglow* 21, no.1 (January–February 1990): 10–12.

44. Heather Harpham, *Daddy, Where Were You?: Healing for the Father-Deprived Daughter* (Lynnwood, Wash.: Aglow Publications, 1991).

45. Marie Sontag, *When Love Is Not Perfect: Discover God's Re-Parenting Process* (Lynnwood, Wash.: Aglow Publications, 1991). Sontag writes that "as many as one out of four adults" are victims of some form of child abuse (p. 14).

46. Kathy Collard Miller, *Healing the Angry Heart: A Strategy for Confident Mothering* (Lynnwood, Wash.: Aglow Publications, 1984), esp. 39–46 (quote from p. 39).

47. Ibid., 46. Another example of this genre published by Aglow Publications is Stanley C. Baldwin, *If I'm Created in God's Image Why Does It Hurt to Look in the Mirror?: A True View of You* (1989); see also "When You Hurt: A Study of God's Comfort" (Aglow Encourager Bible Study series, 1987).

48. Interview, May 18, 1993.

49. Quin Sherrer first published her narrative in "The Song That Changed: A Story of Forgiveness," *Aglow* 76 (May–June 1985): 18–20 (quotes from p. 19); she also told this story in a workshop at the U.S. Women's Aglow Conference in November 1994.

50. Jennie Newbrough [with Carol Greenwood], *Support Group Leader's Guide* (Lynnwood, Wash.: Aglow Publications, 1993), 26.

51. This prophecy has been recounted in numerous places, including the Women's Aglow Prayer Map and *Women of Prayer Released to the Nations* (Lynnwood, Wash.: Aglow Publications, 1993), 9.

52. Metaphors of warfare have been utilized by a wide variety of cultural fundamentalists. See David Snowball, *Continuity and Change in the Rhetoric of the Moral Majority* (New York: Praeger, 1991), esp. 123–49. As Snowball notes, the effectiveness of prowar rhetoric requires optimism that the war can indeed be won (p. 135).

53. Brochure of the Spiritual Warfare Network, coordinated by C. Peter Wagner. This network is part of the United Prayer Track of the A.D. 2000 and Beyond movement and is supported by Global Harvest Ministries, Pasadena, Calif.

54. C. Peter Wagner, *The Third Wave of the Holy Spirit: Encountering the Power of Signs and Wonders* (Ann Arbor, Mich.: Servant Publications, 1988); John Wimber (with Kevin Springer), *Power Evangelism* (San Francisco: Harper and Row, 1986). See also Wimber and Springer, *Power Healing* (San Francisco: HarperCollins, 1987). An evangelical critique of this movement is Michael G. Moriarty, *The New Charismatics: A Concerned Voice Responds to Dangerous New Trends* (Grand Rapids, Mich.: Zondervan, 1992).

55. For recent elaborations of this view by international Aglow leaders, see the essays in *Women of Prayer Released to the Nations.*

56. The passage continues: "Therefore put on the full armor of God, so that when the day of evil comes, you may be able to stand your ground, and after you have done everything, to stand. Stand firm then, with the belt of truth buckled around your waist, with the breastplate of righteousness in place, and with your feet fitted with the readiness that comes from the gospel of peace. In addition to all this, take up the shield of faith, with which you can extinguish all the flaming arrows of the evil one. Take the helmet of salvation and the sword of the Spirit, which is the word of God. And pray in the Spirit on all occasions with all kinds of prayers and requests. With this in mind, be alert and always keep on praying for all the saints" (vv. 13–18 NIV).

57. Other evangelical groups that utilize military imagery have emphasized women as warriors, notably the Salvation Army; see Diane H. Winston, "Boozers, Brass Bands, and Hallelujah Lassies: The Salvation Army and Commercial Culture in New York City, 1880–1918" (Ph.D. diss. Princeton University, 1996). Women have been dramatized as warriors in other cultural and historical settings as well; a particularly interesting study is Dianne Dugaw, *Warrior Women and Popular Balladry, 1650–1850* (Chicago: University of Chicago Press, 1996; orig. pub. by Cambridge University Press, 1989).

58. Quin Sherrer and Ruthanne Garlock, *A Woman's Guide to Spiritual Warfare: A Woman's Guide to Battle* (Ann Arbor, Mich.: Servant Publications, 1991), 12, 58.

59. Ibid., 41.

60. Ibid., 164–65.

61. February 1993. The speaker made this comment during the inspirational talk to a group of about one hundred women.

62. April 21, 1993. This statement was made in an informal group discussion with approximately fifteen women present.

63. Gifford, "Home Protection: The WCTU's Conversion to Woman Suffrage," in *Gender, Ideology, and Action: Historical Perspectives on Women's Public Lives*, ed. Janet Sharistanian (Westport, Conn.: Greenwood, 1986), 95–120.

64. Andrea Dworkin, *Right-Wing Women* (New York: G. P. Putnam's Sons, 1983 [1979]), 26.

65. "Jane Hansen: Waking Up from the American Dream," *Charisma & Christian Life* (November 1987): 18–23 (quote from p. 23).

66. Interviews, September 14, 1993; May 18, 1993; May 14, 1993. Hansen is currently writing a book on this very subject, according to my conversation with her in August 1996. In contrast, some elderly women who were early members of Aglow but are no longer affiliated with the organization emphasized the doctrine of female submission in much stronger terms. Phone interviews, September 16, 1993.

67. Bendroth, *Fundamentalism and Gender*, 7.

68. Goodboy, *God's Daughter*, 27 (in original version) and 29 (in 1991 version).

69. See Radway, *Reading the Romance*, 209–22.

Chapter Nine

GOLDEN RULE CHRISTIANITY: LIVED RELIGION IN THE AMERICAN MAINSTREAM

Nancy T. Ammerman

Vanishing Boundaries, the recently published book by Hoge, John-son, and Luidens,[1] examines the religious lives of a cohort of baby boom-ers confirmed in Presbyterian churches in the 1950s and 1960s. The au-thors look for what has happened to them since and just what sort of religiosity, if any, they are practicing today. Among those who are cur-rently connected to churches, a majority are what they call "lay liberals." This group scores low on "orthodox" Christian beliefs, such as traditional views about the Bible, believing that Jesus is the only way to salvation, and emphasizing the next world over this one. They are, by contrast, very this-worldly and do not think either that the Bible should be taken literally or that Christianity has a corner on the truth. They also attend church much less than others. For all these reasons, lay liberals do not get ringing endorsements from Hoge, Johnson, and Luidens, nor from the many other sociologists and theologians who have recognized similar categories of non-orthodox churchgoers.[2] Implicitly, most observers seem to mea-sure strength of belief and commitment against a norm defined by evangelicalism, equating that with "religiosity" and painting these non-exclusivist, less involved practitioners as simply lower on the scale. In this essay, I suggest that "lay liberals" are not simply lower on the religiosity scale. Rather, they are a pervasive religious type that deserves to be under-stood on its own terms.

I draw here on research originally undertaken as part of the "Congrega-tions in Changing Communities" project, carried out under the auspices of the Institute for the Study of Economic Culture at Boston University, with funding from the Lilly Endowment, and reported in full in *Congre-gation and Community*. While that project was concerned with the re-sponses of congregations to new institutional ecologies, it included atten-tion to the individual religious lives of congregational members. Among the data we collected are survey responses from 1,995 individuals in 23 congregations and extensive observations of activities in those congrega-tions. With the help of Edward Gray, I have also looked carefully at 103 of the over 300 interviews from the study. These include lay people in seventeen of the churches we studied.[3] Sixty percent of these were women, 20 percent were African American (the rest Anglo), and there was a fairly even distribution across the adult age spectrum. Fourteen percent were in Catholic churches, 54 percent in liberal Protestant churches, and 32 percent in evangelical Protestant churches. All the congregations and individuals are from within the Christian tradition, although one, First Existentialist in Atlanta,[4] recognizes that a substantial number of its members do not claim to be Christian. While the patterns I describe may hold in parallel form in other traditions, I cannot directly address that question with the data from this study.

TOWARD DEFINITION AND LOCATION

The first step in describing the religiosity of "lay liberals" is to recognize what these people believe and practice. Their religiosity is not just a paler reflection of evangelical fervor, but different in kind. For that reason, I will not call them "lay liberals." Religious liberalism is usually taken to indicate the opposite end of a scale that is anchored by evangelicalism. That, in turn, indicates that the primary differences we should observe are differences in the certainty with which people hold traditional beliefs: evangelicals are relatively certain, whereas liberals have rejected or reinterpreted traditional ideas about the Bible, Christ's divinity, the second coming, and the like. What I want to suggest, however, is that this category of religious persons is best defined not by ideology, but by practices. Their own measure of Christianity is right living more than right believing. What Hoge, Johnson, and Luidens found, in fact, was that these Christians are characterized by a basic "Golden Rule" morality and a sense of compassion for those in need. It is those practices of doing good and caring for others that we highlight here.[5]

As we looked at the interviews from our study, across all the demographic and ideological categories, the most frequently mentioned characterization of the Christian life was that people should seek to do good, to make the world a better place, to live by the Golden Rule. A smaller group of people—mostly those in evangelical churches—defined the Christian life in terms of being saved, but even those people also talked about the importance of living by the principles taught in the Bible, chief among them the Golden Rule.

In our surveys, we also asked people to tell us how important various practices were to "living the Christian life," as well as what they thought their church's top priorities ought to be. Taking those two lists together, one can identify three clusters of responses. The largest (51 percent of the

TABLE 1
Orientations to Christian Life by Congregation

	Activist	Golden Rule	Evangelical	N =
"Mainline" Protestant				
Hinton UMC, Dacula (suburban Atlanta)	0%	88%	12%	34
Brighton Evangelical Congregational (Boston)	0%	80%	20%	10
Carmel UMC (suburban Indianapolis)	15%	76%	9%	175
Epworth UMC (Atlanta)	13%	67%	20%	30
Good Shepherd Lutheran (Oak Park, Ill.)	31%	63%	6%	67
Incarnation Episcopal (Atlanta)	31%	61%	8%	72
Activist				
Holman UMC (Los Angeles)	33%	47%	20%	147
First Congregational (Long Beach, Calif.)	49%	49%	2%	77
First Existentialist (Atlanta)[a]	79%	17%	4%	48
Catholic				
St. Lawrence (suburban Atlanta)	15%	75%	10%	206
St. Catherine's (Boston)[b]	27%	62%	11%	26
St. Matthew's (Long Beach, Calif.)	32%	60%	8%	73
Evangelical				
Grace (independent Baptist, Anderson, Ind.)	8%	11%	81%	100
City (independent Baptist, Oak Park, Ill.)[b]	4%	21%	75%	82
Northview Christian Life (Assemblies of God) (suburban Indianapolis)	6%	34%	60%	65
South Meridian Church of God (Anderson, Ind.)	5%	39%	56%	168
Berean Seventh-Day Adventist (Los Angeles)	6%	38%	56%	71
Hope Baptist (National Baptist, Atlanta)[b]	14%	45%	41%	49

[a] This congregation is loosely affiliated with the Unitarians, but sees itself as only marginally Christian.
[b] These congregations asked for anonymity. These are not their real names.

total of 1,564 respondents for whom we have complete information) we might call "Golden Rule Christians." It includes people who say that the most important attributes of a Christian are caring for the needy and living one's Christian values every day. The most important task of the church, they say, is service to people in need. They can be distinguished from two other groups. On one side stand more evangelically oriented respondents, comprising 29 percent of the total. They emphasize prayer, Bible study, and witnessing as key Christian practices and, correspondingly, want their churches to give attention to evangelism and helping them resist the temptations of this world, while preparing for the world to come. On the other side are the activists, 19 percent of the total, who emphasize social action and working for justice.[6]

Nine of the eighteen congregations on which we have complete data have majorities of Golden Rule-oriented Christians. But, as table 1 shows, these three types are spread throughout the congregations. Not surprisingly, evangelical Protestant congregations have larger contingents of members who are evangelically oriented, but four of the six evangelical churches have substantial minorities of people who think Golden Rule principles are more important than evangelism. Similarly, in two of the three congregations we identified as "activist," there are substantial minorities of members who put a simple good life ahead of trying to change the world. In almost every congregation, there is appreciable diversity in orientation. Less than half have no minority contingent above 25 percent. And only two—one activist and one evangelical—have fewer than 20 percent who see the Golden Rule as the guiding principle for their lives.

Two of the congregations that are most clearly dominated by Golden Rule Christians are Carmel United Methodist Church, in the suburbs of Indianapolis, and St. Lawrence Catholic parish, in the suburbs of Atlanta. Carmel UMC is as old as the town—over 150 years old—and has grown dramatically as Carmel has been transformed from small town to suburb. It sits on a principal highway with a lovely colonial-style sanctuary, and many of those who move to town make at least one visit to inspect its worship services and programs. They find a full round of activities, especially for children, and worship with polished musical offerings and stimulating sermons. Many decide to stay; the average number of Sunday worshipers at two services totals about six hundred.

St. Lawrence, on the other hand, is brand-new. Twenty years ago, there were barely enough Catholics in Gwinnett County, northeast of Atlanta, to organize a parish. Since then, they have not only organized; they have built a dramatic new building, and are but one of several very large Catholic parishes in the county. Today, there are about one thousand people in the various weekend Masses in St. Lawrence's open, semicircular worship space. As the priest strolls the aisles during the opening portion of the service, greeting visitors, he is likely to tell them about the many family-oriented activities from which they can choose if they make St. Lawrence their home parish. His homily, delivered in equally informal style, is likely to remind them of the importance of loving both others and themselves.

As these congregations suggest, Golden Rule Christianity has an identifiable social location. All but two of the congregations with majorities of this type are also solidly middle-class (the exceptions being the Boston churches), and four of the six suburban churches in our study are dominated by Golden Rule religiosity. What I am describing may in fact be the dominant form of religiosity among middle-class suburban Americans. It certainly is among the middle-class suburban Americans in our study. It is their form of "lived religion." Urban congregations were more likely than suburban ones to be activist, while our evangelical congregations are located in all sorts of settings.

Of the individuals who completed our surveys, Golden Rule Christians, on average, have finished college and have family incomes of about $50,000. (On these measures they are very much like the activists.) They stand in contrast, however, to evangelical Christians who have, on average, some college (but not a degree) and have family incomes just under $40,000. Golden Rule Christians are, then, located disproportionately in the suburbs, are slightly better educated, and are economically better off. They are people with the social resources for making their own choices rather than following a single orthodoxy or narrow institutional commitment.

Golden Rule Christianity is not, however, an exclusively White phenomenon. At the individual level, all of the ethnic groups represented among our respondents have similar levels of the three types of religiosity. At the congregational level, all four of the Black churches in our study have substantial numbers (from 38 percent to 61 percent) of Golden Rule Christians in them. While activism is certainly part of the heritage of the African American churches, there are also substantial numbers of these members who are less ambitious about changing the world.[7] Even when a church attempts to promote activism, protest and social justice may not be the primary reasons people attend.

Nor are these orientations defined by age or gender. Although the Golden Rule orientation puts a strong emphasis on "nurturing" activities, women are no more likely than men to say Christianity should be defined this way. Similarly, although women are sometimes thought to be more "orthodox" than men, that does not translate into a greater propensity to define the Christian life in terms of evangelical practices of Bible reading and witnessing. Taking these eighteen diverse congregations together, men and women of all ages are found, on average, in equivalent proportions in all three orientations.

Among the interviews we analyzed, older people were slightly more likely to include Golden Rule themes than younger people, but there were otherwise no consistent differences by age or gender. This is not, then, a "baby boomer" style of religion. Although Hoge, Johnson, and Luidens found a significant number of "Golden Rule" people among their baby boomers,[8] our data indicate that they would have found just as many if they had interviewed the parents. Indeed, the emphasis on a "good life" above any other religious distinctives (either pietist Bible reading and prayer or activist work for social justice) is reminiscent of the religion of the 1950s. It was celebrated by Will Herberg as the triumph of the American melting pot, and it was bemoaned by others as the triumph of triviality and irrelevance.[9] In 1951, Joseph Fichter described the Catholic parishioners he studied thus: "the practical ideology of the parishioners is in approximate balance with their actual behavior patterns, while both of them are at considerable distance from the complete Christian ideology of the Catholic Church."[10] They might not have known the finer points of the catechism, but they had a guiding moral philosophy by which they lived.

GOLDEN RULE BELIEFS

That guiding moral philosophy is not unrelated to traditional religious beliefs and texts. For Golden Rule Christians, it is grounded in the Bible, but certainly not in a literal reading of it. We asked our survey respondents about their view of the Bible, offering them a wider-than-usual range of possible responses. As table 2 shows, activists are slightly more "liberal" than Golden Rule Christians, while evangelicals are a good deal more "conservative." However, people with all three orientations hold every possible position on the Bible. Slightly more than a quarter of the evangelicals take "liberal" positions on the Bible, while a roughly equal number of the Golden Rule group takes the "conservative" position of calling the Bible inerrant or inspired. Given only those alternatives for beliefs about the Bible, however, the Golden Rule Christians would have looked very unorthodox (as they do in most studies). If we concentrated solely on beliefs and divided positions on the Bible along these liberal–conservative lines, we might see the "culture war" that so many claim characterizes American religion.[11]

However, if we take those "liberal" positions on the Bible as genuine alternative beliefs—not a rejection of orthodoxy, but a different orthodoxy—we may see something different. Note that nearly half of the activists and Golden Rule Christians said that the Bible's "stories and teachings provide a powerful motivation as we work toward God's reign in the world." Another quarter of the Golden Rule Christians (and a higher proportion of activists) said the Bible is a "useful guide for individual Christians in their search for basic moral and religious teachings." Almost no one was ready to throw the Bible out as "irrelevant." Among the interviews we analyzed, about one-quarter, spread equally across different types of respondents, specifically mentioned the Bible as important to their own lives and to what they think their children should learn. Just because they do not accept traditional definitions of inspiration or inerrancy does not mean that they have no use for Scripture.[12] Like the rest of their religious life, their use of Scripture is defined more by choices and practice than by doctrine. They draw from Scripture their own inspiration and motivation and guidance for life in this world. Their knowledge of

TABLE 2
Views of Scripture by Orientation

	Activist	Golden Rule	Evangelical
The Bible is . . .			
the inspired Word of God, without error not only in matters of faith, but also in historical, scientific, geographic, and other secular matters.	7%	15%	53%
the inspired, authoritative Word of God that is without error in all that it says about faith and morals.	6%	14%	21%
the Word of God, and its stories and teachings provide a powerful motivation as we work toward God's reign in the world.	40%	42%	18%
the record of many people's experience with God and is a useful guide for individual Christians in their search for basic moral and religious teachings.	37%	28%	8%
an important piece of literature, but is largely irrelevant to our lives today.	10%[a]	1%	1%
TOTAL	100% N = 284	100% N = 750	101% N = 500

[a] A substantial portion of the activists who gave this response are in the Unitarian congregation that includes many who do not call themselves Christian.

Scripture may not be very deep, but they have at least some sense that the Bible is a book worth taking seriously, especially as a tool for making one's own life and the life of the world better.

Everything we have seen thus far tells us that developing a coherent theological system is not what Golden Rule Christians are concerned about. Even the notion of salvation is a bit fuzzy in their minds. Hoge, Johnson, and Luidens found that their lay liberals were rather uninterested in conversations about the "meaning of life." What I want to suggest, in fact, is that "meaning" for Golden Rule Christians consists not in cognitive or ideological structures, not in answers to life's great questions, but in practices that cohere into something the person can call a "good life." William McKinney refers to this group of people as believers in the "cult of the good person."[13] The description is apt and corresponds to their own words. As one member of Carmel United Methodist Church put it: "I think all He [God] stands for makes you hope that you could be a better person." Said another, when asked to describe the essence of God: "[It's] the way you live your life. By that I mean, what good is it to know God if—you can study, you can be an excellent Bible student, but if you don't practice what you have learned, then you aren't making a better world for yourself or for anyone." The members of St. Lawrence agree. In the class for new members, a discussion of salvation concluded that it was not a one-time experience, but a continuing process of demonstrating with your life the value of what you have learned about God. A small-town newspaper put it this way: "[We] are proud to be labeled a 'Christian' newspaper. We take that to mean readers perceive us as a caring establishment that tries its best to uplift the community."[14] One can imagine similar themes emerging in the eulogies given for admired members of these communities.

GOLDEN RULE PRACTICES

What is this good life for which Golden Rule Christians aim? Most important to Golden Rule Christians is care for relationships, doing good deeds, and looking for opportunities to provide care and comfort for people in need. Their goal is neither changing another's beliefs nor changing the whole political system. They would like the world to be a bit better for their having inhabited it, but they harbor no dreams of grand revolutions.

The emphasis on relationships among Golden Rule Christians begins with care for friends, family, neighborhood, and congregation. In the neighborhood, they value friendliness and helpfulness. Many of these folk know what it is to be mobile and therefore what adjusting to life in a new location involves. "Doing unto others" means welcoming newcomers and offering routine neighborly assistance. Beyond such routine care, they are also convinced that a good person invests in relationships. That means being open and vulnerable, working through difficulties, being there during the hard times. Younger people may talk about building relationships on honesty, openness, and caring.[15] But older people talk about church in similar relational terms. Among those we interviewed, older people were especially likely to describe the church as like a family, a place where people care for each other in times of need. When people of all ages talked about being dissatisfied with a church, it was rarely over doctrinal disagreements, but often over the failure of a congregation to care for someone in need.[16]

This emphasis on caring also defines their picture of God. Just as our interviewees' most common description of the Christian life was living by the Golden Rule, so the most common description of God was as a protector and comforter. God was experienced most often in moments of need. Even beyond times of crisis, these church members talked about seeing God's presence in the ways "things just work out" or feeling more confident about everyday challenges because they know God will care for them.[17] Among the survey respondents, preferred images of God included savior, comforter, and father.[18] These pictures of God as loving, caring, comforting, and protecting largely transcended ideological lines. They are characteristic of Golden Rule Christians, but they are by no means alien to the evangelicals and activists in our study.

These images of God and of the Christian life also have consequences for congregational programming. Both Carmel and St. Lawrence have various formal and informal counseling ministries. Carmel has someone on staff whose primary responsibility is counseling. St. Lawrence sponsors "Stephen's Ministries," a program that is cropping up in various denominations throughout the country. Lay people are trained as "caregivers," taught how to listen and encourage and make referrals when necessary. Even more important, both congregations provide an array of (optional) small fellowship groups.[19] At Carmel there are the usual Sunday school classes and ladies mission groups. At St. Lawrence there are traditional Catholic societies, such as the St. Vincent de Paul group. But in both there are also periodic study groups, fellowship activities, and mission projects. At St. Lawrence there is even an effort to adopt the "small faith communities" developed by Father Baranowski.[20]

Relationships with friends and fellow church members are important, then, but the relationship that perhaps defines the religiosity of Golden Rule Christians more than any other is the relationship of parent to child.[21] A quarter of the interviews we analyzed contained explicit statements linking faith to the upbringing of children. As Anne Brown and David Hall demonstrate (elsewhere in this collection) parents have persistently, throughout much of American history, sought the protection of faith and the good graces of the church for their children—even when they themselves were less than enthusiastic believers.[22] Golden Rule Christians are no exception. They are not in church *only* for their children (as we will see below), but religious training for their children is part of what they see as their obligation to the world. They would not be doing good or making the world a better place if their children were denied the training provided by the church.

The members of Carmel and St. Lawrence recognize, however, that bringing up children is not so easy these days. Stresses in family life are among the items of most concern to the Golden Rule Christians in these two affluent suburban congregations. They spoke often of care for spouse and children as very important to them. They worried about the demands of their jobs and how to balance work and family life. Among the relatively small proportion who participated in various Bible study or discipleship groups at the two churches, discussions about work and family decisions were frequent refrains. Although all of these people were comfortably situated, they worried about the excesses of materialism and said they were willing to consider material sacrifices in favor of the well-being of their families.

This emphasis on caring relationships tends to mean a certain narrowness in the circle of care occupied by Golden Rule Christians. Such a level of intense commitment could not be maintained over a wide domain. It is focused primarily on family, friends, neighborhood, and church. It is, in Stephen Warner's terms, parochial, but an "elective parochialism," chosen rather than ascribed.[23] In some cases, there may be a certain defensiveness in its narrowness, an attempt at protection from threatening "others" who occupy the rest of the urban landscape.[24] In other instances, it may more properly be seen as an attempt to create a community in which mobile people can be rooted. It is a narrow circle, but it is characterized by genuine engagement and caring. Unlike the "moral minimalism" M. P. Baumgartner ascribes to suburbia, these Golden Rule Christians have carved out a space in which the indifference of the suburbs is limited, in which both caring and conflict are possible because the bonds of community are being tended more attentively than those in the larger suburban milieu.[25]

In addition, Golden Rule Christianity seems to have at least some impact on the other domains Golden Rule Christians inhabit. Religiosity is not, for them, utterly "private." In business and in the community, they value honesty, believing that good people give an honest day's work and do not try to cheat others. They say that their faith also means that they treat their co-workers and clients with more care than do others who are not religious.[26] Other studies have found that members of "mainline" Protestant and Catholic churches see their faith as providing them with principles by which they can make ethical decisions at work.[27] While they may not be eager to talk about religious issues while they are at work, and they might find it hard to articulate any coherent theological sense of "vocation," they claim that the practices they put at the center of the Christian life inform their everyday economic and civic activities.[28]

For most Golden Rule Christians, especially those in the suburbs, most of the really big problems of the world lie beyond the everyday world. They have little hope that anything very fundamental will change in the larger world, but they are more than willing to do what small things they can to ameliorate the suffering. Their efforts usually consist of donations and volunteer activity. They give food and clothing to food pantries and clothes closets, and contribute money to charitable causes of all sorts. Some of them spend time working in a senior center or on a soup line or in other volunteer activity. Wuthnow found that nearly half of regular American churchgoers had done some volunteer work at their own church or synagogue, and almost 40 percent had done some other charitable work in the community.[29] The Golden Rule respondents to our survey say that they participate in "community/social ministries" on average "a few times a year."

What I have described so far is a set of caregiving practices that extends from family to neighborhood to larger community. They are practices based in a generalized Christian ethic that calls for people to "love one another" and treat others as they would wish to be treated. Among Golden Rule Christians, these practices are explicitly nonideological, and those two factors taken together lead to another of the characteristics of this mode of religiosity—its tolerance.[30] Hoge, Johnson, and Luidens found that their "lay liberals" were not insistent that Christianity is the only way to salvation, and they are certainly not likely to proselytize. Caregivers in the Stephen Ministry at St. Lawrence talked about seeking to foster spirituality, but not trying to push the Catholic Church with those they counseled. Less than half of all our Golden Rule-style respondents say they ever participate in "seeking converts or new members" for their church. Indeed, members of both Carmel and St. Lawrence specifically mentioned tolerance for diversity as a virtue of their faith tradition. Methodists noted that Methodism (at least in their view) does not impose a rigid creed on its members, and Catholics talked about the diversity of spiritual experience among Catholics—from visions of Mary to charismatic renewal to ordinary Mass-going. They like being part of a church that leaves room for people with different beliefs and experiences.

The basis for unity, then, is an ethic rather than dogma, a principle long acknowledged by ecumenical organizations. In the early years of the Federal Council of Churches, leaders chose to emphasize "the Fatherhood of God and the brotherhood of man," to concentrate on achieving a kind of pragmatic unity through the pursuit of "social gospel" reforms, rather than any doctrinal unity or actual church union.[31] More recently, theologian Leo Lefebure has noted that efforts toward interreligious dialogue seem to be helped by the assumption that "there is a fundamental ethical structure on which very diverse religions can come to at least limited agreement apart from special claims of revelation." Citing the declaration "Toward a Global Ethic" issued by the 1993 Parliament of the World's Religions, he notes that at its center "is the Golden Rule, a principle of wisdom found in various forms in different religions."[32] Those who work from such "principles of wisdom" (practices) rather than from explicit revealed dogma have ground on which to meet. The Golden Rule Christians in our study and the "lay liberals" described by Hoge, Johnson, and Luidens seem to be attempting such a nondogmatic and tolerant ethic.

GOLDEN RULE RELIGION

If Golden Rule Christians are characterized by their moral practices and their lack of creed, why call them Christian (or even religious) at all? Could they not be doing all these things based on an ethic generally available in the culture, the sort of generalized value system Talcott Parsons thought Christianity had become anyway?[33] Are they the perfect proof for secularization theory? They have, after all, given up particularistic beliefs in the face of pluralism, reducing religion to a rather universalistic morality. Could they not be members of a lodge or community club just as easily as of a church?

There are at least two reasons to reject that argument. The first is that they themselves insist on joining churches. They may join community organizations as well, but they talk about how important it is to them to find and join a church. They know they could stay home on Sunday morning; they often do. And they have the resources and social connections to pursue friendships and good deeds through other organizational means. Among our survey respondents, in fact, Golden Rule Christians said they participate in church fellowship activities only a few times a year, on average, while they participate in civic and community groups once a month or more. On average, they find only one or two of their five closest friends in their congregation. Still, they claim that church membership and participation is important to them. Why? In part, it is habit. In part, it is conformity to community norms. But in large measure, it is an extension of their care for their families and communities. They simply see no other organization that puts caring for others so clearly at the center of its life.[34] They are eager for what churches can contribute to the task of bringing up their children and are convinced that churches offer something uniquely valuable not present in other kinds of community and social activities.

The more potent reason to reject Golden Rule Christianity as proof of secularization, however, is that Golden Rule Christians have not given up on transcendence. They were sometimes rather fuzzy on just what it is they experience, and they sometimes had to stop and think when we asked, but they almost always came up with answers to questions about their experience of God.[35] Some said that they feel close to God in Sunday worship, especially in the music and in the opportunity for quiet reflection. Nearly half of those whose interviews we analyzed mentioned some aspect of the worship service as important to them, as a time when they feel God's presence or find new insight and understanding for their lives.[36] Many mentioned the music, and some mentioned Communion. A few mentioned sermons.[37] The parts of the service that involved participation and introspection seemed most important. The church's "sacred space," along with the "sacred time" set aside for worship, seems to combine for many into an opportunity to set priorities in order, to "feed the soul" (as a few put it), and to know that they have been in a presence greater than themselves.

In addition to church, those we talked with often mentioned special places in nature and critical moments in the life cycle as evocative for them. Some had been to retreat centers or had been to special religious events when they needed to put life into perspective. Others mentioned experiences with their children—births, for example—or moments near the end of their parents' lives. One man reflected, "I think He [God] has always been a big part of our life, our married life, and our kids' lives. I think our kids had a lot to do with making Him more real to us, and personalizing Him." As these people encounter the power and grandeur of nature and the mystery of life's formative moments, they again sense that something beyond themselves is present.

Not surprisingly, they also sense this presence in times of special difficulty. Many of those we interviewed mentioned times of sickness and death as moments of particular closeness to God. Rather than eliciting questions or existential anger, these trials seemed to allow Golden Rule Christians to draw on a reservoir of spiritual energy. As one woman put it, "It just seems to me that when I need something, or when things are really difficult and they get worked out right, it's just like somebody had to be helping you do it." An evangelical Christian might have quoted Romans 8:28, "All things work together for good." A Golden Rule Christian is no less sure of God's presence, just less precise in describing it.

The lack of language for describing God (and perhaps even the lack of any discernible ideological center at all) can be linked at least in part, I think, to low rates of participation in church activities, especially in small groups. Golden Rule Christians have little opportunity for developing a sustained religious vocabulary. At both Carmel United Methodist and St. Lawrence parish, those who do participate in Bible study groups, prayer groups, ministry groups, discipleship groups, and the like, were often quite adept in talking about their lives in explicitly religious language.[38] Our Golden Rule Christians, however, only participate in Bible study groups, on average, several times a year. Many never do. Their usual mode of church participation is reasonably regular Sunday morning attendance, nothing more. While that time of worship may offer them a sense of God's presence, it does not offer opportunities for conversation with others about the role of religion in their everyday lives. This lack of ongoing religious conversation may undermine their ability to continue to practice their faith (and, ironically, to pass it on to their children).

GOLDEN RULE CONGREGATIONS

Congregations dominated by Golden Rule Christians are clearly not the high-commitment, sectarian gatherings that some theorists claim are the strongest and most likely to succeed.[39] They do not offer their parishioners distinctive identities, and they do not ask for high levels of involvement. They are this-worldly, downplaying other-worldly rewards. Rather than generating a high level of rewards through the sacrificial contributions of all their members (minimizing the "free rider problem"), they generate rewards by gathering minimal contributions from large numbers of people who engage in a good deal of "free riding." Are they therefore doomed to failure? I think not. Half of the people we surveyed define their faith more in terms of everyday morality than in terms of institutional commitment or theological orthodoxy. They would be likely to find a high-commitment sectarian congregation uncongenial. They value the choices they have in how they spend their time and do not believe that their eternal salvation depends on weekly church attendance. While they are less likely to create the sort of vibrant, high-reward communities more demanding groups may favor, they can create viable congregations. There is, quite simply, a very large "market" for the sort of low-commitment congregations Golden Rule Christians favor.

What do they favor in a congregation? As we have seen in looking at the concerns of individual Golden Rule Christians, three things are essential: opportunities to serve (or contribute to serving) people in need, dynamic worship, and attractive activities for children. As would be expected from the emphasis on child-rearing, Golden Rule congregations are very child-centered. From a bright, pleasant nursery with competent workers, to children's choirs and confirmation classes, to regular teen social gatherings, a good deal of the congregation's energy and money goes into "family-centered" activities. Over and over, when we asked people why they chose a given church, they said they were looking for a place that would be good for their children.

But the parents also want a place where the worship is meaningful for themselves. Both St. Lawrence and Carmel UMC devote a good deal of energy to the planning and execution of worship. At Carmel, where music is important, the choir polishes multiple offerings, and there are often vocal and instrumental solos, too. Sermons are imaginative retellings of biblical stories in light of current situations. They are filled with skillful turns of phrase and insightful use of contemporary literature. Worship leaders at St. Lawrence also give attention to music and sermons, but the Catholic tradition of singing and preaching has a less rich heritage on which to draw. What makes worship at St. Lawrence exciting is the ever-changing pattern of lay and clergy participation and the constant reinvention and reinterpretation of the symbols these Catholics bring with them from a variety of locations into this newly Catholic place. Old traditions about when to kneel, who serves the Eucharist and how, what symbols will be used to celebrate the seasons of the church year take on new meaning as this congregation creates its own heritage.

Finally, Golden Rule Christians want their churches to be involved in serving the community. They like the idea of hosting food pantries or organizing work teams to help elderly people care for their homes. They want the church to collect money to send in times of disaster. They may even participate in tutoring programs or home-building efforts (usually in communities other than their own). Congregations are effective centers for such service activities. They can provide a support structure (space, equipment, mailing lists) for all sorts of volunteer activity and fundraising. Robert Wuthnow has shown that people generally trust churches to use their money well: "They may not know how government programs work, or they may not know what happens when they send a check to United Way, but their congregation is small enough that they can feel directly involved and see the fruits of their labors."[40] While Golden Rule Christians may be involved in service activities beyond their churches, they see the church as a primary means through which they leave the world a better place.

SUMMARY

What I am arguing is that there is a pervasive style of religiosity in the United States today that needs to be better understood. While theologians might want to argue that the people I have termed "Golden Rule Christians" have no coherent theology, and evangelists might worry about their eternal souls, sociologists cannot afford to dismiss a form of lived religion just because it does not measure up to orthodox theological standards. Using the twenty-three congregations in our study (as well as impressionistic evidence from a variety of other sources), it is clear that Golden Rule Christianity is far too prevalent to ignore.

It is also probably not new. While I do not have long-term trend data on which to draw, I am struck by the consistency between what I have described here and what David Hall describes in his history of religion in seventeenth-century New England. He notes that "common sense instructs us that religion (or the church) attracts not only a committed core, but also others who, like 'horse-shed' Christians [those who skip the pastor's Bible teaching to spend part of their Sunday mornings in the horse-shed discussing secular matters], limit their commitment." They were more committed to living a good life, he argues, than to particular Calvinist doctrine.[41] Jon Butler closes his book, *Awash in a Sea of Faith,*with a description of Abraham Lincoln's religion—on the one hand, undeniably deep and pious, but on the other hand, clearly unorthodox and institutionally uncommitted: "Lincoln's religion, then, paralleled that of many of his contemporaries. He faced innumerable religious choices. He understood much of Christianity's appeal. He eschewed church membership and resisted practices and doctrines that distinguished contemporary Christianity. . . . [He] represented the ambivalent spiritual inclinations among America's heterodox citizens."[42] According to Butler, America has always been characterized by a strong strain of unorthodox, yet deeply spiritual religiosity. It is this same unorthodox-yet-spiritual morality that made possible the nineteenth-century cultural success of moralistic novels, Chautauqua, and other religious diversions. By concentrating on basic ethical values and dilemmas, commercial innovators marketed religious products far beyond sectarian bounds.[43] Throughout the history of religion in the United States, something resembling Golden Rule Christians seems to have been a fact of life.

I have argued here that the Golden Rule Christianity we see today is explicitly nonideological. That is, it is not driven by beliefs, orthodox or otherwise. Rather, it is based in practice and experience. God is located in moments of transcendence and in the everyday virtues of doing good. Golden Rule Christianity emphasizes relationships and caring. The good person invests heavily in care for family (especially children) and friends, tries to provide friendly help in the community, and seeks ways to make the larger world a better place. All the while, the ideas of others are respected. Proselytizing is frowned upon, and tolerance is celebrated.

Despite the absence of an extensive theological meaning system, I have also argued that Golden Rule Christians are not utterly unreligious. They still identify with religious institutions, and they find themselves with some regularity in the presence of "something bigger," something most of them are quite willing to call "God." They come to church, at least in part, to find the sacred space and time in which those encounters occur.

The congregations they prefer, then, are likely to be shaped by the need for reflective time, as well as by an emphasis on child-rearing and community service. Congregations are not the only social institution to which Golden Rule Christians belong. These people are likely to have many allegiances and friendships outside their particular congregations, but that does not necessarily mean that their religiosity is constrained to a small slice of life. On the contrary, much of their everyday activity is shaped by Golden Rule religious practices, and those practices are grounded in the stories of Scripture and the experiences of worship and transcendence. If we begin to recognize the dimensions of this Golden Rule mode of religiosity, we may also begin to recognize the ways in which modern religion has more pervasive effects than we might have thought.

NOTES

The idea for this essay originated in discussions at the Center for the Study of American Religion at Princeton University, while I was a visiting faculty member there in 1993–94. My thanks go also to Robert Orsi and Charles Hambrick-Stowe for their comments at the "Lived Religion" Conference at Harvard Divinity School in September 1994. I have since benefited from careful comments by Nancy Eiesland and David Hackett and from discussion in the American Religion "Brown Bag" group at Emory and in the Congregational Studies Project Team. The role of Edward Gray is noted in the text, but deserves elaboration. He carefully culled the transcripts from the project for material relevant to the faith being practiced by the individuals we had interviewed. I am grateful for all of these colleagues.

1. Dean R. Hoge, Benton Johnson, and Donald A. Luidens, *Vanishing Boundaries: The Religion of Mainline Protestant Baby Boomers* (Louisville, Ky.: Westminster/John Knox, 1994).

2. Rodney Stark argues that this-worldly religions are destined to extinction, always being replaced by stronger, other-worldly groups that offer the unique "compensators" that only religion can offer. See Rodney Stark and William Sims Bainbridge, *The Future of Religion* (Berkeley: University of California Press, 1985). The implications of this essay for that argument are taken up below. The people I call "Golden Rule Christians" are the people rational choice theorists would call "free riders."

3. Because we originally focused on congregational issues, and because the interviews were not uniform across the various researchers who conducted them, not all of the people we interviewed talked about their personal faith.

4. All congregational names used in this essay are the actual names and locations, used with permission.

5. Among the many theorists who point us in the direction of studying practices are Wuthnow and Bourdieu. See Robert Wuthnow, *Meaning and Moral Order* (Berkeley: University of California Press, 1987); and Pierre Bourdieu, *Outline of a Theory of Practice* (New York: Cambridge University Press, 1979).

6. These three categories were created using responses to two sets of questions from our questionnaire. One set asked respondents to rank a list of "qualities of a good Christian life" as "essential," "very important," "somewhat important," or "not at all important." The second asked for similar responses to a list of "priorities for your church's activities in the community." The "Golden Rule" items were a Christian life characterized by "taking care of those who are sick or needy" and "practicing Christian values in work, home, and school," plus a church that "provides aid and services to people in need." The activist items were a Christian life characterized by "actively seeking social and economic justice" and a church that

"supports social action groups." The evangelical items were a Christian life characterized by "reading and studying the Bible regularly," "spending time in prayer and meditation," and "seeking to bring others to faith in Christ," plus a church committed to "encouraging members to share their faith," "helping members resist the temptations of the world," "an active evangelism program," and "preparing people for a world to come." Each respondent received a score based on the sum of his or her responses to each of these sets of items. Those scores were then weighted to make them equivalent, and those whose scores were highest on the activism scale were then categorized as activists, those highest on the evangelical scale as evangelicals, and those highest on the Golden Rule scale as Golden Rule Christians. Those whose scores were equal on the Golden Rule and either activist or evangelical scales were placed in the non–Golden Rule category. The four people whose scores were equal on the activist and evangelical scales were placed in the evangelical category (since they were all in evangelical churches), and the seventy-one people who had equal scores on all three scales were divided proportionately among the three categories.

7. C. Eric Lincoln and Lawrence H. Mamiya, in *The Black Church in the African American Experience* (Durham, N.C.: Duke University Press, 1990), 228, note that the political activism of the Black church tradition is always fraught with ambiguity. While a large majority of Black clergy think they should be involved in the community, not all are. Our data indicate that while many church members may support those goals, they put other Christian practices ahead of "seeking social and economic justice."

8. Hoge, Johnson, and Luidens (*Vanishing Boundaries*) never identify exactly how many fit their "lay liberal" category. They say simply that "most of the active Presbyterians we interviewed . . . give voice to a theological perspective that we call 'lay liberalism'" (p. 112).

9. Will Herberg, in *Protestant-Catholic-Jew*, rev. ed. (Garden City, N.Y.: Anchor Doubleday, 1960), especially noted the "activism" of American religion, our conviction that we ought to be doing things to make the world better. He quotes Handlin, saying that Americans tend to believe that "ethical behavior and a good life, rather than adherence to a specific creed, [will] earn a share in the heavenly kingdom" (p. 83, quoting Oscar Handlin, *The Uprooted* [New York: Little, Brown, 1951, 128]). Among those who decried the narrowness of such religiosity were Gibson Winter, in *The Suburban Captivity of the Churches* (Garden City, N.Y.: Doubleday, 1961); and Peter L. Berger, in *The Noise of Solemn Assemblies* (Garden City, N.Y.: Doubleday, 1961).

10. Joseph H. Fichter, *Southern Parish: Dynamics of a City Church* (Chicago: University of Chicago Press, 1951), 270.

11. James Davison Hunter, *Culture Wars: The Struggle to Define America* (New York: Basic Books, 1991).

12. The slipperiness of questions about Bible beliefs is demonstrated in two recent studies. In an attempt to learn more about "lay liberals," the Presbyterian Research Office repeated some of the questions asked by Hoge, Johnson, and Luidens. They discovered a similar level of theological relativism among their respondents. However, they worry that these lay people may not be understanding "the questions in the same way we in Research do." As evidence, they

cite responses to questions about the Bible. Seventy-two percent of those who agree that the Bible is "accurate in every detail" also say that the Genesis creation stories are not "a precise how and when." See Keith M. Wulff, " 'Lay Liberals' and Theology Matters," *Monday Morning* 59 (October 10, 1994): 9–12. In a 1985 survey, fifty-six percent of Southern Baptists answered these same questions in the same way. See Nancy T. Ammerman, *Baptist Battles: Social Change and Religious Conflict in the Southern Baptist Convention* (New Brunswick, N.J.: Rutgers University Press, 1990). Such responses do tend to support the notion that most people take a position relative to the Bible that is not ideologically consistent.

13. Personal communication.

14. Editorial, *The Record Argus*, Greenville, Pa., December 24, 1994, 4.

15. This, of course, is an echo of the baby boomer patterns described in Robert N. Bellah et al., *Habits of the Heart* (Berkeley: University of California Press, 1985).

16. Penny Becker's study of congregational conflict supports the centrality of this emphasis on caring. She found that congregations tended to place their conflicts within a communal logic that puts relationships above truth, process above outcome. See Penny Becker, "Politics and Meaning: Framing Gender Conflicts in Local Congregations," paper presented to the meetings of the Association for the Sociology of Religion, Los Angeles, August 1994.

17. This is not the sort of "instrumental" religion Robert Althuser describes in "Paradox in Popular Religion: The Limits of Instrumental Faith," *Social Forces* 69, no. 2 (December 1990): 585–602. Many of those we interviewed did claim that people should go to church or be religious because it would be "good for them." But those did not seem to be the same people who talked about simply experiencing God's caring presence in their daily lives.

18. People with all three orientations place "savior" and "comforter" virtually tied at the top of their list of images, although evangelicals do so with the highest rankings, followed by Golden Rule Christians and activists, in that order. Both evangelicals and Golden Rule Christians rank "father" as the next most desirable image, although again, the evangelical ranking is stronger. Activists choose "liberator" as their third most likely image.

19. See Robert Wuthnow, *Sharing the Journey* (New York: The Free Press, 1994), for a study of such small groups. His ch. 8 pays special attention to their role in religious life.

20. For a description of such intentional faith communities among Catholics, see William V. D'Antonio, "Small Faith Communities in the Roman Catholic Church: New Approaches to Religion, Work and Family," in *Work, Family and Religion in Contemporary Society*, ed. Nancy Tatom Ammerman and Wade Clark Roof (New York: Routledge, 1995), 237–59.

21. Hoge, Johnson, and Luidens (*Vanishing Boundaries*) found that the presence of children is a strong predictor of who returns to church (p. 168). The continuing tie between congregational life and parenting is a recurring theme in Ammerman and Clark Roof, eds., *Work, Family, and Religion in Contemporary Society*. See especially Penny Long Marler, "Lost in the Fifties: The Changing Family and the Nostalgic Church," in that volume, pp. 23–60.

22. See the essay by Anne S. Brown and David D. Hall on family strategies and religious practices in this volume.

23. R. Stephen Warner, *New Wine in Old Wineskins* (Berkeley: University of California Press, 1988). See esp. 201–8.

24. Robert Orsi suggested this line of analysis in his comments on an earlier draft of this essay. This fortress mentality can be seen quite clearly among an older generation of parents who were the first to move to Carmel in the 1950s (and who have now left Carmel United Methodist over, among other things, its lack of clear boundaries).

25. See M. P. Baumgartner, *The Moral Order of a Suburb* (Oxford: Oxford University Press, 1988).

26. In her study of gender, work, and religion, Tracy Scott has discovered that explicit ideas about work as "calling" are very rare, but both liberal and conservative Protestants are nevertheless convinced that their faith matters. Across all categories, the most common response is that it shapes who they are and how they treat people. "What's God Got to Do with It? Protestantism, Gender, and the Meaning of Work in the United States" (Ph.D. diss., Princeton University, forthcoming).

27. Stephen Hart and David Krueger, "Faith and Work: Challenges for Congregations," *Christian Century* 109, no. 22 (July 15–22, 1992): 683–86.

28. In further study of another of our Golden Rule congregations, Nancy Eiesland has demonstrated the extent to which the ethos and connections created inside the congregation extend into other community organizations. See Nancy Eiesland, "A Particular Place: Exurbanization and Religious Response in a Small Town" (Ph.D. diss., Emory University, 1995). For a similar argument about the role of presumably "privatized" religion in "public" life, see Nancy T. Ammerman, "Review of *A Bridging of Faiths* by N. J. Demerath and Rhys H. Williams," *Society* 31, no. 1 (November–December 1993): 91–93.

29. *God and Mammon in America* (New York: The Free Press, 1994), ch. 8.

30. In this respect, they do echo the "moral minimalism" Baumgartner describes in *Moral Order*. They are extremely reluctant to exercise any sort of social control.

31. See Robert A. Schneider, "Voice of Many Waters: Church Federation in the Twentieth Century," in *Between the Times: The Travail of the Protestant Establishment in America, 1900–1960*, ed. William R. Hutchison (Cambridge: Cambridge University Press, 1989), 105–6.

32. Leo D. Lefebure, "The Wisdom of God: Dialogue and Natural Theology," *Christian Century* 111, no. 30 (October 26, 1994): 988.

33. Talcott Parsons, "Christianity in Modern Industrial Society," in *Sociological Theory and Modern Society* (New York: The Free Press, 1967).

34. If Baumgartner (in *Moral Order*) is right about the "moral minimalism" of the suburbs, these Golden Rule Christians may seek church membership at least in part as a place where the bonds of social cohesion are somewhat stronger, where there are some moral claims to be made.

35. This ill-defined spirituality is reminiscent of the "seekers" Wade Clark Roof describes in *A Generation of Seekers* (San Francisco: Harper–San Francisco, 1993). Like the "counterculture" Steven Tipton describes, they trust what they

experience, not the rules or authorities of any system. They are seekers after a truth that will be intuitively known rather than pronounced. See Steven M. Tipton, *Getting Saved from the Sixties* (Berkeley: University of California Press, 1982). However, the people we interviewed rarely talked about specifically seeking spirituality, other than in their commitment to participating in church worship services and occasional special events or retreats.

36. In an analysis of national survey data collected by Gallup, Marler and Roozen found that high on the list of reasons for joining a particular church are its "warmth" and "meaningfulness." See Penny Long Marler and David A. Roozen, "From Church Tradition to Consumer Choice: The Gallup Surveys of the Unchurched American," in *Church and Denominational Growth*, ed. David A. Roozen and C. Kirk Hadaway (Nashville, Tenn.: Abingdon, 1993), 94. Warmth certainly has to do with the caring relationships we have been describing, and meaningfulness includes spiritual experience and insight. Spirituality and relationships are key elements in church choice.

37. Robert Wuthnow notes, "Even in their preaching, their role is probably to remind people of the basic values contained in scripture and tradition or to give a brief time for people to reflect about their lives more than it is to impart an authoritative interpretation." See *Producing the Sacred* (Urbana: University of Illinois Press, 1994), 60.

38. Daniel Olson studied a small "discipleship" group in a liberal Methodist church. He found that their discussions "function much as they do in more conservative churches. There they are much like testimonies: they make the tradition more plausible and real." See Daniel V. A. Olson, "Making Disciples in a Liberal Protestant Church," in *"I Come Away Stronger": How Small Groups Are Shaping American Religion*, ed. Robert Wuthnow (Grand Rapids: Eerdmans, 1994), 146.

39. This is the "rational choice" model of religion elaborated in Laurence R. Iannaccone, "A Formal Model of Church and Sect," *American Journal of Sociology* 94 (Suppl. 1988): 241–68; Laurence R. Iannaccone, "Why Strict Churches Are Strong," *American Journal of Sociology* 99, no. 5 (March 1994): 1180–1211; and Roger Finke and Rodney Stark, *The Churching of America* (New Brunswick, N.J.: Rutgers University Press, 1992), among others. In their assertion that strict churches are strong, they are testing the hypotheses made famous by Dean M. Kelley, in *Why Conservative Churches Are Growing*, 2nd ed. (San Francisco: Harper and Row, 1977).

40. Wuthnow, *God and Mammon*, 214–15.

41. David Hall, *Worlds of Wonder, Days of Judgment: Popular Religious Belief in Early New England* (Cambridge, Mass.: Harvard University Press, 1990), 15.

42. Jon Butler, *Awash in a Sea of Faith* (Cambridge, Mass.: Harvard University Press, 1990), 295.

43. This is my reading of Laurence Moore's evidence in *Selling God: American Religion in the Marketplace of Culture* (New York: Oxford University Press, 1994).

Chapter Ten

GETTING (NOT TOO) CLOSE TO NATURE: MODERN HOMESTEADING AS LIVED RELIGION IN AMERICA

REBECCA KNEALE GOULD

I BEGIN with a tale of two gardens. The first belongs to Helen Nearing. Helen has been a homesteader since 1932, when she moved to a remote Vermont farm with the socialist writer and activist Scott Nearing and began to make a living from subsistence farming and maple sugaring. In 1952, fleeing the development of the Stratton Mountain area, Scott and Helen relocated to Maine and established a second Forest Farm on a small peninsula jutting into Penobscot Bay. There they continued their ventures together in organic farming and in building houses from local stone.[1] With the encouragement of Pearl Buck in the 1950s, Helen and Scott produced *Living the Good Life*, a report on their homesteading project in Vermont, which created for the Nearings a new, and sometimes overwhelming following, particularly among the youth of the counterculture.[2] In 1983, three weeks after his hundredth birthday, Scott Nearing passed away, having made the deliberate—and revealing—choice to stop taking food when he sensed that his body was wearing out. This is a choice that Helen also plans to make.[3] But for now, still sprightly in her nineties, Helen tends to her garden and proclaims a life of self-sufficiency that is only slightly more dependent on outside help and resources than it was in her younger years with Scott.[4]

Helen's present garden is fifty feet square and is enclosed by a wall that Helen built by hand from stones collected on the shores of Penobscot Bay.[5] It was constructed using the same techniques that Helen and Scott had developed to build their home and outbuildings in Vermont. On the outside of the garden stand several compost bins, each six feet square, spaced evenly apart and arranged in diminishing heights. Within the garden is a series of rows and divisions, much like the original garden, where one segment was for tall peas, the second for pole beans, the third for cucumbers, melons, and tomatoes, and the fourth for a small truck garden.[6]

But let us return to the garden wall. Helen and Scott had kept an open garden in Vermont. Their decision to build a walled-in garden in Maine began, we are told, by the discovery of local deer breakfasting on their grapevines and raccoons snacking on their corn. But Helen and Scott's remarks in their homesteading handbooks reveal that their love of stones and stonework played as much of a role in the decision to wall in their garden as did the deer and the raccoons. Building structures of stone had been, in many ways, Helen and Scott's signature activity during their Vermont years. Over a dozen stone buildings remain as testimony to Helen and Scott's homesteading ventures at a time when going "back to the land" was generally understood as a Depression Era survival measure, rather than a social and spiritual experiment in "sane living in a troubled world."[7] Yet the stonework also betrays Helen and Scott's particular style and approach to their projects. For the Nearings, building in stone enabled them to put into practice the principles that they accepted as crucial to their homesteading plan: to build from local materials, to create structures that are indistinguishable from their surroundings, so that it is difficult to tell where "the environment ends and the building begins," and at the same time, to build in a way that expresses the character of the inhabitants.[8]

Helen and Scott's approach to building reveals an inherent tension—one of several to which we return in the course of this essay—between the pull of human creativity and the desire to humble oneself before the natural world. This tension reveals itself, for instance, in the Nearings' warnings that the placing and pointing of the stones should be done in a way that resists "stylized and formal lines" and lets "each stone tell its own story in its own form and color."[9] This same tension is recapitulated in the decision to build the wall. As the Nearings admit, while hungry animals were a reason for building at least a wire fence, the decision to replace the fence with over four hundred feet of stone wall emerged from the longing to build again in stone and to have an occasional project that carried with it the "absence of any compulsion" and that would serve, in their words, as "our tennis and our golf" for the fourteen years it took to construct.[10] Clearly, the wall was built for Scott and Helen's sake as much as for the sake of the garden—or, to put it more accurately, the wall feeds other human hungers, while a fence would have been only sufficient to protect their food.

The Nearings' judgments on "Stone Walls versus Wire Fences" reveals to us the pattern of what I want to call "the approach–avoidance dance with nature."[11] This is a dance in which most homesteaders participate. In this dance, the desire to get close to nature, a desire that fuels the decision to homestead at all, is countered—often unintentionally—by strategies that impose distance. The strategies may be as richly symbolic as the building of an intricately crafted wall or they may emerge more subtly in the way homesteaders' interpretations of their daily life emphasize preoccupations (professional, psychological, or spiritual) that supersede or even go against a strictly "natural" agenda.

But before we go on to explore this approach–avoidance dance—and the larger personal and cultural tensions to which it points—let us take a quick look at a second garden. This garden belongs to one of Helen's several homesteading neighbors. Sal, together with his wife Kate and their children, moved down to the Nearings' neighborhood on Helen's invitation.[12] Helen had heard of Sal and Kate's homesteading efforts in another state and was aware of the extreme economic limitations under which they were living. At first, Sal worked for Helen, helping her with the garden, though his ideas of gardening were significantly different from hers. Later, another of Helen's neighbors leased some land to Sal (who is not interested in land ownership) and Sal and Kate built their own home and garden, both of which are flourishing after three years.

Sal's home resembles a "yurt," a Mongolian-style structure that became a popular form of shelter among the counterculture "back-to-the landers" of the 1960s and 1970s. Sal's house is a kind of "permanent yurt," a circular dwelling made with wood cut on site. Inside is a large central kitchen and living space, with several bedrooms, a loft, and a composting toilet apportioned in spaces created by partial divisions coming out from the center of the house like spokes on a wheel. Outside, the garden—once it becomes distinguishable—recapitulates the home's circular design. It seems to emanate from the house in increasing circular patterns, as if the home were dropped in a green pond of grasses, grains, and midsummer vegetables.

My difficulty in distinguishing the garden, when I first visited at the height of its July flowering, was an intentional effect on Sal's part. The garden is planted so that low, fast-growing plants, such as lettuces, grow as protective soil-nourishing weeds for taller, sun-seeking beans and peas.[13] Squash, carrots, and radishes seemed to be sprouting randomly. Sal spoke to me of his intention to eventually develop a "walking garden," one that he would plant largely by walking up and down a path and casting the seed abroad. Already, he has planted some of the garden in this manner, and he revels in the way certain plants appear in spaces unexpectedly, each one finding its place of "opportunity." Sal's primary principle is to maintain a "no-till" garden, in which the soil is prepared by mulching and composting only. Seeds, if planted at all, are merely pushed into place in the small compost and mulch hills and the soil is broken only by the water-seeking roots of the plants themselves. As Sal's own words will reveal, the reasons for no-till planting go far beyond the intention of maintaining a fruitful garden, just as Helen and Scott's reasons for building stone walls are complex, if not always openly expressed.

A WIDER VIEW—SOME INTERPRETATIONS OF HOMESTEADING

A look at the gardens and homes of those who are deliberately intending to live close to nature and off the land—that is, an examination of homesteads and homesteaders in the twentieth century—is revealing of the dominant religious and cultural tensions of modern and postmodern times. Some of these tensions—between order and chaos, between "nature" and "culture," between mortality and immortality, to name a few heady possibilities—are age-old. But they are variously inflected, defined, and created by the particular historical and cultural events of the twentieth century, as well as certain nineteenth-century legacies. Moreover, homesteaders' ideas and feelings about nature, control, progress, and self-fulfillment all have a certain resonance with familiar themes in American religious history, particularly in the period since industrialization.

Homesteading, as I have come to define it, is the act of choosing to live a largely self-sufficient life close to nature, usually after having spent some time living otherwise, in the city or in the suburbs. It is not the homesteading of the Homestead Act (1862), it is not growing up on the family farm, nor is it the art of keeping a Victory Garden out back. On the other hand, homesteading is an open term, allowing for a range of possibilities: locating oneself imaginatively within a pioneering tradition, as the Nearings have done; returning *to* the family farm after teaching and writing in the city as farmer and essayist Wendell Berry has done; or extending the idea of the backyard garden to advocate a new practical and moral way of living, as Bolton Hall and Ralph Borsodi variously attempted in the early twentieth century. Such experiments in living demonstrate the practical, as well as metaphorical aspects, of a generalized practice known as homesteading.[14]

Like more conventional religious practices, homesteading comes out of a particular historical and cultural legacy. The many approaches to homesteading that have developed over time can serve, for us, as both window and mirror. Sometimes the practice enables us to see into the times; sometimes it is a reflection of them through the act of dissent. We may develop a typology of homesteading that corresponds in time and "style" to the optimisms and anxieties of the turn of the century and the Progressive Era, the challenges of the Depression and the postwar period, the cultural revolution of the 1960s, and the environmental awakenings of the 1990s.[15] Such a typology reveals homesteading as a kind of parallel movement growing and shifting alongside religious movements such as the social gospel, neo-orthodoxy, the Death of God, and the New Age. In many ways, homesteading represents a kind of "antimodernist" impulse which, like the movements T. J. Jackson Lears describes, reacts against the currents of religious liberalism and secularization while also moving

HOMESTEADING AS LIVED RELIGION

within them.[16] Thus, while homesteading has been a persistent American activity since Thoreau took to the Walden Woods in 1845, it is also a changed and changing activity, embodying and responding to various cultural crises, and frequently providing an "answer" that is as persuasive, as grounded in "Truth," and as personally transformational as are more explicitly religious engagements.

A second way to explore the relationship between homesteading and lived religion is to envision homesteading as part of a larger American story, the story of our long-standing impulse to get "close to" or "back to" nature. Restricting ourselves to the twentieth century alone, we know that getting close to nature has taken a number of forms: the nostalgia for the closed frontier that emerged at the turn of the century; the growing popularity of Fresh Air movements and the Boy Scouts in the 1920s; the rise of wilderness preservation legislation and the development of "land ethic" thinking under the influence of Robert Marshall and Aldo Leopold through the 1930s, 1940s and 1950s; the Woodstock impulse to "find a way back to the garden" of the 1960s and 1970s; and the boom in the 1980s and 1990s of literature on deep ecology, ecofeminism, ecological theology, and radical environmentalism.[17] All of these are signposts, though hardly nuanced descriptions, of the ongoing enthusiasm for, yet ever-changing meanings of getting close to nature. And if we look back still further, we see that from the "howling wilderness" of the Puritans to the oppressed Mother Earth of the ecofeminists, nature has always been a type and a trope for other cultural foundations, and more often for the cracks and shifts within them.[18]

Throughout this larger story of running from or fleeing to the natural world, "the religious" comes to the fore with great clarity. In the twentieth century alone, we can follow a telltale trajectory from the pages of Lyman Abbott's *Outlook*, where nature is portrayed as a place of retreat for spiritual cleansing and as a proving ground for good (usually male) Christians to strengthen their moral values, to more recent religious valuations of nature in which nature itself becomes the object of worship.[19] An extended version of this trajectory has been traced with considerable skill and detail by Catherine Albanese in her work on "nature religion" in America. But my emphasis here is somewhat different. For Albanese, "nature religion" functions as a noun, a civil religious tradition that is traced as a definable "counterreligion" to traditional, institutional forms.[20] A more fruitful interpretive possibility is to leave behind the "what" question with respect to the possible presence of "nature religion," and to pursue some inquiries as to how, and in what cultural circumstances, religion and nature come together.

This brings me to my third point about the ways we can understand homesteading as lived religion. The third approach, the one that underlies both the methods and the arguments of this essay, is to explore home-steading as an act of cultural creation. Here I need to make an important distinction. While the two approaches I have discussed above help us understand the way in which homesteading, as an activity and as a move-ment, may be culturally constructed—especially in terms of its relation-ship with the cultural (and religious) construction of "nature"—what makes homesteading an especially revealing practice to study as an exam-ple of lived religion is that the practice itself involves the creation, or re-creation, of culture.

Of course, we may argue that all of our practices do this. Practice, among other things, involves the art of making choices and the choices we make constitute a significant part of the individual and cultural identi-ties we create. But the practice of homesteading highlights and compli-cates the act of cultural creation in particularly revealing ways. While homesteading, more than many activities, seems like everyday practice, it differs from everyday practice in both intensity and kind. First, it places a conscious emphasis on decisions and decision making. For homestead-ers, all decisions—from how to procure water to whether to buy a car—are understood to be deeply important (hence, the many well-articu-lated rationales and interpretive glosses). The larger choice, the choice to engage in homesteading, thus constitutes a commitment to taking very seriously—though not without humor—a host of smaller choices. Given the total reorientation of life that homesteading demands, we can begin to see homesteading as a kind of conversion. Indeed, the many testimonies of homesteading that I have heard or read are often infused with a kind of evangelical energy, tempered only by the fear that too many converts might jeopardize the spiritual, environmental, and economic benefits of the practice.

But it is also the *kind* of decisions that are made which makes home-steading a distinct and distinctly intriguing practice to consider. However minor some decisions may seem, the decisions homesteaders self-con-sciously make are the same kinds of decisions that have been made over the centuries in Western culture on a grand scale: decisions about tech-nology, agriculture, what and how we eat. These daily decisions inevit-ably lead to or stem from other decisions: whether and how we will control, worship, or disdain natural processes, how we will come to view our bodies and our embodiedness, and how, if at all, we will recognize forces beyond our human selves. These are decisions we are all involved in making, whether consciously or otherwise. But in the ritual context of homesteading, an imaginative circle is drawn in which cultural decisions about technology, progress, nature, and humanity are allowed to be "made again."

Of course, these acts of cultural re-creation must be held in some suspicion. For just as the decision to homestead is conditioned by both individual and cultural circumstances, so all the smaller decisions involved in homesteading are not freely made.[21] A discussion of the particular constraints on these smaller decisions and the kinds of religious and cultural common ground that twentieth-century homesteaders seem to share will constitute the last section of my explorations. But let us return first to the practices themselves, with Helen and Sal as our representative figures for so many homesteaders whose lives and practices must be the subjects of a longer study. In returning to these practices—gardening and eating, uses of time, styles of planning, and ways of learning—I will be attuned to the way meaning is constructed out of them, as well as to the ironies and ambivalences that emerge as these homesteaders attempt to work out deliberate approaches to nature and technology, self and society in the work they do. It is in these ironies and ambivalences that the dynamics of freedom and constraint, progress and return, mortality and immortality come to the fore.

PLANNING, PLANTING, AND
SPENDING TIME

We already have some sense of the differences in the way Helen and Sal construct their gardens. Helen's garden, and, even more so, the gardens she previously developed with Scott, have been created with a strong valuation of order and "system."[22] The "Good Life" books confirm this impression. They report, for instance, that garden rows were always planted running north to south, and each row was marked by a numbered stake.[23] These stakes had corresponding numbers in the Nearings' garden book, which was devoted to mapping the garden in two-year intervals, recording crop rotation and succession, and reporting "bed by bed and row by row . . . the dates of planting, variety and origins of seeds, methods of treatment and results." Compost piles were also numbered, and the treatment and development of each pile were duly recorded.[24]

Much of Helen and Scott's descriptions of the gardens appears not only in the "gardening" sections of their books, but in chapters such as "Plans, Records and Budgeting."[25] Here Helen and Scott report their design for insuring that potatoes will be planted in fresh green sod each year.[26] Here also they describe the maps of their gardens, their approach to bed gardening, and the details of bookkeeping. The Nearings' primary focus in this chapter and throughout their homesteading texts is on the matter "of greatest concern to homesteaders and other experimenters": the art and necessity of bookkeeping and planning. "Every day, week and month," they argue, "should have a working program, put down on paper, and referred to constantly as a guide and determining factor."[27]

Not surprisingly, when Helen and Scott embarked on their first homesteading venture in Vermont, they drew up a twelve-point plan designed to take them through the first ten years of their project. The points in the plan ranged from the commonsense necessities of their task ("12. . . . *we will need a dependable source of sand and gravel*") to the more philosophical foundations behind the project ("7. *We will keep no animals*. . . . We believe that all life is to be respected—non-human as well as human. Therefore, for sport we neither hunt nor fish, nor do we feed on animals. Furthermore, we prefer, in our respect for life, not to enslave or exploit our fellow creatures [by keeping farm animals or pets]").[28] Under each point of the plan is a carefully argued, and often enumerated, elaboration of the rationale and usefulness of the approach. Yet Helen and Scott take pains to inform their readers that their plan was "not made out of whole clothe [*sic*]," but was changed according to experience. "It was flexible," they insist, later adding, "but in principle and usually in practice we stuck to it."[29]

In describing the Nearings' various gardens and their ways of writing about them, my point is not simply to show how organized and precise they were. It is, rather, to bring to the fore the dynamics of freedom and control that are at work in their practices and to suggest that issues of freedom and control, interwoven with the related question of proximity to nature, are at the heart of their homesteading venture. In other words, just as the garden crops are being cultivated through agriculture, freedom and control are being cultivated through the Nearings' creation of a mini-culture. Helen and Scott describe the basis of their homesteading practice as being one of cultural dissent, of becoming free from the "dread implications" of a profit–price economy, which they saw, in the 1930s, as having led the nation into depression, war, and deteriorating social conditions. But their social protest takes the form of two people trying to "live rightly" in the world. Thus, in their personal lives and choices, they sought "an affirmation of those values we considered essential to the good life . . . simplicity, freedom from anxiety or tension, an opportunity to be useful and to live harmoniously."[30] But the Nearings' quest for freedom has carried with it any number of ironies. While seeking freedom from a social structure they considered inherently corrupt and a way of life that brought anxiety and tension, the Nearings responded by consistently developing practices of constraint.

We can see this dynamic not only in their approach to gardening, but in the larger visions of their homesteading project that evolved out of this central activity. For the Nearings, freedom from the limits of contemporary culture meant not only leaving behind the urban life of the majority and rejecting the prevailing economy for a use-economy; it also meant rejecting some of the most tightly held assumptions of consumer culture, such as assumptions regarding the use of time. Time to lecture, write, travel, and make music was something that both of the Nearings wanted and they rearranged time accordingly. But while the practice of home-steading allowed them to break from the prevailing structures of time, those structures were replaced by a well-planned counterstructure. In the early years, the structure was to spend half the day on bread labor and half the day pursuing personal interests from sunbathing to preparing a lecture. Evenings were often spent with one person reading aloud while the other shelled beans or knitted.[31] Later, this pattern of activity was refined into what became know as the "four-four-four" formula: four hours of "bread labor" (maintaining self-sufficiency), four hours of "pro-fessional activity" (reading, writing, teaching), and four hours of "fulfill-ing obligations and responsibilities as members of the human race" by engaging in community and civic activities.[32] In essence, the activities of the four-four-four formula were the same as the ones previously de-scribed, though the "structure" in which they were later placed seems—at least in the description—to allow even less room for spontaneity or for personal pleasure. In both cases, the desire for freedom from the con-straints of time is fulfilled by the creation of a new, fairly rigid schedule, shaped first to the demands of the garden, but extending beyond it to include all the activities of daily life.

As if sensing the disjunction between the freedom that they hoped to attain through homesteading and their self-imposed control, the Nearings write: "We adhered generally to this daily and weekly routine, but not fanatically." "However," they add, "unless there was a good and sufficient reason, we did not depart from it."[33] A certain refrain emerges from the Nearings' writings about homesteading. In the explanation of the garden wall, their remarks on their twelve-point plan for living, and their description of the four-four-four daily schedules, Helen and Scott express an awareness, even contriteness, about the physical or psychological constraints they are placing on their lives lived close to the natural world. At the same time, they continue to insist on the practical and moral utility of their choices. Here the approach–avoidance dance with nature is inter-laced with and sometimes indistinguishable from other kinds of ap-proach–avoidance dances: freedom and constraint, order and chaos, mor-tality and immortality.

In the daily lives of homesteaders questions of meaning are inextricably bound up with the practical problems of self-sufficiency. Indeed, the choice to be self-sufficient is a choice about making meaning. We may nod in agreement that all of the Nearings' plans for their project "make sense," but we do well to ask just what kind of sense they make. More often than not, homesteaders' pragmatic choices are choices that also reveal much about their understandings of "nature" and within that general understanding, particular notions of and concerns about human possibilities and limits, the nature of the body, and of life and powers beyond the self. The negotiation of freedom and control, or order and chaos, becomes, in its most fundamental sense, a negotiation of the human condition.

REJECTING THE PLOW

A return visit to Sal's no-till gardening practices can help us open up the dynamics of these negotiations still further. Sal's approach to gardening is clearly a particular agricultural method, but it reaches beyond practical theory to include a philosophy and a theology.[34]

On the first day that I visited his garden, Sal spoke to me about the practical details and "how-tos" of its maintenance. Even then, Sal hinted about the fact that there is a "spirituality" both in the "walking garden" he is trying to develop and in the gardens he has already made. That "spirituality" is one of digging into the earth, aerating it, and letting things come up into the sun. On the second day I visited, I asked Sal to clarify his remarks on the "spirituality" of till and no-till gardening. His response was, in itself, a kind of cultural history:

> [Tilling] has been part of our past evolution . . . [of] bringing things to light. . . . Tilling the earth was part of that process. [But now] you can recognize forces where they are. . . . In other words, things appeared to be so dark before that it was necessary to throw light and air on things in order to see truth and have order. I think in the future we'll be capable of realizing that there's no need for imposed order—that order is there, it's a chaotic sense of order. It's such a large and interwoven sense that it appears chaotic, but it's a much more divine sense of order.[35]

Sal's comments on his gardening technique suddenly catapult us into his homesteading world, where culture—it appears—is being remade. For Sal, tilling locates itself in a wider complex of cultural moments, moments that Sal would be too generous to label as "errors," but nevertheless moments in history that we would be fortunate to get beyond: the relentless desire for truth and order and the exercise of too much human control over the natural world.

Sal explains his practice of no-till gardening in ways other than his own version of Western cultural history. For example, equally significant, are the "natural facts" that justify the practice. According to Sal, the soil has a tripartite structure: a microbial network of fungi and roots, the earth itself, and "an ethereal, kind of magnetic membrane that overlies the earth's surface."[36] This structure is broken every time the soil is tilled. Thus, argues Sal, tilling the soil is

> a remedial process. [You] bring your garden to a kind of fulfillment by the end of the year. But then you break it again, so that the garden never heals beyond a certain point. You have a limited potential for building the garden and that's because you have a limited potential for it to be healed.[37]

In Sal's view, the health of the garden, the productivity of the garden, and the health of the humans relying on the garden are all intertwined. Thus, no-till gardening is not only representative of a cultural process in which the "need to impose order" is relaxed; it is also a choice to respond to nature on nature's terms, so that both natural health and human health are kept in balance.

Running through both of Sal's rationales for no-till gardening is the assumption that he is responding to the way nature *really is*: a divine sense of order that appears chaotic, a complexly structured environment to which humans should accommodate. For Sal, this understanding of nature—which historians might call a "construction" of nature—emerges from his early experience with formal education. "Ever since I was young," he remarked to me, "there seemed to be a part of the world that was available to me, but the conventional schooling that I was going through didn't seem to offer it."[38] Sal originally selected a college major in wildlife biology, a field that appealed to him because it involved being "out in nature." His decision to switch majors and eventually to leave college in order to pursue wood carving and carpentry full-time came, in part, from disappointment with his original discipline:

> You weren't really out [in nature]. You weren't out in the sense of being available to what was there. You were going out with a predetermination of what you were looking for and a schedule. You know a schedule of things that had to be accomplished and it was all . . . determined already. Nothing entered in except *by accident* . . . [and then] often you aren't prepared for it and you don't have the proper energy to access it.[39]

In this description of his frustrating educational experiences, Sal exhibits an approach to nature in sharp contrast to that of Scott and Helen Nearing. To have a schedule, to make a "plan," to see nature as a "laboratory" for human "experiments," as Helen and Scott often put it, is, according to Sal, a way of closing oneself down to the real lessons—of math and physics, of history and spirituality—that nature has to teach. Sal and Helen share a desire to "learn by doing," and to learn from direct experience with the natural world. Yet he clearly differs from her in both style and approach.[40]

Ambivalence and Common Ground

Attending to the differences between Helen's and Sal's approaches to gardening enables us to see not only the ways in which homesteaders attempt to "re-create culture" in their own backyards, but also their own styles of explicating these practices. In Helen and Scott's writings, we can hear their ambivalence about the need for human control of the natural world, as well as their confidence in designing and executing a plan that will provide both personal and social change. In Sal's oral commentary, we hear the refrain of "being available" and "letting go," of cultivating intimacy with nature on nature's terms, of wanting to learn from "matter itself." But behind Sal's discourse is a logic, as precise as the Nearings', about how, why, and in what way such "letting go" should happen. In an unexpected way, then, Helen and Sal share some significant religious and cultural common ground. That common ground begins with the fact that these two homesteaders—while occupying different places on a continuum—are nonetheless deeply interested in the same larger questions. Whether it is order and chaos, nature and culture, or control and freedom, all are poles of personal and cultural matters in which Helen and Sal are not only involved—as we all are—but are consciously engaged in rethinking and reenacting. But while this self-consciousness is part and parcel of homesteading practice, it is that which is *less* conscious—ironic, unintended, or ambivalent—which often brings Helen, Sal, and many other homesteaders together.

The shared experience of ambivalence I have been referring to throughout this essay is the ambivalence homesteaders have about how close to nature we should (or can) actually get. In the Nearings' case, this ambivalence is more or less explicit, particularly as it comes through in the range of apologies (in both senses of the term) for the literal and symbolic walls they place between themselves and the natural world.[41] In Sal's case, the ambivalence may be less clear, until we begin to see the extent to which his spontaneous, "immediate" relationship with nature is part of a carefully articulated vision of self and of culture.[42]

The history of American religion and culture has shown us that individuals have always painted the canvas of nature with interpretations of life, death, health, sexuality, community, individuality, and freedom. We have, as Robert Orsi observes, certain "cultural hot spots," and nature is often the symbolic locus where these cultural hot spots simmer and burn.[43] Thus, we can read homesteaders' ambivalence about getting close to nature as being ambivalence about any number of other matters: the human body, intimacy with others, death, the existence of a "plan" underlying the structure of the universe, or a force guiding the direction of human lives. The limits of this essay prevent me from pursuing the nature and texture of these ambivalences more fully.[44] We can, however, look more closely at some persistent themes in the limits homesteaders set with respect to intimacy with nature. Despite their differences, both Helen and Sal remain invested in two shared commitments, or longings, which strike me as coming right out of the heart of the American religious story: the commitment to the idea of progress and the related quest for immortality. Attending to the practices pertaining to food and eating will bring these homesteaders' impulses into focus.

EATING RIGHT: TRANSCENDENCE, INCARNATION, AND IMMORTALITY

For homesteaders, the decision to homestead is, in a fundamental sense, a decision about food. To engage in homesteading is to place food at the center of one's life and livelihood, or as many would prefer to put it, to recognize the centrality of food and to appropriately adjust one's life around it. The choices made about food and eating are as various as those that are made about gardening. These range from recognizing that one can reject consumer culture by minimizing the "hype" around food and living simply, to acknowledging the essential spirituality of eating "mindfully" and thus choosing, say, to develop rituals of gratitude around eating, to eat meat from "well-loved" animals, or to make sure one eats "locally" only.[45]

In Helen and Scott Nearing's case, the decision to be vegetarian emerged from their stated principles against the consumption or "enslavement" of animals, as outlined in their original twelve-point plan for living.[46] But a closer look at their words about vegetarianism, mono-diets, and "eating with the seasons" reveals the complex layers of meanings and motivations wrapped up in these decisions.

One or two examples may suffice. On the significance of fasting on water only for ten days at a time, the Nearings write: "We enjoy these days of fasting and look forward to them. . . . Just as shaving the head completely of hair can give one a godlike feeling of lack of clutter, so going without food can give one a feeling of freedom and release that is real emancipation."[47] The Nearings' notion of controlling eating in order to acquire freedom is further developed in the concept of eating according to the seasons (i.e., only eating greens until other vegetables appear in the garden) as a necessary discipline. "There is something extravagant and irresponsible about eating strawberries in a cold climate," the Nearings remark. They go on to assert: "Such practices ignore the meaningful cycle of the seasons. Those who dodge it or slight it are like children who skip a grade in school, pass over its drill and discipline, and ever after have the feeling that they've missed something."[48] Here the Nearings move beyond a focus on nature and the importance of eating (and hence, working and living) in the cycle of the seasons to a judgment of those people who do not live in this way; such people shirk a necessary discipline and a crucial step in their education. This emphasis on maturity, whether personal or cultural, becomes more apparent in the Nearings' remarks about drinking milk, a practice they came to reject:

> Milk is a highly concentrated infant food, especially designed to stimulate rapid growth in the early stages of development. Human milk should normally be for baby humans, cow's milk for calves. . . . Food intended by nature for one is not necessarily a desirable food for the other. Adults of any breed should have been weaned and past the milk stage of feeding.[49]

In these various comments on food and eating, we see again a line of reasoning that begins with an assertion about the way that "nature *really is*," but at a second glance, this reasoning reveals more about the human desire to control the "natural" intake of food and water, to "progress" beyond previous personal and cultural limits, and to attain freedom. For the Nearings, "getting close to nature" also can mean getting above and beyond nature, and, in a sense, reaching for immortality.

As we are beginning to see, the daily decisions of homesteading, like the decision to homestead itself, participate in homesteaders' larger visions of progress, even while "progress" itself might be disdained.[50] These visions may be generalized as the ironic pursuit of "going forward by going back." In some instances, this pursuit is explicitly articulated as a "return to simpler times," which will help human culture perfect and purify itself from the bad habits (such as factory farming) of contemporary life. At other times, homesteaders insist that they are not idealizing the past, yet claim that their particular choices with respect to building, eating, and gardening will lead them individually, if not collectively as a culture, to the realization of the Good Life. That Good Life is variously construed as one of economic independence, spiritual integration, or the pursuit of personal satisfaction.

The individual choices homesteaders make, then, reveal to us not only what homesteaders tend to turn away from—industrial, technological, capitalist, or "mainstream" culture—but also what they hope to move toward: harmony with other humans and other species, a new level of spiritual intensity, a dramatic experience of self-reliance, a more just economic system. All these versions of progress have been pursued before and such pursuits are familiar touchstones in American religious history.

But there are inherent ironies in the larger dynamic of "going forward by going back," particularly for those homesteaders who see American culture's stress on "progress" (material or spiritual) as something they are trying to escape. The paradoxes involved in "going forward by going back" is something that all homesteaders struggle with, though they do not always articulate it directly. While Sal's notion of progress is not as stringently or explicitly expressed as is the Nearings', it still bubbles up to the surface in his discussions about gardens and food.

Sal's decision to eat meat, like his practice of no-till gardening, both emerges from and is supported by those larger views of history and of the self that we have already heard him articulate. In arguing that it is possible to "recognize forces where they are," Sal begins to unfold a vision of personal and cultural progress. "I think it's a further evidence of maturity," he remarked, "when that authority acts in us . . . when you no longer have to pull things out into the light anymore."[51] Sal's belief in "learning from things directly," rather than from books or other people, comes not only from his intense personal experience with this kind of learning, but from his conviction that the "time has passed" in history for people to learn in the context of "guru–disciple" relationships. His decision to light his house with candles and not to insulate it from the winter cold comes not only from his desire to be more in touch with the natural rhythms of time and the seasons, but also from his belief that we have evolved "past technology." Solar power would be an environmentally appropriate choice for light and heat, but "candlelight is more profound," he told me, because of "knowing electricity" and choosing to return to a prior practice.[52] Many of Sal's choices constitute a rejection of what is commonly understood as a "cultural advance" in favor of an earlier method. Yet the larger uses to which these methods are put, the meaning-making that is involved in them, are ironically cast in terms of progress.

Sal's choice to eat meat, after previously being a vegetarian and having once experimented with living on no food at all, locates itself within the larger complex of building and gardening practices and his ideas about nature and culture. Sal understands his own previous experiments with fasting and vegetarianism as a "phase," a test in freeing the body from its dependence on food. Moreover, Sal understands vegetarianism as another aspect of that moment in history when people sought truth and light through strategies of force. Now, Sal and his family eat meat on occasion, pursuing a kind of middle path between the factory farming of consumer culture and the pursuit of "other-worldly" perfectionism that some vegetarians seem to seek. Yet Sal's interest in getting to a "more mature place" personally and culturally—in part by eating meat—resonates (again ironically) with the Nearings' own comments on the vegetarian way of life as an appropriately "grown up" and enlightened practice.

Just as Sal simultaneously resists and participates in ideals of progress as he struggles to make decisions about the growing and eating of food, so also does he seem to seek a kind of immortality, even while objecting to the way Western culture has so actively pursued this goal. Sal's preference for "being available" to the practical and spiritual lessons already present in nature, for cultivating a chaotic sense of order in his garden, for resisting "how-to" books in favor of becoming "a living book," all reveal a Thoreauvian desire to "know by experience." Eating meat in moderation and with awareness of the animal's life and death fits into this schema. It represents a way of accepting the embodiedness of other beings and the interdependence of these bodies, in a way that vegetarianism does not. On the other hand, the desire to progress "past technology," to cultivate a walking garden in which nature *seems* to take the lead, this too represents a desire to solve human problems—both those that emerge from individual biographies and those that belong to the human condition.

As Sal relates his first steps away from conventional education and toward the natural world, we hear these existential strains:

> I never really needed a specific teacher or ever sought one out because I was too busy; there was just too much going on. . . . Everything immediately would lead to the next thing. . . . [With] no one there to lead you . . . you're going purely by either sense or instinct. . . . However, once those things are crossed, the information is, is you. You see what I mean? It is you *fully* and *nothing* can take it away. There's no set of circumstances—accidents or physical death even or whatever that can part you from that information. It becomes your very flesh itself, your bones, your structure of your body.[53]

In Sal's view, knowledge that is attained through self-sufficiency and through living intimately with the natural world is taken into the body. Yet somehow this knowledge outlasts the body and the natural processes of death. This valuation of the body and embodiment is the larger context in which Sal's approach to gardening and eating needs to be understood. In one sense, this valuation is a response to his earlier experiences of formal education. It is a rejection of rational, "head" learning for fully embodied, experiential learning. Yet as Sal's own words reveal, embodied learning and embodied living involve much more than a rejection. They provide an answer, less distinguishable than a conscious pursuit of "Truth," but an answer nonetheless. When he learns from nature directly, "nothing can separate him" from what he has learned. While Sal rejects the kind of perfectionism that the Nearings strive for and with which he himself experimented, he remains invested in both the idea of progress and the quest for immortality. His approach is a more incarnational one, a yearning for the *real presence* of things through direct, spontaneous experience. But his, too, is a practice of living that responds to the fact of dying, a creation of culture that both embraces and resists the processes of nature.

CONCLUSION

Conclusions typically represent a kind of late-September gardening dilemma: Do you reap what you have sown and call it a day, or do you hustle in some lettuces at the last minute before the frost? Most homesteaders practice fall and winter gardening and I would like to follow suit by making a prospective comment about where I think an investigation of homesteading practices can take us.

There are a number of larger stories to which a study of homesteading contributes. One is a story of "nature" in America and what the American landscape has meant both literally and metaphorically in American history. The truism about the American landscape is that it is both wilderness and garden. Historians and literary critics have often accepted this truism and gone on to show us how these readings of nature are variously inflected by religion, politics, constructions of gender, race, and so on.[54] A study of homesteading complicates the "wilderness/garden" polarity by adding a middle element: the homestead as both home and small working farm. Unlike the "garden" that is understood as a paradise in which humans do no work and are fed and served by nature,[55] the homestead is a garden of human effort and thus becomes inscribed not only with metaphors of "going back to nature" and away from a world of human-centered industry, but also with the metaphors of human impact and control.

By focusing on *practice*, a study of homesteading helps us get underneath the layers of metaphor while simultaneously investigating the ways metaphor is used in the making of meaning. By bringing us to a "middle place" between the wilderness and the garden, a study of homesteading allows us to inquire into old polarities in new ways. Nature and culture are brought more closely together, as are production and consumption, progress and nostalgia, male and female.

The second story to which a study of homesteading can contribute emerges from the first. While students of American history and literature sometimes have been "stuck" in the twin paradigms of wilderness and garden, students of American religion have been similarly limited by the old story of "secularization." A study of homesteading can add to the current flood of complications and revisions of the "secularization thesis."

Secularization has been variously defined as the decline of religion, the decline of the social significance of religion, and, more recently, the decline of religious authority.[56] Those who have sought to challenge the secularization thesis have pointed to the popularity of new religious movements, the resurgence of older movements (Pentecostalism, Mormonism, and Christian fundamentalism), the persistence of individual religious beliefs and practices (claiming belief in God, attending church) and, more theoretically, the inadequacy of the very terms of the debate. Amidst these divergent takes on secularization, a shared observation can be found: that while religion may no longer be what it was (before the Reformation, before the French Revolution, before Marxism), religion somehow refuses to go away.

The impulse to go "back to the land" is a case study in both the decline and the persistence of religion in a "post-Christian" culture. Like many movements of the twentieth century, "going back to nature" both shapes and is shaped by religious liberalism and the secularization of American culture. It is a move away from the supernatural toward the natural, away from the church into the world, away from strictly theological explanations of the world to more scientific apprehensions of the processes of life. Yet this move is also a reaction *against* secularization and the presumed children of secularization: capitalism, materialism, rationalization, the absence of ritual, and the dilution of spiritual values and experiences in everyday life.

The practice of homesteading is a cultural gesture that locates itself on the same two-way street as broader "back-to-nature" impulses. While most homesteaders are not churchgoers, they engage in practices that are as spiritual as they are practical. These actions are self-consciously symbolic and invoke existential questions about life, death, salvation, morality, self-transcendence, and "the good." The lives of homesteaders are sometimes highly ritualized. Often, they demonstrate unflagging commitment to the "truths" of nature and of nature's way, however these may be constructed. In this sense, homesteading not only may be "religious," but also may bear some unintended family resemblances to such unlikely relatives as fundamentalism and evangelicalism. Those very aspects of Christian culture that many homesteaders resist—perfectionism, exceptionalism, the quest for immortality—often reappear in the midst of their everyday practices.

Broadly speaking, then, the study of homesteading provides us with a new look at religion and nature in America, while also taking us into other areas of inquiry (gender, the meaning of home, nostalgia, consumerism) that have significant bearing on our larger understanding of "lived religion" and American culture in the twentieth century.

Now for the harvest. Much of this essay concerns itself with what I have called "the approach–avoidance dance" with nature. An underlying thesis has been that getting close to nature literally through the act of homesteading does not necessarily mean getting close to nature in the way of making meaning for one's life. Intimacy with nature may be desired, but it is not always accomplished or sustained. Homesteaders' practices and their theories about them may ironically keep nature at bay. This distancing tends to take place, in fact, in the disjunctions between particular practices and the "readings" of them that we or the homesteaders provide. Another observation I have made is that, for some homesteaders, "the religious" manifests itself in the act of getting close to the natural world. Here begins the second approach–avoidance dance, the approach–avoidance dance with "the religious." The second dance pertains to the first. For even when "the religious" does manifest itself, the particular character or quality of that religious moment—for instance, transcendental or incarnational—may take someone toward nature, away from nature, or both at the same time.

How do we make sense of all of these approach–avoidance dances going on at once? That is a task I have only begun to undertake here. But my interest, both with respect to homesteading particularly and the way we go about religious studies generally, is not only to tell the large stories of American history and culture, but also to explore those moments along the historical lines we know so well, when our preferred categories of "religious" and "secular," "nature" and "culture" intercept each other in the full messiness of human lives. For homesteaders, this happens in the context of lives that are articulated both in particular stances taken toward nature and in the literary and ritual expression of those stances. For the rest of us, the larger questions of "the religious" and "the secular" or of "nature" and "culture" are ones in which we are all engaged and which a study of practice and practices can illuminate. To look beyond these practices, to the ironies and ambivalences they reveal is to come home—somewhat—to ourselves.

NOTES

1. There they also launched "The Social Science Institute," thus giving an umbrella name to their educational efforts and their private publishing ventures. This was Scott's only means of producing what would otherwise have been blacklisted books.

2. The Nearings' "Good Life" books, *Living the Good Life*, first published in 1954 and republished by Schocken in 1970, and *Continuing the Good Life* (New York: Schocken, 1979), were republished in one volume, *The Good Life* (New York: Schocken, 1989). Although the original volumes reflect the Nearings' own aesthetic sensibilities, for the purposes of convenience I am making my citations from the new double-volume. So that the reader may know which of the two texts is being cited—as this is sometimes significant—the first and second texts are hereafter cited as *GL* and *CGL*, respectively, with pagination given from the double-volume.

3. On September 17, 1995 (between the writing of this essay and the final publication), Helen Knothe Nearing died in a car accident several miles from her home. Though she was ninety-one at the time, her death struck many as premature. Helen gave much of her time, energy, and insight to me and to many

others interested in the Good Life. She supported my work with interest and care. This essay is presented with gratitude toward her and in her honor.

Important thanks go to several others who have contributed to this essay and to my larger project on homesteading. My first debts are to my dissertation advisers, David D. Hall and Lawrence Buell, who have graciously and energetically supported my work over the long haul. To the many homesteaders who have welcomed me into their neighborhoods and shared their life-stories with me, I am deeply grateful. While only two of those stories are discussed here, many others inform this essay and my other work on homesteading. I'm also indebted to several close friends and colleagues who have commented on drafts, R. Marie Griffith, Michael McNally, John O'Keefe, and John Saltmarsh. A special thank you to Cynthia Smith who, with both a keen eye and a warm heart, read this piece more than once.

4. Helen has remarked to me and others that her current level of self-sufficiency is "about 70 percent," which would constitute a slight decrease from Helen and Scott's earlier reports on the Maine project, where 85 percent of their food was produced on site, as well as all fuel except gas. See *CGL*, 286. Increasingly after Scott's death, however, Helen became more willing and accustomed to receiving help from visitors and neighbors. She struggled with this issue, because of wanting to continue to uphold ideals of self-sufficiency on the one hand, but on the other, also wanting to benefit—both practically and emotionally—from participating in (and nurturing) a community of people concerned about her welfare. Thus, Helen sometimes portrayed her "self-sufficiency" to be more than it always was.

The difficult relationship between "truth" and "myth" in the lives of the Nearings is a theme I treat in my larger work, while dealing with other ambivalences in this particular essay. The question of truth and myth pertains not only to self-sufficiency but to other issues as well. The nature of Scott's death, for instance, was not as gentle or as freely chosen as Helen portrayed it, for as one of Helen's closest friends informed me, Scott was already "beginning to cross over" when he embarked on his fast. Similarly, Helen's attitude toward her own passing was ambivalent. While she publicly announced that she planned to go as Scott did, she mentioned to others that she would prefer a sudden death.

A sustained analysis of the relationship between "truth" and "myth" is forthcoming from Helen Nearing's biographer, Ellen LaConte. See her article, "The Nearing Good Life: A Perspective on its Principles and Practices," *Maine Organic Farmer and Gardener* (March–April 1989): 11–12, and her book, *On Light Alone: A Guru Meditation on the Good Death of Helen Nearing* (Stockton Springs, Maine: Loose Leaf Press, 1996). I am indebted to many of Helen Nearings' friends and neighbors for shedding light on these issues and to Ellen LaConte particularly for her insightful comments on and interest in my work.

5. Helen and Scott's original Maine garden was sold to a neighbor in 1980 and is not in use. This garden measures a quarter acre and is surrounded by a five-foot-high stone wall. It is this original wall to which Helen and Scott refer in their writings. For the story of the transformation of Helen and Scott's original farmhouse and garden, see Stanley Joseph and Lynn Karlin, *Maine Farm: A Year of Country Life* (New York: Random House, 1991). Helen Nearing's cautious fore-

word to this text hints at the significant differences in "homesteading style" between these two neighbors and the tensions such stylistic differences can produce.

6. *CGL*, 348–50.

7. *GL*, 192.

8. Ibid., 57.

9. Ibid., 78.

10. *CGL*, 383.

11. See the chapter "Stone Walls versus Wire Fences," *CGL*, 318–28. Other chapters in which the Nearings write extensively on the uses and pleasures of working with stone include: "We Build a Stone House," *GL*, 55–91, "Building Stone Structures," *CGL*, 328–40, and (my personal favorite) "Remodeling Old Wooden Buildings: Don't!" *CGL*, 348–58.

12. Here names and some biographical details have been changed to preserve anonymity.

13. The garden works the other way as well, with some tall weeds shading and protecting low-growing vegetables.

14. Wendell Berry, who locates himself in the Jeffersonian agrarian tradition, is an important figure in my larger work on homesteading. He occupies a somewhat "borderline" position in that he has more of an independent income—through teaching and writing—than most of the people in my study. Nevertheless, his prominence as an essayist on the contemporary (1980s–1990s) values of getting back to the land makes him impossible to ignore. Moreover, his own reflections on "right" farming, eating, and writing are central to the study of practice I am engaged in here. Berry's work, like that of John Burroughs and Aldo Leopold before him, contributes especially to my investigations of "literary homesteaders" and to the questions of the reading and writing of homesteading, which I have explored elsewhere. See especially Wendell Berry, "Two Economies," in *Home Economics: Fourteen Essays by Wendell Berry* (San Francisco: North Point Press, 1987), 54–75; "Discipline and Hope," in *Recollected Essays 1965–1980* (San Francisco: North Point Press, 1981), 151–223; "An Argument for Diversity," in *What Are People For?* (San Francisco: North Point Press, 1990), 109–23, "The Agricultural Crisis as a Crisis of Culture" and "The Body and the Earth," in *The Unsettling of America* (San Francisco: Sierra Club Books, 1977), 39–48, 97–140; and "The Making of a Marginal Farm," in *This Incomparable Lande: A Book of American Nature Writing*, ed. Thomas J. Lyon (New York: Penguin, 1991), 356–65. For Bolton Hall, see *A Little Land and a Living*, 3rd ed. (New York: Arcadia, 1908). Ralph Borsodi's father, William Borsodi, both influenced and was much affected by Hall's earlier work. He wrote a letter to Hall (which serves as the introduction) encouraging him to write *A Little Land and a Living*. For Ralph Borsodi, see *The Flight from the City* (New York: Harper and Brothers, 1933). The "postlude" consists of a report on the Dayton, Ohio community homestead experiments, for which Borsodi served as economic consultant. An excellent discussion of Borsodi's mix of agricultural and technological ideals in the pursuit of an economically viable "simple life" occurs in David Shi, *The Simple Life* (New York: Oxford University Press, 1985), 226–47.

15. For early-twentieth-century homesteading texts, see Bolton Hall, *Three Acres and Liberty* (New York: Arcadia, 1907) and *A Little Land and a Living*. In

the same period, John Burroughs' works serve as a kind of literary counterpart to Bolton Hall's more pragmatic manuals of social reform. Burroughs' broadest readings of nature are found in *Locusts and Wild Honey* (1879, 1907) and *The Ways of Nature* (1905), vols. 4 and 12 of *The Writings of John Burroughs* (Boston, Mass.: Houghton Mifflin, 1904–19). The details of his practice of homesteading are more available in such texts as Clifton Johnson, *John Burroughs Talks: His Reminiscences and Comments* (Boston, Mass.: Houghton Mifflin, The Riverside Press, 1922); and Clifford Hazeldine Osborne, *The Religion of John Burroughs* (Boston: Houghton Mifflin, The Riverside Press, 1930). For discussion of Burroughs, see Shi, *The Simple Life*, 198–201, Peter Schmitt, *Back to Nature: The Arcadian Myth in Urban America* (New York: Oxford University Press, 1969), 23–25, and Edward J. Renehan Jr., *John Burroughs: An American Naturalist* (Post Mills, Vt.: Chelsea Green, 1992).

For Depression Era and war-time homesteading, numerous lesser known works may be read alongside familiar texts such as Ralph Borsodi's *The Flight from the City* and Louis Bromfield's *Malabar Farm* (New York: Harper, 1948; republished New York: Aeonian, 1978). See, for instance, Paul Corey, *Buy an Acre* (New York: Dial, 1944), Louise Dickinson Rich, *We Took to the Woods* (Philadelphia, Pa.: Lippincott, 1942), and Henry Tetlow, *We Farm for a Hobby and Make It Pay* (New York: William and Morrow, 1938).

For a classic "sixties" homesteading text, see Raymond Mungo, *Total Loss Farm* (New York: Dutton, 1970). For more recent homesteading experiments from the 1970s to the 1990s, some representative texts are Frank Levering and Wanda Urbanska, *Simple Living* (New York: Penguin, 1992); Gene Logsdon, *Homesteading: How to Find New Independence on the Land* (Emmaus, Pa.: Rodale, 1973) and *At Nature's Pace* (New York: Pantheon, 1994); Peter Matson, *A Place in the Country* (New York: Harcourt Brace Jovanovich, 1977); and Laura and Guy Waterman, *Wilderness Ethics* (Woodstock, Vt.: The Countryman Press, 1993).

16. T. J. Jackson Lears, *No Place of Grace: Anti-Modernism and the Transformation of American Culture 1880–1920* (New York: Pantheon, 1981). Lears first sets out his line of analysis in his preface and later details this dynamic with respect to the arts and crafts movement and related back-to-the-land movements. See pp. xiv and 74–82. While homesteading would fit into Lears' analysis, it also challenges it in several ways. Lears places his analysis in the context of the alienating effects of America's transition from a producing to a consuming culture. But homesteading in some senses resists the production–consumption cultural shift by locating itself firmly in the middle of it. Moreover, by being engaged in the production of food rather than artifacts, homesteaders, perhaps more than other "antimodernists," seem to resist the slide into consumer culture that Lears charts as the fate of other dissenting groups. On the other hand, some homesteaders *are* engaged in the production and consumption of homesteading texts—texts that homesteaders and non-homesteaders alike consume. If we pursue this phenomenon, Lears' thesis rears its head once more. I discuss homesteading in the context of turn-of-the-century "back-to-nature " movements and the notion of homesteaders as "modern antimodernists" more fully in "'Getting Close to Nature: Homesteading, 'Ecology' and Lived Religion in America," paper presented for

the Lilly Endowment Research Group in American Religious History, Harvard University, May 13–14, 1994.

17. For a discussion of the Boy Scouts, Ernest Thompson Seton's Woodcraft Indians, and "fresh air" movements, see Schmitt, *Back to Nature*, 108–19. For the conservation years, see Roderick Nash, *Wilderness and the American Mind*, 3rd ed. (New Haven, Conn.: Yale University Press, 1982) and Donald Worster, *Nature's Economy*, rev. ed. (Cambridge: Cambridge University Press, 1977). For the environmental movements of the 1960s, see Kirkpatrick Sale, *The Green Revolution: The American Environmental Movement 1962–1992* (New York: Hill and Wang, 1993). For the source of deep ecological thinking, see Arne Naess, *Ecology, Community and Lifestyle*, trans. David Rothenburg (Cambridge: Cambridge University Press, 1989) and "The Shallow and the Deep, Long Range Ecology Movements," *Inquiry 16* (1973): 95–100. For American versions, see Bill Devall and George Sessions, *Deep Ecology* (Salt Lake City, Utah: Gibbs Smith, 1985). For a representative sampling of the literature on ecofeminism, see Irene Diamond and Gloria Orenstein, *Reweaving the World: The Emergence of Ecofeminism* (San Francisco: Sierra Club Books, 1990). For broad portraits of radical environmentalism and ecological theologies, see Roderick Nash, *The Rights of Nature* (Madison: University of Wisconsin Press, 1989) and Carolyn Merchant, *Radical Ecology: The Search for a Livable World* (London: Routledge, 1992). Nash tells the tale from an environmental history and ethics perspective, while Merchant leans toward a Marxist analysis.

18. Perry Miller in *Nature's Nation* (Cambridge, Mass.: Belknap, Harvard University Press, 1967) and Leo Marx in *The Machine in the Garden* (New York: Oxford University Press, 1964) tell this story most eloquently.

19. See Leigh Eric Schmidt, "From Arbor Day to the Environmental Sabbath: Nature, Liturgy and American Protestantism," *Harvard Theological Review* 84, no. 3 (1991): 299–323. Schmidt traces the path I am referring to when he places recent environmental theologies in historical perspective by looking at how "abstract intellectual or theological propositions about nature have found ritual expression in the American calendar and Protestant church year." My study of homesteading shares some of Schmidt's interest in ecological praxis, although my intention is to investigate its less "mainstream" and more extra-ecclesial expressions. For Abbott's (often contradictory) views on the "religious benefits" of nature, see Schmitt, *Back to Nature*, 31, 141. For an example of an environmental movement's direct (and evangelical) worship of nature, see Johnny Sagebrush, *The Earth First: Li'l Green Songbook* (Arizona: Nedd Ludd Books, 1986). It includes such favorites as "Give Me That Earth First Religion!" ("It was good enough for redwoods / It was good enough for sage brush / It was good enough for old growth / Well, its good enough for me!") and "Were You There When They Built Glen Canyon Dam" (sung to the tune of: "Were You There When They Crucified My Lord?").

20. See Catherine Albanese, *Nature Religion in America* (Chicago: Chicago University Press, 1990), 7.

21. Drawing on the theoretical work of Michel de Certeau, Pierre Bourdieu, and Catherine Bell, I have treated this issue of constraint in the practice of homesteading more fully elsewhere, particularly in a talk given at the Society for the

Scientific Study of Religion, November 1996: "The Production of Religious Cultures in Everyday Life: Case Studies and Theoretical Implications in the Production of Religious Cultures." Here I discuss the significance of homesteaders' (usually privileged) class and educational backgrounds. For my use of Bell's work, see Rebecca Kneale Gould, "Homesteading in America: Religious Quests and the Restraints of Religion," *Social Compass* 44, no. 1 (January, 1997): 165–78. See also Michel de Certeau, *The Practice of Everyday Life* (1984), trans. Steven Rendell (Berkeley: University of California Press, 1988); Catherine Bell, *Ritual Theory, Ritual Practice* (Oxford: Oxford University Press, 1992); Pierre Bourdieu, *Outline for a Theory of Practice* (1972), trans. Richard Nice, ed. Ernest Gellner et al., Cambridge Studies in Social and Cultural Anthropology 16 (Cambridge: Cambridge University Press, 1977) and *The Logic of Practice* (1980), trans. Richard Nice (Stanford, Calif.: Stanford University Press, 1990).

22. Helen's close friend and fellow gardener, Nancy Berkowitz, has both enlightened and entertained me with tales of Helen's more playful and impulsive attitude toward the garden in the years after Scott's death. Still, these are differences in degree rather than kind, for, in general, Helen continued to adhere to the principles and practices she and Scott established together. My thanks to Nancy for these insights and for many enjoyable hours spent working together in Helen's garden.

23. Even the making and use of garden stakes was a matter of planning and precision. The Nearings report, "In our earlier gardening experiments the stakes were made of sawed lumber and the tops were painted before numbering. Later, we used straight 16 inch sections of hard maple or ash saplings, an inch or a little more in diameter, pointed on one end with an axe and having on the opposite end of the stake, a small blaze . . . on which the number could be written with a lumber pencil." *GL*, 103.

24. Ibid., 104.

25. *CGL*, 348–55.

26. "The third year, potatoes go into plot 3 and squash into plot 2; plot 1 is planted to grass and clover [which by year 4] has a rich green sod" into which the potatoes return in year 5. *CGL*, 349.

27. Ibid., 354. Although their emphasis here is on the first three years of a homesteading project, the Nearings recommend such formulas whenever they are useful—that is, most of the time.

28. See *GL*, 36–39 and the whole chapter entitled, "Our Design for Living."

29. Ibid., 30.

30. Ibid., 31, 14.

31. Ibid., 53.

32. *CGL*, 388.

33. *GL*, 53.

34. The Nearings refer to something like this method when they champion their own practices in contradistinction to "current theories" of letting "everything grow" and picking out the vegetables "when the time comes." *CGL*, 235.

35. Transcription of interview with S. (July 7, 1994), 7.

36. Interview notes, 7.

37. Ibid., 5.

38. Ibid., 1.

39. Ibid.; emphasis added to reflect vocal inflections.

40. Helen Nearing does have a more "mystical" side to her, however, which is rooted in her upbringing as a Theosophist. She considers herself a "water witch" and tells of finding the farm in Maine by dowsing with a map and pendulum. Astrological signs matter to her and she still regularly consults an astrologer. Much of the writing that Helen and Scott have done together reveals a certain tension between Scott's rigid pragmatism and Helen's playful and mystical sides. Helen describes herself as having let Scott take the lead in their projects and the books seem to do the same (though in each case I am quite sure that Helen held her own!). See Helen Nearing's memoir, *Loving and Leaving the Good Life* (Post Mills, Vt.: Chelsea Green, 1992).

41. We might consider, for instance, the intriguing apology with which the Nearings conclude their chapter on "stone walls versus wire fences": "We regret the need for fences, walls and other obstructions to free movement. If they must be built, we would hope that as many of them as possible could be solid, beautiful and provided, like this quarter acre garden, with three gates, closed only when necessary, and available to anyone who has the wit to turn a wooden button." *CGL*, 325.

A slightly different kind of ambivalence is expressed by many homesteaders, which pertains to their fear of how they will be viewed. Borsodi and Tetlow, particularly, express anxiety about not wanting to be seen as part of the "nuts and berries school" of homesteaders, longing for the salve of nature. Yet a close reading of their texts reveals both "nuts and berries" rigor and nostalgia for nature as recurrent themes.

42. Sal's sense of his relationship with nature is sometimes explicitly expressed in terms of salvation and conversion. As he put it to me: "The more I inquired, the more I learned and the more I endeavored to work with these things the more information came to me, more ability and skills and so on. . . . And I found that the only way to go was to go on. In other words, I was learning and why should I give up learning, because if I gave up learning I would just stop. I mean I had learned so much, in a sense, not informational knowledge, but natural knowledge. I realized that . . . I would die otherwise. . . . And so it was an absolute necessity for me to create a certain kind of lifestyle so I could continue to live." Interview notes, 5.

43. See Orsi's comments in "The Decade ahead in Scholarship," in the "Forum" feature, *Religion and American Culture* 3, no. 1 (Winter 1993): 3.

44. My doctoral dissertation, "At Home in Nature: The Religious and Culture Work of Homesteading in Twentieth Century America" (forthcoming, Harvard University, 1997), takes ambivalence as a major interpretive strategy.

45. For one example, see Wendell Berry's essay, "The Pleasures of Eating," in *What Are People For?* 145–52.

46. The foundations for the Nearings' decisions significantly predate their homesteading experiment. Helen was raised by Theosophist vegetarian parents, traveled to Europe, Asia, and Australia to pursue her Theosophical interests, and entered into an intense emotional and spiritual relationship with Krishnamurti. Scott was a devotee of fitness guru Bernarr McFadden and in the summers be-

tween 1906 and 1913 he lived and worked at Arden, Delaware, a single-tax intentional community devoted to organic farming and vegetarianism. See Helen Nearing, *Loving and Leaving the Good Life* and John Saltmarsh, *Scott Nearing: An Intellectual Biography* (Philadelphia, Pa.: Temple University Press, 1991), 50–57.

47. *CGL*, 373.

48. *GL*, 105.

49. Ibid., 141–42.

50. See, e.g., Samuel Ogden, *This Country Life*, rev. ed. (Emmaus, Pa.: Rodale, 1979), 179 and 10 (first published by A. S. Barnes and Company, New York, 1946). Ogden is a follower of both Borsodi and the Nearings and he exhibits a typical stance when he points his finger at progress as "a more bitter brew to swallow than the pap of optimists," while with the other hand he beckons others (if they are "fit") to build lives "more rewarding socially and culturally than [they] have ever dreamed of."

51. Interview notes, 7.

52. Ibid., 9.

53. Ibid., 2, emphasis added to reflect vocal inflections.

54. See, for instance, Annette Kolodny, *The Land before Her : Fantasy and Experience of the American Frontiers, 1630–1860* (Chapel Hill: University of North Carolina Press, 1984).

55. Raymond Williams makes this point in *The Country and the City* (New York: Oxford University Press, 1973), as does Leo Marx in *The Machine and the Garden*.

56. On the problem of characterizing secularization as "the decline of religion" and the difficulty in establishing a satisfactory definition of religion, see Bryan Turner, *Religion and Social Theory*, 2nd ed. (London: Sage, 1991). For the argument that secularization is best understood as the process by which religion loses its social significance, see Bryan Wilson, *Religion in Sociological Perspective* (Oxford: Oxford University Press, 1982.) For the more circumscribed argument concerning secularization as a decline in religious authority, see Mark Chaves, "Secularization as Declining Religious Authority," *Social Forces* 72, no. 3 (March 1994): 749–74. My thanks to Mark Chaves for providing me with this article. For an excellent collection of articles that are representative of debates about the secularization thesis, see Phillip E. Hammond, ed., *The Sacred in a Secular Age* (Berkeley: University of California Press, 1985). See esp. Bryan Wilson, "Secularization: The Inherited Model," 9–20.

CONTRIBUTORS

NANCY T. AMMERMAN, Professor of the Sociology of Religion, Center for Social and Religious Research, Hartford Seminary, has recently published *Congregation and Community* (1996).

ANNE S. BROWN wrote the prize-winning "Visions of Community in Eighteenth-Century Essex County: Chebacco Parish and the Great Awakening," *Essex Institute Historical Collections* 125 (1989); she received her Ph.D. in history from Boston University in 1995.

CHERYL FORBES, Assistant Professor of Writing and Rhetoric at Hobart and William Smith Colleges, spent seventeen years in religious publishing as a writer, editor, and executive; she has written six books and numerous articles on the relationship between art and faith.

REBECCA KNEALE GOULD completed her Ph.D. in the study of religion, Harvard University, in 1997; her essay is drawn from her dissertation. She has published "Homesteading in America: Religious Quests and the Restraints of Religion," *Social Compass* (January 1997).

R. MARIE GRIFFITH, Mellon Fellow in the Humanities, Northwestern University, received her Ph.D. in the study of religion from Harvard University; the fuller study from which her essay is drawn has recently been published as *God's Daughters: Evangelical Women and the Power of Submission* (1997).

DAVID D. HALL, Professsor of American Religious History, Harvard Divinity School, has published, among studies on early America, *Worlds of Wonder, Days of Judgment: Popular Religious Belief in Early New England* (1989).

DANIÈLE HERVIEU-LÉGER, Professor at the Ecole des Hautes Etudes en Sciences Sociales, Paris, directs the Centre d'Etudes Interdisciplinaires de Faits Religieux and edits the journal *Archives de sciences sociales des religions*. Her books include *La Religion pour memoire* (1993) and *Identites religieuses en Europe* with G. Davie (1996).

MICHAEL MCNALLY, Assistant Professor in the Department of History and Philosophy, Eastern Michigan University, has done research and community work with a group of Ojibwa elders and hymn-singers at the White Earth Indian Reservation in his home state of Minnesota. His essay is drawn from his dissertation in the study of religion, Harvard University, which he completed in 1996.

ROBERT ORSI, Professor of American Religious History, Indiana University, is most recently the author of *Thank You, St. Jude* (1996).

STEPHEN PROTHERO, Assistant Professor in the Department of Religion, Boston University, is author of *The White Buddhist: The Asian Odyssey of Henry Steel Olcott* (1996); his essay is drawn from *The American Way of Cremation* (forthcoming, University of California Press).

LEIGH ERIC SCHMIDT, Associate Professor of American Religious History, Department of Religious Studies, Princeton University, has most recently published *Consumer Rites: The Buying and Selling of American Holidays* (1995).

INDEX

Abbott, Lyman, 221, 239n.19
abolitionism, 98, 131n.8
abortion, 186
Abraham, 41
activist. *See* congregations
A.D. 2000 and Beyond movement, 182, 194n.53
Adams, Eliza, 80
Adler, Felix, 107, 112n.23
Adorno, Theodor, 77
African Americans, 3–4, 15, 197, 200, 213n.7
Aglow. *See* Women's Aglow Fellowship International
Aglow (magazine), 161, 162, 188, 190n.4
agnosticism, 98
Albanese, Catherine L., 108, 221
alcoholism, 13, 18, 139, 143, 161–62, 174, 179, 188, 193n.41
Alcott, Louisa May, 73
Althuser, Robert, 214n.17
ambivalence, ix, 11, 37, 91n.36, 223, 228, 236n.4, 241n.41. *See also* practice
American Board of Commissioners for Foreign Missions, 137–38
American religious history, 69–73, 86n.2, 111n.9; and lived religion, vii, ix–x, 10–13
Ammerman, Nancy T., ix–x, 8–10
anamiajig ("those who pray"), 139–43, 148–49, 156n.47
Andean panpipe music, 136
Angier, Mary, 51
anishinaabe, 133–34, 140–49, 151n.1, 152n.9. *See also* Ojibwa
antimodernism, 220–21, 238n.16
Antinomian controversy, 47, 59
April Fool's Day, 70, 110n.5
Arden, Del., 242n.46
arts and crafts movement, 238n.16
Asad, Talal, 158n.66
Asbury, Francis, 72
Assemblies of God, 198
astrology, 39n.15, 241n.40
Atlanta, Ga., 198–99

baptism, ix, x, 8, 41–43, 47–62, 64nn.17 and 21, 70; and family preservation, 50–56, 58, 60–62
Baptists, 47–48, 60, 198
Baptists, Southern, 214n.12
bar mitzvahs, 70
Barton, Bruce, 72
"base communities," 33
bastardy: rate of, 56
Bates, Katherine Lee, 127
Bauberot, Jean, 33
Baumgartner, M. P., 205, 215nn.30 and 34
Beatitudes, Les, 29
Becker, Penny, 214n.16
Beecher, Henry Ward, 112n.23, 127
Bell, Catherine, 134, 147–49, 239–40n.21
Bendroth, Margaret Lamberts, 187, 191n.15
Berkowitz, Nancy, 240n.22
Bernadette of Lourdes, 3–4
Berry, Wendell, 220, 237n.14
Beverly, Mass., 56–57, 66n.28
Bible 71–72, 167, 176, 216n.37; and charismatics, 15, 31–38; and control, 32–33; and evangelicals, 198, 200–201; and fundamentalism, 33–35, 117, 131n.8; and Golden Rule Christians, 196–97, 201–5, 209–12, 213–14n.12; and reading, 31–38, 117–23, 125–27, 161, 171, 198, 200
biblical criticism, 107, 117
bimaadiziwin, 157n.56
bimaadjiwewin, 157n.56
birthdays, 70, 77, 80, 82, 85
Blavatsky, Helena Petrovna, 99
Blinman, Richard, 52
Boardman, Cornelia, 154n.35
body, 7, 29–30, 158n.66, 232; and cremation, 94–97, 100–101, 105–8, 111n.9
Bolo, Fernando, 33
Bongo, Susan, 155n.36
books, devotional, 118–19
Borsodi, Ralph, 220, 237n.14, 241n.41, 242n.50
Borsodi, William, 237n.14
Boston, Mass., 52, 106, 198, 199

Boston Public Library, 93
Bottome, Margaret, 127
Bourdieu, Pierre, 16, 35, 85, 86n.1, 134, 146, 147–48, 158nn.66 and 67, 239–40n.21
Boy Scouts, 221
Bradstreet, Anne, 66n.32
Breck Memorial Episcopal Church, White Earth, 149
Brooklyn, N.Y. health board, 100
Brooks, Phillips, 112n.23, 117
Brown, Anne S., ix–xi, 8, 11, 17, 204
Browning, Ophelia G., 127
Browning, Robert, 119
Buck, Pearl, 217
Buddhism, 99
Bunyan, John, 42, 117, 120, 129
Burder, G., 131n.7
burial. See cremation
Burridge, Kenelm, 147
Burroughs, John, 237n.14, 238n.15
Burton, Frederick, 155n.39
Butler, Jon, 211
Butler, Judith, 14, 16
Butterfield, Mary, 129

calendar, Protestant, xi, 239n.19
Calvin, John, viii
Calvinism, 127, 211
Cambridge, Mass., 48–49
Cambridge, Mass. testimonies, 51
Cambridge Platform, 42, 45, 47–48
camp meeting, 138
cancer, 143, 161
capitalism, 9, 14–15
Caplow, Theodore, 82
Carmel United Methodist Church, 198, 199, 202–6, 208–9, 215n.24
Carnegie, Andrew, 112n.23
Carrier, James G., 86n.1
Carter, Stephen, 116
Carter, Sybil, 154n.34
casino: proposed at White Earth, 143–44
Catholicism. See Roman Catholicism
cemeteries, rural movement, 105
Chambers, Oswald, 119
chapel, voluntary college, 117
charismatic movement (French Roman Catholic), vii, 15, 26–38, 39–40n.20
charitable donations: by Golden Rule Christians, 205–6, 210

Charlestown, Mass., 65n.27
Chaucer, Geoffery, 127
Chautauqua, 211
Cheal, David, 82, 90n.30
Chemin Neuf, le, 29
Cheney, Elizabeth, 127
Chiang Kai-Shek, 116
Chicago, Ill., 12, 156n.50
Child, Robert, 52
child abuse, 179–82, 186, 188, 193n.45
childbirth, 53–54, 66n.28, 208
children, 179–82, 199, 204, 208–9, 211, 214n.21. See also baptism; church membership
Chippewa, 140, 151n.1. See also Ojibwa
Cho, David (Paul) Yongii, 182
cholera, 94
Christianity. See religion
Christmas, 71, 74, 76–77, 80–81, 84–85
Christmas tree, 76
church membership, ix, xi, 29, 41–61, 66n.28, 67nn.38 and 45, 124, 196, 199, 204, 206–8, 210–11, 215n.34, 216n.36, 233–34
Church of England: parish system of, 41, 44, 51, 53
Church of the Apostles (United Church of Christ), Lancaster, Pa., xiiin.1
church year, 210, 239n.19
Cincinnati, Ohio, 106
civil disobedience, 144
Clarke, Mary, 73, 90n.33
Clay, Cassius M., 112n.23
clergy and lay relations, vii–viii, xii, 12, 31, 37, 41–62, 118, 122, 146, 154n.27, 159n.71, 163, 199, 213n.7
Coakley, Sarah, 178, 193n.38
Coles, Robert, 10, 13
Collins, Edward, 51
colonialism, ix, 133–34, 144–45, 147, 149, 152n.7
Communion. See Lord's Supper
compost, 217, 223
Comunione e Liberazione, 26
confirmation, 70, 196, 209
Congregationalism, 41–68, 96, 198
Congregational Way, 44–47, 49, 52, 60–61
congregations: study of, ix, 209–11, 214n.16, 215n.28; types of, 198–202, 213nn.7 and 9
Connerton, Paul, 145
consumerism, 72, 234

conversion, 28–29, 138, 157n.56, 158n.70, 241n.42
Conway, Moncure, 112n.23
Cooper, Darien B., 172–74, 187, 189
I Corinthians, 36; (11:27–29), 46; (11:28–29), 49
II Corinthians (9:7), 78
Cornell, Joseph, 78
Cotton, John, 41, 48, 52, 64n.17
counterculture (1960s), 26–27, 215–16n.35, 217, 219
Counter Reformation, 39n.12
covenant, x, 8, 50, 60–61; church, 44, 50; external, 41–43, 47–50, 54, 60–61; of grace, 42, 48, 60–61; renewal of, 43, 50, 52–53, 55–60, 66n.28
Cowman, Mr. Charles E., 117, 119, 131n.10
Cowman, Mrs. Charles E., ix, x, xii, 17, 116–30
Crapanzano, Vincent, 16
Cremation Association of America, 97
cremation movement, viii, x, 10–13, 92–109, 110n.5, 112n.23; and body, 94–96, 100–101, 104–5, 108
Cremation Society (New York), 92
cultural studies, vii, ix, 14, 19n.10

Dakota Indians, 139
dance, 29, 141, 145, 148, 153n.21, 159n.71
Daniel, Yves, 38n.4
Davenport, John, 45, 64n.17
Dawson, John, 182
Dayton, Ohio, 237n.14
deacons, Episcopalian Ojibwa, 139–40, 154n.27
Death of God, 220
death practices, 70, 92–115, 160, 164, 203, 208, 235–36n.3, 236n.4; ancient, 94–95, 97, 103–4; Asian, 95, 97, 103–4, 108; at White Earth, 134–36, 140, 143–44, 158n.71
Deborah, 186
de Certeau, Michel, 39n.17, 239–40n.21
dechristianization, 24, 104–5, 108–9, 114n.49
declension, xi, 59, 61
Deerfield, Mass., 56
Deland, Margaret, 112n.23
Delattre, Roland, 158n.65
Demos, John Putnam, 65n.23

demythologization, 107–8
denominationalism, 7
Densmore, Frances, 151n.4, 153n.21
De Palm, Baron Joseph Henry Louis Charles, 11–13, 92, 98–106, 109
DeRose, Mrs. C. S., 119
Derrida, Jacques, 73
De Sales, Francis, 127
desert: image of, 120, 122–23, 127
Deuteronomy, 121
Devil. See Satan
devotional practices, x, 6, 16, 24, 116–30, 131n.7, 140–42, 148, 154nn.28 and 35, 155n.36, 156n.50, 171
dewe'igan, 155n.37
discernment, 36–37
disenchantment. See secularization
dispensationalists, 117
divorce, 164–65, 169–70, 179, 181, 188
Dobson, James C., 192n.31, 193n.41
Dobson, Shirley, 193n.41
Dominican Republic, 3
Dorchester, Mass., 53–54
Dorfles, Gillo, 77
Douglas, Mary, 75
dream songs, 141
drum, Ojibwa, 141, 145–46, 148, 155n.37, 158n.61, 159n.71
Duby, Georges, 24
Dunn, Mary M., 66n.30
Durkheim, Emile, 38–39n.9, 62; school of, 24, 37
Dyer, Ellen, 119

earthquake of 1727, 59
Easter, 13, 17, 70, 77, 80–82
Eastman, Dick, 182
eating. See food
ecofeminism, 221
ecological theology, 221
ecology, 221
Edwards, Jonathan, 43, 45, 59–60, 117, 127, 131n.6
Ehrenreich, Barbara, 174
Eiesland, Nancy, 215n.28
elders, Ojibwa, 140, 152n.9
Eliot, Charles William, 112n.23
elites, 19n.10, 39n.12
Ellenwood, Mary, 57
Emerson, Ralph Waldo, 73–76, 82–83, 88n.11, 117, 128, 131n.8
Emmanuel, l', 29, 30

England, 100
Enmegabowh, 154n.27
environmentalism, radical, 221
Ephesians (5:13–18), 194n.56; (5:22), 177; (6:11–12), 183
Episcopalians, 96, 198; and Ojibwa, 133, 138–42, 146–49, 151n.3, 152n.8, 154n.28, 155n.40, 156n.51, 159n.71
Erichsen, Hugo, 97
eschaton, 44
Essex County, Mass. baptism records, 53
Esther, 186
Ethical Culture, 96
ethnology, 24
ethnomusicology, 155n.39
Eucharist. See Lord's Supper
eulogies, 203
evangelicalism, 72, 196–97. See also Women's Aglow Fellowship International
evangelicals, 163, 168–69, 172, 183, 187–88, 191n.15, 198, 200–202; and homesteading, 234, 239n.19
evangelism, 49, 162, 198–99, 206
evolution, 107, 117
Exodus (3:1–2), 132n.19; (23:8), 74

family, 82–83, 160–64, 168–71, 179, 181–82, 184–87, 191n.15; and Golden Rule Christians, 203–5, 207, 209, 211; and strategies of preservation, 8, 41–43, 50–62, 63n.5. See also children; parents
farming, 98, 241–42n.46. See also homesteading
fast days, 58
fasting, 229, 231
fathers, 161–62, 179–82
feasting, Ojibwa, 136, 140, 142, 148, 156n.43, 159n.71
Federal Council of Churches, 206
Field, Kate, 112n.23
Finke, Rodger, 71
Finney, Charles Grandison, 72
first communion, 70
Fish, Stanley, 118–19
Fitchter, Joseph, 201
Flint, Annie Johnson, 127–30
flowers, 76, 101–2, 105, 108, 169
folklorists, 24
Folsom, Dr., 102
food, 136, 140, 142, 148, 156n.43, 159n.71, 217, 223, 229–32

Forbes, Cheryl, x, 17
Forest Farm, Maine, 217
Foucault, Michel, 14
France, xi, 15, 22–40, 100
Frazer, Persifor, Jr., 93–94, 96–98, 101
Freemasonry, 98, 103, 113n.48, 185
free religion, 96
Free Religious Association, 95
"free riders," 209, 212n.2
French Revolution, 234
Fresh Air movements, 221
Freud, Sigmund, 17
friendship: Emerson on, 75
Frothingham, Octavius B., 93–97, 99, 101
Fuller, Margaret, 112n.23
Fuller Theological Seminary, 182
Full Gospel Women's Fellowship (Women's Aglow), 162
fundamentalism, 10, 26, 33–35, 117, 127–28, 168, 187, 191n.15, 233–34
funerals, 80, 99, 149, 159n.71, 160. See also wakes
fur trade, 138–39, 142

Garden River, Ont., 155n.39
gardens, 11, 217–20, 223–24, 229, 231–33, 236n.5, 240nn. 22, 23, and 27
Garlock, Ruthanne, 183–85
Geertz, Clifford, ix–x, 16, 19n.5
gender, xii, 82, 163–69, 172–78, 183–88, 191n.15, 192n.31, 200, 233–34
Generals of Intercession, 182
Genesis: creation account in, 214n.12; (17:7), 41–42, 45–46, 48, 51
gentility, 90n.33
Germany, 100
germ theory, 105
gestures, 145
Gifford, Carolyn DeSwarte, 186
gift economy, x, 11, 69–91
gift-giving, 74–85; alienation from, 74–78; appreciation of, 78–83; and holidays or rites, 70–71, 74, 76–78, 80–82, 84–85; and Romanticism, 73–85, 86n.1; and Shakers, 71, 87n.5
Gilfillan, Joseph A., 138, 140, 154nn.27 and 29
Ginzburg, Carlo, 19n.10
Global Harvest Ministries, 194n.53
glossolalia, 26, 29–30, 32, 34, 71
God: as comforter, 204, 214n.18; Cowman's view of, 120–30; as Father, 166,

169, 179, 204, 206, 214n.18; and
  Golden Rule Christians, 203–4, 207–8,
  211, 214nn.17 and 18; as husband, 169–
  70; as liberator, 214n.18; as savior, 204,
  214n.18; tribulations from, 127, 129–
  30; and Women's Aglow, 160–63, 165–
  79, 182–85
Godin, Henri, 38n.4
God's Daughter, 176, 188
Golden Rule Christians, 196–212; practices
  of, 203–7, 210–11
Goodboy, Eadie, 176
Goodhue, Sarah (Whipple), 55
Goodwin, John, 55
gospel songs, 117
Gould, Rebecca Kneale, viii, x, 10–11, 17
grace: Reformation theology of, 117
graduations, 144
Gramsci, Antonio, 134, 152n.5
Gray, Edward, 196, 212
Great Awakening, 42, 59–60, 67n.45,
  131n.6
Green, Joseph, 64n.21
Greenberg, Clement, 77
Greenhouse, Carol, 168
Greenwood, Grace, 112n.23
greeting cards, 13, 80–81, 83–84
Griffith, R. Marie, x, 8, 13, 18, 132n.14
groups, small, 204–5, 208, 214n.19,
  216n.38
Gull Lake, 140
Gwinnett County, Ga., 199

Habenstein, Robert W., 112n.23
habitus (Bourdieu), 16, 147–48, 158nn.66
  and 67
Hale, Edward Everett, 112n.23
Hale, Sarah Josepha, 73, 76, 82, 90n.33
halfway covenant. *See* church membership
Hall, Bolton, 220, 237n.14, 237–38n.15
Hall, David D., ix–xi, 8, 11, 17, 118, 124,
  204, 210
Hall, Joyce C., 83
Hallmark cards, 80, 83
Halpert, Mrs. C. A., 90n.33
Handel, George Frederick, 120
Handlin, Oscar, 213n.9
Hansen, Jane, 182, 183, 187
Hansen, Karen V., 89n.27
Harper Brothers publishers, 119
Harvard University, vii, 49, 117
Havergal, Frances Ridley, 127

healing practices, ix–x, xii, 24, 30, 71,
  160–95
hegemony, redemptive, 147
Henry, Matthew, 117, 131n.7
Herberg, Will, 200, 213n.9
Hertz, Robert, 24–25
Hervieu-Léger, Danièle, vii, ix–xii, 15
Higginson, Thomas Wentworth, 112n.23
Hoge, Dean R., 196–97, 200, 202, 206,
  213nn.8 and 12, 214n.21
Holiness movement, 71, 132n.14
Holy Spirit, 26, 31–32, 34–36, 44, 47, 55,
  59, 104, 109, 135, 165, 167, 182, 184;
  baptism in, 32, 37, 71, 165; gifts of, 28,
  30–31, 36, 71
home, 84, 108, 130, 163, 165–66, 168–69,
  191n.15, 217, 234
Homestead Act (1862), 220
homesteading, viii, x, xii, 10, 217–42; as
  practice, 222–23, 233–34; and seasons,
  229–31, 233
homesteading practices: of the Nearings,
  217–19, 223–26, 228–29, 229–31; Sal's,
  219, 226–27, 228–29, 231–32
homily. *See* sermon
homosexuality, 186
Hooker, Richard, 117, 131n.5
"horse-shed" Christians, 210–11
housework, sacred, 175
Howe, Julia Ward, 112n.23
Hubert, Henri, 24
Hughes, John, 131n.7
husbands, 160–61, 163, 164–78, 181–82,
  184–85, 186–90
Hutchinson, Anne, 47
hymnody, 117, 142, 144–46, 151n.3, 160;
  history of, 133, 136–39
hymn-singing, ix, x, 13, 133–61; as practice, 146–50; and remembering the
  past, 144–46; and wakes, 134–36, 144,
  148–50; and worship, 133, 137–38

Immaculate Conception, 4
immortality, x, 101, 105, 229, 231–32, 234
imperialism, ix
India, 99, 102–3
Indianapolis, Ind., 199
Indian Reform policy, U.S., 139
individualism, 30, 35, 74–75, 82–83
industrialization, 38n.4
"intellectual religion": rejection of, 30
intercession, 182, 184

Ipswich, Mass., 55
Isaiah (35:6), 120
Isambert, François André, 25

Jackson, Michael, 8–9, 16, 20n.11
Jacobs, Cindy, 182
Jamaica, 3
Jefferson, Thomas, 237n.14
Jehovah's Witnesses, 15
Jesus Christ, 42, 75, 81, 120, 129, 161,
    163, 165–67, 175, 177, 183–84, 196–
    97; as husband, 169–70; second coming
    of, 183, 197; as Shepherd, 176; suffering
    and death of, 155n.39, 157n.56, 176,
    180
Jews, 93, 106
Johnson, Benton, 196–97, 200, 202, 206,
    213nn.8 and 12, 214n.21
John the Baptist, 120
Jones, Jenkin Lloyd, 112n.23
Jones, Peter, 137–38

Kah-O-Sed, Edward, 151n.4
Kakabishigwe, 154n.35
Kegiosh, 155n.36
Kelley, Dean M., 216n.39
Kelly Longitudinal Study, 164
Keswick movement, 131n.10, 132n.14
II Kings (4:4), 125; (6:17), 127
kinship, 42, 50, 82. See also family
Kircher, Julius, 106
Kirkland, Caroline, 73, 77–80, 82, 89n.26,
    90n.33
Komarovsky, Mirra, 164
Krishnamurti, 241n.46

ladies aid societies, 122
Ladurie, Emmanuel Le Roy, 19n.10
Lamb, Charles, 79–80
Last Judgment, 42
Laurens, Henry, 109n.1
"lay liberals." See Golden Rule Christians
Lazarus, 107
Lears, T. J. Jackson, 78, 89n.22, 220–21,
    238n.16
Le Bras, Gabriel, 22–23, 38n.1
Leech Lake reservation, 141–42, 154nn.28
    and 35, 155n.36
Leeson, Ted, 126
Lefebure, Leo, 206
Le Moyne, Francis Julius, 98, 101–3, 106
Le Moyne crematory, 98, 99–103

Leo XIII, 104
Leopold, Aldo, 221, 237n.14
liberalism, Protestant, xi, 103–4, 197, 211,
    220, 234
liberation theology, 33
Liberty Party, 98
Lilly Endowment, vii, xii, 196
Lima, Peru, 142
Lincoln, Abraham, 211
Lion de Juda, Le, 29
liturgy 9, 25, 84, 93, 145, 199, 207–10
lived religion, vii–xii, 7–9, 13–15, 18, 19–
    20n.10, 22–25, 57, 62, 72–73, 84–85,
    107, 118, 189, 199–200, 210, 220–23,
    234. See also practice
Living the Good Life, 217, 235n.2
Longfellow, William Wadsworth, 127
Lord's Supper, x, 12, 23, 70, 147, 207,
    210; and church membership, 48–49;
    participation in, 43, 46, 49–50, 56–60
Lourdes, France, 3–6, 18n.1
Luidens, Donald A., 196–97, 200, 202,
    206, 213nn.8, and 12, 214n.21
Luke (8:48), 161; (9:10), 124–25
Luther, Martin, viii
Lutherans, 106, 151n.3, 198

Madonna of 115th Street, The, x
Maendjiwena, Mrs., 154n.35
mainline churches, 162, 198
man, ideal Christian, 166–67
Manchester, England, bishop of, 94
Maori, 83
market economy: and gift-giving, 71–78,
    82–85, 90n.32
Marler, Penny Long, 216n.36
marriage, 160–61, 164–78, 181–82, 184–
    90; and church membership, 53, 60
Marsden, George, 127
Marshall, Robert, 221
Marx, Karl, 16–17
Marxism, 33, 234
Masonic Temple, 99, 105
Mass. See Lord's Supper
Massachusetts Board of Health, 100, 102
mass culture, 85
Mather, Cotton, 43, 56
Mather, Increase, 43, 64n.17
Mather, Richard, 53, 64n.17
Matthew (6:6), 120
Mauss, Marcel, 69, 73, 79, 82–83, 86n.1,
    158n.66

May, Elaine Tyler, 164
McFadden, Bernarr, 241n.46
McGuire, Meredith, xii
McKinney, William, 202
McNally, Michael, ix–x, 13
meaning, ix–x, 26. *See also* narrative
meditation, 31, 118, 125, 207
megachurches, 72
memory, 145, 149
mental illness, 160–61
Messiah, 120
Methodists, 138, 198–99, 202–6, 208–9, 215n.24, 216n.38
Meyer, Melissa, 156n.45
Middletown, 82
midéwiwin, 140–41, 146, 154n.29
midéwiwin songs, 141
Milford, Conn., 65n.26
Miller, Perry, 61
Minneapolis, Minn., 149, 156n.50
Minot, James: wife of, 54
miracles, 16, 128
Missionary Alliance, 151n.3
missions, 117, 121–22, 131n.10, 132n.14; to Ojibwa, 133–59
Mitchel, Jonathan, 49, 60
modernity, 24, 26–27, 38n.4, 62, 77
Moran, Gerald, 65n.26
Morgan, Edmund S., 65n.26
Morgan, Larry Cloud, 144, 157n.58
Mormonism, 233
Mother Earth, 221
motherhood, 53, 168
Mother's Day, 77, 82
Mueller, George, 127
music, 134–50, 157–58n.59, 199, 207, 209, 239n.19
Muskogee, 154n.24. *See also* Ojibwa

narrative, x, xiiin.1, 45, 116–32, 160–95
National Prayer Embassy, 182
Native Americans, death rates of, 156n.51
nature 208; and homesteading, 217–42; and worship, 221–22, 239n.19
Nearing, Helen Knothe, 11, 217–19, 223–32, 235nn.1 and 2, 235–6n.3, 236n.4, 240nn.22 and 34, 241nn.40 and 41, 241–42n.46
Nearing, Scott, 11, 217–19, 223–32, 235nn.1 and 2, 236n.4, 240nn.22 and 34, 241nn.40 and 41, 241–42n.46

neo-orthodoxy, 8, 220
New Age, 220
New Haven, Conn., 45
New Lights, 59–60
New London, Conn., 52
New Year, 70, 74, 77, 80, 128
New York City, 92–94, 98–102, 106
Nietzsche, Frederick, 88n.11
Northampton, Mass., 43, 57, 59–61

Oberlin College, 153n.19
occult phenomena, 185
Ogden, Samuel, 242n.50
Ojibwa, 133–59; drums of, 141, 145–46, 148, 155n.37, 158n.61, 159n.71; and feasting, 136, 140, 142, 148, 156n.43, 159n.71; language of, 135, 137–38, 143–44, 152n.8, 155n.39, 157nn.57 and 58; meaning of religion for, 134, 146–50
Ojibwa Singers. *See* White Earth Ojibwa Singers
Olcott, Henry Steel, 13, 99–105
Olson, Daniel, 216n.38
O'Meara, Frederick, 138
Onigum, 155n.36
Opus Dei, 26
Oriental Missionary Society, 117, 131n.10, 132n.14
Orsi, Robert, ix–x, xii, 215n.24, 228
Otis, George, Jr., 182
Overseas Missionary Society, 131n.10

paganism, 24
Pain de Vie, Le, 29
parasciences, 39n.15
Paray-le-Monial, 30
parents, 17, 42, 50, 161–62, 179–82, 204, 208, 193n.41
parish system, 44, 47, 52
Parker, Theodore, 117, 131n.8
Parliament of the World's Religions (1993), 206
Parris, Samuel, 45–46
Parry, Jonathan, 86n.1
Parsons, Talcott, 206
Pasteur, Louis, 105
patriarchy, xi
Paul, the apostle, 36
Paul VI (pope), 113n.48
Peabody, Elizabeth P., 112n.23
Penobscot Bay, 217

Pentecostalism, 10, 26–27, 71, 151n.3, 168, 182–83, 233
perfectionism, 234
pilgrimages, 24
Pilgrim's Progress, 42, 117, 120, 129
Pine Point village, 159n.71
pipe ceremony, 147
Pitman, Jane, 106
Pittsburgh, Pa., 98, 100
popular religion and popular culture, vii–xii, 9, 19–20n.10, 22–27, 39nn.10 and 12
potlatch, 69
practice, vii, x–xii, 7–8, 13, 22–23, 146–50, 197, 206, 222–23, 233–34
practices. *See* baptism; church membership; death; gift-giving; Golden Rule Christians; healing; homesteading; hymn-singing; prayer; reading; ritual
prayer, 27–31, 118–20, 123–24, 198, 200; group-based, 27–30, 35–37, 140, 155n.36, 208; and healing, 160–68, 171, 178, 180, 182, 188; at White Earth, 156n.50; and Women's Aglow, 160–68, 171, 178, 180, 182–83, 186–90
Presbyterianism, 98–99, 103, 196, 213n.8
Presbyterian Research Office, 213n.12
Primano, Leonard, 20n.10
Proctor, Adelaide, 127
prophecy, 26, 30, 71
Prophet, the Shawnee, 153n.21
Prothero, Stephen, viii, x, 9–11
Psalms (105:5), 121; (109:4), 123
public health, 105–6
Puerto Rico, 3–4
Puritans, ix–xi, 8, 17, 41–68, 70, 118, 125, 210, 221

Quakers, 70

race, 4, 200, 233
Radway, Janice, 170, 187
Ragon, Michel, 109–10n.2
Ramsbottom, Mary McManus, 65n.27
"rational choice" model of religion, 216n.39
reading, x, 116–32, 171
recovery movement, 181
Red Lake reservation, 141–42, 158n.71
Reformation, Protestant, viii, 44, 116–17, 124, 132n.21, 234
regulation, xii, 15–16, 27–38

"relation" of the work of grace, 45, 47–48, 53
religion, vii–xii, 5–18, 19–20n.10, 22–38, 38–39n.9, 107, 117, 148–49, 196–97, 214n.17, 215n.28, 233, 235, 242n.56
renewal of covenant. *See* covenant
resistance, 134, 148, 157n.58
restitutionist movements, 26
retreats: and Golden Rule Christians, 208, 215–16n.35
revivals, Protestant, 10, 31, 59, 66n.28
Richwood, Minn., 139
rites of passage, 70
ritual, ix, 10, 101, 120, 158n.65, 171, 234; and practice, x, 32, 134, 145, 147–49
Ritual Healing in Suburban America, xii
Rock, Reuben, 149
Rock Memorial Hall, White Earth, 149
Roman Catholicism, 3–6, 12, 15, 23, 25–26, 93, 104, 113n.48, 198–99, 203–6, 209–10, 214n.20
Roman Catholicism and charismatic movement, 27–38; at White Earth 151n.3, 152n.8, 153n.17, 159n.71
romance literature, 170
Romans (8:28), 208
Roof, Wade Clark, 215n.35
Root, Mary, 79
Root, Sophia, 79
Roozen, David A., 216n.36
Rose, Susan D., 191n.7
Rossetti, Christina, 127–28
routinization, 31, 38
Roy, Mrs. Alex, 154n.35
Roy, Suzanna, 140
Rubin, Lillian, 164
Ruskin, John, 127
Ryan, Mary P., 68n.45

Sabbath, 70
sacrifices: logic of, 71
St. Lawrence Roman Catholic parish, 198, 199, 203–6, 209–10
St. Lucy Church, Bronx, N.Y., 3–5, 9, 18n.2
St. Nicholas of Toletine Church, Chicago, 12
St. Valentine's Day, 76–77, 79, 80
saints: devotion to, 6, 16, 24
Salem, Mass.: and church covenant, 45; witch-hunt in, 66n.33
Salt Lake City, Utah, 106

salvation, 127, 157n.56, 198, 241n.42
sanctification, 71
Sangster, Margaret, 117
sanitary movement, 98, 106, 114n.53
Santa Claus, 82
Sarah, 41
Sartre, Jean Paul, 6, 16, 18
Satan, 54–55, 99, 127, 160, 164, 184–88
Schlafly, Phyllis, 174
Schmidt, Leigh Eric, x–xi, 6, 8, 10, 16–17, 239n.19
scholasticism, Reformed, 61
Schopen, Gregory, 19n.10
Schwitters, Kurt, 78
science, 12–13
Scopes trial, 117
Scotland, Church of, xi
Scott, Tracy, 215n.26
Seattle, Wash., 162
secularization, 9, 26–28, 37; and crema-tion, 104–5, 108–9, 114n.49; and Golden Rule Christians, 206; and home-steading, 220, 233–34, 242n.56
"seekers," 215–16n.35
self-help, 172
"Separates," 60
sermons, 32, 45, 94, 116, 118, 199, 207, 209, 216n.37
service, community: and Golden Rule Christians, 205–7, 210–11
Seventh-Day Adventists, 198
Sewall, Samuel, 57
Shay-day-ence, 140–41, 147, 154n.29
Shepard, Thomas, 48–49
Sherrer, Quin, 180, 183–84
sickness, 140, 164, 208
Simpson, A. B., 127
Singing and Praying Bands, Ojibwa, 140–42
sisters: Aglow use of term, 170
slaveholders, 70
slaves, African-American, 70
smallpox, 139
Smith, Hannah Whitall, 127
Smith, Jonathan Z., 9
social gospel, 117, 206, 220
social justice, 198, 200
Social Science Association of Philadelphia, 93
Social Science Institute, 235n.1
sociology, ix, 196, 217; and French school of, vii, 22–27, 39n.10

solitude, 123–26
songs, 141, 153n.21, 239n.19
soteriology, Protestant, 70
Sparhawk, Mary, 51
Spiritualism, 39n.15, 103–4, 108
spirituality, 116, 120, 128, 226–27
spiritual warfare, 182–86, 187
Spiritual Warfare Network, 182
spontaneity, 32–37
Spurgeon, C. H., 127
Stacey, Judith, 169
Stanton, Elizabeth Cady, 112n.23
Stanton, Maura, 84–85
Stark, Rodney, 71, 212
Stephen's Ministries, 204, 206
Stoddard, Solomon, 43, 57
Stokes, Frederick M. (publisher), 119
Stone, Lucy, 112n.23
Stowe, Harriet Beecher, 127–28
Stratton Mountain, Vt., 217
Streams in the Desert, ix–x, xii, 116–32
submission, 137; and transformation xi, 13, 160–78, 185–90
suburban life, xii, 205–6, 215n.34
suffering, 118, 124–25, 127–30, 162, 205
suicide, 143, 150, 164
Sumner, Charles, 112n.23
Sunday, Billy, 131n.10
Sunday schools, 71, 72
superstitions, 24
support groups, 171, 181
surrender, 160–62, 164–68, 172, 178, 182, 184, 186–90
survey methods, 38n.3
survival, 150
synod of 1662, 49

Taunton, Mass., 58
technology, 221–23
Tecumseh, 153n.21
testimonies, 162–63, 216n.38
Tetlow, Henry, 241n.41
Thanksgiving, 70
theology, vii, 9, 117, 127, 196, 211; and environment, 239n.19
Theosophical Society, 99, 102
theosophy, 98–99, 102, 104, 108, 241nn.40 and 46
Therborn, Goran, 14
Thoreau, Henry David, 221, 232
Thorndike, Mrs., 57
Tileston, Mary W., 119

timber industry, 139
time, 124, 137, 225
Tipton, Steven, 215–16n.35
Tokyo, Japan, 119
Toronto, Ont., 138
Tournier, Paul, 83
tradition, 37–38, 143, 149, 152n.7, 216nn.37 and 38
Transcendentalism, 74–75, 83, 95, 131n.8
tribalism, Puritan, 52–53, 65n.26
Trinidad, 3–4
Troeltsch, Ernst, 35
tuberculosis, 139
Turell, Jane, 54, 57
Turino, Thomas, 136, 142, 157n.59
Turner, Victor, ix
tutoring: and Golden Rule Christians, 210
Twain, Mark, 112n.23

Underground Railroad, 98
Unitarianism, 95, 96, 131n.8, 198
United Way, 210
urbanization, 38n.4

valentines, 70, 79, 81. See also St. Valentine's Day
Van Dyke, Henry, 127
Vanishing Boundaries, 196
Vatican Council, Second, 6, 25
Vecsey, Christopher, 156n.41
vegetarianism, 229–32, 241–42n.46
Victorians: and culture, 116, 121, 127
Victory Garden, 220
Virgin Mary, 3–4, 6, 85, 206
visible saints, 42, 45, 47
visiting: practice of, 89n.27, 140
Vizenor, Erma, 134, 157n.54
volunteer work: and Golden Rule Christians, 205–7, 210–11

Wagner, C. Peter, 182–83
Waits, William B., 90n.33
wakes, Ojibwa, 157nn.52 and 55, 158n.71; and hymn-singing, 134–36, 144, 148–50
Walden Woods, 221
Warner, Stephen, 205
Washington, Pa., x, 92, 98–106, 107
water, healing, 3–5
Watt, David Harrington, 191n.15
Watts, Isaac, 135

Weber, Max, 29, 62
weddings, 70–71, 76, 77, 80, 82
weeping, 162, 166, 179
Weiner, Annette, 87–88n.8
Wesley, John, 155n.36
West Indies, 3
Whipple, Bishop Henry, 133, 139, 141, 142, 156n.47
White Earth Ojibwa Singers, 135–36, 143–46, 149–50, 152n.8, 158n.61
White Earth reservation, 133–36, 138–50, 156nn.45 and 51
Whitefield, George, 72, 124, 127
Whitefisher, Emma, 154n.35
Whitman, Walt, 76
Wigglesworth, Michael, 42, 46
Willard, Frances, 112n.23
Windsor, Conn. church covenant of 1647, 45
Winona Lake Bible Conference, 131n.10
Winslow, C. F., 106
witchcraft, 185
witches, 50, 65n.23
witch-hunt (Salem Mass.), 66n.33
witnessing, 200
wives, 53, 160–61, 163–78, 185, 187–89
Wolfe, James, 102
Wolin, Richard, 16
Woman's Christian Temperance Union, 186
women, xii, 13, 96, 112n.23, 116–32, 140, 154n.35 160–95
Women's Aglow Fellowship International, ix–xi, 12–13, 18, 132n.14, 160–95; publications by, 162, 167, 169, 174, 188, 190n.4
Woodstock, 221
Woolman, John, 70
work, 204–5, 215n.26
World War II, 191n.15
worship, 9, 84, 199, 207–10, 212, 216n.35; and hymn-singing, 133, 137–38. See also devotional practices
Wright, Charles, 151n.4
Wuthnow, Robert, 206, 210, 216n.37

Youth with a Mission, 182

Zondervan Publishing House, 117, 119, 131n.1

About the Editor

DAVID D. HALL is Professor of American Religious History at the Harvard Divinity School. His books include *Worlds of Wonder, Days of Judgment: Popular Religous Belief in Early New England.*